THE 1600s
New York, Boston, Newport, Philadelphia, Jamestown, Charles Town—the gathering points of colonial America, building an economy and an identity from which a new nation would be born.

THE 1700s
From settlements to booming pre-industrial cities locked in competition for the shipping trade that was the lifeblood of the colonies.

THE 1800s
American expansion—industry, railroads, and canals promote the growth of old cities and the creation of new ones.

THE 1900s
The cities in crisis—crime, race riots, pollution, unemployment, and financial peril spearhead the movement away from urban centers.

THE FUTURE
Can our cities survive the current cycle of decay and abandonment? Will smaller communities or megapolises be the wave of the future?

URBAN LEGACY
The Story of America's Cities

All three authors are professors of history specializing in urban affairs. IRA LEONARD teaches at Southern Connecticut State College and lives in Hamden, Connecticut; DIANA KLEBANOW teaches at the University of Connecticut and lives in Forest Hills, New York; and FRANKLIN JONAS teaches at Long Island University and lives in the Bronx, New York.

MENTOR Books of Related Interest

☐ **AMERICAN SKYLINE by Christopher Tunnard and Henry Hope Reed.** A fascinating panorama of American civilization as shown in the growth and form of our cities and towns, from log cabins to skyscrapers and the latest innovations of modern urban living.
(#MW1275—$1.50)

☐ **BREAD—AND ROSES: The Struggle of American Labor 1865-1915 by Milton Meltzer.** The Living History Library / General Editor: John Anthony Scott. The tumultuous years when American workers battled for a living wage and unions fought to survive. (#ME1574—$1.75)

☐ **BROTHER, CAN YOU SPARE A DIME? The Great Depression 1929-1933 by Milton Meltzer.** The Living History Library / General Editor: John Anthony Scott. America's years of hardship—from the stock market crash to the New Deal. With photos, songs, and personal accounts from the period. (#ME1577—$1.75)

☐ **AMERICA FEVER: The Story of American Immigration by Barbara Kaye Greenleaf.** A splendid chronicle of the peoples who came to our shores from many lands. It is the story of why and how each came to this country, the hardships and prejudices they had to ovecome after their arrival, and their major contributions to the rich diversity and enormous vitality of our country and our culture. (#MJ1279—$1.95)

☐ **LOOKING FAR WEST: The Search for the American West in History, Myth, and Literature edited by Frank Bergon and Zeese Papanikolas.** Here in song and story, myth and firsthand report, analysis and eulogy, is an anthology that gives full expression to the West in all its complex meanings. With 16 pages of photographs.
(#ME1645—$2.50)

If you wish to order these titles, please see the coupon in the back of this book.

URBAN LEGACY

∞∞∞∞∞∞∞∞∞∞∞∞∞∞∞∞∞∞∞∞∞∞∞∞∞∞

The Story of America's Cities

by
Diana Klebanow,
Franklin L. Jonas,
and
Ira M. Leonard

A MENTOR BOOK
NEW AMERICAN LIBRARY
TIMES MIRROR
NEW YORK AND SCARBOROUGH, ONTARIO

NAL BOOKS ARE ALSO AVAILABLE AT DISCOUNTS
IN BULK QUANTITY FOR INDUSTRIAL OR SALES-PROMOTIONAL USE.
FOR DETAILS, WRITE TO PREMIUM MARKETING DIVISION,
NEW AMERICAN LIBRARY, INC.
1301 AVENUE OF THE AMERICAS, NEW YORK, NEW YORK 10019.

Copyright © 1977 by Diana Klebanow, Franklin L. Jonas, and Ira M. Leonard
All rights reserved

ACKNOWLEDGMENTS

"Colonial Town Statistics" and "Foreign-Born and Blacks in Selected Cities: 1860." From Bayrd Still, URBAN AMERICA: A HISTORY WITH DOCUMENTS. Copyright © 1974 by Little, Brown and Company Inc. Reprinted by permission of Little, Brown and Company Inc., Boston.

"Map of New York Neighborhoods." From "Neighborhoods of New York, 1760–1775," by Carl Abbott, *New York History*, January, 1974. Copyright © 1974 by The New York State Historical Association. Reprinted by permission of the author and publisher.

"Schematic Map of Boston and Environs," "Schematic Town Plan of New Haven," "Schematic Town Plan of New Amsterdam," "Schematic Town Plan of Penn's Philadelphia," "Schematic Town Plan of Washington, D.C.," "Schematic Town Plan of Cincinnati," "Schematic Town Plan of New York City," by Steven M. Fix. Copyright © 1976 by Steven M. Fix. Reproduced with permission of Steven M. Fix.

"Generalized Model Showing the Pivotal Role Played by Seacoast Urban Merchants in the Communication Network," "Model of the 'Multiplier Effect' Showing the Mutual Stimulation of City Size, Growth, and Industrial Diversification," "An Example of the Circular and Cumulative Growth Process: Brass Production in Connecticut 1800–1850," "American Metropolitan District Growth: 1920," by David E. Hunter. Copyright © 1976 by David E. Hunter. Reproduced with permission of David E. Hunter.

"The Atlantic Trading Region," "The Evolving Urban Network, 1680–1730," "Major Cities of the Ohio-Mississippi Valleys," "Main Northeast-Midwest Railroad Trunk Lines," "Railroad Trunk Lines Forming the Continental Urban Network, mid-1880s," by Peter P. Sakalowsky. Copyright © 1976 by Peter P. Sakalowsky. Reproduced with permission of Peter P. Sakalowsky.

"First Telephone Directory." From the Southern New England Telephone Company, New Haven. Reprinted with permission of the Southern New England Telephone Company.

Library of Congress Catalog Card Number: 77-080810

MENTOR TRADEMARK REG. U.S. PAT. OFF. AND FOREIGN COUNTRIES
REGISTERED TRADEMARK—MARCA REGISTRADA
HECHO EN CHICAGO, U.S.A.

SIGNET, SIGNET CLASSICS, MENTOR, PLUME and MERIDIAN BOOKS
are published *in the United States* by
The New American Library, Inc.,
1301 Avenue of the Americas, New York, New York 10019,
in Canada by The New American Library of Canada, Limited,
81 Mack Avenue, Scarborough, Ontario M1L 1M8

First Mentor Printing, November, 1977

2 3 4 5 6 7 8 9

PRINTED IN THE UNITED STATES OF AMERICA

DEDICATION

To Ruth Klebanow, and
in loving memory of Irving Klebanow

To Blanche Jonas, Doris Jonas and
in memory of Oscar Jonas

To Myrtle, Andrew and
Christopher Leonard, and
in memory of Harold J. Kushner

Contents

INTRODUCTION ix

1. The Urban Frontier 1
2. Rising Centers of Commerce and Industry 39
3. Urban Turmoil 70
4. Growing Pains of City Government 105
5. The Emerging Metropolis 137
6. Continuing Patterns of Community Development 177
7. A Taste of Reform 217
8. The Era of the Metropolis 249
9. Black Urbanites in a Changing City 298
10. Dilemmas of Urban Policy 331

NOTES 375

SELECTED BIBLIOGRAPHY 395

INDEX 409

Introduction

Are the major cities of the United States presently in a state of dissolution? Or, to put the question another way, is there an urban future for the American people? It is the contention of the authors that in order to understand the role that cities can play in succeeding years, it is imperative to know how they have functioned in the past. Consequently, this book attempts to set forth an account of the forces that have shaped American urban development, as well as to focus on various socioeconomic, ethnic, and racial conflicts that have plagued cities throughout the country's history. Although the authors are mindful that the present urban crisis is unique in several respects, they also recognize that many similar problems have existed in the past. As a result, they take a certain degree of comfort in the fact that the United States has had a measure of success in dealing with the various dilemmas that have accompanied the growth of the city in America.

Many people believe that the importance of cities in America is limited to relatively recent times. As this book will demonstrate, this notion is unwarranted. Cities have always figured prominently in American life, and, in the process, have altered the course of the nation's development. While the nature and scope of urban growth have undergone modifications with the passage of time, cities nevertheless have been able to provide a nucleus for the material expansion of the United States. Their impact on the social and economic class structure of the population has been no less significant. They created opportunities for virtually all groups in the community, including rural migrants, immigrants, and blacks. Viewed from this perspective, it can be asserted that the history of the United States never can be fully understood without considering its urban dimension.

One of the themes explored at the beginning of this book is

how the dynamic quality of urban life affected the history of the American people during the colonial and revolutionary periods. Many of the country's earliest cities, such as Boston, New York, Newport, and Philadelphia, were already centers for trade at the time of the American Revolution, providing commercial services for the surrounding agricultural areas and contributing to the growth and prosperity of the rural portions of the country. The vitality shown by these cities played a key role in the economic success of the colonies and helped to make possible the kind of exuberant attitude on the part of the American people that made the movement for Independence inevitable. Their influence is particularly striking in terms of the relatively small number of people who lived in cities. The census of 1790, which was the first census ever taken in the country, reported that only 5 percent of the American population could be classified as "urban"—the term being defined as an incorporated village of 2,500 people or more.

The impact of America's first cities vis-à-vis the rest of the nation was far-reaching in other respects. Cities were the centers of most of the cultural pursuits in the country, and their citizens started to develop an *esprit de corps* that set them apart from their rural counterparts. One manifestation of this urban way of life was a spirit of commercialism and a desire for personal gain. Indeed, it was partly a reaction against the materialism associated with city living that led many observers to view the growth of the city with alarm, and, as a consequence, to develop an anti-urban bias that has never completely disappeared from American ideology or belief.

The early American cities accommodated a variety of socioeconomic groups, but social mobility served to mitigate the conflicts that might otherwise have arisen over class. While these cities had their rich and poor classes, the greater portion of the people belonged to the middle levels, consisting principally of artisans and shopkeepers. The mercantile elite, which comprised the bulk of the urban upper class, held the major positions in municipal government and came to have a preponderant influence on matters of local policy. Nevertheless, there was little challenge to their leadership, for these years still constituted a period when the interests of the merchants appeared to coincide with many of the broader interests of the entire community.

Another factor contributing to a feeling of cohesiveness

within the cities was the geographic proximity which offset the pervasive spirit of individualism that characterized economic endeavors. A large number of facilities in the city were within walking distance from the center of the town, so that different groups of people were accustomed to mingling together. In similar fashion, most neighborhoods housed people who came from different occupational levels, which helped to break down the barrier of class. Thus, a sense of community permeated many of these early towns, enabling urban residents of that era to withstand the divisive forces that already were at work to challenge the somewhat tenuous bonds holding them together.

In the beginning of the nineteenth century, the ability of individuals to forge an urban society was everywhere in evidence. When the War of 1812 disrupted normal channels of commerce, urban merchants were quick to exploit new areas of trade in the southern and western portions of the country. In their quest for continued commercial prosperity, they recognized the importance of improved methods of transportation. As a result, the first few decades of the nineteenth century witnessed the extensive construction of new roads, followed by the building of canals, steamboats, and railways. The rush to build internal improvements often resulted in poorly constructed projects which were abandoned after slight use, but the country was blessed with an abundance of such overwhelming proportions that it could afford the luxury of waste.

During this same period, many cities were engaged in fierce rivalry with each other in attempting to gain new railroad facilities and attract settlers to their areas. They were frequently aided in their schemes by land speculators and town-site promoters, who reflected the entrepreneurial spirit that figured so decisively in shaping the country's urban destiny. Although many of these town-site speculations ended in failure, failure was relative, and it was clear that cities were the wave of the future. It was only in the South that the growth of cities did not keep pace with the pattern in the rest of the nation, and it was not until a later era that urbanization in this region began to take on the dynamic quality that had been demonstrated earlier in other sections of the country.

It was fortunate that the economic success accompanying the rise of the American city in the nineteenth century was able to blunt the sharper edges of urban growth in many respects. As cities became less homogeneous, their social structure oftimes appeared to be on the verge of collapse. The increasing magnitude of immigration in the decades beginning with the 1840s, coupled with the fact that a majority of the foreign-born were Roman Catholics, convinced scores of Americans that these newcomers constituted an undesirable element in society. Tense situations developed periodically between native and foreign-born workers, and nativist groups complained that the rapid increase of disease, disorder, and crime in the cities was directly attributable to immigrants. Economic opportunities and social mobility served to lessen the impact of these antagonisms, and they played an important part in easing some—but not all—of the upheavals in these transitional years.

Friction between white and black workers also figured prominently throughout the nineteenth century. Although black migration did not reach the huge proportions of the following century, a substantial number of blacks in the North already lived in cities by this time, and there were sizable clusters of black people in the leading cities in the South. Significantly, the largest-scale riot of this era—New York City's Draft Riot of 1863—involved violence that was chiefly directed at the city's black population, and resulted in more deaths and injuries than all the race riots of the 1960s.

The conflicts arising from the heavy migration of foreigners and blacks in the nineteenth century suggest that various cities had tended to become mere aggregates of population, in which any sort of transcendent spirit of community was comparatively rare due to divisions in race, ethnic group, religion, and social class. The decline of community was further affected by the extraordinary migration patterns of the people. Recent scholarship indicates that throughout most of American history the migrations into and out of the cities far exceeded in size the net changes in their populations. With the remarkable acceleration of immigration and of urban growth by the 1840s, the size of this turnover of population increased markedly, thereby adding to the turmoil and confusion of the period. Squalid living conditions and soaring crime rates also had the effect of exacerbating urban tensions, and created an air of pessimism and despair in certain parts of the community.

Another current urban problem—the inability of many cities to furnish essential services to their residents—also reached crisis proportions in the nineteenth century. The sheer magnitude of city growth severely taxed the ability of municipalities to provide adequately for the safety and welfare of their residents. In the field of health, cities were particularly vulnerable to large-scale epidemics of diseases like cholera and yellow fever by virtue of their concentrated population. This situation was compounded by the fact that medical care was still in its most rudimentary stages. Municipalities eventually made considerable strides in improving health facilities and providing for the general welfare, but in certain areas, such as housing, pollution, and environmental control, the remedies adopted were far too inadequate.

In spite of the vast array of social and physical problems that plagued urban development in the nineteenth century, it was the crisis in government that aroused the greatest concern on the part of municipal reformers. These reformers usually came fom a middle and upper class background and had an essentially *laissez-faire* approach to many urban problems. However, they became incensed at the degree of graft and corruption in municipal government and put most of the blame on the urban bosses who dominated local affairs in a majority of the nation's largest cities in the period immediately after the Civil War. These bosses had replaced the commercial gentry as the leaders in government, and their well-organized machines purported to speak for the immigrants. Bosses provided a variety of services, particularly to the foreign-born and businessmen, and brought a measure of order to the community amid the disrupting forces of urbanization. But virtually all the machines practiced some form of corruption, and in the Tweed Ring scandal of 1871—the most famous municipal scandal of the age—New York's Boss William M. Tweed and his associates may actually have succeeded in stealing as much as $300 million. In spite of revelations of this kind, bosses remained very popular with their constituents, and several early attempts to defeat them ended in failure.

At the beginning of the twentieth century, there was renewed cause for both optimism and concern. The expanding city of the streetcar, elevated railway, and commuter railroad was pushing beyond its previous boundaries, and in 1910 the census bureau used a new term, "metropolitan district," to designate central cities and their surrounding ring of smaller cities and towns. It was ironic that just when the United States appeared to be adjusting to the transition from a rural to an urban nation, it experienced changes that led to the metropolitization of America and the resultant growth of the suburbs. Until this point, cities had varying degrees of success in coping with their own problems, but they would henceforth carry the additional burden of having to meet many of the demands of their metropolitan components.

In 1920, the census bureau reported that 51 percent of Americans were classified as urban dwellers, which marked the first time that a majority of people lived in cities. The date is significant as a watershed mark in American development, but it is only an arbitrary turning point. The city had already become one of the controlling forces in American life by the latter part of the nineteenth century, if indeed not earlier.

The economic and social transformations of the early twentieth century were as spectacular as those that had previously taken place. Urban technology not only continued to provide jobs for workers but produced goods that sparked the consumer culture of modern American society. The growing demands for products in an increasingly nationwide market altered the structure of business transactions and led directly to the emergence of a white collar urban working class. The mass transit network which operated in virtually every city facilitated access within the central city and made it possible for urbanites to take up residence in suburban communities on a scale not previously envisioned. The growth of residential suburbs also went hand in hand with the emergence of industrial suburbs, or rings of industrial cities on the periphery of the larger cities. Within the metropoltan cities themselves, the appearance of office buildings, skyscrapers, electric power plants, and telephone lines lent a commercial and industrial tone to urban life—all at a time when newly created city planning boards and agencies attempted to create a more functional and harmonious urban environment.

In demographic terms, the growth of the early twentieth-century city was largely attributable to migration and immigration, as was the case in earlier periods. Immigrants continued to make up a significant portion of the urban population, as did migrants from other parts of the United States. Between 1880 and 1920, most of the immigrants came from southern and eastern Europe, adding even greater ethnic diversity to the already heterogeneous American city. While not as successful economically as native-born white Protestant groups, a majority of immigrants nevertheless were able to move up the occupational ladder. This mobility once again helped to ease urban unrest and resulted in a general lessening of tension and discord.

Politically, the early twentieth century saw the further spread of municipal progressivism, which was the largest movement for urban reform in the history of the United States. One important initial achievement was the defeat of many of the political machines and the election of reform candidates to local office. Although their regimes were frequently of short duration—they were not always adept at tackling the intricacies of municipal government and they proved vulnerable to charges that they were more interested in efficient government than in dealing with social problems in the city—their overall impact on municipal government cannot be denied. Even as some of the bosses returned to power, the struggle between the machines and the reformers led to certain modifications in municipal politics. On another level, the number of structural changes which were begun during the Progressive period paved the way for improving the effectiveness of local governments and represented another step forward in correcting some of the weaknesses in municipal administration.

While urban Americans could take pride in much of the progress that they had made by the early decades of the twentieth century, later generations would come to view the rapidly changing urban scene with a sense of alarm and of crisis. On one hand, the "exploding metropolis" continued to move beyond its previously defined boundaries, resulting in a spread of its population—or urban sprawl—and the accompanying uneconomical use of its land. On the other hand, the development of the megalopolis—long, uninterrupted stretches of urbanized land—led to a concentration of population in giant-scale cities within a specific geographic area. These super cities, along with their modern technologies, have placed great strains upon the available supplies of clean air and water and have posed a veritable nightmare with regard to questions of planning, traffic control, and land-use policy. Of equal concern are the hazards to the environment which have poisoned the air, polluted the streams, and threatened the water supply in many of the nation's urban centers and their adjacent regions. It is debatable whether these problems are any more serious than the ones that existed in the past, but many critics nonetheless take a pessimistic view about the future of the American city.

Their pessimism is justified to the extent that a day of

reckoning appears to be at hand, and the nation may need to decide whether the environment can continue to be sacrificed in the interests of economic growth. The recognition of this problem comes at a particularly perilous time insofar as cities are concerned, for they have already lost jobs and industry to the suburbs and desperately need a way of maintaining their economic base. In viewing the priorities in a community, however, the repeated pressures by groups favoring proposals that might adversely affect the environment must be balanced against the health, safety, and comfort of the residents. By the 1970s, it was estimated that 60 percent of all atmospheric pollution was caused by automobile emissions. Other well-known urban "landmarks," notably incinerators and smokestacks, further reduce the level of clean air and contribute to the problem of pollution. On occasion, air pollution has reached alarming proportions. A temperature inversion in New York killed at least 170 people in 1953, and another which occurred ten years later caused about 400 deaths. Unfortunately, once the immediate danger has passed, the problem tends to be ignored. In the meantime, the use of automobiles has increased, highways have been built without sufficient attention being paid to their effect on pollution, and factories and public utility companies have spread layers of smoke throughout metropolitan areas. As the levels of pollution continue to mount, cities may be compelled to re-examine their options. If some of the experts are correct, the environmental crisis will reach a point where the situation cannot be reversed—no matter what measures are taken or how much money is spent.

There are urbanologists who maintain that decisions pertaining to matters like environmental control can best be dealt with at the regional or metropolitan level, even though the federal government has come to play an increasingly active role by passing legislation such as the Environmental Quality Act (1969), Clean Air Act (1970), and the Water Pollution Control Act (1972). In some cases, the machinery to tackle certain aspects of the problem has already been created. Regional planning associations, which began to proliferate in the early decades of the twentieth century, began to receive substantial funds from the federal government in the 1960s to focus on transportation, land use, housing, and community development. The proposals for metropolitan government—the consolidation of municipal governments into one unit with authority to govern an entire metropolitan area—have not been so fortunate and remain largely in the blueprint stages. Nevertheless, several cities have been successful in pooling their resources to control a specific problem. Metro Council, or the Metropolitan Council of the Twin Cities, was established by Minneapolis and St. Paul in 1968 to deal with sewage pollution and has made remarkable progress in cleaning up the area. One of the reasons Metro Council has performed so effectively is that the Minnesota state legislature stipulated it would have its own funding, thereby enabling it to function as a regional body free of the dictates of local authorities.

The growing awareness of the importance of the environmental crisis should not divert attention from the serious racial problems besieging the modern metropolis. The mounting clashes between whites and blacks as more and more blacks have moved into urban areas indicate that the cities are no more successful now in resolving tensions between different ethnic groups than they have been in the past. Blacks are sometimes (if erroneously) referred to as the "last of the immigrants." While comparison with the immigrant experience helps to lend historical perspective, it must be remembered that blacks are native-born and, in some cases, have lived in cities for long periods. The evidence clearly shows that blacks still face more discrimination than any immigrants, yet their upward mobility in recent years suggests that their situation is more hopeful now than it ever has been. At the same time, this overall success is closely linked to the vitality of the American economy. The recession of the 1970s demonstrated once again that economic setbacks are more apt to have a disastrous effect on blacks than on any other segment of the working force.

It is likely that the status of blacks will be affected by the presence of large numbers of Hispanics, whose migration to cities has risen sharply within the last few decades. The income of Hispanics—they earn more than blacks but considerably less than whites—would indicate that in social mobility patterns their experience may more closely resemble that of immigrants than that of blacks. Their migration also serves as a reminder that virtually all mass movements of minority groups into the American city have resulted in the periodic unleashing of violence.

Many of those who remain optimistic about American cities have come to hope that the federal government will assume some share of the responsibility for revitalizing urban areas. As of the present time, the federal government has failed to devise and implement a comprehensive national urban policy, although it has passed a number of important pieces of legislation concerning urban America. However, not all of this legislation has been successful, and some acts have had the unintended effect of intensifying the problem. Urban renewal is a prime example of how government funding for housing has often worked to the advantage of powerful real estate interests, while the groups who presumably should have benefited from such programs were inadvertently victimized. Hailed in the 1950s as the answer to inner city decay, urban renewal sometimes had the effect of destroying cherished neighborhoods and uprooting communities, while at the same time failing to make any provisions for housing the people whom it displaced. In contrast, the government offered enough inducements to builders of urban renewal projects to enable many of them to reap handsome profits.

The results of programs like urban renewal reinforced the arguments of those persons who believed that federal involvement in municipal affairs must be either toned down in scale or directed to other channels. This was the approach of President Richard M. Nixon, who sought to modify the Great Society programs of his predecessor, Lyndon B. Johnson. Admittedly Nixon's task was made much easier because of the shifts in population that were clearly evident during his administration; by the 1970s, the United States had become a nation of suburbs, with more people living in suburbia than in the central cities.

This loss of population came at the very time when cities were finding that their depleted revenues were no longer sufficient to provide essential local services. Suburbanites and rural dwellers tended to see the problem in another way, and blamed the cities for inefficiency and waste in the management of their finances. When New York was on the verge of default in 1975, the immediate response in many sections of the country was to allow the city to go bankrupt. The federal government eventually went to New York's rescue, but its future remains uncertain. Moreover, its plight is not unique, and other large cities, particularly those located in the northeastern and north-central regions, are finding that their revenues are grossly inadequate for the services that they are called upon to provide. Hopefully, the nation will find a way to solve its urban crisis; an understanding of what went wrong can be useful in weighing future courses of action, provided that there is still time in which to make changes.

The authors would like to acknowledge, on an individual basis, their gratitude to their friends, families, and colleagues who helped them with this project, while assuming full responsibility for any errors in the text.

Diana Klebanow wishes to express her appreciation to Lionel Ovesey, M.D., for his encouragement during the writing of the book. Her mother, Ruth Klebanow, read the manuscript and offered many helpful suggestions. Ella N. Pinsker, her aunt, graciously consented to type several chapters. Among those who offered assistance were her sister, Sheila Klebanow, M.D.; her aunt, Nettie Baim; and Lucille Chappelle of the National Urban League. She enjoyed having the help of her nephew, David Isaac Klebanow, in selecting several of the illustrations used in the book.

Franklin L. Jonas would like to thank Dr. Lester Jackson and Mrs. Dorothy Swanson, Librarian of Tamiment Library at New York University, for valuable criticism and suggestions, and Mrs. Grace Sitt and Mrs. Leona Singer for typing his chapters.

Ira M. Leonard would like to express his gratitude to Stephen Brown, Professor Max Mintz, and Gerard Paul for their insightful comments on drafts of the manuscript and their encouragement throughout the writing. Dr. David E. Hunter conceptualized and designed many of the graphics in Chapters 1, 2, and 5 and provided invaluable advice at every stage of the project. Friends and colleagues at Southern Connecticut State College rendered assistance in a variety of ways. Dr. Peter P. Sakalowsky prepared most of the maps used in these chapters. Professor Steven M. Fix executed the schematic town plans. Henry Gorski, Irv Leveton, Stephanie Russell, and Amy Eastland volunteered their time and talents to prepare many of the graphics in the book. A special debt is owed to Mrs. Maryann Franco for her helpfulness, sunny disposition, and proficient typing.

The authors wish to express their thanks to those individuals and institutions that allowed the reproduction of copyrighted materials.

Chapters 1, 2, and 5 were principally written by Ira M. Leonard; Chapters 3, 6, and 8 by Franklin L. Jonas; and the Introduction and Chapters 4, 7, 9, and 10 by Diana Klebanow.

1

The Urban Frontier, 1600–1800

Urban centers—cities and towns—have always played a major role in shaping the life and culture of American society.* America took form during the colonial era when the main urban centers were seaports on the Atlantic Ocean or on navigable rivers such as the Hudson, Connecticut, Delaware, and Savannah. Begun as trading posts or forts for European expansion in the New World, they soon became integral parts of an Atlantic Ocean-wide trading economy centered in the major cities of western Europe. During the 1600s and 1700s the seaport communities stimulated, organized, and directed the settlement of the interior of the continent, accelerating the economic, social, and cultural development of the North American mainland. Goods, people, and ideas were channeled into the rural backcountry areas from these centers along the coast. Largely because of their success in performing these varied activities, the coastal towns of Boston, New York, Newport, Philadelphia, Charles Town, and a host of secondary inland towns grew into substantial communities, some of which during the 1760s began to rival English cities in size.

As long as harmony existed within the British trade and commercial system, these cities seemed destined to prosper. But this harmony was shattered when the English imperial managers tightened controls over the colonial economy and introduced major taxation schemes. Resistance to British au-

---

*The United States Census Department defines "urban" as a settlement with a permanent population of at least 2,500. By the eighteenth century, if not even earlier, the main colonial towns had well over 2,500 residents; and they may properly be defined as cities because of the variety of specialized services they provided for themselves and within their regions.

thority during the 1760s and 1770s was centered in these seaport cities, as was much of the leadership during the War for Independence and, later, during the drafting of the U. S. Constitution.

Basic Sources of Urban Growth in the Colonies

The discoveries of Columbus, and the great Spanish Empire that followed, had an electric effect upon the other mercantile powers of Europe. They established their own imperial outposts in the new American world, viewing it as a great "resource region" to exploit as they saw fit. In the seventeenth century, various trading posts and other forts were established either on the first-rate harbors along the Atlantic coast, at or near the confluence of two or more navigable bodies of water, or at the crossing of key wilderness trails. At the site of some of these outposts would later emerge some of the great American cities, New York and Chicago among them. These outposts were to play a prominent role in the economic and social processes through which Holland, Great Britain, and France had, in the words of historian Bernard Bailyn, "flung their commercial frontiers westward to the new world and made of the whole Atlantic basin a single great trading area."[1] (See Map 1.1.)

These outposts, which would later be the nucleus of the United States, took the form of towns and from the outset performed many of the same economic, governmental, and cultural functions as the cities of Europe. They served as fortresses against foreign rivals and hostile Indians, as centers of government supervision and control, and as places where goods were exchanged and ideas transmitted. The Puritans, Quakers, and others who migrated for religious reasons also adapted the town form, while reshaping it into a community of like-minded believers. The growth of towns was also prompted by cultural considerations. Seventeenth-century Europeans regarded cities and towns (words used interchangeably at the time) as essential for civilized life and for the maintenance of social order. Ultimately it may well have been the very vastness of the New World environment itself that seemed to demand the creation of tightly organized, ordered communities, some initially under semi-military discipline.

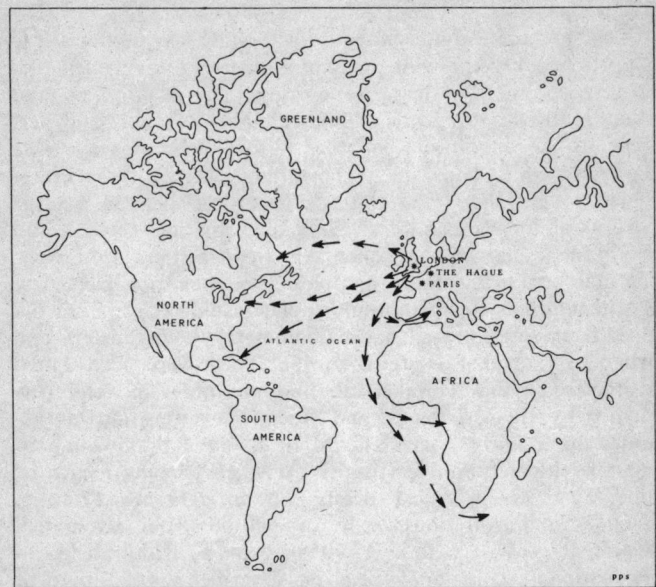

Map 1.1 The Atlantic Trading Region

Whatever the reason, "America was an exercise in community development, an experiment in social order," as historians Kenneth Jackson and Stanley Schultz viewed it.[2]

The sources of urban growth, however, are to be found in the broad economic functions these seaports performed for Europe and America. Western Europe underwent an extraordinary period of sustained growth during the 1600s and 1700s, and the New World played a vital role in that process. Much of that growth was dependent upon enormous quantities of North American farm, forest, and sea products, all of which were shipped from these Atlantic coast seaports. Acting as "economic hinges," these seaports linked the interior of the North American continent with Europe.[3]

The seaports also performed a wide variety of indispensable services for their surrounding areas, encouraging rapid agricultural development. Actually a characteristic feature of cities has always been the performance of commercial functions—marketing, exchanging, storing, processing, distributing, and transporting of goods—for a surrounding territory; what urban geographers describe as "central place" functions.

The preparation of farm, forest, and sea products for export encouraged a wide array of industries to evolve. These, in turn, required a large supporting base of workers and other industries to provide food, clothing, shelter, and services to the city itself, enabling it to function as a viable economic unit. Thus, the export industries of these cities, together with their central place functions, defined a large portion of their inhabitants' everyday activities.

The character of the North American settlers during the colonial era made these complex processes possible. New World migrants were culturally sophisticated people from the most technologically advanced, commercially organized, and urbanized areas of western Europe. They were accustomed to the economic, commercial, and cultural functions performed by villages, towns, and cities. They were also accustomed to a fairly high standard of living and unwilling to put up with a primitive frontier existence for any length of time. To the New World forests, they brought urban values, attitudes, and aspirations. As historian Julius Rubin explained, "Colonial America, though 90 percent agricultural in an occupational sense, may also be described as 90 percent urban in a cultural sense."[4]

Urban Growth in the South

The American South has always been less urban than the North; this pattern had already begun to emerge in the colonial era. Jamestown, established in 1607 as the American headquarters of the Virginia Company, became the first successful British colony in North America. The colony grew very slowly; Jamestown was the only important town to emerge in either Virginia or Maryland until the eighteenth century, despite continued urging by the Crown and its colonial governments. As late as 1790, when the southern states still contained about half of the new nation's population, they had only about a fifth of its urban residents.

The most important city to emerge in the lower South during the colonial era was Charles Town, South Carolina, which was founded in 1680 by the Carolina Proprietors. Situated on the peninsula between the Ashley and Cooper rivers, and fronting on the Cooper, Charles Town was laid out in checkerboard or gridiron fashion following the pattern of nine squares initiated in New Haven, Connecticut, in 1638, continued in Philadelphia, Pennsylvania, in 1684, and followed by scores of other towns set up in the wilderness during the next century. One of the squares was reserved for the market, church, and courthouse, but the most built-up parts of the town were near the waterfront facing the numerous docks and wharves, some of which extended into the Cooper River. Surrounding the town was a line of fortifications. Charles Town was destined to become one of colonial America's most cultured and affluent centers during the eighteenth century, when rich rice planters underwrote the building of theaters, clubs, and racetracks.

The other major southern towns—Savannah, Georgia, Norfolk, Virginia, and Baltimore, Maryland—were not established until the eighteenth century. Both Norfolk and Baltimore were created to service the increased needs of the Chesapeake region. Norfolk was set up under royal direction in the 1720s as the export center for the lower Chesapeake; Baltimore was founded in 1729 by a group of entrepreneurs to act as a port for the shipment of tobacco from the upper Chesapeake area of Maryland and Virginia. Lastly, Savannah was planned by the colonial proprietor James Oglethorpe in 1732, to serve as the administrative, commercial, and governmental center of the Georgia colony.

Urban Growth in the North

Farther to the north, in the New England region, urban development was rapid and of considerable importance. A small but influential colony was established at Plymouth, Massachusetts, in 1620 by a group of religious separatists known to history as the Pilgrims. Sponsored by a London merchant group, the Pilgrims promised to repay the cost of their expedition and return a profit as well. The Mayflower Compact, drawn up the night before disembarkation, served as the basis for the community's social organization and is usually regarded as the "first municipal charter in America."[5] Its signers were themselves the voters, officeholders, and government. This kind of community arrangement, the product of a "voluntary association of like-minded believers," became the method by which other New England towns were later created as well as the colonies of Connecticut and Rhode Island.

In contrast to the founders of Jamestown, the basic motivation of the Massachusetts Bay Puritan settlers was religious, as had been the case with the Plymouth Pilgrims. Each town was a single religious congregation, and the inhabitants regarded themselves as having made an agreement—a covenant—with one another and with God to do his work on earth. Through the creation of truly Christian communities in the New World, the Puritans believed they could act as beacon lights for western European Christians who had strayed from the Lord's word. In so doing, they believed they could secure their own individual and collective salvation. These "covenanted communities" viewed themselves collectively as a "city on a hill" for the rest of Christendom.[6]

Boston

The Massachusetts Bay Company settlements soon overshadowed Plymouth and were destined eventually to absorb it. Boston, the product of extremely careful planning, was founded in 1630; it became the nucleus of the colony of Massachusetts and the bridgehead from which more than 20,000 Puritan colonists would rapidly disperse during the 1630s throughout Massachusetts, Connecticut, Rhode Island, Maine, New Hampshire, and parts of New York. Boston was the first settlement to employ the town form that was to become typical in New England. Strategically located on a hilly peninsula jutting into the Charles River, Boston had a good harbor which afforded natural protection against Indian attack, and it soon became the major New England center (see Figure 1.1). The two focal points of the early town were Dock Square, where the town dock was located, and the common, the center of town where the open market, church, and houses were situated. In addition to Boston, the Massachusetts Bay Company laid out the neighboring towns of Charlestown, Watertown, Roxbury, Medford, Saugus, and Dorchester, and within a dozen years there were an additional twenty similar towns.

The Other New England Towns

Like its old English village counterpart, the New England town was designed to be a complete rural-urban unit encompassing the residential area where all members of the con-

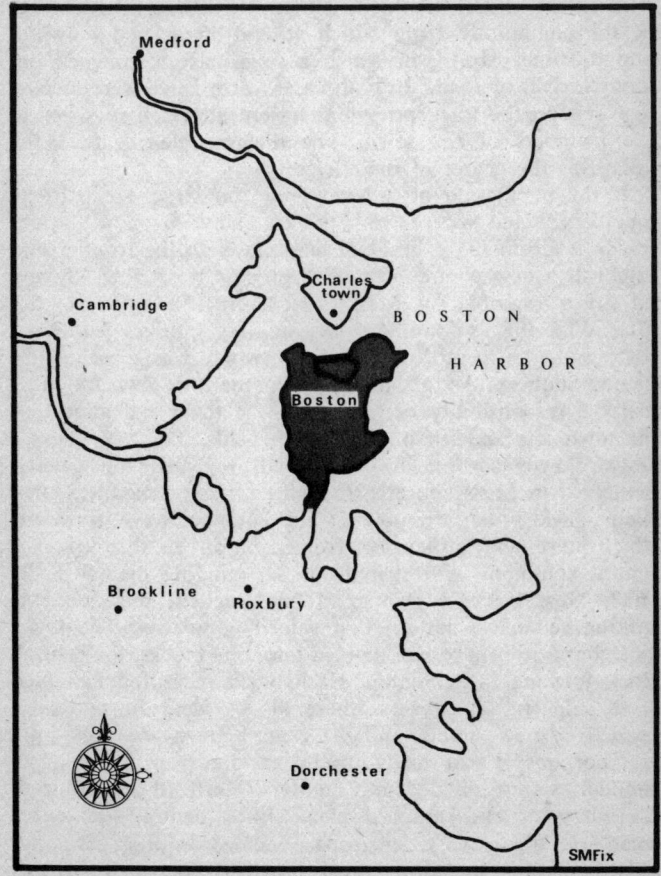

Figure 1.1 Schematic Map of Boston and Environs c. 1650

gregation lived and the farm fields just beyond the village. Initially there was no uniform community plan. In some places people clustered around the meetinghouse, in other communities people were relatively dispersed, and sometimes "outlivers" were allowed to erect homes away from the center of the village. But eventually most New England towns, regardless of location, fell into one of two general town-form plans: the blocklike compact or "squared" form, in which the house and garden lots were marked off from each other next to the central common, a green or square in the center of the community from which several streets led outward; and the linear form, in which a single street stretched out along a river or road.[7] In both cases, farm fields were located just beyond the town proper and were allocated in strips to the members of the town. The townspeople regarded the village as the center of their lives.

If the population of a town grew too large, some of its members would secure from the company (by now the colonial government) a grant of land closer to the frontier and establish a new community. This process was called "hiving off." For example, in Massachusetts in 1637, seven years after Watertown's founding, fifty to sixty families petitioned for permission to settle a new town, which was subsequently named Sudbury. As in the other communities, town founders had the responsibility of laying out the town and allocating the town lots and surrounding farm fields.

The towns set up in Connecticut repeated the pattern pioneered in Massachusetts, though with some modifications. Wethersfield is an example of the compact town form, in which home and garden lots fronted on streets that led to a central common, with strip fields surrounding the town. In 1638, New Haven's planner, John Brockett, introduced a striking geometric pattern that gained popularity. The town took the form of a square divided into nine blocks, the central block forming the common. Each block measured 825 feet on a side. In later years, these blocks were further subdivided by new streets, and the central green was split into two portions. Farm fields up to a mile from the village boundaries were divided into quarters. Hartford also utilized a gridiron or checkerboard plan with a central square or green (see Figure 1.2). Since space seemed limitless, virtually every seventeenth-century town provided for open spaces, such as common lands, garden plots, market areas, and farms.

Religious divisions in Boston led to the development of

THE URBAN FRONTIER, 1600–1800

Newport, Providence, and Portsmouth, Rhode Island, in the 1630s. In 1638 William Coddington and his friends chose the site for Newport because of its excellent year-round harbor on Narragansett Bay. Newport, which was to become one of the five main seaport towns during the colonial era, was laid out following the gridiron plan used in New Haven and Hartford, Connecticut. Providence, which was founded by Roger Williams, the most famous of the religious dissenters

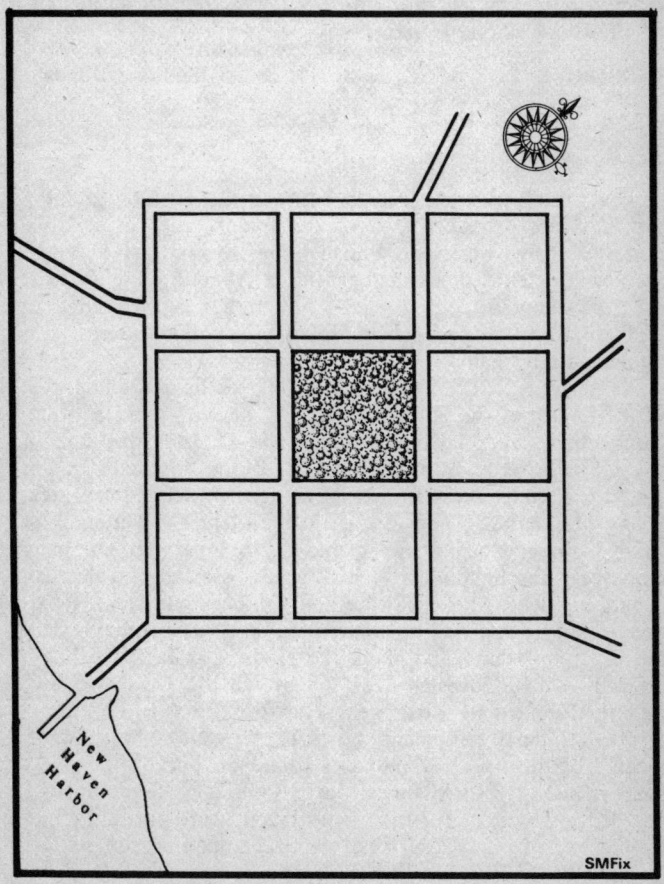

Figure 1.2 Schematic Town Plan of New Haven c. 1745

from Massachusetts, followed a linear pattern. For the convenience of settlers who wanted water frontage for trade purposes, Williams laid out the houses on one side of Towne Street, the north-south road that followed the shoreline. And to retain a close grouping of dwellings, very long and narrow house and garden lots were designed, extending to the farm fields beyond the village proper.

Small settlements along the Piscataqua, Merrimack, and Kennebec rivers in Maine and New Hampshire developed less quickly but in much the same manner as had those in Connecticut and Rhode Island.

New York

The Middle Atlantic region between the Hudson and Potomac rivers produced two of the major cities of colonial America, New York and Philadelphia. In contrast to towns in New England, those in the Middle Atlantic colonies were not "covenanted communities" but rather aggregations of individual fortune-seekers whose only common interest was quick material gain.

As early as 1614, Dutch merchants set up a trading post at the mouth of the Hudson River. Along with the Delaware, Connecticut, and Savannah rivers, the Hudson was one of the major arteries into the interior of the continent and it gave the Dutch access to a vast and fertile backcountry area. Using Manhattan Island as the headquarters, the Dutch West India Company began in the mid-1620s to scatter company employees throughout its New World possessions, which lay roughly between the Delaware and Connecticut rivers. Fortified trading posts and small communities were quickly laid out on Long Island and along the Hudson as far as Albany, as well as in Gloucester, New Jersey, on the Delaware, and on the Connecticut River near Hartford.

The principal settlement, however, was New Amsterdam, located at the tip of Manhattan Island on one of the finest harbors along the Atlantic coast. Some of the company's detailed instructions for the town's layout were put into effect by engineer Cryn Fredericks, who accompanied the settlers in 1625 or 1626. (See Figure 1.3.) Located within a four-pointed fort, New Amsterdam contained a square for market, school, church, and hospital buildings; a street connecting the two gates of the fort; and provision along this street for twenty-five house lots. As the town developed, however, the original plans were quickly abandoned. Streets were laid out as needed, usually following local lanes between houses, farms, and the fort. Before long, thirty houses were constructed on the East River shore front, including a small countinghouse that served as company office and storeroom. The Broad Way was the first main street to be laid out; it

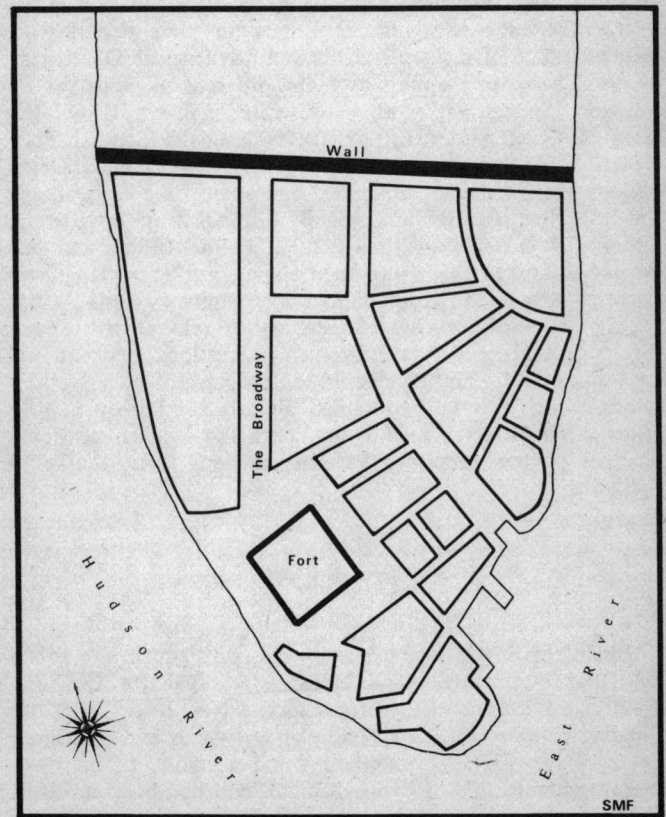

Figure 1.3 Schematic Town Plan of New Amsterdam c. 1660

ran north from the fort for a quarter of a mile to the edge of town, Wall Street, which was a line of fortifications from the Hudson to the East River.

Few Dutch wished to migrate to the New World despite the generous land grants, or patroonships, available along both sides of the Hudson River, so the company grudgingly tolerated the wide variety of other nationalities that increasingly filtered into the colony. French-speaking Walloons and Africans, the latter company slaves, had been among the earliest arrivals, but soon Scandinavians, Germans, Flemish, English, Irish, Scottish, Bohemians, Spanish, and Portuguese were in residence. Significantly, most of these people were granted some of the same rights and privileges as Dutch residents. There were almost as many different religious groups in New Amsterdam as there were nationalities: Dutch Reformed, Congregationalists from New England, Scottish Presbyterians, Lutherans, French Huguenots, Jews (from a Dutch colony in Brazil and Holland), and some Catholics, among others. New Amsterdam steadily increased in population, from 270 in 1628 to almost 2,000 in the 1660s, and one visitor estimated that more than eighteen different languages were spoken in the cosmopolitan community by 1643.

The English government, seeking to remove the Dutch presence and consolidate its own possessions, sent an expedition in 1664 and conquered the province of New Netherlands, which by then contained almost 5,000 people. New Amsterdam was renamed New York. The English now had control of the American eastern seaboard from Maine to Virginia.

Philadelphia

Philadelphia was established by William Penn in the 1680s to enhance his fortune and provide a refuge for Quakers. Penn had been one of the proprietors of New Jersey after the English conquest of New Netherlands (which included large parts of New Jersey), but he wanted a colony of his own. Before gaining title to Pennsylvania, Penn had been involved in establishing two towns in New Jersey, Burlington (1677) and Perth Amboy (in 1683). He drew upon this experience and the plans of previously established American communities such as New Haven, when he planned the capital of his new province. Recognizing that Pennsylvania would not be successful unless towns were created to facilitate trade and commerce and help maintain social order, Penn chose the site and formulated the town plan carefully. Because Penn wished to make his city not only large but also spacious, beautiful, and scaled to human needs and dimensions, he directed that:

> every house be placed, if the person pleases, in the middle of its plat [or lot], as to the breadth of it, that so there may be ground on each side for gardens or orchards or fields, that it may be a green country town, which will never be burnt, and always wholesome . . .[8]

The site, between the Delaware and Schuylkill rivers, stretched for two miles in length and almost a mile in width. (See Figure 1.4.) The town was laid out on the gridiron or checkerboard pattern, with wide streets intersecting at right angles. The principal feature of the plan called for four streets, one of which was 100 feet wide, to intersect the middle of the sides of five squares. In the center of the city was a ten-acre open square for schools, markets, and public buildings; four other squares were situated in each quarter of the city for similar purposes. Due to Penn's skillful planning and superb advertising campaign all over Europe, Philadelphia was an instantaneous success; though building did not begin until 1683, there were 600 houses and approximately 2,500 people in the town by 1685. Like New York, Philadelphia's population almost from the beginning was quite heterogeneous and the city exuded a distinctly cosmopolitan air.

Penn and his family created cities and towns as a means by which to encourage trade and commerce. Therefore, they chose sites that were central in their counties, accessible to Philadelphia, and adequately spaced from other county seats and towns. (What was planned in Pennsylvania apparently unfolded in other colonies more slowly and far less systematically.) These inland towns facilitated internal commerce and functioned as central market and exchange centers for their localities while Philadelphia supplied the same functions on a wider scale.[9]

Penn's plan for Philadelphia was more successful than even he would have believed. The rectangular pattern of Philadelphia's street plan provided a simple, easy to duplicate

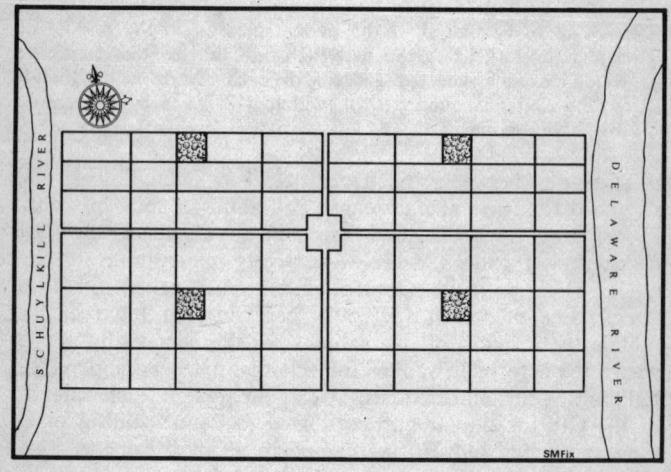

Figure 1.4 Schematic Town Plan of Penn's Philadelphia c. 1680

pattern which later surveyors and real estate developers superimposed on the most irregular sites throughout Pennsylvania and elsewhere in the country. There are dozens of towns in Pennsylvania that eventually incorporated Penn's plan, among them Lancaster (1721), York (1741), Reading (1748), Allentown (1762), and Pittsburgh (1780s). Each was originally laid out with open squares or rectangles having four streets intersecting the middle of the square's sides.

The Colonial Urban Network

By the end of the seventeenth century, the principal seaport towns linked the interior of the North American continent with the far-flung English trade and commercial system that encompassed the Newfoundland fisheries, the West Indian sugar islands, the Madeira, Azores and Canary wine islands, the British Isles, and the continents of Europe and Africa.[10]

At the center of the trade and transportation-communication network within each of the main regions (with the exception of the Chesapeake Bay area) was a major seaport town which provided a host of specialized goods and services to the region (see Map 1.2). Within these towns merchants drew the diverse commodities produced inland to the coast, sold some locally, warehousing the rest until suitable markets could be found. These seaports were sophisticated exchange centers—or entrepôts—receiving, processing, and exporting all kinds of products from American farms, forests, and fisheries.

The southern colonies produced major cash crops (tobacco in Maryland, Virginia and North Carolina; rice and indigo in South Carolina and later Georgia) which were sought-after in England and on the continent of Europe. Apart from lumber products and furs, England did not want—or need— the cereal grains, meat, livestock, and fish produced in the New England and Middle colonies. Therefore, the merchants of the northeastern seaports—with Boston leading the way as early as the 1640s—scoured the Atlantic Ocean trading region seeking markets capable of absorbing these diverse commodities and supplying in return hard coin, finished products, or raw materials that could be fabricated into products acceptable to English merchant firms. The principal purpose of this search originally was to find ways and means to reimburse English merchants for imported goods (such as guns, gunpowder, bar iron, axes, saws, hammers, knives, nails, pots, pans, books, cloth, etc.) which the colonists wanted in order to make their lives more comfortable, but which they could not make.

By providing markets for surrounding farms and for grist mills and sawmills and by distributing imported goods, the seaport towns stimulated agricultural and extractive pursuits in inland regions, particularly in New England and the Middle colonies, and thus made these areas even more attractive to prospective settlers who wished to remain in contact with townspeople, markets, cultural fare, and the English homeland. Farmers who were close to seaports or inland towns

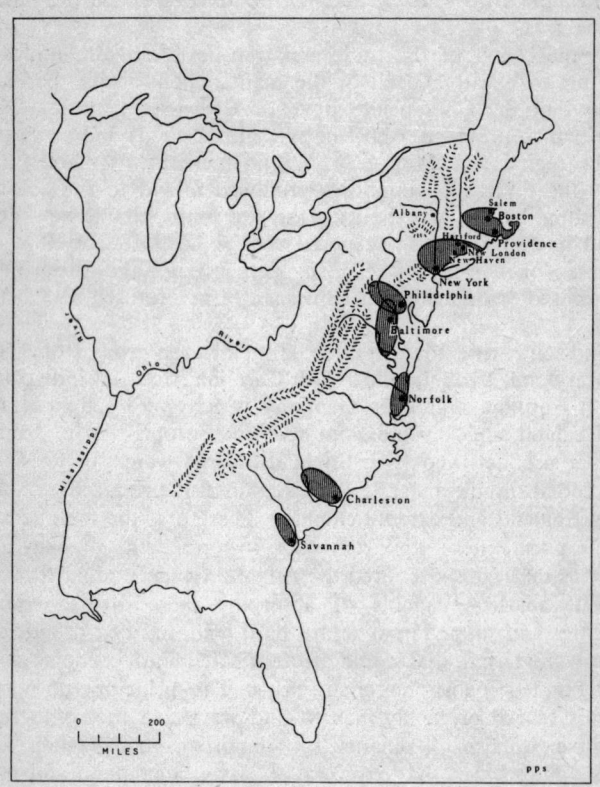

Map 1.2 The Evolving Urban Network, 1680–1730

were able to specialize in dairy products, fresh vegetables, and fruits for the urban population.

Even farmers in distant villages and frontier settlements were brought into the commercialized world of the Atlantic economy through a series of complex interchanges. Country storekeepers concluded dozens if not hundreds of small trades with local farmers in order to accumulate sufficient inventory which, in turn, could be exchanged with a town merchant in places such as Salem, Massachusetts, New London or Hartford, Connecticut, Albany, New York, or Lancaster, Pennsylvania, for supplies of "West Indian" goods (sugar, molasses, rum, or spices) or English commodities.

The chief economic function of these inland towns or secondary port towns was to collect interior products and ship them to the main seaports and distribute imports. An Albany merchant, for example, would forward to merchants down the Hudson River in New York furs from Canada, lumber from the mountains, wheat from the Mohawk Valley, plus other diverse commodities from country storekeepers. Merchants and shopkeepers in these towns were both local retailers and suppliers of country storekeepers in distant villages and frontier settlements. Equally important, these inland communities helped generate a diversified regional economy, providing, in addition to markets for farm specialties, a wider range of occupations and industries for farmers and settlers—blacksmiths, craftsmen, tavern keepers, gristmill and sawmill proprietors, and workers.

Some of these rapidly growing secondary port towns actually became "small-scale reproductions" of the port cities and began to engage in ocean trading as well. New Bedford and Nantucket specialized in whaling, Newburyport in fish, Salem in East India goods. New London opened up trade with Barbados, shipping horses, livestock, and barreled pork in exchange for sugar, molasses, and rum.

Indeed, Newport, Rhode Island, grew from a satellite of Boston to one of its major New England rivals. Newport residents turned to shipbuilding because of abundant inland timber resources, and town merchants began to distribute European and West Indian goods obtained from Boston for locally produced grains, cattle, horses, and mules. From there, they branched out to the coastal trade, shipping Rhode Island barreled beef, pork, dairy products, horses, lumber, and candles to the Carolinas and thence to the West Indies. By the late seventeenth century, the production and exportation of rum (distilled from West Indian sugar and molasses) became a Newport specialty. Shortly thereafter, these same merchants began trading rum for African slaves who were shipped to the Chesapeake Bay area, the Carolinas, and West Indian plantations. By 1720, Newport was the principal North American slave trade center.

By the end of the seventeenth century, the scattered villages and small towns, each with its own particular character, population, and local trade patterns, were drawn into the Atlantic trading system. The nature of the New England and Middle Atlantic commodities partly explains the growth of this urban-based network, the complexity of these interactions, and the vitality of these cities and towns. Fish, lumber, and farm produce required a considerable amount of specialized servicing and processing prior to exportation. Grains such as wheat, for example required milling into flour, grading and sorting, packing in hogsheads (airtight, watertight barrels that held up to one thousand pounds) or baking into biscuits, storaging, and loading on wagons, before shipment to market.

On the other hand, tobacco, the dominant Chesapeake region crop, required very little specialized servicing prior to transshipment to market in England—and this in part accounts for the scarcity of important towns in the upper South during the seventeenth century. Also, the numerous navigable rivers that flowed near the larger plantations in Virginia and Maryland permitted first British and then colonial ships to put in directly at the wharves of the major planters. Tobacco was generally stored in the planter's barns, loaded into hogsheads (which were either produced on the plantation by slave craftsmen or imported), carefully rolled to the planter's wharf, ready for transit to market by a merchant vessel.

A planter so situated could himself perform the storaging, distributing, processing, and marketing that elsewhere was provided by towns. Significantly, by the early 1700s, the top 1 percent of the Chesapeake planters—whose holdings were in excess of $25,000—were engaged in a wide variety of economic activities both for themselves and for many small farmers and planters. These included acting as brokers for locally produced commodities, as lawyers writing deeds and wills, as bankers lending money or providing credit or insurance, and also as retailers, selling or exchanging tobacco for imported good.[11] However, as the volume of trade grew, in the eighteenth century, Baltimore and Norfolk were created, and these towns began to emulate the patterns already developed in the New England and Middle Atlantic cities.

As it had in Virginia and Maryland, the plantation-slave system developed rapidly in South Carolina; it was adopted first for the raising of rice in the mid-1690s and was then used for indigo culture in the 1740s. Rice was cultivated along rivers that afforded cheap transportation to Charles

Town or, later, Savannah, Georgia. Farmers up the Ashley and Cooper rivers floated their crops down to Charles Town, and from there pork, corn, lumber, cattle, and rice, as well as deerskins from the interior, were carried to the West Indian island of Barbados. Because many of the original settlers had migrated from the West Indies, Charles Town merchants were oriented toward the Caribbean. Sugar from Barbados was shipped to England and exchanged for manufactured articles that were sold back in Charles Town, up the Ashley and Cooper rivers, and into the back country. However extensive the system of trade and commerce, Charles Town was fundamentally oriented to servicing the needs and whims of inland rice planters, so despite its affluence, Charles Town was not destined to become a major economic rival for the New England and Middle Atlantic seaport cities.

The relative lack of towns in the southern colonies where plantations specialized in cash-crop farming had profound social consequences. The scattered population made it extremely difficult for craftsmen to find a settled market for their skills and make a living from their trades. This had the effect of further retarding the diversification of economic activities, many of which tend to be urban-based. Small planters and farmers had to improvise, do without, or buy expensive imported goods. As Chesapeake tobacco farmers became more specialized, they became more dependent on importation of foodstuffs, lumber, and manufactured goods which New Englanders and Middle Atlantic shippers, who were closer, could more easily and quickly provide than English merchants. Moreover, the slowness of urban growth in the South resulted in power and wealth being concentrated in the planter class, rather than being diffused, as it was in the northern colonies, among a number of economic and occupational groups, including merchants, lawyers, craftsmen, and white collar workers.

The Role of the Urban Merchants

The success and rapid growth of Boston, Newport, New York, Philadelphia and, to a lesser extent, Charles Town, testified to the ingenuity and aggressiveness of the seaport merchants who orchestrated the transfer of all goods and services within their special trading areas and throughout the

Atlantic trading region.[12] The first New England merchants had gained their experience as merchants or tradesmen in London or other English cities before their departure for the colonies. This pattern was duplicated in New York, Philadelphia, and Charles Town as well. (See Figure 1.5.) Besides being efficient middlemen in the distribution of goods and services, they performed a wide variety of other crucial services that promoted economic growth and urbanization. Since they owned or rented the ships and hired the captains, the merchants provided the transportation for most of the exported goods. They also supplied information about markets and served as financial intermediaries. Most important, with the profits derived from marketing, shipping and warehouse charges, insurance premiums, commissions on goods sold and credit services, they generated investment capital unavailable elsewhere in the colonies to set up grist mills and flour mills

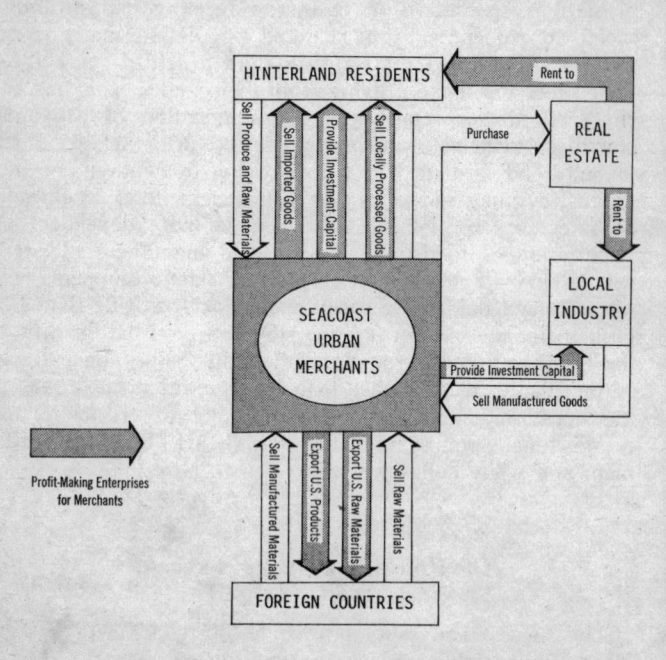

Figure 1.5 Generalized Model Showing the Pivotal Role Played by Seacoast Urban Merchants in the Communication Network (Copyright D. E. Hunter)

and local industries, and to help local and country storekeepers, craftsmen, and farmers. In addition, they invested in ships, land, and other profitable commercial ventures in their communities.

The key to the position of the merchant, however, is to be found in his relations with small farmers within his trading region. By assuring markets, these mercantile leaders drew farmers out of subsistence agriculture toward production for market and directly stimulated farmers to put more land under cultivation. Surplus capital provided credit to local farmers to purchase land, tools, building materials, livestock, clothing, and utensils. These varied activities explain the merchant's major role in his community and the regional economy as well as the accumulation of investment capital in these commercial towns. Without these capital resources, the colonial economy would have grown very, very slowly.

Another prime reason for the leadership exercised by seaport towns in shaping the direction of American inland growth was their control over the circulation of ideas and information. Out along the economic networks flowed not only goods and services but news and gossip from Europe, the other colonies, and elsewhere. Ships sailing to these seaports brought word of the latest in European politics, art, music, literature, religion, medicine, and science as well as new happenings in the other colonies. Along with their wares, inland traders and merchants carried news and gossip of the day. Newspapers first evolved in the seaports (for example, in Boston in 1704) as adjuncts of trade and commerce—to circulate business news and information about ship sailings, cargoes, goods and services available, but editors quickly introduced news sections to acquaint a news-hungry population with details of the outside world; though at first newspapers circulated locally, they, too, rapidly found their way inland along the trade routes. The towns represented a different way of life than the settled farm communities and the restless backcountry frontiers; through their role as transits of culture from the Old World to the New, they helped radiate urban values and a greater cultural breadth to the settled rural farm areas.

Urban Population Growth

The American urban foundation had been laid by 1700, and these colonial towns had developed into bustling communities. Although social and cultural activities were important, the main attractions of the urban centers were the wide range of supportive industries and services encouraged by trade and commerce. These activities offered a diversity of economic opportunities and were the underlying reason for the steady, if not in some cases, spectacular growth of urban populations. Boston's population had grown steadily from 1,200 in 1640 to more than 6,700 by the end of the century. New York, meanwhile, jumped from 300 in 1630 to more than 5,000, while Newport, with a population of 96 in 1640, grew to more than 2,600, Charles Town, 700 (1680) to 2,000. (Virtually all population figures are approximate because the actual populations of these seaports exceeded the town census or tax assessment rolls. The best recent approximations are to be found in Table 1.1.)

But it was Philadelphia that consistently demonstrated the most rapid patterns of growth. Within a few years of its founding, it had a population of 2,500 (1685), reaching 5,000 by 1700. And Philadelphia's eighteenth-century growth was spectacular; by 1760 it had jumped ahead of its rivals with over 23,000 residents. New York, with 18,000, and Boston, with 15,631, were relatively close behind, while Newport, with 7,500, and Charles Town, with 8,000 (half of whom were black slaves) were far behind.

Competition among cities prompted booms and economic declines. Baltimore became America's first "boom" town as its population soared from 200 to 5,934 between 1752 and 1775. Baltimore merchants after 1750 moved quickly to service the Maryland and Virginia wheat and rye producers, tapping Philadelphia's Susquehanna River hinterland trading area. Competition between Philadelphia and Baltimore merchants for backcountry farm commodities spurred farmers there to produce even larger yields.

Boston found itself losing ground and stagnating by the 1740s and 1750s, however, as Philadelphia, New York, and Newport seemed to surge ahead. Several Massachusetts towns, like Newburyport and Portsmouth, had become shipbuilding

TABLE 1.1*

Urban Population Growth in Colonial America

MAJOR CITIES

Year	New Amsterdam (New York)	Boston	Newport	Philadelphia	Charles Town
1630	300				
1640	400	1,200	96		
1650	1,000	2,000	300		
1660	2,400	3,000	700		
1680	3,200	4,500	2,500		700
1685				2,500	900
1690	3,900	7,000	2,600	4,000	1,100
1700	5,000	6,700	2,600	5,000	2,000
1710	5,700	9,000	2,800	6,500	3,000
1720	7,000	12,000	3,800	10,000	3,500
1730	8,622	13,000	4,640	11,500	4,500
1742	11,000	16,382	6,200	13,000	6,800
1760	18,000	15,631	7,500	23,750	8,000
1775	25,000	16,000	11,000	23,739 (7,179 suburbs†)	12,000
1776	5,000	3,500	5,299	21,767	12,000

SECONDARY CITIES ABOUT 1775

New Haven	(1771)	8,295	Hartford	(1774)	4,881
Norwich	(1774)	7,032	Middletown	(1775)	4,680
Norfolk	(1775)	6,250	Portsmouth	(1775)	4,590
Baltimore	(1775)	5,934	Marblehead	(1776)	4,386
New London	(1774)	5,366	Providence	(1774)	4,361
Salem, Mass.	(1776)	5,337	Albany	(1776)	4,000
Lancaster, Pa.	(1776)	5/6,000	Annapolis	(1775)	3,700
			Savannah	(1775)	3,200

*Adapted with permission, from Bayrd Still, *Urban America: A History with Documents*, p. 12. Copyright © 1974 by Little, Brown and Company, Inc.
†Suburb in this context meant adjacent communities that were economically linked but governmentally independent of the city.

specialists, while Newport took control of large portions of Boston's Long Island Sound traffic as well as the Narragansett Bay trade in cattle, horses, and grains.

The greatest period of urban growth during the colonial era occurred between 1760 and 1775. Led by Philadelphia, whose population reached about 30,000 (including its adjacent suburban districts), all of the major urban centers also showed growth: New York rose to 25,000, Boston, to 16,000, Charles Town, to 12,000, and Newport, to 11,000. Secondary seaports and inland towns had grown correspondingly by the 1770s. New Haven and Norwich, Connecticut, led with 8,295 and 7,032, while Norfolk, with 6,250, Baltimore, with 5,934, and Lancaster, Pennsylvania, with 5,500, were relatively close seconds. Salem, Massachusetts (5,337), New London, Connecticut (5,366), Providence, Rhode Island (4,361), and Albany, New York (4,000) were somewhat further back. Small by comparison to America's principal seaport cities, these urban centers nonetheless played a generative role in the interior of the country.

The Pre-Industrial American City

These communities were compact "pedestrian" or "walking cities," and the principal mode of transportation was walking. Because they had grown in a helter-skelter fashion, occupational and residential areas were, for the most part, mixed.

In the center of Philadelphia, for example, just beyond the dockside wards lay the middle ward. Within slightly less than twenty-five acres of land, as Sam Bass Warner, Jr. has shown, 1,401 men, women, and children of every condition from slave to William Penn's descendants lived and worked. This represented at least 346 families with 469 children, 17 hired servants, 65 indentured servants, 78 black slaves, and 80 tenants.

Within this ward also could be found a cross-section of the city's occupations. Along with five colonial government officers, nineteen merchants, two doctors, and twenty-nine shopkeepers could be found thirteen hatters, eleven innkeepers, thirteen tavernkeepers, ten bakers, ten carpenters, six coopers (barrelmakers), five schoolmasters, two silversmiths, two butchers, two bookbinders, as well as fifteen shoemakers, eleven watchmen (police), a watchmaker, printer, and goat keeper, and two carters and seventeen laborers.[13]

High building and land costs rather than strict municipal regulations kept houses small, narrow, cramped, and in short supply. Wood construction was expensive because a highly skilled carpenter and an army of assistants were necessary just to put up the building frame. Sixteen-inch square posts and beams were laboriously fastened together, lifted into place, and to them were nailed heavy planks, clapboards, and shingles. It was not until the 1830s that a new method—known as the balloon frame—was developed in Chicago which revolutionized construction in wood.

The availability of lumber and nails made this form of construction possible. Instead of heavy timbers fitted together, lighter, sawn lumber posts of smaller dimension—2x4s and 2x6s—were used to create the outer frame, while exterior boarding provided the structure's rigidity and strength. Using this method—sometimes referred to as early prefabrication—amateur builders rather than skilled carpenters were able to quickly construct housing. During the colonial era an artisan's or shopkeeper's house was generally about seventeen feet wide and twenty-five feet deep, a story and a half high, with a back area for gardens and a shed of cows, chickens, and perhaps even a horse. The owner and his family plied the trade in the largest front room.

The striking economic maturity of these pre-industrial cities was reflected in the gradual emergence, between the 1730s and 1760s, of specialized residential and occupational areas. (See Figure 1.6.) Near the center of the seaports, as Carl Abbott has shown, could be found the commercial section which included the retail establishments, major commercial institutions, and important merchant firms.[14] In Philadelphia, New York, and Boston, these zones were usually a few blocks from the public harbor, wharves, and warehouses. This was generally an area devoted to shipyards, where ship carpenters, sailmakers, longshoremen, and transient sailors lived and worked along the rivers or Atlantic Ocean. In Philadelphia, this maritime band was situated along the Delaware, in New York along the East River, and in Boston along the north end. While much of the local light manufacturing was carried on in small shops, such workshops tended to concentrate along or near the main commercial areas of these cities. Because of their noxious odors and the dangers they posed to public health, tanneries, distilleries, slaughterhouses, ropeworks, and similar industrial activities were generally concentrated on the edge or outside the town and city limits.

The city was already in the process of subdividing into

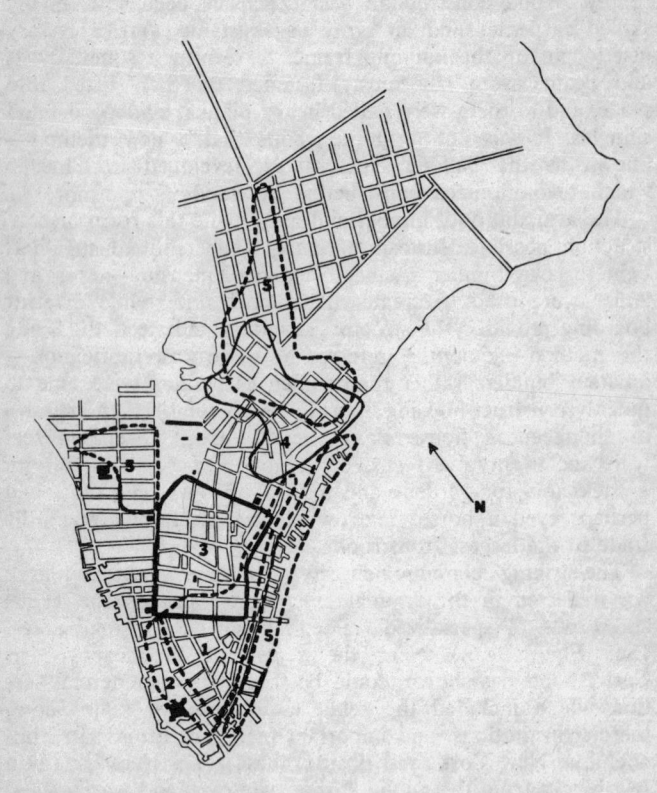

Neighborhoods of New York City before the American Revolution:
  1. *Commercial activity and upper class residences*
  2. *Upper class residences*
  3. *Artisanal manufacturing and residence*
  4. *Manufacturing*
  5. *Slums*
Map by Margery P. Abbott

Figure 1.6 Neighborhoods in Manhattan, 1760–1775 (Reproduced from Carl Abbott, "The Neighborhoods of New York, 1760-1775," *New York History* LV [January, 1974], p. 53. Courtesy of the author.)

sectors devoted to trade and commerce, light manufacturing, and heavy manufacturing, and there is considerable evidence that residential neighborhoods of different status were also developing. Basically, the upper class of merchants, professional men, and governmental officials concentrated near the main business streets in the center of town while the poor stayed on the fringes of the business district and the middle classes of prosperous craftsmen, small shopkeepers and grocers were in between. Areas with the poorest housing, and the highest incidence of crime, immorality, and poverty were also to be found along the waterfronts in all the larger seaports. As time passed, these characteristics would become more and more pronounced features of city life.

By the time of Revolutionary era, the pre-industrial city was the center of extensive manufacturing. Shipping and the preparation of foodstuffs and lumber for export along the Atlantic coast and the West Indies were the basic industries in every seaport. Most ports became centers for shipbuilding, flour milling, processing of lumber into naval stores (tar, pitch, turpentine), sugar refining, distilling, and barrel-, keg- and case-making. These occupations required skilled craftsmen such as ship carpenters, sailmakers, millers, and coopers, among others.

The expanding urban population also required a wide range of consumer goods and services provided by tailors, weavers, bakers, butchers, shoemakers, candlemakers, blacksmiths, brewers, paper makers, newspaper printers, and glass makers. Craftsmen-shopkeepers (such as tailors, bakers, gunsmiths, saddlemakers) were the small businessmen of the colonial period—part workingman, part property-holding entrepreneur—who manufactured goods largely for the inhabitants of the town and the immediate vicinity. Other manufacturing shopkeepers and artisans who produced for local sale and for export inland and along the coast were tanners of leather, coopers, metalsmiths (silversmiths, tinsmiths), and furniture makers.

This broad pattern of urban growth illustrates the theory of "circular and cumulative" causation put forth by economists. Local manufacturing and processing industries initially developed in seaport communities as adjuncts of trade and commerce because of locational and other advantages. But once established, these local industries (called "threshold industries") attracted individuals and businesses engaged in similar or linked activities, providing new jobs and creating new local needs for nonindustrial consumer goods and services such as food, clothing, housing, public buildings, and entertainment facilities, among other things. As the industry grew, the city population expanded, and the community became large enough to support more local or regional threshold industries, thus giving rise to another round of growth. (See Figure 1.7.)

Simultaneously, a second chain of circular and cumulative reactions tended to take place, setting the stage for technological growth and change. Dynamic urban centers attracted talent, new innovations and inventions, and were generally more open to new ideas, knowledge and skills brought in by immigrants and rural-to-urban-migrants. The adoption of new inventions or innovations in turn helped enlarge industry, attract more population growth, and continue the circular and cumulative process on a somewhat higher technological level. It is the multiplier effect underlying these two broad reaction-chains that helps explain rapid urban and economic growth during the colonial era. In short, success bred more success.

Due to the shortage of investment capital and European-produced machines, these industrial activities were unmech-

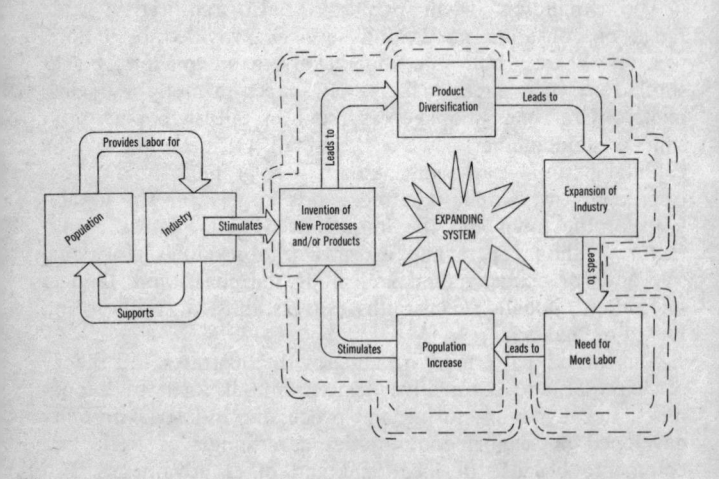

Figure 1.7 Model of the "Multiplier Effect" Showing the Mutual Stimulation of City Size, Growth, and Industrial Diversification (Copyright D. E. Hunter)

anized and basically dependent on handicraft production and manual power—a system of production usually referred to as the "cottage-and-mill" system of manufacturing. Household crafts were practiced most commonly by farmers and their families who made such articles as were necessary for their own use as well as some for sale; these included soap, cheese, candles, and wood products. Urban-based butchers, carpenters, shoemakers, candlemakers, weavers, blacksmiths, watchmakers, silversmiths, furniture makers, and other craftsmen and artisan shopkeepers produced goods with the aid of primitive tools and small numbers of apprentices, journeymen, and unskilled employees. Even the largest commercialized industries of the time were relatively small-scale, although they employed dozens of craftsmen and semiskilled workers. At least half of Philadelphia's work force in 1774 was engaged in various kinds of processing activities, among which were lumber and flour mills, sugar refineries, breweries, distilleries, tanneries, cheese and packing houses, fisheries, shipyards, ropeworks, slaughterhouses, iron foundries, and brick-making facilities.

Though small and based on hand labor, these industries did manage to produce significant quantities of manufactured goods. As an example, in 1768, New York City had seventy-seven distilleries which produced more than 540,000 gallons of rum for use in trade and commerce. Germantown, near Philadelphia, produced more than 60,000 pairs of stockings in a year during the 1760s, while Lynn, Massachusetts, made about 80,000 pairs of shoes in 1767 alone. The only other economic activities requiring large numbers of workers were the tobacco, rice, and indigo plantations. With the exception of a few of the commercialized industries and plantations, then, the basic characteristic of work within the colonial towns and cities was its individualized structure.

Urban Economic Stratifications and Social Structure

Detailed regulations of the economic life and activities within the municipalities were enforced until the eve of the Revolution. Like the city's social structure, the economic regulations were modeled closely upon those which had been traditionally exercised in European cities. The purpose was twofold: to safeguard the rights and the incomes of local merchants, tradesmen, and craftsmen as well as consumers. Limitations were set on wages, prices were regulated, and the quality of goods bought and sold in public markets was fixed. As early as 1640, for example, New Haven enacted legislation setting the maximum wages and prices for the important occupations (carpentry, building, and agricultural labor) and products (plants, boards, fencing, and lime). With varying degrees of success, this kind of regulation was attempted in all cities and towns during the seventeenth and eighteenth centuries. The three consumer commodities most frequently singled out for regulation were the price, weight, and quality of bread, meat, and firewood. In licensed inns and taverns, the price and quantity of all beverages was to be clearly posted. Since seaport town and city prosperity was dependent on exports, municipal inspectors examined and graded the quality of flour, salted fish, furs, and lumber.

This kind of minute inspection and regulation of economic activities extended to land use as well. The most complete land use controls were exercised in New England towns since the fundamental intention was the creation of a tight-knit community, but this kind of control was adopted elsewhere, too. Streets were planned, building sites specified, although the height and size of construction were generally left to the builder or owner. By the 1760s and 1770s, however, all kinds of economic and land use regulations were under attack because they hindered the free flow of trade, commerce, and economic activity. Militating against strict economic regulations throughout the colonial era was the dynamic process of growth and change, an acute labor shortage, the availability of land, and the each-against-all pursuit of individual gain that characterized the colonial towns and inland areas.

The everyday economic interactions of the urban populations directly affected the cities' social structure as well as their physical structures. The eighteenth century, no less than the seventeenth, was a highly stratified world of clearly defined classes or groups, each one of which was expected to defer to the next higher class on all social, political, economic, and religious matters.

At the apex of the colonial city and town structure were the "persons of quality," a small group consisting of royal officers, the most successful merchants or rich planters, high governmental officials in the colony, lawyers, and eminent clergymen (from the highest status denomination—the Anglican Church—to which this elite belonged). Men of less wealth and less eminent merchants, lawyers, doctors, clergymen, and urban-dwelling landowners comprised "the better sort." Though these cities, particularly Philadelphia and New York, were quite cosmopolitan, each was dominated by an Anglo-American merchant elite.

Not only did the merchant elite dominate in each city, but interurban information and economic ties between merchants in each major city also helped weld them together into a distinct intercolonial group. Merchants, whose incomes were indissolubly linked to the economic growth of the municipality, were anxious to maintain their monopolies of trade. Thus, all issues related to municipal projects, such as construction of wharves, docks, harbor renovation, bridges, roads, location of warehouses, laying out of new streets, taxation and local financial practices were of direct concern to the merchant elite, and they usually had their own way before the Revolution. As long as the elite's self-interest generally coincided with the broader needs of the community there were no real challenges to their domination.

Below the elite and better sort were the "middling sort." Perhaps one half to two thirds of all cities' inhabitants occupied the middle status of craftsmen, artisans, shopkeepers, and white collar workers in merchant firms. The "inferior sort" consisted of half-vagrant unskilled laborers, seamen, apprentices, indentured servants, freed slaves, mulattoes, and slaves. At the time of the Revolution, black slaves represented as much as one fifth of the local population of New York, Boston, and Philadelphia and one half in Charles Town.[15] For the most part, they were house servants or menial laborers (barbers and longshoremen), but many were also skilled craftsmen.

The degree to which economic and social class lines had hardened by the Revolution could be seen in Boston. Between 1687 and 1771, according to historian James Henretta, the share of the taxable wealth of the community controlled by the lower half of the propertied inhabitants declined from 12 to 10 percent. In 1771 the middle group of property holders owned only 12.5 percent of the taxable wealth, a decrease from the 21 percent held in 1687. However, the wealthiest 25 percent of the taxable population by 1771 controlled 78 percent of the assessed wealth—a gain of 12 percent from the end of the seventeenth century. Moreover, fully 29 percent of the adult white male population did not own *any* taxable property![16]

This situation was fundamentally the same in Philadelphia. The top 10 percent of the Philadelphia population controlled 54 percent of the city's taxable wealth, while the poorest 40 percent of the free adult inhabitants owned a pitiful 4 percent of the total wealth. Sam Bass Warner, Jr. has shown that only 19 percent of the local families in 1774 owned their own houses, while close to 80 percent lived in rented dwellings.[17] These findings for Boston and Philadelphia seem representative of the situation to be found in the other major seaport cities as well as inland towns.

The Goal of the Colonial City

The quality of a city depends on the motives behind its existence and the tendencies which shape its structures. As it evolved, the American colonial city increasingly became a highly stratified population of individuals all bent on private gain rather than a community concerned about all its citizens. In these commercially oriented cities and inland towns, the basic assumption was that each man was to make it on his own—a value which Sam Bass Warner, Jr. termed "privatism," and which he felt was the essence of the American urban experience. Privatism meant

> that the individual should seek happiness in personal independence and in the search for wealth; socially, privatism meant that the individual should see his first loyalty as his immediate family, and that a community should be a union of such money-making, accumulating families; politically, privatism meant the community should keep the peace among individual money-makers, and, if possible, help to create an open and thriving setting where each citizen would have some substantial opportunity to prosper.[18]

The goal of the colonial city, then, was to be a "community of private money-makers," and the "first purpose of the citizen" was the private search for wealth. It was thus material success that translated itself into other forms of prestige in the city.

But the urban dwellers did have some sense of local community identity and of shared interests that tended to blunt some of the sharper edges of this quest for material success. Through their economic interactions had come an awareness of their interdependence, and this helped foster a willingness to respond to their mutual needs. Geographical proximity helped reinforce these tendencies. All social classes and groups mixed together to some extent in these preindustrial walking cities and had some face-to-face contact. They shared the same few public facilities, such as stores, churches, taverns, and coffeehouses, and the children of different classes generally played together. Work patterns, too, tended to reinforce the "sense" of a cohesive, stable, orderly community, since the vast majority of men worked in small shops with a few other apprentices and journeymen and the shop owner. Despite differences in economic status, historian Gerard Warden wrote that Bostonians "still retained a remarkable sense of community spirit, a familiarity with one another that transcended the class or economic lines which divided larger European towns. There were very rich people and very poor people in Boston, but very few insuperable barriers between them."[19]

Without overly romanticizing the conditions in these preindustrial colonial cities, it is nonetheless possible to suggest that *some* sense of community existed. But this, too, was destined to wither away rapidly as the preindustrial city gave way to the nineteenth-century industrial city.

The Effects of the Revolution on Colonial Cities

Until the 1760s, the British government seemed more interested in trade and commerce than imperial control, and the North American colonies were able to grow and develop quite rapidly. The genius of the American colonial merchants, as economic historian George Rogers Taylor pointed out, was their ability to work autonomously but nonetheless within the framework of the British Empire.[20]

However, after England defeated France in the ruinous Seven Years War (1756–1763) and became the possessor of an expanded domain encompassing Canada and the Mississippi Valley, British leaders gave up the policy of "salutary neglect" that had characterized the 1720s to the 1760s. Beginning in 1763 they took steps to reorganize the entire structure of their New World empire, and for the first time Britain attempted to impose substantial taxation upon the colonists. This inevitably led to clashes with the American colonists, who had for so long been allowed to direct their own local affairs. Resistance centered in the seaport cities—facilitated by their concentrated urban populations and the ease of communication provided by the more than thirty-six newspapers flourishing by the beginning of the War for Independence.

New York Journal editor John Holt described the crucial role played by the city press in firing-up the Revolution, when he wrote in 1776 that "it was by means of newspapers that we received and spread the Notice of the tyrannical Designs formed against America and Kindled a Spirit that has been sufficient to repel them."

The Proclamation Line of 1763, restricting settlement of the region beyond the Allegheny-Appalachian Mountains, was quickly followed by the Sugar Act of 1764 and the Stamp Act of 1765, all of which demonstrated to the colonists the intent of the British to control their lives and local economies. Led by the seaport merchant class, who were beginning to suffer heavy losses, America began to resist the efforts of the King and Parliament.

Among the first cities to resist was Boston whose trade and prosperity were already suffering as a result of intense competition from Philadelphia, New York, and Newport. Merchants in Boston and other cities joined merchants' associations which provided local and then intercolonial leadership in the early phases of the resistance movement.

The Sons of Liberty was the other intercolonial resistance organization. Founded in 1765, it was composed of urban workers, mechanics or craftsmen, and sailors (who comprised the largest population group in these cities), but it was generally led by men of wealth and high position. This organization did not hesitate to resort to violence to prevent implementation of the Stamp Act. Within the year, it sprouted local chapters in Albany and White Plains in New York—spreading soon after to Boston, Baltimore, and Newport. Clashes between urban dwellers and Boston troops soon grew into armed encounters—as in the Battle of New York's Golden Hill and the Boston Massacre, both in 1770—which helped push colonies and mother country even further apart.

Many seaport towns suffered severe economic dislocation and heavy loss of population during the war years (1775–1783) as people sought to flee the unknown terrors of occupation by British troops. The population of Philadelphia dropped from about 40,000 to 21,767 in one year, while New

York (occupied throughout the war) fell from 25,000 to 5,000, and Boston lost some 5,000. Charles Town and Baltimore, however, were more fortunate. During the Revolution, Baltimore was the largest American seaport left open by the British, and after the war its mercantile operations continued to flourish. Its population more than doubled between 1775 and 1790, from 5,934 to 13,503.

Not until 1783 when the British evacuated New York City, however, were the Americans able to begin the long recovery from the war. In honor of independence, Charles Town was changed to Charleston.

During the 1780s merchants, shippers, craftsmen, and townsmen as well as planters understood how important it was to develop new markets. The struggle to regain the prosperity of the prewar period was made more difficult because American merchants were frozen out of the British West Indies and English markets. Salem and Boston merchants, as a consequence, pioneered the trade around the Cape of Good Hope to Mauritius (1784), Canton (1784), Bombay (1788), and Manila (1796). New Englanders developed the Pacific Northwest sea otter trade to find items that could be exchanged for Far Eastern goods. Well before 1820, then, they would have resident traders along the coast in Spanish California. Also seeking new markets were the New Yorkers and Pennsylvanians. The *Empress of China,* a cooperative venture of New York and Philadelphia merchants, sailed from New York City in 1784. It returned in 1785 with a cargo of silk and tea from Macao. Some of the French and Spanish ports were opened to American ships by the mid-1780s, as were the British West Indian Islands. By 1788 trade with the West Indies was as brisk as on the eve of the Revolution.

America's first national government—the Articles of Confederation—was adopted in 1781, but the states jealously retained all actual power within the system. And the Confederation Congress seemed unable to deal effectively with European nations. In the mercantilist world of the 1780s, it was also understood largely by urban economic groups that foreign trade, commerce, and shipping could only survive if there were a strong central government, strong enough to arrange mutual trade treaties with foreign nations and provide naval protection. Equally as important, westerners beyond the Allegheny-Appalachian Mountains desired a national government capable of militarily controlling the Indians, exerting pressure on Spanish and French to allow settlement of the Ohio Valley, and securing free navigation down the Mississippi River and the use of New Orleans, at its mouth.

Underlying all, however, was the desire for a stable national framework within which farmers, planters, craftsmen, merchants, shippers, and other key economic groups could expand their activities. Those groups most sensitive to these needs tended to be urban-based or economically dependent upon trade and commerce, and they proved the most important elements in the movement for the drafting and ratification of the United States Constitution. Of the fifty-five delegates to the Constitutional Convention in Philadelphia during the summer of 1787, twenty were urban dwellers, and another twenty were lawyers and merchants with urban contacts. At a time when only 5 percent of all Americans lived in cities, this is more than coincidental.

Following the adoption of the Constitution, no American city seemed to rebound more rapidly than Philadelphia, which reached the peak of its eighteenth-century influence by the end of the 1790s.[21] Its population—44,096 in 1790 and 61,559 in 1800 (including its contiguous suburbs)—made it the largest city in North America. Philadelphia served both as the state's capital and the national capital during the 1790s.

Washington, D. C.

Probably the most important urban development of the 1790s was the planning and construction of Washington, D. C.—a new national capital to reflect the future greatness of the American experiment in republican government.[22] Although Philadelphia had served as the first capital, between 1783 and 1790 the national capital had been moved from Philadelphia to Princeton, then to Annapolis, Trenton, New York, and back to Philadelphia. Washington was chosen in 1790 as the permanent site of the nation's capital because it was midway between the North and South. Beginning in the early 1790s, George Washington, who in his youth had been a surveyor, Thomas Jefferson, a talented amateur architect, and architect Pierre L'Enfant helped design the new, permanent national center of the United States. Important aid was

THE URBAN FRONTIER, 1600–1800

rendered by black mathematician Benjamin Banneker, who served as surveyor and engineer, and architect Bejamin Latrobe, who supervised construction of the city's public buildings.

The intention of the planners was to create a community whose members were to work or live not together but apart from each other, following the three main sections of the Constitution; one area for Congress, one for the President, and a third for the Supreme Court. Upon the familiar gridiron plan of parallel streets and right angles, L'Enfant superimposed a bold pattern of diagonal streets and wide avenues or promenades that radiated out from each of the two major centers of the community, the Congress and the President, and opened directly to the hinterland beyond. (See Figure 1.8.) The highest spot north of the Potomac River between the Anacosta River and Rock Creek was selected as the focal point where the Capitol building would stand, while the President's house was to be built a mile to the west near the shores of the Potomac. Another focal point within the city was the Great Mall, where the Washington and Lincoln monuments

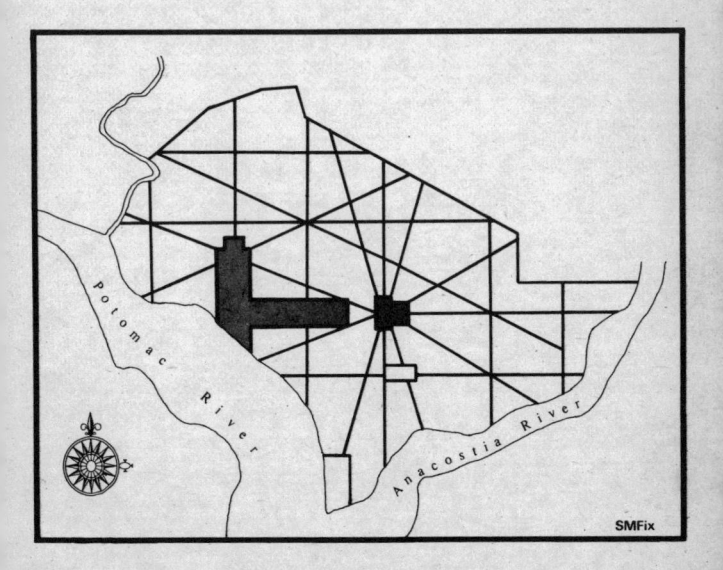

Figure 1.8 Schematic Town Plan of Washington, D.C. c. 1800

are now located, but other great open spaces—squares or circles—were provided for future city growth.

Washington, D. C., was the most carefully planned and constructed—and for most of its history one of the most beautiful—of America's cities. Created to provide government, not become a self-supporting economic unit, the planners did not set aside any part of the city for commercial or industrial activities or even market sites for the local needs of its future population. And without a significant geographical location, extensive agricultural hinterland, or sizable local population to service, Washington did not attract an energetic corps of merchants, craftsmen, and entrepreneurs. Washington thus remained an administrative center—a city of federal government employees, office-seekers, and a small service sector composed mainly of hotel, tavern, and innkeepers.

With a thriving economy, a growing population, a host of bustling regional cities, a new capital under construction, and expanding western territories, the new nation had achieved a great deal in a short time—yet the most astonishingly rapid period of growth lay just ahead.

2

Rising Centers of Commerce and Industry

During the first thirty years of the new American nation, urbanization continued at a very gradual pace. Indeed, from 1810 to 1820, the decade of the semi-disastrous War of 1812, the rate of urban growth showed a very slight decline. From 1820 on, however, the American people advanced rapidly toward an urban civilization. Cities developed and grew faster during the next four decades than in any other period of American history. The urban population soared upward from 693,225 in 1820 to more than 6,216,518 (or 19.8 percent of the total population) by 1860; and between 1860 and 1870 the number of urban dwellers rose to 9,902,000, representing 25.7 percent of the total population. Indeed, the rate of urban growth was striking—62.6 percent between 1820 and 1830, 63.7 percent between 1830 and 1840, 92.1 percent between 1840 and 1850, and 75.4 percent between 1850 and 1860; between 1860 and 1870, the rate was 59.3 percent, representing an increase of some 3.5 million people. In 1830 there were 23 cities with a population of 10,000 or more; by 1860 there were more than 101. The number of places containing 25,000 or more inhabitants rose from five to thirty-five, and the number of cities with 100,000 jumped from one to nine.

Factors Contributing to Urban Growth

One of the chief factors promoting such growth was the expansion of commerce. Between 1792 and 1815, the war in Europe, by greatly stimulating the demand on the continent and in the West Indies for American surpluses of grain and meat, had proved highly profitable for American farmers and

TABLE 2.1
Population Growth of Regionally Important Cities, 1790–1870*

	1790	1800	1810	1820	1830	1840	1850	1860	1870
NORTHEAST									
New York	33,131	60,515	100,775	130,881	214,995	348,943	515,500	813,600	942,292
Philadelphia	44,096	61,559	87,303	108,809	161,271	220,423	340,000	565,529	674,022
Boston	18,320	24,937	38,746	43,298	61,392	93,383	136,881	177,840	250,526
Brooklyn				11,187	20,535	47,613	138,882	279,122	419,921
Rochester					9,207	20,191	36,403	48,204	62,386
Albany	3,498	5,289	10,762	12,630	24,209	33,721	50,763	62,367	69,422
Newark			5,008	6,507	10,953	17,290	38,894	71,941	105,059
Lowell					6,474	20,796	33,383	36,827	40,928
Providence	6,380	7,614	10,071	11,767	16,833	23,171	41,513	50,666	68,904
New Haven	4,487	4,049	5,772	7,147	10,180	12,960	20,345	39,267	50,840
MIDWEST									
Chicago						4,470	29,963	112,172	298,977
St. Louis					4,977	16,469	77,860	160,773	310,864
Cincinnati		750	2,540	9,642	24,831	46,338	115,435	161,044	216,239
Pittsburgh	376	1,565	4,768	7,248	15,369	31,204	67,863	77,923	139,256
Buffalo			1,508	2,095	8,668	18,213	42,261	81,129	117,714
Detroit				1,422	2,222	9,102	21,019	45,619	79,577
Cleveland				606	1,076	6,071	17,034	43,417	92,829
Milwaukee						1,712	20,061	45,246	71,440
Minneapolis								2,564	13,066
SOUTH									
Baltimore	13,503	26,514	46,555	62,738	80,620	102,313	169,054	212,418	267,354
New Orleans		9,650	17,242	27,176	46,082	102,193	116,375	168,675	191,418

Table 2.1 (continued)

Washington		3,210	8,208	13,247	18,826	23,364	40,001	61,122	109,199
Richmond	3,761	5,737	9,735	12,067	16,060	20,153	27,570	37,910	51,038
Norfolk	2,959	6,926	9,193	8,478	9,814	10,920	14,326	14,620	19,229
Charleston	16,359	18,924	24,711	24,780	30,289	29,261	42,985	40,522	48,956
Savannah		5,146	5,215	7,523		11,214	15,312	22,292	28,235
Atlanta							2,572	9,554	21,789
Memphis					5,566		8,841	22,623	40,226
Nashville	200	359	1,357	4,012	10,341	6,929	10,165	16,988	25,865
Louisville						21,210	43,194	68,033	100,753
PLAINS & MOUNTAINS									
Omaha								1,883	16,083
Kansas City, Mo.								4,418	32,260
Denver								4,749	4,759
Galveston								7,000	13,818
San Antonio							2,396	6,000	13,000
Houston								4,845	9,382
PACIFIC									
San Francisco							34,766	56,802	149,473
Los Angeles							1,610	4,385	5,728
Portland								2,874	8,293
Seattle									1,107
Total of Urban Dwellers	202,000	322,000	525,000	693,000	1,127,000	1,845,000	3,543,700	6,216,500	9,902,000
Percent Urban	5.1	6.1	7.3	7.2	8.8	10.8	15.3	19.8	25.7
Total U.S. Population	3,929,000	5,308,000	7,240,000	9,638,000	12,866,000	17,069,000	23,191,800	31,433,300	39,800,000

*These statistics are derived from U.S. Censuses in 1850, 1860, and 1910 (Washington, D.C.: U.S. Government Printing Office).

shippers alike. After the Napoleonic Wars had ended, there was a great increase in the volume of inter-regional trade between eastern seaports and manufacturing centers and the rapidly growing South and West. Thus, after 1815, there was, in the telling phrase of George Rogers Taylor, "a great turnabout" in the nation's commerce, as shippers and manufacturers became less dependent on the European markets, from which most of their business had formerly come, and expanded their commerce to the southern and western regions of the nation.[1]

Before long, the three major sections of the nation—the Northeast, the West, and the South—were producing specialized commodities and services for sale elsewhere in the country. The West produced foodstuffs, the South raw materials for industry, especially cotton, and the Northeast became the manufacturing and financial center of the nation. The nation was being transformed from a small, agricultural society into an increasingly urban and industrial one. (See Figure 2.1.)

Both the volume of trade and urban growth were promoted by new and improved roads and by the era's revolutionary innovations in communication. Canals and steamboats reduced both the costs of shipping goods and the time required for commodities to reach distant markets to a mere fraction of what they had formerly been. Distances and costs were

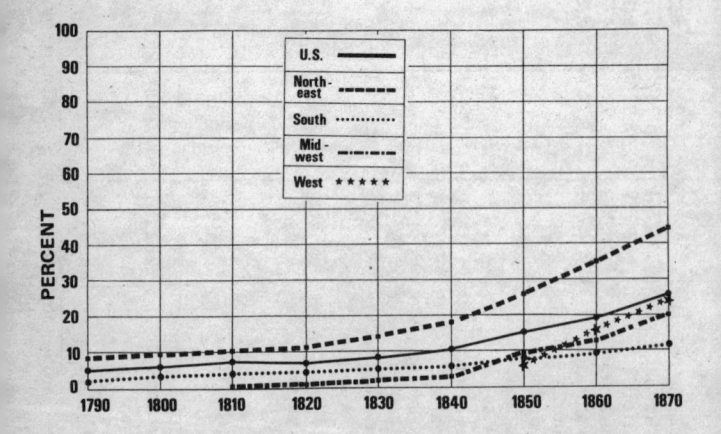

Figure 2.1 Urban Growth by Section, 1790–1870

cut even further by the most revolutionary of all the era's innovations, the railroad. Finally, the telegraph made it possible to communicate virtually within seconds with quite distant areas.

The rapid spread of these new forms of communication had been spurred by the fierce intercity rivalries for markets that had been characteristic of America's cities and that was typified by the rivalry between Philadelphia and Baltimore in the later eighteenth century (see pp. 48–52). By the 1790s, city leaders had already become convinced that improved transportation was the key to the continuance and growth of commercial prosperity. Consequently, merchants and politicians in the established eastern seaports raced to extend their hinterland connections through the construction of new roads, canals, and railways.

Many of the emerging cities also engaged in the construction of new transportation systems and frequently came to regret it. Many of their hastily undertaken projects failed to attract enough traffic to allow the repayment of their construction costs. In the end, these doomed projects were quickly abandoned, as were many of the communities that had grown up near them. Thus, despite the heavy expenditure on canals (some $250 million by 1840), some were jettisoned when the railroads, with their greater efficiency, speed, and cheaper rates, invaded their territory.

The crazy-quilt pattern of canal and railroad construction was governed almost entirely by local feelings, urban pride, and capricious governmental decisions. Although substantial capital for construction of railroads was raised in local areas (along the railroad rights-of-way), most came from the major eastern cities, the state governments, and European investors. The cost of railroad construction was incredibly high: $2,000,000 was expended in 1830, $80,000,000 by 1840, and $1,000,000,000 by 1860. Railroad building stimulated the entire economy since there was a need for prodigious amounts of manpower, iron, lumber, and financial resources, as well as organizational and managerial talents. Urban rivalries, far more than any other force, shaped these economic developments.

In bringing every part of the nation within reach of every other, the revolution in communications provided great encouragement to the development of manufacturing. By 1830 there was a sizable textile industry in New England and by mid-century there were ironware and agricultural processing industries as well. Various technical innovations starting with Eli Whitney's invention of standardized parts early in the century, had by the 1850s helped to create the "American system of manufacturing"—mass production in factories of standardized, and therefore interchangeable, parts. Although, as late as 1860, fast-flowing waterfalls were still the chief source of mechanical power, the steam engine was being used increasingly after 1830 in such major industries as agricultural implements, shoes, clothing, textiles, and agricultural processes.

Growth of the Atlantic Ports

Thanks to these advances, several of the Atlantic seaports were able to add extensively to their hinterlands and were also able to control their areas more than before. As a result, the population in several of the leading eastern seaports expanded rapidly. Philadelphia's population increased from about 87,000 in 1810 to roughly 565,000 as of 1860, while that of Baltimore increased from 46,000 to about 212,000. Even Charleston, which failed signally in this period to maintain its position as the South's leading seaport, saw its population increase from about 24,000 in 1810 to over 40,000 in 1860. Finally, the number of Boston's residents also increased, going to just under 178,000 on the eve of the Civil War.

BOSTON AND THE MILL TOWNS

The growth of Boston was accomplished despite many factors that pointed toward its decline. After 1790 Boston's maritime industries tapered off. Its narrow hinterland, the lessening importance of its West Indian trade, the restricted resources of its fisheries, the uncertainty of the newly opened China trade, and New York's aggressiveness in capturing much of the Connecticut Valley business all seemed to forecast Boston's rapid decline to the status reached by Newport, Rhode Island, several decades before.

Such, however, was not to be the case. Soon after the Embargo of 1807, Boston merchants began to invest some of their accumulated capital resources in textile factories, which were expanded by the War of 1812. Applying the technology pioneered in England, the Boston Manufacturing Company began textile production in Waltham, Massachusetts, in 1813. Here the complete textile operation, from spinning raw cotton to dyeing the finished cloth, was mechanized and combined under one roof. By 1816 more than eighty such mills were situated along the swift-flowing rivers in Massachusetts, Connecticut, and Rhode Island, giving rise to a new kind of urban community in New England. Towns began to spring up around these factories providing shelter and services for the mill workers. Boston in turn benefitted greatly from the increase in raw materials and finished goods that flowed through the city's port.

After 1815 the growth of New England mill towns was largely in the hands of absentee corporate interests in Boston. Although at first the Boston investors were concerned about the welfare of their workers, they soon came to regard the factory, town, and workers as little more than figures on profit-and-loss statements. During the 1820s and 1830s, Boston investor groups set up factory towns all over New England to produce textiles, woolens, furniture, paper products, shoes, and tools. Planned mill towns were established in Lowell, Lawrence, Chicopee, and Holyoke in Massachusetts, and at Manchester and Nashua in New Hampshire. Lowell, situated on the Merrimack River, grew from 2,500 in 1823, to 18,000 by 1836, to 41,000 in 1870.

The most distinctive feature of these mill towns was the long row of houses or tenements near the factory buildings, all grouped around the river site. In his description of Lowell, Massachusetts, in 1846, Henry A. Miles, a Unitarian minister, captured the essence of these company-owned, tightly organized factory towns:

> The superintendent, from his room, has the whole of the corporation under his eye. On the one side are the boarding-houses, all of which are under his care, and are rented only to known and approved [worker] tenants; on the other side are the mills, in each room of which he has stationed some carefully selected overseer, who is held responsible for the work, good order, and proper management of his room. Within the yard, also are repair shops, each department of which, whether of iron, leather [for pulleys], or wood, has its head overseer. There is a superintendent of the yard, who, with a number of men under his care, has charge of all the out-door work of the establishment.[2]

The human dimension is ably described by historian Constance M. Green who provides a portrait of Holyoke, Massachusetts, between the 1860s and 1870s.

> Mill whistles sounded at six in the morning and at six at night, and walking through heavy snow in winter or mud in spring meant that people must live within a mile or two of their work. People crowded into tenements, sometimes ten to twelve families in a house built for two or three. The charming spot just above the dam with a beautiful view of the river and hills became a slum. The newcomers were usually ignorant of the most elementary rules of health and sanitation, and, had they been educated, poverty and lack of facilities would still have made their quarters uncomfortable at best, foul at worst.[3]

These mill towns were not only the first true factory towns in America but also the first "company" towns as well—a phenomenon generally associated with mining and railroad communities in the trans-Mississippi West later in the century.

NEW YORK: THE COTTON TRIANGLE AND THE ERIE CANAL

The incredible growth of New York was made possible largely because of its initial advantages. It possessed the finest deep-water harbor on the Atlantic coast, its merchants were as experienced and aggressive as any in America, and its immediate hinterland in New York States and eastern New Jersey had begun filling up rapidly with new settlers during the early nineteenth century.

The excellent connection of New York's commercial community with London commerce permitted them to take advantage of the massive "dumping" campaign launched by Great Britain after the War of 1812 in order to smash the newly budding American textile industries. Since British manufacturers chose New York as the port to unload their surplus textiles and thereby undermine American mills, wholesale buyers flocked to the city for bargains which they could, in turn, sell to merchants up and down the Atlantic coast and to country storekeepers inland. New York merchants devised a new auction system in 1817 which, by eliminating the middleman and requiring that all goods offered at auction *had* to be sold, made Empire City imports cheaper than those in other seaports. Eventually British merchants and manufacturers retreated from their policy of economic warfare, but American wholesalers continued to buy from New York City importers and merchants.

New Yorkers also introduced, in 1818, the first transatlantic "packet" line—*The Blackball Express*—between America and England; sailing on a regular monthly schedule not only meant fast, dependable service and more extensive business information, but also made New York City the principal port-of-entry for European immigrants. Those Europeans passing through on the way west were outfitted by New York merchants and manufacturers, while the rest, who remained, added immeasurably to the city's vast labor pool and consumer population.

A network of commercial agents and fast ships enabled Empire City merchants to outdistance their competitors in the speed with which they could obtain information about markets and prices, a critical factor in a commerce-based economy. New Yorkers in 1818 knew what was happening as far away as Norfolk, Virginia, Syracuse, New York, and Portsmouth, Massachusetts, whereas it took their nearest competitors in Philadelphia the same amount of time to obtain news from Richmond, Virginia.

Equally important, New Yorkers expanded their coastwide trade, taking command of the South's new cash crop, cotton. As early as 1785, New Yorkers exported southern cotton to Europe, but it was not until 1793, when Connecticut inventor Eli Whitney created the first cheap, practical, easy-to-use cotton gin, or engine, to remove the seeds from the cotton boll that southern planters began to specialize in cotton production.

Half of all cotton produced in America was grown in South Carolina as of 1801, the rest in Georgia, North Carolina, and Virginia. In search of new cotton land, Southerners extended the plantation-slave system southwestward along a narrow strip across Alabama, Mississippi, and Louisiana. Between 1794 and 1820, cotton production rose from 5 million to 160 million pounds. Cotton exports had risen in value to $15 million by 1810.

New Yorkers aggressively solicited southern cotton business through the provision of financial services—credit, insurance, and investment capital. New York ships picked up cotton from Charleston, Savannah, and New Orleans, carried it to Liverpool, bringing back European cargoes to New York, and these imports were distributed throughout the New York hinterland. By 1811 New York led the field in cotton export and was well on the way to becoming the principal commercial city for the South.

New York City's commercial supremacy was strengthened by the Erie Canal which, under the leadership of Governor De Witt Clinton, was constructed by New York State between 1817 and 1825 at a cost well over $10,000,000. Even while it was being constructed, the Erie, sometimes referred to as "the Mother of Cities," transformed a series of inland villages along the Hudson-Mohawk Valley corridor in New York State—Buffalo, Syracuse, Rochester, Utica, and Rome—into thriving centers of trade, transport, and later of manufacturing.

Freight costs from Buffalo to New York City were cut from $100 a ton to $10 and travel time from twenty to six days! In the decade following 1815, a mounting stream of wheat, flour, corn, pork, beef, and livestock began pouring from the Ohio and Mississippi valleys into the East through the Erie Canal. The canal not only made it possible for northern Ohio farmers to supply goods directly to New York City, instead of sending agricultural commodities down the Ohio and Mississippi rivers to New Orleans; it also decisively shifted the trade axis from north-south to an east-west direction.

The success of the Erie touched off a canal construction craze during the 1820s as cities and towns in eastern and midwestern states vied for east-west or west-east connections. Most of these ventures did little, however, to change the direction of internal trade, and the great majority failed to make money. Nevertheless, the Erie and other east-west canals fostered the specialization and commercialization of western farming, since large quantities of heavy agricultural commodities could be shipped cheaply over a few direct routes to distant markets in the East.

Philadelphia and Baltimore: Two Rivals

Vigorous growth characterized the other established seaports as well. Philadelphia's continued growth was tied to the exportation of foodstuffs from its trading areas in western New Jersey, southern New York, Pennsylvania, Delaware,

RISING CENTERS OF COMMERCE AND INDUSTRY

and the backcountry. This broad hinterland stimulated Philadelphia's consumer manufacturing industries to such a degree that in 1810 its products were valued at $16,000,000. Baltimore had replaced Boston in 1800 as the third largest city, primarily as a result of its booming wheat business. During the 1790s Baltimore had become the country's leading flour milling center. Its merchants drew upon a trading area composed of Virginia, Maryland, Delaware, western Virginia, and the Susquehanna Valley of Pennsylvania for wheat, tobacco, and cotton. Both Baltimore and Philadelphia vied for control of the overland trade with the expanding Ohio Valley population.

The growth of Philadelphia and Baltimore was also prompted by improvements in transportation. As early as the 1790s Philadelphia and Baltimore business leaders hoped to capitalize upon the Cumberland Gap through the mountains into the Ohio Valley. Baltimoreans helped persuade the United States government to build a road from Cumberland, Maryland, to Wheeling (now West Virginia) on the Ohio River. Begun in the 1790s, the National Road was completed in 1818, and a Maryland highway connected Baltimore, providing that city's merchants—and Philadelphia's as well—with the first major overland route into the continent's interior. As cities grew along its path, the National Road had been extended by 1840 through Columbus and Dayton in Ohio, Indianapolis and Terre Haute in Indiana, to Vandalia, Illinois.

In the 1820s, Philadelphia, already a booming center of commerce and manufacturing, undertook several major canal projects. The Pennsylvania Main Line, which ran through Harrisburg to Pittsburgh in the Ohio Valley, proved less successful than the Erie Canal. But another canal system, completed in 1825, linking Philadelphia to Pennsylvania's Lehigh Valley coal deposits in the northwest, was a major boost to the city's economy. Philadelphia began to export large quantities of high-quality, long-burning clean coal to New York and other eastern cities where it was used both for household heating and a variety of industrial purposes.

The availability of inexpensive coal accelerated the adaptation of the steam engine to power river boats and textile mill machinery. Significant amounts of coal were shipped to Boston for use in the textile mill satellite towns of southern New England, many of which used stationary steam engines to supplement water power. Steam-powered factories appeared rapidly in Philadelphia, New York, and Baltimore during the late 1820s and early 1830s. In Bridgeport and New Haven, Connecticut, for example, factories using steam power produced such common consumer items as brass clocks and locks as well as various agricultural implements and tools to make machines (see Figure 2.2 for the broad indications of these developments). Many of these plants throughout the Northeast employed mass-produced, interchangeable-parts technology to make these commodities.

Apparently the crucial function of building and maintaining steam engines and mill machinery was performed initially by a host of farmer-mechanics and talented tinkerers who received their training in the New England, New York, and Pennsylvania grist mills and sawmills and blacksmith shops. During the 1820s and 1830s, clusters of shops and plants producing steam engines and turbines, mill machinery, machine-making tools and power lathes appeared in every major city. Near these shops could generally be found dozens of specialized parts producers and auxiliary service trades. With the introduction of the railroad in the late 1820s, these American shops began producing and repairing railroad loco-

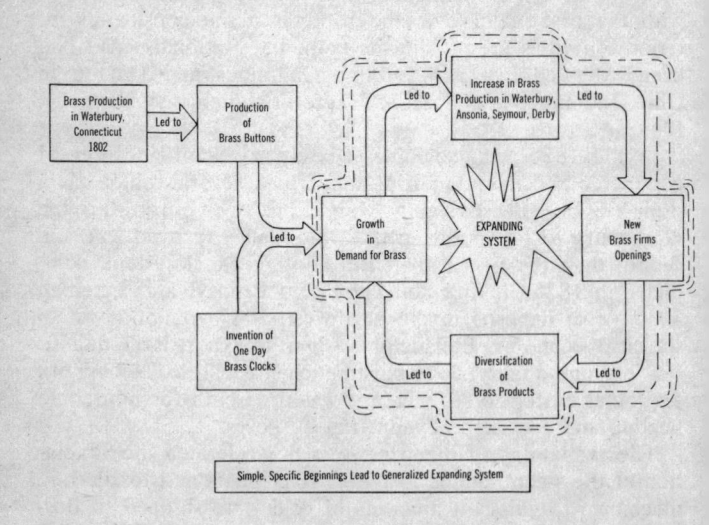

Figure 2.2 An Example of the Circular and Cumulative Growth Process: Brass Production in Connecticut, 1800–1850 (Copyright D. E. Hunter)

motives and cars. Had it not been for these domestic shops and the pool of skilled mechanics, American factories and railroad companies would have been dependent upon expensive European-produced machinery and European-trained craftsmen, and the nation's industrial growth would have been much, much slower.

In 1827, the bankers and businessmen of Baltimore, the nation's leading flour-milling center, decided that their city could best strengthen its waning hold upon its markets by constructing a steam-powered railroad, such as had recently been developed in England. Baltimore businessmen prepared a plan, obtained a company charter, raised $3.5 million, and hired an engineer to start construction of the 380-mile Baltimore and Ohio Railroad. To assure their town's selection as the Ohio River terminus, citizens in Wheeling raised $1 million to pay for building costs. By 1830, a double track had been laid from Baltimore to Ellicott's Mills, thirteen miles away; within five years, this line gave Baltimore undisputed commercial control of most of Maryland's trade, creating a railroad construction mania throughout the nation during the 1840s. When the B.&O. reached the Ohio River in 1850, Baltimore was again a major outlet for western products, second only to New York and New Orleans. Meanwhile, Philadelphia's leaders co-sponsored with the Pittsburgh counterparts construction of a railroad link to Pittsburgh, which was completed in 1852. Baltimore redoubled its efforts, and the B.&O. reached Cincinnati in 1858.

The hinterlands of all the major Atlantic seaports were extended by the construction of railroads leading West. Boston had experimented with short rail lines to Lowell and Worcester, its industrial satellites, and then began construction of a railroad west to Albany on the Hudson (completed in 1842), so as to use the Erie Canal. Albany's citizens sponsored a $1 million bond issue to support construction of the railroad line. This, among other reasons, prompted New Yorkers to project a railroad (virtually paralleling the Erie Canal) from New York City to Albany and Dunkirk on Lake Erie, which was completed in 1851.

With the construction between 1849 and 1854 of four trunk lines—the B.&O., the Erie, the Pennsylvania, and the New York Central—connecting the Atlantic Ocean with western river cities, railroad development took on all the aspects of a great race. By 1858, New York, Boston, Philadelphia, and Baltimore were connected by rail with the major cities of the Middle West. Thus, as Richard Wade has written, "New York, Philadelphia, Baltimore, and Boston promoted all kinds of water and rail enterprises into the Ohio Valley . . . and speeded the transformation of the continent from a wilderness into a modern civilization."[4]

The Inland River Towns and Cities

Soon after the Revolutionary War settlers began pushing across the Appalachian Mountains into America's vast inland domain. Fueling the westward migrations was a veritable city-building mania as town boosters and real estate promoters attempted to transform western river sites or prairie land into great cities. In contrast to responsible promoters who tried to sell legitimate town lots or "package" an entire town, there were a vast array of hucksters and confidence men who swarmed all over the West as early as the 1780s and 1790s. Settlers were induced to go west not only by the prospect of acquiring fertile farmland but also by the promise of success in these emerging western towns. Yet as these towns grew, they not only hastened the settlement and commercialization of the surrounding agricultural areas, they also imposed something of an urban quality on the agrarian West.

Before 1800 all of the major towns of the Old Northwest and Great Lakes region, with the exception of Chicago, Indianapolis, and Milwaukee, had been surveyed, the grid system applied, and the land cleared (see page 66 for a description of the gridiron system of urban land use). Geographical location helps explain the initial success of many western communities (see Map 2.1). Before the advent of the railroad, the chief artery of interior trade and travel was the Ohio River and its tributaries flowing into the Mississippi and down through New Orleans into the Gulf of Mexico. Situated strategically at the juncture of the Monongahela and Allegheny rivers, which joined to form the 980-mile Ohio River, was Pittsburgh, originally the site of Fort Duquesne, which commanded the whole upper-Ohio Valley. Four hundred and fifty miles down the Ohio in the heart of the trans-Appalachian region was Cincinnati, destined to become the major distribution center for the interior because of its access to the rich farmlands of Kentucky and Ohio. At the falls of the Ohio, some ninety miles downstream from Cincinnati, was

RISING CENTERS OF COMMERCE AND INDUSTRY 53

Louisville, whose major business was transshipment of goods around the falls, the river's major obstruction. The fourth major inland river city was St. Louis, located on the west bank of the Mississippi River just below the juncture of the Mississippi, Illinois, and Missouri rivers.

Dependent at first upon local market needs, the Ohio Valley river towns' growth stemmed from the westward migrations. By the 1780s and 1790s they functioned as frontier way stations supplying the United States Army Indian ex-

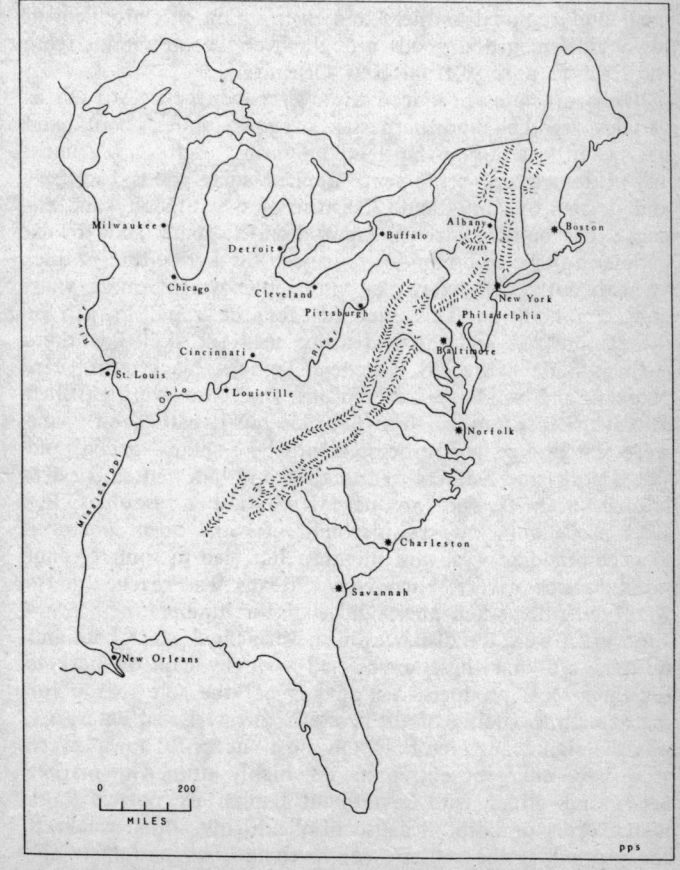

Map 2.1 Major Cities of the Ohio-Mississippi Valleys

peditions and outfitting the seemingly endless flow of migrants and transients, those passing through and those who settled nearby. (Despite the Indian threat, the population in the trans-Appalachian West soared to 200,000 in 1790, 400,000 in 1800, and a million in 1810.) Although little more than clusters of taverns, gristmills or sawmills, small blacksmith and workshops, around the rivers, these small towns, like their colonial predecessors in the seventeenth century, were, almost from the outset, amazingly complex and multipurpose. They were commercial centers whose principal activities lay in trading with their hinterlands, gathering up the output of local and regional farmers and distributing the products of town craftsmen and goods brought over the mountains from the East or upriver from New Orleans.

The workshops produced the everyday necessities such as candles, saddles and harnesses, wagons, shoes, boots and hats, a little clothing, household utensils, and soap. Almost any little western settlement supplied such goods for itself and its nearby hinterlands. Because of the difficulty and expense of long-distance transportation, farmers and townspeople in these communities processed the agricultural staples (wheat, corn, and livestock) into lighter-weight, more valuable commodities. This accounts for the rapid growth of these industries and the increasing need for skilled workers such as millers, brewers, butchers, tanners, blacksmiths, carpenters, and saddlemakers. Grains and corn were distilled into whiskey or milled into flour or meal; cattle and swine were slaughtered and processed into beef, hams, bacon, and salted pork; and leathers were tanned and hides cured. Lastly, lumber products were produced from timber resources. Besides processing, townspeople built rafts and boats, not only to accommodate westward migrants but also to ship regional products downriver. When New Orleans was reached, rafts were generally taken apart and sold for lumber.

So great were the distances in the pre-canal, steamboat and railroad era that these towns had virtually captive markets for their local products. Yet that is not the sole reason for the economic vitality of the western towns. Local enterprise was the significant factor. In the most successful towns were a corps of energetic entrepreneurs, highly attuned to market needs and gifted with investment capital or possessed of scarce skills or both. Because of the highly commercialized background of the settlers, entrepreneurs had extremely sophisticated consumer demands to satisfy, and they began to

RISING CENTERS OF COMMERCE AND INDUSTRY

produce a wide array of manufacturers and specialties for local use and regional distribution. Lexington manufactured hemp sacks and rope for the cotton trade, Louisville cured and marketed tobacco, while Cincinnati processed grain and livestock.

Drawing wholly upon local capital and talent, Pittsburgh businessmen developed a glass factory, shipyard, iron foundries, and five nail factories well before 1812. Local metal workers produced household utensils and tools. So rapidly did the value of Pittsburgh's manufactures increase, from more than $350,000 in 1803, to $1,000,000 in 1810, to more than $2,600,000 in 1815, that the town earned the title "the Birmingham of America."[5]

Before the advent of canals, the trans-Appalachian West's annual imports and exports reached an appreciable figure. In 1817, for example, 13,000 wagons came to Pittsburgh from Philadelphia and Baltimore. The value of such goods purchased in the East and brought down the Ohio River was estimated at between $16,000,000 and $17,000,000. This did not take into consideration the merchandise that came up the Mississippi River by way of New Orleans. As for exports, between 1801 and 1816 the value of western goods shipped downstream rose from $3,700,000 to $8,000,000.

Despite these early successes, the mortality rate among these towns was high. Ghost towns littered the Ohio and Mississippi Valley landscape; when expected transportation schemes failed to materialize, or local industries petered out, settlers and promoters simply left for more promising towns up or down river or farther west. For every successful interior city, there were dozens of others that failed—or died. Edwardsville, Illinois, never grew to rival St. Louis; Pittsburgh overcame Steubenville, Ohio, and Wheeling, West Virginia; Jeffersonville and New Albany, Indiana, never matched Louisville; Cincinnati outdistanced North Bend, Louisville, and Manchester. Cairo, Illinois, never quite grew large despite vigorous promotional efforts throughout the century. Somehow their original promise never quite equaled that of cities which became important. Even some that thrived, such as Louisville, could not duplicate the success of Cincinnati. (See Figure 2.3.)

Urban rivalries, too, contributed to the growth of some towns and the stagnation of others. "One of the most striking characteristics," says Richard Wade, "was the development of an urban imperialism which saw rising young giants seek to spread their power and influence over the entire new country." If possible, western rivalries were more intense and openly ferocious than in the East. One of the most bitter of the early struggles for regional supremacy was that between Pittsburgh and Wheeling over which would serve as the terminal point of the Ohio River. Soon thereafter a duel ensued between Pittsburgh and Cincinnati. "Poor Pitts," exclaimed a jubilant Cincinnati newspaper in 1818, "your day is over, the sceptre of influence and wealth is to travel to us."[6]

Had it not been for the advent of the steamboat in 1811, however, the trans-Appalachian West would have remained for many years a relatively undeveloped, isolated inland

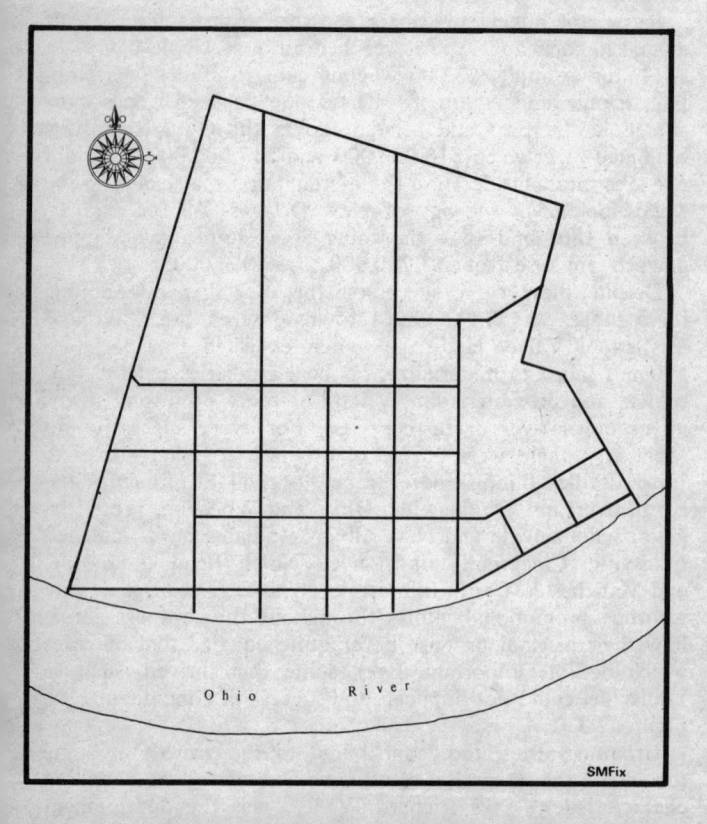

Figure 2.3 Schematic Town Plan of Cincinnati c. 1815

region, dotted with small river towns and adjacent agricultural areas. Soon after Robert Fulton's *New Orleans* steamed down the Mississippi in 1811 from Pittsburgh, where it had been built, steamboat construction fever hit the river towns. By 1818, steamboats could be found on the inland river systems, becoming by 1830 the most important factor in the Mississippi Valley.

Steam navigation, in the words of Richard Wade, "telescoped a half century's development into a single generation."[7] The 1,500-mile trip up from New Orleans to Cincinnati, for example, was cut from seventy-eight to twenty-five days. During the 1820s and 1830s, as upriver travel became more rapid and dependable, Pittsburgh, Cincinnati, Louisville, and St. Louis grew from small regional towns into dynamic cities. Because the initial investment was relatively small, the steamboat industry in the western towns was financed by local merchants, farmers, traders, and speculators who were the principal users of the steamer.

CINCINNATI

All towns and cities along the navigable rivers and lakes benefitted from the intensification of port activities brought about by the steamboat—but none more than Cincinnati. Local entrepreneurs began to build steamers in 1818, and by 1825 the town became the steamboat construction and maintenance capital of the Ohio River system. Iron foundries, forges, and machine-making shops sprang up as part of the new steamboat industry, and soon Cincinnati was a machinery manufacturing center as well. Not just the first true city of the trans-Appalachian West, Cincinnati was also the first major inland rival of the eastern seaboard cities. By mid-century, Cincinnati was the "economic colossus" of the entire west with a population well over 110,000. Cincinnati, in the words of Louis Tucker, had become "the largest inland port in the nation; the supreme pork producer in the world; the leading beer and liquor producer in the nation; the prime soap, candle, furniture, shoe, stove and boat manufacturer in the west, and the principal printing center in the west."[8]

ST. LOUIS

Though located near the center of the great midwestern river networks, St. Louis, high up on the Mississippi River, lagged well behind Cincinnati. However, the discovery of gold in California (early in 1848) sparked the gold rush of 1849, and changed that. By the end of the 1840s and early 1850s, steamboats heading north from New Orleans, west from Cincinnati and Louisville, and south from the upper Mississippi all converged on St. Louis, bringing thousands of prospectors, settlers, transients, and speculators, among others, from all over the country—all destined for the California gold fields and the burgeoning towns of San Francisco and Los Angeles. As the equipment and supply center for the cross-country trip, St. Louis quickly became one of the fastest-growing cities in the country. Its population jumped from approximately 16,000 in 1840 to 77,000 in 1850. By 1854, St. Louis was the river trade center of the West with more than 150,000 inhabitants, and its economic leaders believed that the continued preeminence of their city was assured, thanks to its location and to the burgeoning steamboat traffic of the Mississippi.

The Great Lakes Cities

Runaway, explosive urban growth characterized Buffalo, Detroit, Cleveland, Milwaukee, and Chicago during the 1840s and 1850s as these Great Lakes communities became major commercial and industrial cities. Boosterism, real estate speculation, and new transportation systems came together to promote the phenomenal rise of these Great Lakes cities. What the steamboat did for the river cities, the Erie Canal and railroads accomplished for these strategically situated towns.

Because of their proximity to the Pennsylvania coal fields, Lake Superior iron ore reserves, and Lake Michigan copper deposits, the Great Lakes cities quickly turned to iron production and the manufacturing of stoves, guns, saws, pots, pans, scythes, plows, reapers, and harvesters, among other metalwork products, employing interchangeable parts techniques. These products were distributed along the Ohio and Mississippi rivers. But no sooner had the impact of canals and steamers begun to reverberate throughout the trans-Appalachian West than railroads were introduced into the Lakes region, a development which dramatically accelerated urban growth during the 1840s and 1850s. By 1860 the area north of the Ohio River had become not only a "manufacturing belt" but the second most populous section of the nation.

CLEVELAND

Characteristic were the conditions found in Cleveland, Ohio, and Milwaukee, Wisconsin. Favorably located at the mouth of the Cuyahoga River and on Lake Erie, Cleveland underwent boom conditions in the 1830s. "We have nine large warehouses and several others are being constructed," the *Cleveland Herald* exclaimed, "a steam flouring mill, an air furnace [for iron ore processing] and steam engine manufactory, a dry dock, a paper mill, twenty different kinds of stores, two printing offices, a brewery, and a nail factory soon to be erected."

Population, meanwhile, began to outstrip the local community ability to supply provisions. "The various trades are pursued with profit," the paper announced, "and journeymen have been in demand, particularly carpenters and joiners to which may be attributed the fact there is not even a room to be rented and families have been compelled to take shelter in barns."[9]

Water-born transportation had been the chief stimulus to its mercantile growth, but after 1850 the railroad and industry provided the principal impetus. Cleveland became the terminus of railroad lines from the south and was an important way station on the lakeshore route farther west. From the south came the Cleveland, Columbus and Cincinnati Railroad in 1851, which was followed by two more roads from the east, the Cleveland and Pittsburgh in 1852 and the Cleveland and Erie. The processing of iron ore from the Lake Superior area and the manufacture of iron and steel products for railroad construction became Cleveland's principal industries. By 1857 Cleveland was connected with Youngstown, Ohio, and assured a constant supply of coal to feed its rapidly booming iron manufacturing plants.

MILWAUKEE

Similar developments took place in Milwaukee, Wisconsin, which, until the 1830s, was a small fur trading post located on the western shore of Lake Michigan. After the Black Hawk Indian War ended, in 1833, the southeast parts of Wisconsin were opened to settlement. Land speculators were attracted to Milwaukee as a potential Great Lakes harbor and flour mill site. Competition from Racine and Southport (Kenosha) prompted town leaders to build wooden plank roads to reach outlying agricultural hinterlands, and the town's population jumped to 20,061 by 1850. By the mid-1850s, Milwaukee had beaten its competitors to become the major flour and wheat shipping center on Lake Michigan, although Chicago was the most important shipping center on the lake. Then, during the 1850s, Milwaukee experienced another major growth spurt as a result of transportation developments. Railroad connections to the Mississippi River assured Milwaukee's position as a trade and budding manufacturing center.

Widening its functions as an entrepôt for farm and lumber products for the northwest, the city's economy tilted toward a diversified industrial one, and by 1870 its population had reached 71,440. Of the 1,466 workers employed in manufacturing in 1850, 331 were in the processing industries (flour milling, liquor distilling, leather tanning, construction materials, and meat packing); approximately 560 were in the household-consumer clusters (shoes and boots, clothing, and furniture making); and 104 were in the heavy industries group (iron and iron goods)—the value of these products was estimated at $812,196. By 1860 the population engaged in manufacturing and increased to 3,492, of whom 908 were employed in processing, 1,113 in household goods, and 205 in heavy industry—and the value of products had jumped to $2,958,591.[10]

CHICAGO

Chicago, of all the trans-Appalachian cities, experienced the most spectacular nineteenth-century growth—from a town of 3,200 in the early 1830s to a city of 112,172 by 1860. Chicago, which was originally a fort, was the product of the interior canal-building mania during the 1830s, for it was the plan to build a canal through Chicago, linking Lake Michigan with the Illinois River and the Mississippi that touched off a wave of land speculation there.

Speculators and promoters, aware that the canal would provide an all-water route from the East Coast through the Great Lakes to New Orleans, flocked to the area with the intention of making Chicago the region's principal center. A key figure in the city's early growth was the real estate speculator William B. Ogden who, after arriving in Chicago in the early 1830s, almost singlehandedly promoted the construction of the railroads which later became the basis of the city's success. The Galena and Chicago Union Railroad, which was completed in 1849, connected the city with Galena's lead mines and with the Mississippi River.

Another reason for Chicago's extraordinary population growth was the revolutionary new wood-building technique, pioneered in the early 1830s, that made possible the rapid construction of housing from lightweight wood. Called the "Chicago" or balloon frame, it rapidly spread to Cleveland during the 1840s and eventually to all the other American cities.

Like Cleveland and Milwaukee, Chicago developed a diversified manufacturing base, but its basic eastern export was grain and livestock. However, the key factor in Chicago's growth was transportation. Reaching out with rail and water connections, Chicago seized control of trade, commerce, and industry in every conceivable direction. Its promoters' intentions were no longer merely to create an urban center that would be regionally important but one that would be of national significance. They met their first challenge by besting Milwaukee, Racine, and Kenosha, Wisconsin, for control of the grain markets of northern Illinois and southern Wisconsin. In so doing, Chicago's leaders carved out a hinterland for their city consisting of all of Illinois, Indiana, and Wisconsin. In defeating Milwaukee, Chicago became the primary commercial and transportation center of the Midwest, second only to St. Louis.

Chicagoans then proceeded to challenge St. Louis's upper-Mississippi commerce through the simultaneous construction of two railroad lines, both of which were completed in 1856. The Illinois Central Railroad linked Chicago to Cairo, Illinois, at the southern tip of the state, to the Ohio River and to Mobile and New Orleans, while the Rock Island Line would connect the city with the Mississippi, thereby diverting much of St. Louis's upper-Mississippi commerce. In addition to its railroads, Chicago also had water connections with Toledo, Detroit, and New York. Before 1840, Chicago's grain exports were less than 10,000 bushels. In 1845, this figure reached 1,000,000 bushels, soared to 31,000,000 in 1860, and skyrocketed to 56,000,000 just two years later.

With ten trunk lines and eleven branch lines leading into and out of the city, by 1858 Chicago was the railroad capital of the United States and well on the way to overcoming St. Louis's primacy in the Midwest (see Map 2.2). By 1870 Chicago had achieved that position.

Rivalries for control of trans-Appalachian markets had led to the creation of a transportation-communication network linking the Atlantic Coast cities with regional cities along the Ohio-Mississippi river system. These interregional connections

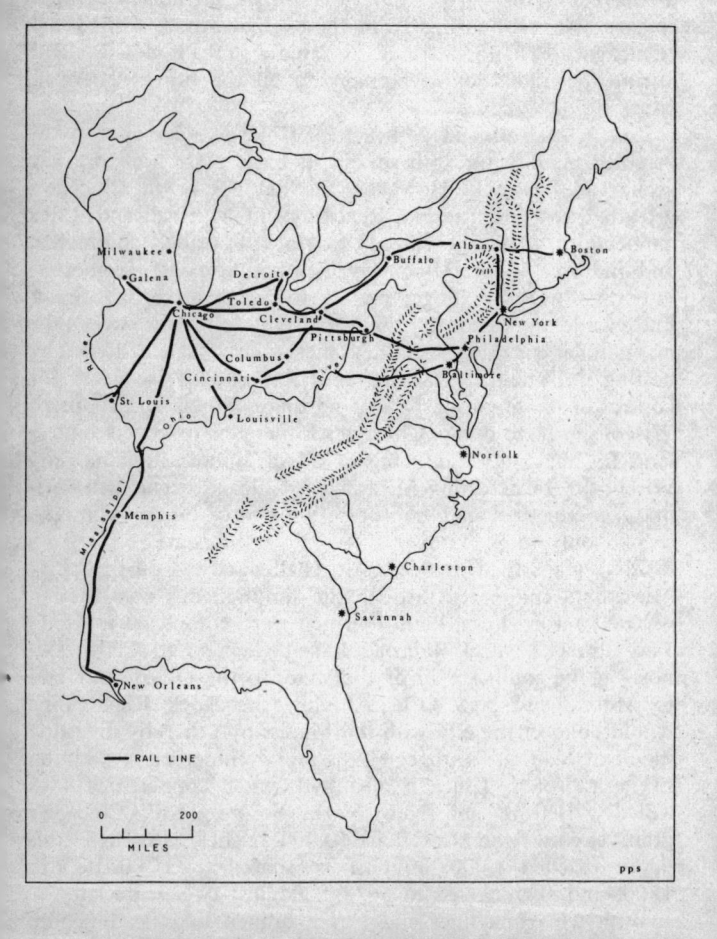

Map 2.2 Main Northeast-Midwest Railroad Trunk Lines

stimulated broad economic growth in both areas and underlay the extraordinary expansion of the factory method of production.

Lagging Southern Urbanization

The dynamic pattern of urban growth in the Northeast and Midwest was not matched by the South. As cotton culture moved southwest, Charleston gave way to Mobile on the Gulf of Mexico, and Memphis, Nashville, and New Orleans on the Mississippi, all of which were closer to the newly emerging areas of economic activity. New York had captured some of Charleston's potential trade, as had Savannah, Georgia, along the south Atlantic.

As settlers moved into the Southwest, small towns appeared on the major navigable southern streams, connecting inland southwestern areas with seaport cities and providing hinterland farmers with collection, storage, and transport centers. By the eve of the Civil War there were several small manufacturing centers, such as Harper's Ferry, Frankfort, and Richmond, manned by both slave and free laborers.

However, the South remained less urban than other regions. With the exception of Baltimore and New Orleans, the slave states before the Civil War had almost no large cities, and few that had a population of 15,000. In 1850, Charleston, with a population of 42,985, Richmond, 27,570, Louisville, 43,194, Norfolk, 14,326, Savannah, 15,312, Nashville, 10,165, were large by southern standards. Richard Wade has shown that the large numbers of slaves in every southern town sharply reduced the proportion of its citizens and limited the range of their enterprise. Southern investment capital was tied up in buying slaves rather than used for developing resources and activities that could broaden these cities' economic and urban bases.[11]

Baltimore, with a population 102,313 in 1840, was not a typical southern city, however, since only about one fifth of its families owned slaves. Until the late antebellum period, no other border city had so low a percentage of slaveholders.

The region's only other truly sizable city, New Orleans, was authentically southern. Even before its acquisition from France as part of the Louisiana Purchase of 1803, New Orleans had served as the point of deposit and transshipment for the farm surpluses of flour, grain, and corn liquor produced by American farmers in the Ohio and Mississippi valleys and for the cotton, sugar, and tobacco of nearby plantations. After 1800, the growing migration of dirt farmers into the upper-Mississippi Valley and the establishment of many new plantations in Alabama, Mississippi, and Louisiana greatly added to the volume of New Orleans trade. As a result, its population rose from 9,650 in 1800 to 17,242 in 1810 and had reached 168,675 by 1860.

Most southern towns and cities did not play a major generative role in southern economic life; unlike urban centers in the Northeast and Midwest, they neither helped to develop the wealth of interior regions nor stimulated a diversified regional economy with a wide range of occupational activities.

For much of its history, the South was a producer of raw material—tobacco, rice, and indigo during the colonial era; cotton, tobacco, and sugar during much of the nineteenth century. At the center of the slave states' economy were not small farms as in the Northeast and expanding Midwest but the plantation-slave system of production which, more than any other factor, thoroughly inhibited agricultural diversification and urban growth. Virtually all southern investment capital was put into new cotton land and slaves—relatively little into city-building, transportation systems, and industry.

The inability of the South to develop viable inland towns and cities was clearly a by-product of an obsessive concern with the slave-based plantation system. Cassius M. Clay, a Kentucky anti-slave advocate, gave voice to this condition, when he remarked:

> Lawyers, merchants, mechanics, laborers, who are your consumers; Robert Wickliffe's two hundred slaves: How many clients do you find, how many goods do you sell, how many hats, coats, saddles, and trunks do you make for these two hundred slaves? Does Mr. Wickliffe lay out as much for himself and his two hundred slaves as two hundred freemen do? . . . All our towns dwindle, and our farmers lose, in consequence, all home markets. Every farmer bought out by the slave system send off the consumers of the manufacturers of the town: when the consumers are gone, the mechanic must go also. . . . A home market cannot exist in a slave state.[12]

Without an expanding urban population there was little or no stimulus or market for diversified agricultural products such as wheat, vegetables, or dairy products; nor was there any need for an urban middle class of merchants and craftsmen to provide commodities for local and regional consumers. Except for those farmers close to the cities of the free states, the southern backcountry population was isolated, self-sufficient, and economically, politically, and socially backward. For the most part, southern urban centers, regardless of location, were little more than adjuncts of the plantation system whose primary economic function was the processing of the staple produced on the plantation. Secondarily, they provided marketing facilities for slaves (particularly true in New Orleans), distributed imported manufactures and foodstuffs produced in the Northeast and West, made available banking and financial services, and functioned as recreational centers.

Southern cotton producers of the nineteenth century relied on New York merchants, bankers, and shippers as heavily as tobacco planters and West Indian sugar growers had relied on all the northeastern port cities during the colonial era. But as we have seen, New York's control of southern trade during the first sixty years of the nineteenth century was *not* the fundamental reason for the relatively slow rate of urban growth in the South or its inability to develop diversified local economies.

The Emerging Industrial City

America had big, sprawling, populous cities well before the Civil War, and all of them had a similar thrown-together and dreary appearance. The extraordinarily rapid growth in population was the chief reason, but the spreading impact of railroads, factories, and manufacturing and the universal adoption of the gridiron city plan contributed in significant ways as well.

Basically each city was composed of a series of distinctive areas. At the heart of the city's economy was the downtown business district of offices, wholesale and retail stores (including the recently developed "department store"), banks, insurance companies, and law firms. Alongside these commercial activities in the central business district were factories and manufacturing clusters. Next were the residential areas, in which fashionable neighborhoods and streets were in proximity to congested slums. And, lastly, each large city had many mixed-use districts scattered throughout in which industrial, commercial, and residential streets were mingled together. Although these areas seemed to have an internal unity, they had simply grown in an uncoordinated and completely uncontrolled fashion.

The nineteenth-century American city was "treated not as a public institution," according to Lewis Mumford in *The City in History*, "but a private commercial venture to be carved up in any fashion that might increase the turnover and further the rise in land values." Since urban land was "a mere commodity, like labor[—]its market value expressed its only value," the gridiron plan admirably fulfilled the desires for rapid expansion.

The checkerboard pattern (see page 8) treated all land similarly and gave priority to the individual enterpriser whose planning was on a piecemeal basis for his own limited needs. Its attractiveness lay in its standard-size lot, standard-size city blocks, and its standard-size widths, which could be adapted to any kind of terrain, whether flat or hilly.

Thus, the rectangular building block became the unit for extending the city. But in the plan "no section was planned for a specific purpose; instead the only function was the progressive intensification of use, for the purpose of expanding business needs and raising land values."[13] Although the grid plan fulfilled the need for rapid economic expansion, it failed to fulfill other critically important human purposes adequately. When the need arose for sites for public uses within these large, populous cities—for parks, open spaces, recreation, and public buildings—the appropriate parcels of land were privately held, extremely costly to obtain, or unobtainable.

New York and Boston adopted the grid early in the nineteenth century for their old towns of crooked streets. (See Figure 2.4.) But New York's streets, laid out at right angles, had no breaks or focal points; one block was the same as the next, or the last. Those small squares that existed by the 1860s—when the city's population was well over 800,000 inhabitants—were residential districts in the older parts of the city. These were ringed with fashionable houses, and because there were few convenient public meeting areas set aside in the city plans, men in the poorer districts could only gather in saloons to talk. In spite of its carefully devised city plan, oriented originally around five large open spaces, Philadel-

RISING CENTERS OF COMMERCE AND INDUSTRY 67

phia, too, fell victim to the same situation. Struck by the dreary effect he found, British novelist Charles Dickens remarked in 1842 that Philadelphia "is a handsome city, but distractingly regular. After walking for about an hour or two I felt that I would have given the world for a crooked street."[14]

Philadelphia, like New York, seemed an endless series of right-angle streets, narrow house lots, row houses, interior alleys, rear yard houses and shacks. Stores, schools, saloons, police and fire stations, churches, shops and houses cropped up next to one another all over the city. In every big city neighborhood, shops, homes, immigrants, native Americans, manufacturing clusters, occupational groups, slums, ghettoized blacks, and occasional class and nationality enclaves seemed crowded and jumbled together.[15] The situation was little different in Boston, Brooklyn, Chicago, Baltimore, or Cincinnati by the 1860s; other rapidly growing cities like Milwaukee, Buffalo, and San Francisco were undergoing the same process of internal change—or would undergo it later in the century.

The railroad also played a decisive role in changing the physical appearance and life of the city. Railroads carved out rights-of-way through established cities disrupting the traffic arteries; terminals, train yards, repair facilities, and steam en-

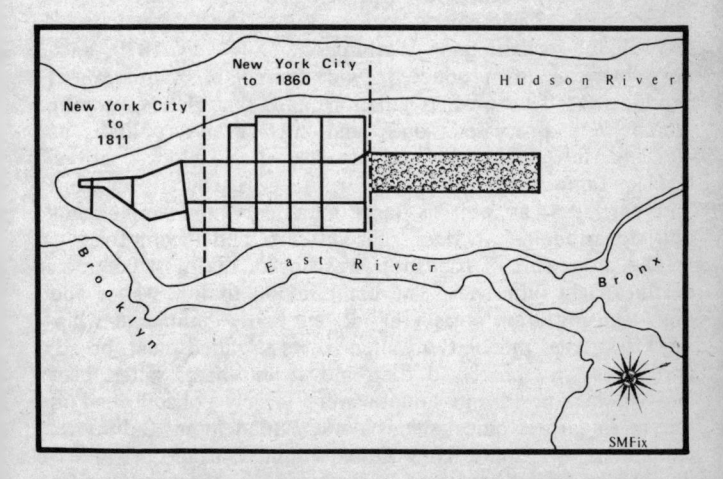

Figure 2.4 Schematic Town Plan of New York City c. 1860

gines produced cinders and smoke which blanketed the areas adjacent to the tracks. The Cleveland and Pittsburgh line cut diagonally across Cleveland's most fashionable street. The string of factories and industries which the railroad stimulated and encouraged naturally chose to locate near the railroad right-of-way, on what had till then been a residential street.

But it was the factory and manufacturing plants that *most* dramatically changed the face of the American city. Superimposed upon the commercial base was an industrial component of factories and large and small plants. By 1860 manufacturing was a mainstay of each big city's economy. In 1859, 30 percent of New England's population was engaged in manufacturing, as was 42 percent in the Midwest, 13 percent in the Great Lakes region, and 10 percent in the South—virtually all of which were urban-located. Philadelphia and Cincinnati had the largest percentage of their total populations engaged in manufacturing activities, 17 percent and 18 percent, respectively, whereas New York had 10 percent, Boston 11 percent, and New Orleans only 3 percent. Small predominantly manufacturing cities and mill towns were situated all over the Northeast, the most important of which included Newark, New Jersey, 26 percent of whose population was engaged in industry, Lowell and Lynn, Massachusetts, with 36 percent and 45 percent, and Providence, Rhode Island, with 22 percent.

With the exception of Washington, D. C., by 1870, each big American city produced a wide variety of manufactured products for its own population and hinterlands, among which were processed foods and such everyday items as clothing, tobacco (snuff and cigars), shoes, clocks, stoves, bricks, lumber, kitchenware, furniture, hardware, wagons and carriages, as well as farm machinery and implements and steam engines, boilers, railroad cars, and locomotives.

The processing of foodstuffs was one of the most common of the urban industries. The combination of low wages and high transportation costs (for all but flour, grain, and whiskey) restricted most city dwellers' diets to salted meat, bread, and beer. The processed food industries (beer, salted beef and smoked pork, and liquor) were largely concentrated in the seven largest cities—New York, Philadelphia, Baltimore, Cincinnati, St. Louis, New Orleans, and Chicago. (For example, Cincinnati's total meat production in 1860 was valued at $4,525,000, but it was closely followed by Philadelphia

($4,409,000) and New York ($3,212,000). St. Louis ($1,699,000), Chicago ($1,626,000), and Baltimore ($928,000) also produced substantial amounts. New York and Philadelphia led in the manufacture of beer, followed by St. Louis, Cincinnati, Chicago, Buffalo, Pittsburgh, Boston, New Orleans, and Baltimore.) Only rarely did the urban dweller supplement his diet with midwestern potatoes and locally grown apples, fresh vegetables, and some dairy products (unpasteurized milk, for example, was generally watered down and sold door-to-door by street vendors.)[16]

Until the early 1900s when significant numbers of large industrial cities had emerged, the big city had a diversified economic base consisting of commercial, mercantile, and industrial components. As Sam Bass Warner, Jr., explained, "Manufacturing had not settled into the pattern whereby each speciality located at its best site and from such a single base or cluster of bases sold its products throughout the nation."[17]

By the eve of the Civil War, then, the foundations of an urban-industrial society had been laid along the northeastern seaboard and within the great interior basin between the Great Lakes, Ohio River and Mississippi River.

TABLE 2.2

Value of Food Processing in Selected Cities, 1860*

City	Distilled Liquor	Beer	Smoked & Salted Meat
New York	$658,000	$1,240,000	$3,212,000
Philadelphia	344,000	1,027,000	4,409,000
Cincinnati	812,000	562,000	4,525,000
Chicago	257,000	357,000	1,626,000
Buffalo	224,000	218,000	[none for export]
St. Louis	154,000	729,000	1,699,000
Baltimore	101,000	105,000	928,000
Boston	78,000	153,000	[none for export]
New Orleans	72,000	117,000	[none for export]
Pittsburgh	62,000	204,000	[none for export]

*Adapted from Sam Bass Warner, Jr., "The Feeding of Large Cities in the United States, 1860–1960," *Third International Conference of Economic History*, Munich, Germany, 1965, pp. 85, 86.

3

The Urban Turmoil

Americans have always been a mobile people, reluctant to put down permanent roots in any one spot. The procession westward has been going on now for three hundred years and shows no sign of stopping. The greatest of all our migrations, however, has been the gradual shift from country to city which has transformed a land of farmers into the metropolitan nation of today.

Moreover, historically, a high proportion of those who have at some time resided in one of the nation's major cities have not remained there permanently. According to the recent findings of social historians, the bottom layer of American urban society has consisted largely of long-term transients, those who, after failing to establish themselves in one city, have proceeded to try their luck in another. According to Stephan Thernstrom, a leading student of this question, it has always been "the probability that only between forty and sixty percent of the adult males to be found in an American community at one point in time would still be located there a decade later."[1]

In 1820, the major cities of America were the established but still expanding seaports of the Atlantic coast and the recently founded, yet already important river ports of the Ohio and Mississippi valleys. In these cities, nearly everyone still walked the short distance from their homes to their work. As in the colonial era, most manufactured products were still fashioned in small lots by skilled artisans who were the largest single class in these communities. Below this class were the unskilled workers, such as the sailors, teamsters, servants, and general laborers.

The Urban Elite and Rural Migrants

In each city, there was an established elite consisting of its oldest and most prominent families. In the Northeast and in the Ohio Valley, these elites were almost exclusively Protestant, but in other cities, like Baltimore and in such originally French settlements as St. Louis and New Orleans, they would also include a number of Roman Catholic families. Throughout the nineteenth century, the social elite would continue to set the tone in the realms of fashion and manners. Aspiring young men, sometimes of quite humble origin, sought, as part of their plan for advancing themselves, to imitate the manner and dress of the gentry. With the triumph of universal manhood suffrage in the 1830s and the emergence of mass parties, the members of old patrician families found it increasingly distasteful to run for office and ever more difficult to get elected. As a result, many of them lost interest in politics, choosing instead to devote most of their leisure time to social gatherings, cultural activity, and social reform.

As Daniel Boorstin has noted, America has often rewarded with great wealth those with the foresight or the good fortune to identify themselves with an important city while it was still at an early stage in its development.[2] This observation is particularly applicable to those, whether native or foreign-born, who were endowed with special skill or with significant amounts of capital. Thus, many well-to-do businessmen from the British Isles and from New England readily found places for themselves within the business community of New York City. In most cities, skilled labor was in great demand, especially in the West. In Cincinnati and other midwestern cities during the 1830s craftsmen could sometimes command wages several times as high as those paid in eastern cities.

Throughout the nineteenth century, most of the increase in urban population was the result of migration from the nation's villages and farms which historically have had higher birthrates and lower death rates than those of urban areas. The urban trend was accelerated by the transformation of farming that began in the late 1840s. The application of new machines and improved methods made it possible for one man to produce more grain than had been produced formerly by two. These advances combined with their exceptionally fertile land permitted farmers in the Middle West to outproduce and undersell the competing grain-growers of other regions. By 1860, the bread eaten by many farmers of New England was made from wheat that had been grown in Kansas and Nebraska.

As a result of these changes, some of the eastern farm population was displaced. The majority of those who left their family farms sought new lands farther to the west. Others abandoned farming altogether and took jobs in villages, cities, and towns. "In 1860," writes economic historian Clarence Danhof, "less than half of the population lived on farms; the 392 cities by the Census definition accounted for 20 percent of the population. The other 32 percent of the population lived in small towns and villages or in the open country, but not on farms."[3]

Urban Black Settlements

There were enclaves of native-born blacks in most of the nation's major cities, but especially in those of the South. As of 1830, there was a black majority in New Orleans and Charleston, more that half of which were slaves. Among southern free blacks, a majority were to be found by 1840 in towns and cities, and by 1860, about one out of every four were dwelling in cities with populations of 10,000 or more. They were therefore the most urbanized group in the nation's least urbanized region.

In the two decades that preceded the Civil War, there was a decline in the proportion of blacks in the cities of the South due mainly, according to historian Richard Wade, to the fact that slaves who lived in cities were more difficult for the master class to control. An urban slave would, of necessity, often find his own employment and lodging and could choose his own associates including free blacks whose legal status and somewhat greater self-assertion set an example subversive to slavery.[4] The era of the Civil War and Reconstruction witnessed a temporary reversal of this downward trend as some of the former bondsmen exercised their newfound liberty by migrating to nearby cities. In 1860, in fourteen southern cities there were 142,000 blacks and 610,000 whites, while in the same cities ten years later, there were 270,000 blacks as compared with 712,000 whites.

In the North, where by 1830 slavery was all but extinct, the great majority of blacks had long been living in urban districts. By that year, there were black populations numbering in the thousands in Boston, New York, Philadelphia, and Cincinnati.

However, due to an exceedingly high death rate and to the tremendous influx of whites from rural America and Europe, the percentage of northern cities that was black declined even more rapidly than in the urban centers of the South. Indeed, the number of blacks living in Manhattan actually declined during each of the three decades prior to the Civil War. Where, in 1750, 16 percent of New York City's population was black, by 1860 this figure had declined to 1.5 percent. Even in Philadelphia, which had by far the largest black community of any northern city, the proportion of the population that was black had declined from 12 percent in 1830 to 4 percent three decades later.

In the major northern cities, a higher percentage of the black population had been born in other states than was the case among native-born whites. Thus, in Philadelphia in 1860, fewer than one ninth of the city's American-born whites had come from outside of Pennsylvania, whereas more than one third of the city's blacks had come from other states. Other cities in the North showed a similar pattern, due in part to the Underground Railroad which, in guiding fugitive slaves to safety in the North, maintained "stations" in various northern cities. However, for decades to come, the northern migration of southern-born blacks would remain on a very small scale, consisting primarily of the most desperate and the most adventurous and ambitious members of the race.

In the larger cities of the antebellum era, whether southern or northern, there were small groups of black professionals and entrepreneurs, including the owners of some of the era's most fashionable restaurants and hotels, but these upper and middle class elements were far less numerous than their urban white counterparts. Early in the century, blacks had been employed in a wide variety of trades, many of them as skilled artisans, but after 1830, they were increasingly relegated to the worst paid and least esteemed jobs. Although in a few southern cities, such as Savannah, Georgia, blacks were barred by law or by white pressure from the more desirable trades, economic opportunities remained greater for free blacks in southern cities than in those of the North.

In both regions employers would usually not hire blacks if

white workers were available, and when an employer departed from the norm, he was often forced by labor boycotts and other forms of pressure from whites to dismiss his black employees. By means of such methods, urban blacks were ultimately reduced to three major avenues of employment—working as seamen, as domestic servants, and as general laborers. Even in these areas, they gradually lost ground in the face of the most blatant prejudice and the growing competition from the foreign-born, especially the Irish. "Every hour," wrote Frederick Douglass in the 1850s, "sees the black man elbowed out of employment by some newly arrived immigrant whose hunger and color are thought to give him a better title to the place."[5]

Despite their small numbers, the free blacks were often brutally mistreated in both South and North. By 1870 it had become customary in both regions either to exclude blacks or to keep the races segregated in all public places, save Catholic churches. Most northern states and cities either excluded black children from the schools or required them to attend separate ones. By 1840, 93 percent of the nation's free black population resided in areas in which only whites had the right to vote.

Their very right to reside in a locality was, at times, called into question. In 1800, the authorities in Boston ordered the deportation of 240 blacks. Although this episode was not repeated either in Boston or in any other eastern city, in most of the new states of the Northwest, laws were passed which "either explicitly barred Negroes or permitted them to enter only after they had produced certified proof of their freedom and had posted a bond, ranging from five hundred dollars to one thousand dollars, guaranteeing their good behavior."[6]

Although these statutes normally went unenforced, occasionally an ugly episode would take place. In 1829, the government of Cincinnati ruled that each of the city's black residents must, in compliance with a long-unenforced state law, either post a bond of $1,500 or leave the city within thirty days. Convinced that the city fathers would no longer protect the blacks, a mob of white hoodlums entered the black section bent on riot and pillage. Although the black community resisted the mob and was eventually backed up by the authorities, more than 1,000 blacks, including most of the more prosperous and established, departed shortly for Canada. In the end, however, the law in question was never enforced, and Cincinnati remained a key station on the Underground Railroad.

While the areas of black residence in this era could not accurately be described as ghettos, Negroes in most cities were more segregated both socially and residentially than was any other group. Most urban blacks were housed in cellars, shanties, and other slums, and every epidemic took a heavy toll of the black community. From the beginning of the century, their exclusion from white institutions had compelled urban blacks to create organizations of their own. The refusal of mutual aid societies and regular lodge chapters to admit blacks led to the formation of their own mutual aid associations, which, like most such organizations, supplied its members with companionship and with assistance in caring for the sick, raising orphans, and paying for funerals. A separate black press had also begun to emerge. By 1860, there were some two dozen black newspapers in the northern states and eight in New York City alone.

The most important of all the black institutions were the churches. The racial segregation practiced by the Protestant congregations of the North was directly responsible for the formation of the African Methodist and Abyssinian Baptist churches, each of which had branches in most of the larger northern cities, as well as for a diversity of other separate congregations. As with most Protestant churches, new schisms often developed, resulting in still more churches. Nevertheless, the black minister was, as Leon Litwack has written, "undoubtedly the most important and influential figure in the antebellum Negro community."[7]

The churches supplied the black communities with a variety of services including schools, recreational facilities, and meeting halls and also helped to lead the agitation for the abolitionist cause.

The Immigrant Tide

Many times larger than the black population in the cities of this era was the huge influx of immigrants, almost entirely from the nations of northern and western Europe. After a gradual rise in the 1820s, immigration accelerated markedly with the 1830s, as 600,000 Europeans disembarked at American ports. Between 1840 and 1860, over four million foreigners came to the United States, more than 90 percent of whom had been born in either Germany or the British Isles.

Major cities throughout the world have generally derived the bulk of their populations from migration rather than from natural increase (the surplus of births over deaths). Nowhere, however, has this tendency been carried further than in the United States, "the nation of nations," where urban centers have, since 1820, drawn a high proportion of their residents from a variety of foreign countries. In fact, the foreign-born have traditionally settled in cities more readily than other Americans. In 1870, the percentage of immigrants in the national population was less than 15 percent, but in the fifty largest cities, the foreign-born comprised approximately 34 percent of the total population.

Until 1840 the immigrant population was made up primarily of farmers and skilled workers, most of whom were responding to the modernizing and mechanizing forces that were transforming society in both Europe and America. As a result of the revolutions in industry and agriculture, thousands

TABLE 3.1

Foreign-Born and Blacks in Selected Cities: 1860

City	Total Population	Foreign-Born	(%)	Blacks	(%)
New York	805,651	383,717	48	12,472	1.5
Philadelphia	565,529	169,430	29	22,185	3.9
Brooklyn	266,661	104,589	39	4,313	1.6
Baltimore	212,418	52,497	25	27,898	13.0
Boston	177,840	63,791	36	2,261	1.3
New Orleans	168,675	64,621	38	24,074	14.0
Cincinnati	161,044	73,614	46	3,731	2.3
St. Louis	160,773	96,086	60	3,297	2.0
Chicago	109,260	54,624	50	955	0.9
Buffalo	81,129	37,684	46	809	1.0
Newark	71,941	26,625	37	1,287	1.8
Louisville	68,033	22,948	34	6,820	10.0
Washington	61,122	10,765	18	10,983	18.0
San Francisco	56,802	28,454	50	1,176	2.1
Detroit	45,619	21,349	47	1,403	3.1
Milwaukee	45,246	22,848	50	106	0.2
Cleveland	43,417	19,437	45	799	1.8

SOURCE: Adapted with permission from Bayrd Still, *Urban America: A History with Documents*. Copyright © 1974 by Little Brown and Company, Inc. pp. 118–119.

of these independent farmers and artisans, finding their standards of living imperiled, had come to America. A majority of these new arrivals had paid their own passage and had sufficient funds to journey farther west and, often, even to establish businesses and farms.

Most of the immigrants of this era did not remain long in the Atlantic ports, departing almost immediately for the farms and the rising towns of the interior. Of those who did linger in the seaports, many had either the skill or the capital to fit in readily as part of the urban economy. By 1830, various nationality groups in the cities of the Atlantic Coast and Middle West had established immigrant aid societies which assisted newcomers from the homeland to find lodgings and jobs. In the words of Robert Albion, these organizations followed a policy of "keep them moving," whereby immigrants were generally encouraged to settle in the West where land was available and labor was often in great demand.[8] They maintained employment agencies which sent inquiries to every part of the nation in order to advise their recently arrived countrymen as to where they stood the best chance of finding work.

Among immigrants, the obstacles to acceptance were not so formidable as they were for blacks, and for many, assimilation and intermarriage were conceivable goals. As long, therefore, as immigrant groups remained small and consisted almost entirely of Protestants from northern Europe, the cities had, to an extent, functioned as "melting pots." Thus, in the early 1800s the Episcopal churches in New York City and elsewhere had absorbed various Lutheran, Huguenot, and Dutch Reform congregations. This is especially noteworthy in view of the well-known fact that of all immigrant institutions, the churches tend to last the longest. After 1803, the Dutch Reform ministers of New York City gave sermons exclusively in English. Finally, Jewish immigrants from Germany abandoned many of the religious customs and practices which had set them apart from their Christian neighbors, sometimes even intermarrying with Christians.

Even in the early decades of the nineteenth century, the cities of America, especially those on the Atlantic Coast, had also begun to attract immigrants who were thoroughly impoverished and possessed little training or skill. By the 1830s this group was contributing noticeably to the social problems of the cities. The number of immigrants in this category was massively increased by the amazingly rapid expansion of

American immigration after the 1840s, especially after the onset of the Great Famine of 1845 in Ireland.

Between 1846 and 1850, Ireland alone sent 900,000 men, women, and children to America, nearly all of whom were on the brink of starvation when they arrived. In their desperation, these immigrants had booked passage on any outward-bound ship, regardless of its destination, and they disembarked wherever their ship had taken them, too poor and often too confused to journey any farther. While some of the poorest and least healthy of the immigrants would remain for some years in the ports where they had landed, most in time moved farther inland. The most graphic example of this was in New York City, where from 1820 to 1860 more than two thirds of all the European immigrants had disembarked. Although more than two millions aliens arrived in New York harbor during the 1850s, the foreign-born population of New York City and Brooklyn in 1860 was only 484,000, or 44 percent of the total population.

Despite their peasant background, the vast majority of Catholic Irish, like both the free blacks and the Jews of this era, tended to settle in cities. By 1860, there were colonies of Catholic Irish in every important city, but they were particularly numerous in the Atlantic ports. Thus, by 1860, people from Ireland comprised 28 percent of New York City's population and 26 percent of the population of Boston. Predominantly unskilled, they, like the urban blacks, were employed primarily in the more menial lines of work, such as construction, domestic service, and as casual labor. Indeed, for a time, the Irish of Boston, New York, and other cities had even less status than the local blacks.

As in the case of the blacks, prejudice impeded their progress in this period when the legend "No Irish need apply" regularly appeared at the bottom of classified advertisements in big city newspapers. However, because the prejudice against them rested not on color but on qualities which could more readily be changed, many of the Irish families were able, within a generation or two, to raise their occupational status and acquire some property as well.

The Germans, who comprised the second largest immigrant group of the period, were, generally speaking, less impoverished than the Irish and had a higher level of skill and education. While there were significant German enclaves in various eastern cities, most had settled in the Middle West, at the urging of the immigrant aid societies maintained by their countrymen. Many became farmers, but others came in great numbers to the youthful cities of Cincinnati, St. Louis, and Milwaukee. Unlike the Irish, the German immigrants, who tended in the main to be artisans and shopkeepers, worked at a wide variety of occupations. Many achieved secure positions in American cities within a few years of their arrival, and a few attained success of outstanding proportions.

The immigration of this era was marked by a preponderance of Roman Catholics. Of the nearly one million members added by the Roman Church in the 1840s, over 700,000 were immigrants, more than 500,000 of them from Ireland. It was at this time that the Irish first became dominant in the American branch of the Roman Church. By 1852, the archbishops of the four most important American sees, those of New York, Baltimore, Cincinnati, and St. Louis, had all been born in Ireland.

Unskilled Workers and the Beginnings of the Labor Movement

Whatever their race or birthplace, survival was difficult for urban residents who were lacking in capital and skill. In the antebellum era, there were few steady jobs for such workers, most of whom had to settle for whatever work there was, however menial. It was common for the unskilled to work only part of the week and even to go unemployed for weeks at a time. Many would wander from place to place in search of work or would sign up with a contractor to labor for months at a time on a railroad or canal project in a remote section of the nation. The meager earnings of these unskilled "breadwinners" were frequently supplemented by small amounts earned by their wives and children through such work as taking in laundry or shining shoes.

Many thousands of unskilled workers of both sexes and all ages were employed in manufacturing, either producing commodities at home, for which they were paid by the piece, or working as hands in the sweatshops and factories. For a work day that ran from "sunrise to sunset," amid conditions that were usually unhealthy and uncomfortable, adult workers would typically earn less than a dollar, while children often got as little as twenty-five cents.

After 1820, the labor force in many of the newly established factory towns of New England, such as Lowell and Holyoke in Massachusetts, consisted of the young and unmarried daughters of neighboring farm families. Although worked very hard and paid very little, these factory girls were treated rather paternalistically by their employers in the early years of the factory towns. Housed in dormitories and subjected to a strict 10 P.M. curfew, the girls were normally required to attend church at least once a week. In several of the factory towns, the girls were given the opportunity to attend lectures and concerts, and even to publish a newspaper.

During the 1830s, the terms and condition of labor in the New England factory towns began to deteriorate due to the growing intensity of competition among the region's textile firms. By 1840, the social reformer Orestes Brownson could write that most of the mill girls "wear out their health, spirit, and morals without becoming one whit better off than when they commenced labor."[9] It is possible that Brownson was exaggerating, but no student of the subject doubts that conditions in the factory towns worsened when the farm girls were supplanted by Irish immigrants, or that conditions in big-city sweatshops and factories were substantially worse. By keeping labor costs low, these unskilled workers were helping to expedite industrial progress.

The shift toward larger-scale methods in industry and commerce also served to undermine the status and prospects of many skilled artisans. As goods were produced in larger batches for more distant markets, competition grew more intense and the efforts of employers to organize production became ever more extensive. As more capital was now required to go into business, it became increasingly common for aspiring artisans to remain wage earners permanently.

The old camaraderie between the employer and his men gave way to the impersonal quest for gain, with the "boss" trying to economize on wages while the "hands" sought, through closing ranks, to increase their earnings. Unions of skilled workers became increasingly common in the larger cities after 1820. The labor movement of the 1830s appears to have been a genuine mass movement with a total membership, at its peak, of at least 100,000. Citywide labor federations were established in a dozen cities in the 1830s, some of which were instrumental in obtaining the ten-hour day.

Throughout this era, labor organizations oscillated between the generalized goals of social reform and the more particularized goal of bettering conditions for workers in a given locality or in a particular trade. The workingmen's parties of the 1820s and early 1830s, which had sought such democratizing reforms as universal public education and the abolition of imprisonment for debt, had drawn a sufficiently large vote to induce the major parties to take up much of their program. Labor historian John R. Commons has argued that when times were good and there were more jobs than there were workers to fill them, labor had been concerned primarily with wages and hours, but that when times were bad and jobs scarce, labor had been unable to maintain powerful unions and had turned to political action.[10] With every major economic downturn, most trade unions would disappear as would most of labor's recently won gains.

Urban Blight

The rapid growth of commerce and industry also led to the transformation of urban residence patterns. Prior to 1840, it had been typical for the well-to-do to live in the city's oldest districts, within walking distance of the docks and their places of business. However, with the emergence of large and growing warehouse and manufacturing districts, these once comfortable areas were filled with dirt and noise resulting from the encroachment of new warehouses, lumber yards, and other commercial and industrial establishments. These areas were also blighted by the boarding houses and cheap hotels that had arisen to supply shelter to an impoverished and largely foreign labor force.

Because of the lack of mass transit before 1850, only a small percentage of the urban population did not reside within walking distance of their places of employment. The central and most built-up district or "walking city" was limited in each direction to the distance that could readily be traversed by a pedestrian journeying from his home to his place of work. In cities such as Boston and Chicago, the maximum distance from the city's center to the outer boundary of the "walking city" was approximately two or three miles. Since there were hardly any buildings above six stories, certain districts became increasingly congested as urban economies grew and their immigrant populations increased.

The presence of numerous aliens and the pollution and blight that accompanied economic development soon drove out many of the wealthier families who now sold their houses and formed new communities farther "uptown" or in suburbs just beyond the city line. The development of horse-drawn bus lines and street railways expedited the procession uptown, and the development of the suburbs was encouraged by the establishment of steam-powered ferries and commuter railroads. As early as 1848, about one fifth of the businessmen of Boston were commuting daily via railroad from their uptown or suburban houses to places of business in the central areas of Boston.

As has so often been the case in American urban history, such changes were followed by the rapid deterioration of the older neighborhoods. The houses of those who had moved were purchased mainly by profit-hungry landlords who divided them into one-room apartments, each of which would be rented to a family and sometimes to two. With the tenements and warehouses advancing rapidly toward them, more of the original residents fled the area and their homes too were subdivided and rented to the laboring poor. As newcomers continued to arrive, shanties were constructed at the rear of these properties, and as the demand for housing increased, additional floors were tacked onto both structures until some of the mansions had reached heights of six stories and the rear houses sometimes attained four.

In the older districts, it was not only homes that were so utilized but every available building, regardless of its original purpose. Outhouses, warehouses, and even breweries were subdivided and rented to the poor. In the Five Points district of New York City a former brewery provided housing to more than forty families in the 1840s.

There was also a great deal of new construction in the cities with many new houses being built in middle and working class districts. As not all workers could be accommodated in the central areas, many were compelled to seek both jobs and housing in other districts. Those with too little money to pay the going rentals would often squat illegally on vacant land just beyond the built-up portions of the city where they would erect one-room wooden shanties. Here were to be found a high proportion of the city's transient, criminal, and pauper populations and also those who, lacking any other occupation, eked out a livelihood as ragpickers or as gatherers of cinders and bones. Shanty-dwelling families had a semirural existence in which they often grew vegetables and kept a few pigs and goats. In New York City, as of 1860, an estimated three fifths of the recipients of public and private charity were shanty dwellers.

After 1850, the demand for housing near the manufacutring and warehouse district continued to rise, and shrewd contractors in New York and other cities began to demolish the older houses and to supplant them with new structures designed to make maximum use of the available space. Whether they were the barrack tenements adopted in New York City or the four-floor wooden tenements common to both Boston and Chicago, the new buildings quickly became as overcrowded as the old. Like the earlier forms of working class housing, these too were repeatedly subdivided until it again became typical for a tenement-dwelling family to occupy one room.

The central districts would have been still more congested had it not been for the construction and increasing use of many new horse-car lines. In 1860, Chicago, with a population in excess of 100,000, already had three street railways, and as of 1866, New York City had sixteen in addition to seven omnibus lines. As a consequence of these new means of transit, additional residential areas became available to the more prosperous wage-earning families. By 1860, according to Sam Bass Warner, Jr., "perhaps a third of Philadelphia's manufacturing workers were commuting to jobs in the manner of the majority of their successors in the twentieth century metropolis."[11]

For those too poor to afford the daily carfare and higher rents that the better neighborhoods required there was no alternative to residence within the central areas. By 1860, there was scarcely any city without its slum district where, write Tunnard and Reed, "the houses are so run-down, below standard, and unhealthy that they are declared to be a menace to the occupants and the community."[12] As many tenants as possible were crowded into these buildings, which generally went unpainted, were frequently without heat, and usually had no more than one window per home and, on occasion, no windows at all.

Urban Services

Urban growth and the congestion of central city areas were accompanied, as always, by severe environmental and social problems which were perhaps even more serious in the early nineteenth century than in later periods because Americans had acquired as yet so little experience in dealing with them. Gradually, workable innovations began to spread across the urban landscape. With their long tradition of limited government, Americans sought at first to cure their urban maladies exclusively through private individuals and groups, but in one field after another, they increasingly found it necessary to accept governmental intervention and supervision.

WATER SUPPLY

A good example of the shift from the private to the public sector is furnished by the history of urban water supply. Through most of the eighteenth century, water had posed no problem for most urban residents, who were generally able to meet their requirements either from nearby bodies of water, from cisterns (rain barrels), or by digging wells. Such personally obtained supplies were augmented by the water bought from the "tea-water" men, those who made a business of physically transporting pure water from distant streams and selling it to the residents of New York, Charleston, and other cities. Additional water was supplied by the public pumps that were installed in the eighteenth century in all of the principal seaports.

After 1770, several communities constructed waterworks systems, and in the 1790s, Philadelphia, prompted by the most destructive yellow fever epidemic in its history, built America's first steam-powered waterworks.* Shortly there-

---

*It is interesting to note that the construction of the Philadelphia waterworks was motivated in part by the incorrect theory that yellow fever and indeed most diseases were caused by the vapors supposedly given off by filth, the so-called miasma theory which held sway in American medical and scientific circles until the 1880s.

after, Boston and New York also constructed such facilities. As the cities grew larger, it became necessary to pump water from a distance in order to meet the requirements of industry as well as the needs of ordinary consumers. In 1835, New York City began the construction of the Croton system of reservoirs, aqueducts, and waterpipes, which, when completed seven years later, made water available to New Yorkers from the Croton River, some forty-two miles away. By 1860, 148 cities had equipped themselves with comprehensive systems of running water although cities as large as Milwaukee and Providence still did not have such systems.

As would later prove true of other public utilities, initially most waterworks were privately owned. Of the sixteen cities with public water systems as of 1817, only Philadelphia's was publicly owned. By mid-century, however, private water companies were becoming unpopular due to inadequate service and rising rates. Of the nation's sixteen largest cities in 1860, twelve had municipally owned waterworks, although, overall, private water firms outnumbered the publicly owned by a margin of eighty to sixty-eight. Thereafter, the trend was to move in the direction of municipally owned waterworks.

Many people were doubtful that the new tap water was fit to drink. Sometimes an early subscriber was startled by the sight of a tiny animalcule or even a fish coming through his faucet. Some observers fretted over the supposed danger of growing bullfrogs within the human body as a result of drinking tap water, but others regarded the presence of tiny animals in the water as a positive sign, reasoning that if they could survive in it, then the water must be safe to drink.

In the early water systems, subscribers not only paid fees for their water but also were required to arrange their own hookups with the public water mains. Consequently, running water remained primarily a convenience of the upper and upper middle classes until after the Civil War. In townhouses and luxury hotels, running water and indoor water closets were widely adopted by 1850.

Among the working classes, however, there was often a scarcity of water. It was said in the nineteenth century that a poor man got a good bath only twice in his life: from the midwife after he was born and from the undertaker after his death. In the tenements of the 1850s, there were sometimes no privies at all, or only a single facility for a dozen families. In the New York tenements of the 1860s and 1870s, there were often one or two toilets per floor, but it was not until decades later that they were connected to city water. As of 1860, most city dwellers were still relying on outdoor privies which leaked whenever it rained.

Fire Protection

Protection against fire was another area in which municipal governments eventually came to take a more active role. In the eighteenth century, the ever-present menace of fire in the new, largely wood-constructed cities had inspired the principal cities to purchase hand-pumped fire engines and to establish volunteer fire departments. Men of property had at first predominated in these organizations, but by the early 1800s, many firemen were being recruited from the middle and lower classes. Many a young worker found in firefighting a source of diversion and excitement and a means of impressing the ladies.

Resplendently dressed in their multicolored outfits, the rival fire companies would race each other to every blaze, and should two of them arrive at the same time at the hydrant nearest the fire, they would engage in a lengthy brawl to determine which would have the privilege of combatting the fire. At one such brawl in Baltimore, "the fight raged on for an hour and a half during which bricks were torn up from the sidewalk and showered like hail, pistols were fired in every direction."[13] Frequently, of course, the building would burn down long before the brawl was over. The fire companies also figured in politics, helping to corrupt the political process by serving the local political organizations as repeaters (men who voted several times in elections) and sluggers. By

Figure 3.1 Chicago Fire Department hook-and-ladder truck modeled on those used in the city's famous fire of 1871, in which a vast number of the city's wooden buildings were destroyed.

mid-century, the volunteer departments seemed to many city dwellers to be more of a menace than an asset to the community.

From time to time, there were terrible fires such as the one that took place in Pittsburgh in 1845 in which nearly 1,000 buildings covering some fifty-six acres were destroyed. Such disasters served to arouse interest in the establishment of fire departments made up of paid professionals. The development of the steam fire engine and of improved pumping equipment also necessitated a less amateurish approach to firefighting. Finally, the rising value of urban property and the growing volume of urban business made it essential that fires be dealt with as efficiently as possible. In 1853, Cincinnati became the first major city to make firefighting a paid professional service. By 1860, several of the nation's largest cities had followed suit, and by 1880, in the major cities, the volunteer fireman, one of the stock figures in the early cities, had largely passed from the scene. However, not even firefighting professionals, were able to halt the great Chicago fire of 1871, nor the one that struck in Boston the following year; these conflagrations destroyed a substantial portion of both cities. (See Figure 3.1.)

POLICE PROTECTION

Law enforcement was another area in which the cities, after relying initially on ordinary citizens, resorted increasingly to paid and specially trained professionals. In the cities of the eighteenth and early nineteenth centuries, ordinary citizens had taken their turns as constables who kept order by day or as watchmen who patrolled the streets at night. Although they were sometimes paid, they remained amateurs to whom such temporary duty amounted to a costly sacrifice of time from their true occupations. The rising incidence of crime and violence after 1840 led one city after another (with New York the first in 1844) to follow the example of London in creating a fully professional police force that was semimilitary and centralized in its administration. (See Figure 3.2.) By 1860, most of the nation's major cities had formed police forces modeled after that of New York. Although at first the practice met with some resistance, it soon became common for policemen to wear uniforms.

Despite the new police departments, the cities of the antebellum era were probably no safer than those of today. Certain districts, like the French Quarter in New Orleans and San Francisco's Barbary Coast, were so saturated in vice and crime that the local authorities made no real attempt to enforce the law. According to social historian Herbert Asbury, the New York City police in the 1850s would not enter the city's Fourth Ward in groups of less than six, even in broad daylight.[14] The Barbary Coast and New York's "Murderers Alley" are both believed to have averaged a murder a day in the 1850s and 1860s. In 1870, George Templeton Strong, a prominent New York lawyer, recorded in his diary: "Crime was never so safe as it is this winter. . . . Municipal law is a failure in New York, and we must soon fall back on the law of self-preservation."[15]

ENVIRONMENTAL PROBLEMS AND PUBLIC HEALTH

For the majority of their residents, the cities of this era were crude and uncomfortable places to live. In some cities, air pollution was already a problem. "In Pittsburgh, Cincinnati, and other cities west of the Alleghenies," contended an article in the November, 1865, issue of the *Scientific American*, "the smoke that constantly hangs in the atmosphere is

Figure 3.2 The New York City police first began to wear uniforms in 1853, nine years after the police department was founded.

a very great nuisance."[16] Another urban affliction of this era was the great quantities of manure deposited daily by the innumerable horses on which the cities were forced to rely for the transport of goods and people. As the great majority of urban thoroughfares in 1860 had neither pavements nor sewers, the streets would turn to mud whenever it rained. Thus, the ladies of New Orleans sometimes found it necessary to wade to a ball in their bare feet, with their dresses tucked up to keep them out of the mud.

Adding to the urban environmental problems of the period were the extremely primitive methods utilized for the disposal of sewage and garbage. Some of the cities disposed of their sewage and other filth in the very lakes and rivers from which their water supplies were obtained. For a few years, Chicago was in this category, dumping its waste products into Lake Michigan, upon which most Chicagoans relied for the water they used in their cooking and cleaning.

In many urban districts at mid-century, offal and garbage were generally thrown out the windows to be consumed in the streets by animal scavengers, generally pigs or dogs, although in New Orleans, it was vultures, and in Charleston, buzzards who performed this useful function. "Without them," wrote Mrs. Trollope, the English traveler and mother of the noted author, commenting on the pigs of Cincinnati, "the streets would be clogged with all sorts of substances in every stage of decomposition."[17] In several of the larger cities, private contractors were engaged by well-to-do citizens to remove the waste from their privies and by the city to clean the streets. Conditions remained dismal, however, in the poorer districts of the major cities where, throughout the 1800s, water remained scarce and the streets were seldom swept. In 1865, Dr. Stephen Smith, the director of a comprehensive survey of sanitary conditions in New York City and the leader for half a century of that city's public health movement, told a committee of the New York State Assembly about conditions in the city's Sixth Ward where the roadbeds were covered "sometimes to a depth of two or three feet" with "house slops, refuse, vegetables, decayed fruit sweepings, ashes, and dead animals."[18]

Such conditions, combined with the overcrowded housing of the urban poor, brought about a sharp increase in the death rate in most of the leading cities. Thus, the average death rate in New York City rose from 28.1 per thousand in the quarter century after 1815, to 32.6 in the period from

1840 to 1865, while Boston's average death rates over these two periods were 21.3 and 25, respectively. Worst of all was the record of New Orleans where, from 1815 to 1865, an average of better than 5 percent of the city's population perished each year. The incidence of death tended to be highest among infants, blacks, and the poor generally. Thus in New York City between 1850 and 1854, one out of every six of the city's infants died each year. The higher death rate among blacks is illustrated by the fact that in 1821 in New York City, 15.5 percent of the deaths occurring in the city were accounted for by the city's blacks, who comprised only 8 percent of the overall population. Finally, the lower the social class, the higher its death rate. Thus, the mortality rate among the upper class, largely native-born residents of Boston's Beacon Hill was less than one fourth as high as that in the Third Street district near the city's wharves where the population was 96 percent foreign-born.

The very high death rates in the nineteenth century were in large part due to the prevalence of infectious disease. Until about 1870, there were periodic epidemics in the nation's cities that resulted in thousands of deaths. The most dramatic of these scourges were yellow fever and cholera, which would strike suddenly and spread with amazing rapidity. The yellow fever epidemic of the 1790s claimed the lives of thousands of residents of the eastern seaports, and in Philadelphia did away with one tenth of the city's population. In the summer of 1853 New Orleans, nearly always more vulnerable to contagion than other major American cities, was struck by an epidemic of yellow fever which in four weeks in August was reported to have claimed the lives of nearly 5,000 victims. The three transatlantic cholera epidemics, in 1832, 1849, and 1866, were equally destructive. In the one in 1832, 3,500 people in New York City died of the disease over a period of four months, while in New Orleans, 6,000 people, over 10 percent of the city's population, died of it in just 20 days.

Almost equally dangerous to the city dwellers of this era were such diseases as typhus and dysentery, which were constantly present, occasionally in epidemic proportions. Finally, it is highly probable that more city dwellers died in this period from endemic diseases like malaria and tuberculosis than from all the epidemics combined.

Epidemics would result normally in the appointment of boards of health in the cities they infested. Consisting generally of the mayor and the town council, these boards were

THE URBAN TURMOIL 91

given broad powers to eliminate whatever they considered harmful to the public health. Once the crises that had led to their creation had passed, however, they would become largely inactive. In some instances, politicians obstructed the enforcement of local health laws. (See Figure 3.3.) A departure from the norm occurred in 1820 in Baltimore with the appointment of a health board consisting of three doctors who were given the power to see to it that the streets were cleaned and that all health hazards were removed, but who depended on the city's police for the enforcement of their rulings. By 1860, most of the larger cities had administrative committees that supervised local sanitation, but the health measures of these bodies, like those of the boards of health that had preceded them, were usually enforced only during epidemics.

The public health movement in America began in the 1840s with the formation in a number of cities of voluntary associations patterned after those of Great Britain, bringing together leading citizens, prominent doctors, and government officials. As the specific causes of most infectious diseases were not yet known, the public health activists sought a general

Figure 3.3 A cartoon from the 1850s accuses three New York City aldermen of covering up (whitewashing) for a cow barn owner whose diseased cattle had been fed contaminated feed. From *Frank Leslie's Illustrated Newspaper*, July 17, 1858.

cleanup of the environment and the enactment of measures dealing with a wide variety of social and health questions, ranging from the regulation of slaughterhouses and the interment of the dead to house construction, child labor, and the need for public parks.

The movement's principal breakthrough came in 1866 with the establishment by the New York State legislature of the Metropolitan Board of Health, a reorganized health administration for the New York City region modeled after that of London, which, independently of other administrative bodies, was empowered to adopt ordinances, carry them out, and sit in judgment on its own acts. This legislation was triggered in part by the results of an investigation of sanitary conditions in New York by a medical subcommittee, headed by Dr. Stephen Smith of the Citizens' Association, the coalition of anti-Tammany reformers led by Peter Cooper. Another factor in the measure's adoption was an impending epidemic of cholera.

Once created, the new board sprang immediately into action. Hundreds of cow barns and piggeries were ordered out of the city and all the slaughterhouses below 40th Street were forced to move uptown. Within its first eight months, the board issued more than 23,000 orders and over 5,000 warnings to abate nuisances. The establishment of the Metropolitan Board of Health was a turning point in the history of American public health.[19] Similar agencies were established in Chicago in 1867, in Boston in 1872, and in several other cities by 1880.

To the public health activists of the 1860s it seemed obvious that the high rates of disease and mortality in the slums were closely linked with their congestion, inadequate plumbing, and poor ventilation. In 1867, they persuaded the New York State legislature to enact the New York Tenement House Law which required that all tenement houses were to have fire escapes, that all their sleeping rooms were to be ventilated either by a window or transom, and that there was to be at least one water closet for every twenty inhabitants. This law proved inadequate to cope with the problem, however, and some of the city's worst slums were constructed after its passage. The movement for public parks was another attempt to redeem the urban environment. In the early 1800s, few citizens had seen any necessity for the maintenance of open space within the cities, but as cities became increasingly built up, some prominent leaders, including the poet and newspaperman William Cullen Bryant and the architect Andrew Jackson Downing, began to agitate for public parks. In 1855, Philadelphia opened the 4,000-acre Fairmount Park, the first sizable public park in America. Two years earlier, the New York State legislature had authorized a great public park in New York City. Frederick Law Olmsted, a young landscape architect who was chosen superintendent of the project by the Park Commission, had also, as it happened, collaborated with Calvert Vaux on the design selected by the commissioners for the park.

Olmsted saw parks as an instrument for promoting both the health and morality of the working class who might otherwise be drawn to more vicious forms of amusement such as the saloon. In this, he was not alone among the reformers of his day. Indeed, whether for tactical reasons or out of sincere conviction, the elevation of the morals of the working class and of the poor was one of the principal themes stressed by advocates of public health measures and housing reform. "Outward impurity," observed one reform advocate in 1851, "goes hand in hand with inward pollution."[20]

Public Education

The promotion of "good" morals was also one of the principal objectives of the drive in many parts of the nation to establish public schools. Educational reformers like Horace Mann and Henry Barnard advocated universal education not just for democratic and humanitarian reasons, but also because they believed that public schools would teach the young to be honest, industrious, and respectful of property. The schools would teach their pupils to obey the rules of the game and not to try to change those rules or depart from them.

Early in the nineteenth century, free education had been available only to children whose parents had admitted to being paupers. Free, tax-supported schools were established in Boston in 1818, in New York City in 1832, and in Philadelphia in 1836. By 1860, nearly all the children in northern cities were entitled to a free elementary education. As of 1870, the system of a citywide school board and a superintendent of schools had been widely adopted in American cities.

The education movement was strongest in the cities because wealth and power were concentrated here, as were the most severe social problems. In addition, many urban artisans were zealous advocates of the public schools, and their organizations added greatly to the movement's political clout. Where only a minority of the wealthy had supported public schools out of enlightened self-interest, the working class believed that public education insured that knowledge would no longer be a monopoly of the upper class and also promised greater opportunity for their sons.

Public Assistance

From the colonial period on, American cities and towns, maintaining the policies that had been developed in Elizabethan England, had supplied a combination of private charity and public assistance to those in need. This aid had taken diverse forms, but the municipalities usually had sought to "bind out" or apprentice orphans, to discipline and reform the able-bodied vagrants, and to supply more lenient forms of assistance to the elderly and the disabled among the poor. After 1730, when the trend toward "indoor" relief was beginning, the able-bodied or vagrant element was consigned increasingly to workhouses while a growing minority of the helpless poor were being cared for in almshouses where the obligation to perform work of some kind was less severe. Nevertheless, the most typical form of relief for the poor, who were regarded as "deserving," was the dole or outdoor relief, generally in the form of a small annual payment.

By the 1830s the rising cost of poor relief and the example set by Great Britain's reform of its poor laws (1834) were key factors in the adoption of an increasingly harsh approach to the problem of poverty in the cities of the United States. Outdoor relief was severely curbed and the great majority of the poor were compelled to choose between residence in the local almshouses and the loss of all assistance. Moreover, even the orphans, the elderly, and the disabled were increasingly being compelled to work. Products of a society that was both much less affluent than ours and far more confident of its standards of morality, the taxpayers of that era thought these measures justified, as they were convinced that most paupers had brought their poverty upon themselves through sloth or self-indulgence or other moral failings.

They believed that even the blameless, such as orphans and the disabled, must be made to work or they would inevitably become morally corrupt. In order to save money, drunkards, prostitutes, criminals, and the insane were frequently housed in the same almshouses with young orphans and the indigent aged. Sometimes, the poor were sold at auction to whoever would accept the lowest sum of money for their support. The men who assumed the burden of caring for the poor were entitled to extract any labor that they could from their charges. After 1830, these conditions were increasingly publicized and denounced by humanitarian reformers, led by the redoubtable Dorothea L. Dix. By the Civil War, a variety of specialized institutions for welfare and correction had been established in many cities, including asylums for orphans and the insane, hospitals and dispensaries, schools for the handicapped, and juvenile reformatories. Finally, by 1850, imprisonment for debt had been virtually done away with and the use of the death penalty had been limited in many places to a few, quite serious offenses.

Community Divisions and Conflicts

Aside from the foregoing actions, taken in the name of "the common good," and the common involvement of city dwellers with local and national political and economic systems, the cities of this era were more internally divided than ever. Other than political parties and public schools, the only institutions to cut across religious and ethnic divisions were the trade unions and even these were often greatly hampered by inter-ethnic hostility. Native-born workers were often unwilling to join forces with immigrants, and every antebellum union excluded nonwhites. In turn, the sheer presence of competing groups of workers, who were often willing to work for less than the prevailing wage, served at times to undermine the living standards of native workers. Wherever ethnic antagonism existed, it strengthened the hand of the employer, for, should his employees strike, he could replace them with workers of another ethnic group.

As of 1860, the inhabitants of the major cities were already maintaining distinctive residential clusters based upon social class, race, ethnic identification, religious affiliation, and even upon regional background. In the larger cities, of course, there was at this time no single Protestant community, but rather a variety of denominational communities based in large part upon distinctions of social class. Thus, in antebellum New York City, such religious groups as Quakers and New England

Congregationalists had tended to cluster residentially in the vicinity of their houses of worship. Such sectarian divisions were especially significant because the churches in this period were the focal point of community life and were of crucial importance in charitable and educational endeavors. Finally, in several cities, including New York, St. Louis, and Cincinnati, there were New England Societies which, in addition to serving their members as social clubs, also provided them with life and accident insurance and helped pay for their members' funerals.

In their new "uptown" neighborhoods, the wealthier white Protestants had, on the whole, continued to maintain distinctive communities on the basis of church membership and regional backglound. Such tendencies were even more marked among blacks and immigrants. The latter, especially the Irish Catholics and the Germans, were now too numerous and too culturally different from the Anglo-Saxon Protestants to assimilate as readily as in the past. In the face of an environment that often seemed to alternate between indifference and hostility, most of the members of each group tended, out of mutual need, to huddle near their own kind.

The Immigrant Community

While few urban neighborhoods were as segregated as the black ghettos of today, in most cities each of the more numerous ethnic groups tended to have at least one district where, as the principal group, it had set the tone for the community. In most major cities, there were Little Irelands and Little Germanys and, frequently, smaller enclaves for less numerous groups. Pre-Civil War Pittsburgh contained such areas as Hayti (the black section) and Scotch Hill, and in certain cities, there were compact areas known simply as the Ghetto, or Jewish quarter. However, the degree of cohesion varied greatly from group to group and from city to city. Although in Cincinnati and Milwaukee, there were huge enclaves in which were concentrated the greater part of each city's German population, the Germans of St. Louis, Philadelphia, and other centers were far less concentrated, due partly to geographic peculiarities.

In the United States, the immigrants in time came to regard themselves as having a national rather than a provincial identity, as being Irish or German rather than natives of Cork or Bavaria. As historian Earl Niehaus has put it, "by grouping together immigrants from Ireland, America lifted them out of the littleness of countyism into the broad feeling of nationalism."[21] Even the readily assimilated British immigrants established separate organizations and assiduously celebrated the national saints' days which they had always ignored at home.

As their numbers rose and their ethnic consciousness increased, the immigrants increasingly tended to form distinctive institutions. In New York City as of 1870, at least fourteen different ethnic and religious groups had formed organizations. Often modeled after the organizations maintained by native Americans, these institutions were in the American tradition of voluntary social action and served to alleviate the insecurity of dwelling in a strange city among alien groups. Clubs like the German Red Men and fraternal orders like the Jewish B'nai B'rith were both openly based on American models. Most large immigrant communities established their own militia companies and here too they were modeling themselves on American practice. Many mutural aid societies were also established even by such relatively small groups as the Welsh, the Scots, and the French Canadians.

Some of the larger immigrant groups also created their own networks of charitable institutions, maintaining orphan asylums, homes for the aged, hospitals, and other establishments to aid the needy. Much of this activity was sponsored by synagogues and churches. In every diocese, the charitable institutions founded by the various Roman Catholic communities were often initiated, and always supervised by the local church. Such action was motivated in part by traditional Christian ideals, but also by the fear that the Catholic faith might be weakened among the poor unless steps were taken to relieve their sufferings. The Roman Church also encouraged separate Catholic institutions because it feared that those that were dominated by Protestants would undermine the faith of the non-Protestants they assisted.

Certain communities had also established a variety of cultural organizations with the intention of maintaining the culture of their native lands in their new homes. For example, there were Catholic churches where the faithful were instructed in French or German because that was the language of the community. As the principal foreign-speaking group, the Germans were particularly active, establishing separate schools, bookstores, newspapers, theaters, singing groups, and physical culture societies.

Frequently, the public schools were mistrusted by the foreign-born who perceived all too accurately that one of their principal goals was the assimilation of all immigrants. To many German immigrants, for example, the public schools seemed an implicit threat to their beloved *Kultur*, which might, in Americanizing their children, alienate them from the ways of their parents. In certain cities, such as Cincinnati and Milwaukee, whole systems of private schools were maintained by the German community. In these schools German was for many years the principal language of instruction. In other cities, the German element sometimes obtained important concessions from the local system of education. Thus, according to immigration historian Robert Ernst, special German-speaking teachers were hired by New York City during the 1840s, the first bilingual teachers in the history of that city's public schools.[22]

Fearing that the public schools might be used as a means of converting their children to Protestantism, many Roman Catholics and Jews helped support separate, religiously oriented schools. During the 1840s, the Roman Catholic bishops of New York, Philadelphia, and other cities demanded that their parochial schools obtain a share of local school taxes, triggering a controversy that split these cities into warring camps, divided generally along sectarian lines.

RELIGIOUS CONFLICTS AND EARLY NATIVISM

In this era, there was more to the hostility between Protestant and Catholic than the question of the schools. From the colonial period on, most American Protestants had regarded Catholicism as a body of barbarous superstition, and by the nineteenth century, they had also come to regard it as anti-republican and as generally anti-progressive. Badly frightened by the mounting influx of Catholics from Germany and Ireland, many native Protestants came to fear for the soul of the nation and increasingly gave vent to their anti-Catholic views. That such opinions were to be found even among educated and respectable citizens served to strengthen the hostility of the community at large toward Catholics. After 1830, there were occasional anti-Catholic riots in a number of cities, including Boston, New York, New Orleans, and Philadelphia. The worst of these outbreaks took place in Philadelphia in 1844 when Protestant mobs went on a rampage of looting, arson, and assault which lasted three days and cost sixteen lives.

Anti-Catholicism overlapped with, and was reinforced by, nativistic (anti-foreign) movements which sought to curb the influence and sometimes the civil rights of the foreign-born. From time to time, in all of the seaport cities, nativist politicians would point to the disproportionate number of aliens in the local almshouses and prisons and would blame them for rising taxes. Like later minorities, the immigrants themselves were also blamed for the poverty and squalor in which many of them lived. To many, these evils seemed symptomatic of a deeper malaise which imperiled the republic itself. "A nation of freemen," warned a congressional committee in 1856, "cannot long continue without religion and morality, industry and frugality; for these are indispensable supports of popular government. Crime and pauperism are the bane of a republic."[23]

The conflicts between the native-born Protestants and the immigrants could also assume a cultural form. Nativists charged that in establishing neighborhoods that were distinctively German or Irish and in founding their own organizations rather than joining those of the native-born, the immigrants were resisting Americanization. Native Protestant zealots also tried to impose temperance upon the immigrants, most of whom saw no harm in an occasional drink, and they also took issue with the immigrant practice of treating Sunday, once one had been to church, as a day of relaxation and merriment. (See Figure 3.4.) When the government of Chicago in 1855 attempted to impose a $300 license fee on the city's saloons, a crowd of several hundred, mostly Germans and Irishmen, marched on the courthouse and the police had to be reinforced by the National Guard before order could be restored. In New York City in 1867, another coalition of Germans and Irishmen opposed and defeated an ordinance designed to force the closing on Sundays of the city's grogshops and saloons. "After the fall elections," writes immigration historian Carl Wittke, "in which their votes helped defeat 'the Republican-Puritan Excise Law,' hilarious Celts and Teutons gathered in Tompkins Square to fire artillery salvos to celebrate the defeat of the narrow-minded 'Yankees.' "[24]

Nativists also blamed Roman Catholic immigrants for the widespread fraud and violence in the urban politics of the period. Many were affronted by the fact that immigrants had often voted, or more accurately had been voted by politicians, while actually not yet citizens, and therefore ineligible under the law. In 1868 alone, 68,000 fraudulent certificates of naturalization are said to have been issued in New York city by politically appointed Tammany judges. (See Figure 3.5.) Nativists also made much of the fact that gangs made up largely of Irish-born laborers or volunteer firemen were frequently used by political organizations in cities like Boston, New York, and New Orleans to keep opposition voters from the polls. "Foreign felons," declared a congressional committee in 1856, "are the stuff that mobs are made of in those cities, who invade the sanctity and purity of the ballot-box, and destroy the freedom of the elective franchise."[25]

Critics of the immigrants normally overlooked the fact that the foreign-born were themselves often the victims of intimidation, assault, and, on occasion, mob violence. During the 1830s and 1840s, anti-Catholic and anti-Irish riots occurred sporadically in many American cities, during which churches and other Catholic institutions were damaged and houses resided in by Irish immigrants were wrecked by mobs. On many an election day in the antebellum era, bands of young working-class nativists, the counterpart among the na-

Figure 3.4 Immigrants "defile the Sabbath"—a German beer garden in New York City on a Sunday evening in 1859. From *Harper's Weekly*, October 15, 1859.

THE URBAN TURMOIL 101

tive-born white Protestants of the Irish and German gangs, would attempt through violence to prevent Catholics, and particularly the Irish, from voting. One such group of nativist hoodlums were the "plug-uglies" in Baltimore, whose name was derived from the fact that on election days during the 1850s, they would "plug" (hit in the solar plexus with a fist containing a carpenter's awl) any man who attempted to vote without giving the password of the nativists.

In the spring of 1844, anti-foreign mayors were elected in both Philadelphia and New York City. During the 1850s, antebellum nativism reached its peak with the Know-Nothing movement which proposed to bar all men born abroad from voting and to extend to twenty-one years the period of residence required for naturalization. While neither of these measures was widely adopted, for a few years the Know-Nothings threatened to become one of the nation's major parties. Most recent scholars feel that the movement was more the product of the sectional crisis touched off by the slavery issue than it was of hostility to the immigrant. According to this view, Know-Nothingism obtained most of its support from its appeal to national feeling rather than its

Figure 3.5 Immigrants throng the Naturalization Office on the day before elections. From *Harper's Weekly*, November 7, 1857.

strictures against Catholics and foreigners. Finally, the nativist attacks upon political corruption and chicanery held great appeal for those segments of the public that favored reform.

Anti-Black Feeling

The urban working class, especially its Irish-Catholic component, was also antagonized by the growing strength of the antislavery movement in the northern states. To unskilled urban workers, the Abolitionist movement, which was often supported by the same people who were backers of nativism, seemed a threat to their jobs, their wages, and their standard of living. These fears were heightened by the practice, followed by some employers, of hiring black replacements, sometimes specially imported for the purpose, whenever their workers went on strike. Thus, most of the era's worst race riots took place as part of the struggle of white and black workers for available work on the docks and in the warehouses of the major urban centers. In 1863, there was a fight between black and white stevedores in Buffalo, touched off by the attempt of employers to replace white strikers with blacks; it resulted in the death of three of the blacks and serious injury to twelve more.

The bitterness and sense of grievance among poor urban whites as well as their hostility toward blacks were all deepened by the Civil War, a cause for which most of the poor in the northern cities felt little enthusiasm. On January 1, 1863, President Lincoln issued his Emancipation Proclamation, thereby seeming to confirm the worst fears of the unskilled urban whites: that the war would result in adding ex-slaves to the labor force who, by competing with them, would either take away their work or force their wages down. Already angry, the poor in the northern cities were stung to fury by the adoption of the military conscription law, especially by the provision that exempted from military service every young man who paid a $300 fee or hired a substitute.

In July, 1863, the federal government opened recruitment centers and began drafting men into the army. As a result, riots took place in a number of cities, the worst of which occurred in New York where, for four days, beginning on July 13th, the city's poorest element, led by local, largely Irish

THE URBAN TURMOIL 103

gangs, looted, burned, and killed. (See Figure 3.6.) The mob burned down an orphanage for black children and murdered at least two dozen people, most of them Negroes and Abolitionists, before they were clubbed into submission by the police and federal troops. It has been estimated that the great Draft Riot, as it is called, resulted in more than 1,000 deaths and 8,000 injuries, most of them suffered by the rioters themselves. Thus, the toll taken by this one outbreak resulted in more deaths and injuries than all of the riots of the 1960s combined.

By 1870 the problems of the cities were rooted in the rapidity with which they had grown. Divided by religion, birth, language, and race, the cities had supplied the setting

Figure 3.6 Rioters in New York City loot a drug store during the Draft Riots of 1863. From *Harper's Weekly*, July, 1863.

for a vigorous, brutal, and sometimes desperate struggle for existence. Widespread poverty and economic instability had led to such phenomena as slums, periodic riots, and the virtual surrender of particular districts to criminal elements. In sheer self-defense, many supplemented their strivings as individuals by joining with others in private groups, formed usually along ethnic or religious lines.

Another factor that powerfully affected the cities of this era was the great mobility of their inhabitants and of the American people generally. The modern tendency of urban residents to "solve" their social problems by moving away from them was already in evidence. The frequent migration of individuals and families to other neighborhoods, and even to other cities, may sometimes have contributed to the easing of urban tensions, but by that very fact, it also deprived urban residents of an incentive to deal comprehensively with the problems of their communities. As of 1870, the cities had only begun to develop the amenities and institutions that would in a later era ease the suffering of the poor and soften the brutality of the urban scene.

4

Growing Pains of City Government

While urban America was seeking to solve the problems resulting from the rapid influx of migrants and immigrants and the need for expanded services, the government of American cities suddenly became a subject of keen interest to viewers of the municipal scene. In spite of the fact that cities had undergone innumerable crises in the course of their development, the first upheaval to attract national attention took place in the latter part of the nineteenth century, in a period in American history that is referred to as the Gilded Age. This period, which spanned the years from 1865 to 1895, has been described by some observers as the "dark ages" of city government.[1]

As critics of the Gilded Age were quick to point out, there was an overall collapse in the conduct of public affairs; the federal government was plagued by the scandals of the Grant administration, while the individual states were experiencing political turmoil. In 1871, the governor of Nebraska was removed from office for embezzlement, and the next two years in Kansas were marked by disclosures of bribery in the senatorial elections. Nevertheless, it was corruption in city government that generated the most concern, and it was an Englishman who made one of the definitive comments about it. In *The American Commonwealth* (1888), English author James Bryce referred to city government as "the one conspicuous failure of the United States."[2] Municipal government had attracted scant attention until the "growing pains" stage of urban development led contemporaries to view the situation with alarm.

Municipal Government in Colonial Times

Although the situation would change dramatically by the Civil War period, the early stages of municipal government were marked by relative accord and efficiency, insofar as its limited functions were concerned. Cities were first given a form of government during the colonial era, when the royal governors of the colonies gave charters to twenty boroughs, or cities; among them were New York in 1686; Albany, 1686; Philadelphia, 1691; Annapolis, 1696; Norfolk, 1736; Richmond, 1742; and Trenton, 1746. In granting the charter, the governor sometimes acted upon the request of the colonists or their chosen representatives, although in general the English government welcomed the formation of municipalities. Occasionally, these charters were submitted to the freemen, or property holders, for their approval. The government of these boroughs was similar in several respects to that of municipal corporations in England, where charters of incorporation were issued by royal grant rather than by an act of Parliament.

The charters designated the common council as the chief governing body. The council consisted of a mayor, a recorder, a small number of aldermen, and a larger body of councilmen. This council acted as a single body, but a quorum was necessary before it could take action. The legislative powers of the council were limited to establishing local ordinances pertaining to matters such as the paving of streets or the preservation of law and order in the town. All laws, however, had to conform to the laws of England or the assembly of the province.

Since the charters were usually explicit in their grants of authority to the municipalities, municipal corporations lacked the power to expand their functions. When they wished to exercise additional authority, they petitioned the local assembly for a grant that was not originally provided for in the charter. By the end of the eighteenth century, municipalities had received special grants from the assemblies to undertake needed services, such as the purchase of fire engines, construction of drains, and the power to levy taxes.

The most important municipal official was the mayor, who was usually appointed by the governor. Aldermen and councilmen, who were elected by the male property owners, came to be subordinate to the mayor by the end of the colonial period. The terms of office were short; the mayor, aldermen, and councilmen were chosen for terms of one year. Frequently the mayor was reappointed, and by the middle of the eighteenth century several of the mayors of New York and Albany had held their positions for ten years. Officials generally served without compensation. Municipal service was regarded as a civic responsibility, and the leading citizens of the town were expected to formulate decisions in matters of importance to the community. In spite of the essentially democratic nature of colonial town life, a feeling of noblesse oblige permeated the thinking about the qualifications of officeholders in city government.

The only cities in which all the local officials were appointed were Philadelphia, Annapolis, and Norfolk, where the governing authority was a close corporation. The aldermen and councilmen in a close corporation held their positions for life, and the aldermen elected the mayor. Although the English municipalities during this period were governed by close corporations, the strong feeling among the colonists for elective assemblies limited the acceptance of the close corporation in America.

The judicial functions of the boroughs were undertaken by the mayor, the recorder, and the aldermen, who served as justices of the peace. They had jurisdiction over minor civic and criminal cases and also functioned as a local court of record, which had stated sessions and tried cases brought up before it. They often were members of the county courts as well.

In New England, where there were no active chartered boroughs, the town meeting came into existence. It was a form of government in which the members of the established church in the town, or in some cases all the inhabitants of the town, took part. Questions like the assessment of taxes, the distribution of land, and the establishment of schools were brought before the meeting. Within a short time after the town meeting originated, selectmen were chosen by the townspeople to carry out specific governmental functions. Although the town meeting ostensibly was democratically run—and traditionally has been regarded as an excellent example of grass roots involvement in the political process—in actuality it was dominated by a coterie of upper class merchants. However, because their interests frequently coincided with those of a majority of the inhabitants, potential areas of conflict tended to remain quiescent.

Despite the widespread practice throughout colonial America of having elective rather than appointive officials, the demand for mass participation in local affairs was minimal. As was true in the town meeting, government was in the hands of a small commercial aristocracy. Many urban dwellers were too occupied with earning a living to give much thought to municipal government, and there were few rival economic interests to challenge the dominance of those who were engaged in trade and commerce. Furthermore, as historian Sam Bass Warner, Jr., pointed out in his study of colonial Philadelphia, "by modern standards the town was hardly governed at all."[3] The limited functions of the town governments, together with the fact that cities were small and few in number, meant that the major issues that split the American colonists internally were not apt to pertain to matters undertaken at the municipal level. On the other hand, urban workers, who were generally content to accept the leadership of their "betters," were not wholly without political influence in the colonies, for prior to the American Revolution, it was this group that supplied most of the participants in the acts of violence and intimidation that helped to precipitate the break with England.

City Government: 1776–1850

Independence neither enhanced the political position of the American city, nor resulted in a shift of power within the community. The commercial elite continued to govern, and even the emergence of national political parties made little impact on local politics. However, the spirit of '76 did have a bearing on the structure of city government, and its form was altered in order to reflect some of the ideas about ruling bodies that had gained currency during the revolutionary age. Significantly, it was not sufficiently altered to enable the newly created central governments to exercise any degree of control, since the overwhelming preponderance of rural sections precluded any serious thinking about the responsibility of the federal government to the municipality. It was the state government that determined the destiny of the American city, and the precedent, once established, remained.

After the American Revolution, municipal charters were granted by the state legislatures, as sovereignty over the former colonists passed from the royal crown to the states. In terms of the desire of the American people to avoid arbitrary government, it was not surprising that these new charters made provision for a system of checks and balances and the separation of executive and legislative authority. The belief that executive power should be curtailed—a carryover from the distrust of royal governors during colonial times—also had popular support. Therefore, the powers of the aldermen and councilmen were expanded at the expense of the mayor. The close corporation also was dealt a death blow after the Revolution, and Philadelphia, Annapolis, and Norfolk received new charters which provided for the election of most of their public officials.

Although a majority of the colonial councils had been unicameral, bicameral councils came to replace them, particularly following the ratification of the United States Constitution in 1789. Many of these local councils consisted of an upper and a lower house, emulating the Senate and the House of Representatives which were established on the federal level. Members of the lower municipal house were elected at large; delegates in the upper house were selected on a ward, or district, basis.

As in the past, the mayor was more likely to be appointed than elected. Although property qualifications for voting were reduced, this provision did not necessarily stimulate interest in local politics to any extent. In New York, for example, only a small fraction of those eligible voted in municipal elections during the late eighteenth and early nineteenth centuries.

Several modifications took place in city government between 1825 and 1850, some of which were an outgrowth of Jacksonian democracy, or "the Age of the Common Man." First, the office of mayor became elective, reflecting the continuing wishes of the people to select their own officials. Second, suffrage was further liberalized, as universal white male suffrage was adopted throughout the country. Third, new administrative positions were created to provide municipal services to the community. Fourth, the spoils system was introduced. Fifth, state supervision of municipal affairs became stricter.

In practice, many of the changes were more apparent than real. The method of selecting the mayor was altered, but he still had only minimal power in such crucial areas as making appointments and vetoing legislation. The spoils system, by means of which members of the victorious party appointed their friends and associates to office, made government jobs available to a wider group of people but probably had little effect on the power structure of American city government. While the lower and middle classes secured the ballot and gained access to some positions as a result of the spoils system, it is questionable whether they participated in the decision-making process to a greater extent than they had in the past.

In cities like Pittsburgh, Cincinnati, Lexington, Louisville, and St. Louis, artisans and tradesmen occasionally won places on municipal boards prior to 1830. However, officeholding was a luxury for them in view of their limited time, and it had only minor appeal since most cities in this period paid no salaries. Consequently, municipal officials tended to come from the wealthy merchant classes of the community. They were usually honest and well known, and had been active in many areas of town life before being elected to public office. After 1830, spokesmen for the cities gained entry in state politics, but many of them were from the rising business and professional classes.

Studies undertaken by Edward Pessen of the socioeconomic background of the mayors, recorders, aldermen, councilmen, selectmen, and other municipal officials in New York, Brooklyn, Philadelphia, and Boston between the years 1825 and 1850 revealed that the vast majority of officeholders were merchants, attorneys, and upper class businessmen. Although unskilled laborers and journeymen mechanics comprised about three fifths of the total urban population in these four cities, few of them held office. As the election returns from wards in the poorer sections of the cities indicated, they continued to look to the upper classes for leadership. Although the evidence is by no means conclusive as far as an overall pattern in urban America, other historians have demonstrated that the situation was similar in several cities other than those Pessen studied. In Natchez, Mississippi, government was in the hands of the middle classes during the first half of the nineteenth century; the Jacksonian years brought no major change in the class background of the men elected to office, and local government remained the province of merchants, lawyers, and businessmen. Although the suffrage had been liberalized, voter apathy prevailed. Aldermen in Springfield, Massachusetts, in 1850 were primarily lawyers, bankers, businessmen, merchants, manufacturers, and builders; the representation of artisans and workingmen among the aldermen was 30 percent. Interestingly, this percentage had shrunk to 6 percent by 1870.[4]

If "the Age of the Common Man" was somewhat of a misnomer when applied to city government, Jacksonian America was not without stirrings that would have an effect on municipal politics in the future. Even though urban workers were not elected to municipal office in large numbers, some of them started to participate more actively in politics. Workingmen's parties came into existence in New York, Philadelphia, and in a number of eastern and midwestern cities during the 1820s and 1830s. These parties demanded a variety of statewide reforms aimed at bettering the conditions of workers and improving their overall opportunities for advancement. While the workingmen's parties were short-lived, they sometimes had held the balance of power between the major parties in municipal elections. By 1850, virtually all of their programs had been enacted by the more urbanized states, and the vote of urban workers was being courted by party politicians.

Urban Growth and City-State Relations

During the end of the Jacksonian period, urban governments had started to expand their functions in the community. This change was not dictated by any new philosophy concerning the nature of the municipality, but by the fact that cities were in the process of rapid transformation. Especially striking was the urban population shift that had occurred since the beginning of the nineteenth century. In 1800, there were only six cities that had as many as 8,000 inhabitants, and the combined population of all six was less than 211,000. Writer Horace E. Deming argued that as late as 1850, the United States had almost no cities, with the exception of a few harbors on the Atlantic seaboard and in one or two favorable situations on the banks of large rivers, and those that it did have were more like overgrown towns than cities in the modern sense of the word.[5] In 1860, the United States began to experience the start of its urban age, at least from the point of view of what can be identified as an awareness of the city as a significant factor in American development. By that date, there were 141 cities with a population of 8,000 or more. A decade later, the total had climbed to 226 cities, and by 1890, it had reached 445. Between 1860 and 1890, the number of urban dwellers increased from over 6,000,000 to approximately 22,000,000, which marked an increase from 19.8 percent to 35.1 percent of the national total.

In order to accommodate the needs of their growing populations, cities—sometimes independently and sometimes assisted by state funds—endeavored to provide new or expanded services for education, health, sanitation, water supply, lighting, fire, police, public utilities, and recreational facilities. Unfortunately, in their attempts to provide these services the municipalities were hampered by outmoded governmental machinery, and urban government entered into what could be called its first "chaos" stage.

One of the main difficulties lay in the nature of the relationship between cities and states. In strictly legal terms, the city is a municipal corporation created by the state. In the United States, the city has been subservient to the state from the time that city charters were first issued by the state legislatures following American independence. As a consequence, the American city lacked the power to function as a separate entity and was placed in a position of perpetual dependence upon the state. These restrictions were confining enough in earlier periods when, for example, the city was obliged to go to the state for permission to undertake a new service, but they proved to be an overwhelming burden in an era in which city growth was unparalleled and municipal problems multiplied at an unprecedented rate.

The federal and state courts consistently have upheld the general right of the state to legislate for the city, although there are certain limitations on this right. In the first place, the United States Constitution imposes restrictions whereby no legislature—federal or state—can take away private property in the city for public use without adequate compensation. Secondly, there are limitations contained in the state constitutions, which by the late nineteenth century had begun to provide for some measure of modified home rule for the cities. Nevertheless, the ability of the city to look after its own affairs was seriously impaired. When a municipal reformer complained in 1909 that "the citizens of Birmingham [England] govern Birmingham; the legislature of Pennsylvania governs

Pittsburg[h],"[6] he was describing a problem that has never been entirely resolved.

The states made use of their power to legislate for the cities, often to the point of absurdity. For example, the charter of Jersey City was revised ninety-one times between 1835 and 1875, and at one point, in the 1860s, the date of municipal elections in St. Paul was changed three times in four years. New York had eleven charters between 1846 and 1890, without any appreciable change in the quality of the city government, and the New York legislature passed more municipal laws in the three years from 1867 to 1870 than were passed in all of England during the fifty years from 1835 to 1885. Ohio passed 545 special and local acts between 1849 and 1850 for cities in the state, and in later years the legislature of Kentucky was equally obliging. In 1890, it enacted only 176 public acts, whereas it passed 1,752 private acts for municipalities.

Occasionally, state officials had misgivings about the wisdom of this "special legislation," as it was called, and there were attempts to substitute general legislation for it. In 1851, Ohio and Virginia revised their constitutions in order to outlaw special legislation, and in 1852 Ohio passed the first general municipal Corporations Act in the United States. This act set forth certain areas in which the cities might act independently of the states. Ohio's effort to outlaw special legislation was less successful. Cities were classified by population, but these groupings frequently evaded the constitutional provision outlawing special legislation. Cincinnati was put in a class by itself, and its taxing and borrowing powers were curtailed to the extent that it was unable to meet the demands of its growing community.

Other states followed the example of Ohio. In the years between 1857 and 1869, Iowa, Kansas, Florida, Nebraska, and Arkansas outlawed special legislation. The effectiveness of the act went untested, however, since none of these states had any large cities. On the other hand, when, in 1870, Illinois drafted a constitution giving broad powers to cities, the law, as enacted, proved to have many shortcomings. For example, Chicago's local officials were unable to grant concessions for the checking of hats or the selling of popcorn on the city's new municipal pier without a special act from the state legislature.

The nature and extent of the supervision exercised at the

statehouse could depend on what political party controlled the city, as opposed to the actual needs of the municipality. Throughout the 1860s in places like Chicago, Boston, New York, and St. Louis, the city was controlled by one party and the state by another. This led to bitter partisanship, as is illustrated by what happened in Chicago to the police department in the wake of interparty rivalry. When the Republicans emerged triumphant on the state level in 1861, they decided to reorganize the police department in Chicago, where the Democrats were the majority party. They placed the department under a board, the first members of which were to be appointed by the governor for a six-year term. Two years later the Democrats were victorious in Illinois, and they enacted legislation reducing the term of the police board to three years. By 1865, the Republicans came back into state office. The party restored the six-year term, placed the fire department under the supervision of the police department, and passed an act specifying that police commissioners should be elected by the voters of Cook County, since Cook County was considered less likely than Chicago to fall into Democratic hands.

The fact that the cities were grossly underrepresented in the state legislatures was another obstacle to effective municipal government. The inequities that stemmed from unequal representation were apparent in the composition of the Connecticut General Assembly in 1870, as well as in other state legislatures in the country. The Connecticut Assembly had not been reapportioned since 1818, when cities like Bridgeport and New Britain did not even exist. Although Connecticut changed its apportionment system in the 1870s to include cities with 2,500 or more inhabitants, the existing towns, regardless of size, retained their original representation. States also made use of gerrymandering, which enabled the legislature to divide election districts or political subdivisions in such a way as to reduce the representation of urban areas.*

It sometimes appeared that members of the state legislatures looked upon their urban brethren with a mixture of

*The problems stemming from unequal representation continued until the 1960s when the Supreme Court, in *Baker* v. *Carr* (1962) and *Reynolds* v. *Sims* (1964), directed the states to reapportion their legislatures. As a result, gerrymandering came to an end and cities finally were entitled to receive their proportionate share of representatives.

hostility and contempt. Some of them lived in the rural parts of their states, had scant knowledge of municipal life, and were indifferent to the plight of the cities. It was this kind of attitude that caused editor E. L. Godkin, referring to the New York State legislature in 1887, to complain that it was a "body of obscure men" who "get together every four or five months to play ducks and drakes with the great interests of a great community . . . and then sneak back to their villages and farms, with their tongues in their cheeks, to live on their booty, laugh at the indignation of their victims, and be forgotten."[7]

Municipal Debts and Administrative Agencies

The situation confronting American municipalities was further aggravated by the rising debts of cities. Fifteen of the largest cities in the United States had a population increase of 71 percent between 1866 and 1875, but their debts increased by 271 percent. In Cleveland, the rise in municipal expenditures amounted to 355 percent. During the decade from 1860 to 1870, New York's debts increased from $18,000,000 to $73,000,000, or about 301 percent. Its population rose only 16 percent, growing from 813,600 to 942,292. The huge indebtedness on the part of the municipalities brought some of them to the brink of bankruptcy. A few cities, including Selma, Mobile, Houston, and Memphis, were forced to repudiate their debts in 1878. Memphis had had a debt of $6,000,000 in 1876, and when a yellow fever epidemic broke out two years later, the city went bankrupt.* New Orleans and San Antonio went to the opposite extreme. They had excellent records in paying off their debts after the Civil War, but by doing so they had inadequate resources for other levels of community endeavor.

Municipal debts increased partly as a result of funds allocated to furnish services for the expanding population. However, the states began to conclude that the cities were guilty of fiscal mismanagement. Even though state indebtedness rose greatly during the second half of the nineteenth century,

---

*The state of Tennessee took over its financial operations and revoked its charter in 1879. Another major change occurred in 1909 when Memphis was given a commission government.

there was a disparity between city and state appropriations. The census of 1880 showed a total state indebtedness of $259,964,045. The city and town indebtedness amounted to $765,875,258. To prevent these debts from getting further out of hand, the states began to exercise strict control over city budgets after 1870. Up until that date, municipal budgets usually had come within the jurisdiction of the city council. In 1872, Illinois passed one of the most important laws regarding state supervision over city fiscal policy. Its legislature stipulated that all municipal appropriations had to be specified, and that there would be no additional funds spent unless sanctioned by popular referendum. Similar laws were adopted by Michigan in 1873 and Colorado in 1877. As of 1890, fourteen states had adopted measures to limit the borrowing power of their cities.

State control was welcomed by several municipalities, but it was not an unmixed blessing. Many cities had to rely on special legislation before they could undertake needed functions, and the final judgment rested with the state legislature. New Yorkers complained in the late 1860s that their council had control of less than one sixth of all municipal expenditures, and their protests continued to mount in the decades that followed.

State supervision of budgetary affairs was an outgrowth of an earlier trend, occurring around 1850, toward stricter control of municipal affairs. As municipalities expanded their public improvements, it was impossible for the city councils to exercise close supervision over these various projects. The administrative functions relating to the improvements were taken away from the council by the state and given to specially created boards and agencies. In many instances, they were wholly or partly independent of the council. The cities regarded these changes as an unwarranted usurpation of state power, and they retaliated by establishing their own agencies. The immediate effect was to create even more confusion, since many of these latter agencies functioned as semi-autonomous bodies that were not even subject to the supervision of the council.

Once these city boards and agencies were established, questions arose as to how their officials would be selected. In the past, city administrators had been chosen by the council, but beginning in 1850 many of these positions became elective rather than appointive. An 1849 charter for New York specified that officials in charge of city departments should be chosen by popular vote. In 1852, a board of improvements was set up in Cleveland. The board, which had charge of the supervision of all public works, consisted of a mayor, the city engineer, and three elective commissioners. Two years later, the Pennsylvania legislature made the office of the city treasurer elective in Philadelphia, and created another elective position, the city controller. By the late 1850s, however, some states began to doubt the wisdom of having administrative positions subject to the will of the city electorate. There was a return to the view that members of city departments should be appointed, although not by the council. Within a few years, many mayors were given the right to name administrative officials, with the provision that the appointments were subject to confirmation by the upper chamber of the city council. New York adopted this procedure in 1857, as did Chicago and Baltimore a few years later.

One consequence of all these changes was that as of the mid-1860s many cities had an overabundance of local and state agencies and boards, some of which had overlapping powers and some of which had virtually no authority at all. Further difficulty arose from the failure of municipal charters to fix responsibility on any given official or group. Whenever a controversy arose, the board or agency blamed the council, the council blamed the mayor, while the mayor maintained that he was unable to act without authority from the governor. In 1866, James Parton made a comment about municipal government in New York that was applicable to several of the other large cities in the United States at the time. After observing the workings of the numerous independent legislative bodies in the city and their various commissioners, he wrote: "Was there ever such a hodgepodge of a government before in the world?"[8]

Expansion of Municipal Services

In view of the obstacles to effective municipal government, it is significant that the cities were able to accomplish as much as they did insofar as public facilities were concerned. As time passed, however, many observers became convinced that the city was remiss in providing for the welfare of the community. By the late 1850s, allegations had already been made in several state legislatures about the inefficiency, waste, and dishonesty connected with the dispensing of municipal services, but the charges became more frequent in the period after the Civil War. While not unaware of what had been accomplished by American municipalities in a relatively short span of time, the prevailing attitude was the one expressed in 1876 by New York attorney William M. Evarts. He maintained that the money expended in New York on paving, piers, sewers, and buildings would have been sufficient to provide for necessities and conveniences in the city for many generations, but the work done was so inferior that most of the money had been misappropriated and wasted.[9]

As more facts and statistics became available about municipal expenditures, there was a widespread belief that cities were spending more money than they could afford, and that much of it fell into the hands of corrupt politicians and businessmen. In 1899, the American Society of Municipal Improvements sent a questionnaire to the 212 cities in the United States with a population of 15,000 or more. Seventy-eight replied and listed their expenditures for 1898. They included a total of $49,301,187 for streets; $32,867,458 for water supply; $14,057,142 for sewage; $26,779,847 for public lighting and building; $22,198,566 for parks and bridges; and $66,330,023 for police and fire protection. The figures did not include money spent for waterfront improvements, education, libraries, museums, public baths, markets, charities, and penal institutions. In spite of the vast sums that were appropriated, citizens complained about the dirt, disorder, and other inconveniences of city life. By the end of the nineteenth century, articles appeared in leading journals like *Forum, Harper's Weekly*, and *The Nation* alleging that American cities were poorly run, and suffered by comparison with their European counterparts. The alleged mismanagement in municipal affairs usually was attributed to bossism and machine politics, and it was this aspect of urban politics that became the target of critics of city government.

Origins of Machine Politics

In many respects, bosses and machine politics were logical outgrowths of urban development in the mid- and late-nineteenth centuries. A power vacuum was created amid the diffusion of responsibility in municipal government, offering an opportunity for someone who could get the system to work. Improvements in public transportation made it possible for a central political organization to function in the city, providing it could bridge the gap in communications that had led to the fragmentation and disorganization in urban communities. The changing nature of the city population altered the ethnic composition of the municipality, placing many of these newcomers in a position to demand spokesmen representing their interests. The sheer magnitude of this swelling population also made politicians aware of the advantages that would accrue to the person or persons who could gain their support. By the latter part of the nineteenth century, a substantial number of large cities were ruled by a political machine—an organization coexisting within the framework of political parties which, by its control of election machinery and patronage, became a significant political force in the community. The person who controlled the machine was the boss, and he became one of the most powerful figures in American municipal politics.

A case can be made for the argument that the machine existed before the Civil War. Tammany Hall, one of the strongest political organizations in New York politics, originated in 1789 as a fraternal club. By the early 1800s, it had become identified with the party of Thomas Jefferson. The first boss of Tammany was Aaron Burr, who used the society as a base when he helped to organize Jefferson's party in New York. As early as the 1820s, Philadelphia had an identifiable boss, Joel Barlow Sutherland. Operating out of the neighboring Southside district, he put together an effective machine by supporting measures that were appealing to the lower classes in the area and to the business groups in the community. Fernando Wood, who served as mayor of New York in the 1850s, had many of the attributes of a boss because of his ability to control the vote of the city's immigrants. On the whole, however, most of the large-scale machines did not make their appearance until after the postbellum period, and it was not until then that the boss became a dominant figure in urban politics. The machine survived because the bosses knew how to deal with three factors that accompanied the emergence of modern America—immigration, industrialization, and urbanization—all of which came into focus at a time when the ruling elite was withdrawing from active participation in municipal politics.

By the end of the nineteenth century, the machine was

strongest in the industrial cities in New York State, Pennsylvania, New Jersey, Maryland, Ohio, and Illinois, and in control of local politics in the cities of St. Louis, Louisville, Minneapolis, San Francisco, and New Orleans. The area involved in its domination contained approximately one third of the nation's population and three fifths of its economic interests, even though the geographic area was comparatively small. While the machine was of relative insignificance in rural, homogeneous communities, the degree of influence that it had in urban areas depended on factors like the size and nature of the populace, the degree of industrialization, and local traditions. Stamford, Connecticut, avoided boss rule in the last part of the nineteenth century because of its small population (16,000 in 1893), the orderly nature of its industrial growth (its major factory employed one out of sixteen of the town's inhabitants), and its strong New England heritage of representative government (the town meeting continued to play a central role in the community).

The machine was of minor importance in the southern portions of the country. The South, unlike the North, in general, or New England, in particular, never had a strong tradition of local self-government. In addition, the South had a tendency to rely on the state government to insure the maintenance of white supremacy, which had the effect of strengthening the state at the expense of the locality. The South also was predominantly rural. In 1890, when New York, Philadelphia, and Chicago each had over 1,000,000 inhabitants, only New Orleans and Louisville had a population in excess of 100,000. Boss rule did come to dominate New Orleans politics, but not until 1897, when the city had a substantial number of Irish, German, and Italian immigrants. It was the center for statewide industry, and was second only to New York in being the largest port in the country.

The Bosses and the Machines

Some of the most well-known bosses of the "dark ages" were men like New York's William Marcy Tweed, St. Louis's Edward R. Butler, Philadelphia's James McManes, and Pittsburgh's Christopher L. Magee, but urban politics was controlled by a vast array of lesser known figures as well. Many bosses had control that extended over a district, and the more powerful ones ruled the entire city. There were several whose control of the city enabled them to dominate state politics, while a few headed machines that were a vital factor in the national political party. The bosses who held elective office were in the minority, because most preferred to work on the sidelines in order not to endanger their following by chancing an election defeat. By the use of techniques that included taking only calculated risks, seeking to consolidate intraparty factions, and, if necessary, courting the favor of the opposition party to offset defection within their own organization, the very successful bosses managed to enjoy long periods of rule.

Bosses were found in both the Democratic and Republican parties, and they were largely uninterested in political philosophy, per se. Their main interest was staying in power, and they had a greater commitment to their own personal advancement than they did to questions of social reform. On the other hand, they were capable of fierce loyalty and friendship, even as they meted out their favors with discretion. Cincinnati's boss George B. Cox boasted that "I never violated a pledge in my life," and "I never supported a man . . . without being asked to do so."[10] Their reluctance to take a stand on an issue is related to a story involving Charles F. Murphy, one of Tammany Hall's bosses. Noting that Murphy had remained silent during the singing of "The Star Spangled Banner," a reporter asked one of his assistants why the boss did not sing. "Perhaps he didn't want to commit himself," the aide explained.[11]

The ethnic background of the bosses was varied, although many came from the same background as did a majority of the residents in their districts. Harold Zink's study of twenty bosses holding power during the late nineteenth and early twentieth centuries revealed that fifteen were native-born. A large number had Irish-born fathers or mothers, and the group numbered ten Catholics, five Protestants, one Jew, and four who were indifferent to religion.

Few bosses came from wealthy families, and politics became an avenue to financial success. "Men ain't in politics for nothin'," said Tammany boss George Washington Plunkitt. "They want to get somethin' out of it."[12] It was not unusual for an influential boss to have a partnership in a business, and political connections proved to be a valuable asset in the conduct of his financial dealing. At the same time, personal integrity was not an unknown quality. Boss James McManes fully repaid depositors of a defunct bank in which he had an interest, although it cost him $500,000 to pay them back.

Of the twenty men in Zink's study, several ran afoul of the law. Two bosses served terms in prison, and six others were indicted for crimes ranging from perjury to murder. Some of the men had personalities that differed drastically from the affable, extroverted boss in Edwin O'Connor's award-winning novel, *The Last Hurrah* (1956).* Most bosses, however, were fascinated with politics, and displayed great skill in the conduct of it. Their professional ethics were not above reproach, but their personal lives usually were marked by close family ties.[13]

As the power of the bosses and machines increased, their modes of operation altered the conduct of municipal politics. One aspect of electioneering to which the bosses directed their energies was the primary, for this election was essential to the machine's survival. During the early period of American municipal growth, there were no laws providing for the nomination of public officials, and it was not until the 1890s that voters had an opportunity to choose the nominees directly. In the interim, it was customary for party members to vote at a primary for delegates. These delegates would, in turn, select the candidates at a nominating convention. The primary did not generate much interest among voters, many of whom never even knew when it was held. The machine therefore had little difficulty in putting forward a list of sympathetic delegates. When the party convention met, these delegates did the bidding of the machine. The subsequent election of candidates often would be a foregone conclusion, because voters generally selected municipal officials on the basis of their party affiliation.

If the machine faced strong opposition in the election, it might resort to fraudulent voting procedures to maintain its political power. Although not all bosses tampered with the ballot boxes, a majority of the large-scale machines engaged in some form of election manipulation. The secret ballot was not used until 1888, and votes were openly bought and sold in public. Raising money for this purpose did not present

---

*The protagonist in the novel, Frank Skeffington, allegedly was modeled after Boss James Michael Curley. Curley, who was a leading figure in Boston politics, was first elected mayor in 1913. In the late 1940s, he served five months in prison for using the mails to defraud.

a problem, since many officeholders were required to pay a certain percentage of their salaries to the machine. Another device was the use of repeaters, who were men hired by the machine to vote several times in an election. Lincoln Steffens claimed that in Philadelphia in the late 1890s voting lists were padded with the names of dead dogs, children, and nonexistent persons, and he contended that its "machine controls the whole process of voting, and practices fraud at every stage."[14] Padding of election lists became so common that in the early 1890s California's legislature came up with a plan to end it. The legislature passed an act requiring a voter in San Francisco to give his age, height, weight, and the color of his eyes when he registered to vote.

Rings and Graft

Machine politics sometimes led to the formation of rings. They were associations of politicians and public officials engaged in illegal activities, who were frequently assisted by business groups. Philadelphia's Gas Ring, or Gas Trust, formed in 1841 and taken over by Boss McManes in the late 1860s, purportedly ran the city's municipal gasworks; it was able to distribute patronage jobs and managed to cheat Philadelphia out of vast sums of money in the course of its operations. Following the ouster of the McManes machine in 1881, several members of the ring were sent to jail.

New York's Tweed Ring, headed by Boss Tweed, became implicated in the best-known scandal of the era. Tweed, who held the position of president of New York City's Board of Supervisors, worked in conjunction with Mayor A. Oakley Hall, Controller Richard B. Connolly, Park Board President Peter B. Sweeny, and City Auditor James Watson. They succeeded in getting contractors doing business with the city to raise their bills anywhere from 55 percent to 85 percent. The city paid these inflated bills, the contractors were given a share of the proceeds, and the ring pocketed the difference. Estimates of what Tweed and his associates stole from New York range as high as $300,000,000 over a five-year period. (See Figure 4.1.) The operation ended abruptly in 1871 when the ring was exposed. Tweed was tried, convicted, and sent to jail, but he later made a statement in defense of what he had done:

The fact is New York politics were always dishonest—long before my time. There never was a time when you couldn't buy the Board of Aldermen. A politician in coming forward takes things as they are. This population is too hopelessly split up into races and factions to govern it under universal suffrage, except by the bribery of patronage, or corruption.[15]

There were less blatant types of corruption, some of which, as Tweed noted, existed before the advent of machine politics. "Honest graft," so named by Boss George Washington

Figure 4.1 Reform cartoonist Thomas Nast directed his talents in a concerted attack on New York's Tammany Ring headed by Boss Tweed. In what was probably Nast's best-known caricature, Tweed is depicted as "The Brains." For contemporary audiences the diamond stickpin, bloated body, and the moneybags instead of a head had become established symbols of Boss Tweed. From *Harper's Weekly*, October 21, 1871.

Plunkitt, was one form. It was a method by which a boss turned his firsthand knowledge about the city into personal gain by making profitable investments. Plunkitt, who was a leading figure in Tammany Hall from the 1860s until his death in 1924, was in the habit of buying up land whenever he learned that the city was going to undertake a construction project in a particular area. "Honest graft" helped to make him a millionaire, for as he said: "I seen my opportunities and I took 'em."[16]

"Dishonest graft" involved the outright acceptance of money by public officials, and temptations to engage in it operated on virtually every level of community endeavor. Members of local boards of assessors had countless opportunities to be led astray, since businessmen were willing to hand over substantial sums in order to avoid paying taxes on their property. Saloon owners paid bribes to keep their places of business open on Sundays, and in some cities the head of a crime syndicate made regular payments to politicians if they would refrain from enforcing laws against gambling and prostitution. This kind of corruption was not directly attributable to machine rule, but chances for personal enrichment were enhanced by the accelerated growth of cities in the late nineteenth century, and the machines and bosses exploited them to the hilt. As Plunkitt himself admitted in 1905, "A big city like New York or Philadelphia or Chicago might be compared to a sort of Garden of Eden, from a political point of view."[17] Yet, as Plunkitt and others also realized, machines provided a number of highly important services in the community.

Community Services

The machine capitalized on the fact that it recognized the value of securing the allegiance of the newly arrived immigrants. Part of the population increase that large cities experienced during the nineteenth century was due to immigration, as the foreign-born began to make up a substantial portion of the urban population. European cities had not experienced anything that approached this influx. Only 6.3 percent of the population in London in 1881 was foreign-born, and a decade later the figure for Paris was 6.1 percent. In contrast, 29.9 percent of the people in fifty of the largest cities in the United States in 1880 were of foreign birth, and by 1890, immigrants made up more than two fifths of the population in New York, Detroit, San Francisco, and Chicago.

Whereas many European cities limited the franchise to property owners, American cities had restrictions that were minimal and often overlooked. The foreign-born were sometimes able to vote shortly after their arrival, even though the federal government had established a five-year waiting period for citizenship. James Bryce contended that many immigrants participated in elections three or four years after they arrived in the United States, since individual states had the right to establish their own voting requirements and often granted aliens full voting privileges. In several instances where immigrants were prohibited from participating in elections, fraudulent practices occurred. In *The American Commonwealth*, Bryce recorded the process whereby the machine turned the immigrant into a voter:

> I was long ago taken to watch the process of citizen-making in New York. Droves of squalid men, who looked as if they had just emerged from emigrant ships, and had perhaps done so only a few weeks before, for the law prescribing a certain time of residence is frequently violated, were brought up to a magistrate by the ward agent of the party which had captured them, declared their allegiance to the United States, and were forthwith placed on the roll.[18]

Once his vote was secured, the immigrant tended to remain loyal to the machine. Machines offered friendship at a time when measures like social security, unemployment insurance, and welfare did not exist, and when there were few social services agencies equipped to handle community problems. Because of its close connection with business groups and politicians, the machine was able to accommodate the foreign-born when they needed the kind of help—ranging from a license to do business or a permit to peddle goods—that could be secured most expeditiously through political influence. Patronage jobs represented another important domain of the machine's activities. Tammany Hall endeared itself to numerous voters in the 1880s by its ability to fill 12,000 municipal jobs from the ranks of its supporters.

In addition, there were several bosses who were accustomed to spending part of the day in court in order to be on hand when members of their district got into trouble. Martin Lomasney, a ward boss from Boston's West End district, commented on the importance of this type of assistance when he told Lincoln Steffens that "I think that there's got to be in every ward somebody that any bloke can come to—no matter what he's done—and get help. Help, you understand; none of your law and justice, but help."[19] On another occasion, Lomasney reiterated the philosophy that kept him in power. "From the standpoint of politics," he said, "the great mass of people are interested in only three things—food, clothing, and shelter. A politician in a district such as mine sees to it that his people get these things. If he does, he hasn't got to worry about their loyalty and support."[20]

The quasi-political, or humane, work of the boss was as varied as it was time-consuming, and it sheds light on the comment made by Richard Croker that a boss "might as well give up the idea for all time of having fun" because "there is no end of work in it."[21] James Pendergast, younger brother of Kansas City boss Thomas J. Pendergast, served as the boss in the West Bottoms district in Kansas City from 1892 to 1910. He was an alderman, the owner of a local saloon, and a good neighbor. The number of immigrants in West Bottoms was small, but the poorer members of the district turned to Pendergast for aid. He left instructions with local merchants to see to it that there was no suffering among the needy, and to send all unpaid bills to him, if necessary. Since money was in short supply in the community, he cashed checks in his saloon every month for anyone who wished to avail himself of this service. In this case, his deeds assured his re-election as alderman, brought grateful customers into his saloon, and won him the admiration of the town. Although he was known for his ability to find employment for people in his district, many of them went to see him, according to William Reddig, "for more than jobs. They went to him when they were in trouble and needed someone to soften the stern hand of justice."[22]

In similar fashion, John Powers, who controlled Chicago's Irish-dominated Nineteenth Ward from 1888 until his retirement in 1927, supplied sympathy, friendship, social gatherings, moral support, and jobs for his constituents. He sponsored ward dances, parades, and picnics; supported bazaars and other functions staged by local churches; gave presents at weddings and christenings; furnished bonds for local residents charged with crimes; and offered consolation at funerals and wakes. His appearances at the latter were so frequent that he was nicknamed "the Mourner." He claimed that his ward had 2,600 people on the public payroll, which in 1898 represented approximately one third of its registered voters. During Christmas in 1897, he distributed an estimated six tons of turkeys and four tons of geese and ducks throughout the ward.

Boss Tweed, whose Tweed Ring scandals made his name infamous, was not without philanthropic inclinations. Characteristically, he dispensed them out of the state treasury. Tweed was elected to the New York State Senate in 1868, and in 1869 and 1870 was able to secure $500,000 in public funds, albeit illegally, for the religious schools of some of his Catholic supporters. As a result, this period was the only time in New York's history that Catholic parochial schools received public money that was earmarked for general institutional purposes. His charitable works were not limited to parochial schools. As a member of the State Committee on Charitable and Religious Societies, he was instrumental in obtaining an appropriation of over $2,000,000 in state aid to local charities between 1869 and 1871. His efforts led John W. Pratt to praise him for helping to "soften some of the rigors of urban life years before the majority of Americans were persuaded that the public had a continuing responsibility for the welfare of society's unfortunates."[23]

The Boss as Broker

To a large extent, the boss brought a measure of order to the city during a time when its physical growth not only caused a breakdown in communications but created a corresponding loss of kinship. Lincoln Steffens' description of Chicago at the turn of the nineteenth century may well have been an accurate description of many other communities in the Gilded Age:

> Criminally it was wide open; commercially it was brazen; socially it was thoughtless and raw; it was a settlement of individuals and groups and interests with no common city sense and no political conscience. Everybody was for himself; none was for Chicago.[24]

A similar situation prevailed in the late 1880s in Cincinnati, where the bonds of community had broken down. According to one Methodist minister, every Sunday in Cincinnati became a "high carnival of drunkenness, base sensuality, reeking debauchery, and bloody, often fatal crime."[25] The pattern of the city was altered during the twenty-six-year reign of Boss George B. Cox, who controlled Cincinnati politics from 1885 to 1911. By the time Cox fell from power, he had established a professional police force, reorganized the fire department, suppressed Sunday saloons, pushed through a $6,000,000 waterworks program, and helped reform the public utilities field by favoring privately owned, publicly regulated monopolies. Although the tactics that he used caused Frederick C. Howe in 1905 to charge that "Boss Cox rules the servile city of Cincinnati as a medieval baron did his serfs,"[26] bosses like Cox did alleviate some of the upheavals caused by industrialization.

Business groups found the machine helpful at times and made use of the broker services of the boss in securing legislation, contracts, franchises, and political favors. The rapid expansion of industry provided the urban entrepreneur with a vast number of opportunities, but there was a need to deal with a centralized agency in order to maximize profits and minimize risks. Since urban government in the large postbellum city was ineffectual and diffuse, the machine served as a broker between businessmen and the government. Relying on their machine connections, men like Thomas Fortune Ryan, William C. Whitney, and Charles T. Yerkes* not only built street railways but were able to control electric-light factories in over eighty communities as far apart as Philadelphia, St. Augustine, Vicksburg, Kansas City, Minneapolis, and Syracuse.

Their efforts were aided considerably by their ability to secure franchise rights and to gain the establishment of favorable rates, which were the kinds of political favors the machine was able to provide. The system usually worked to the satisfaction of both parties. The boss was well compensated for his endeavors, and, as business firms in Pittsburgh indicated to Lincoln Steffens, it was much easier to work with a boss in promoting their corporate interests than it was to deal directly with the people's representatives.[27]

---

*The career of Yerkes became the subject of a trilogy of novels written by Theodore Dreiser about the American businessman. Dreiser patterned his central character, Frank Cowperwood, after Yerkes; the books were *The Financier* (1912), *The Titan* (1914), and *The Stoic* (1917).

The case of the Home Telephone Company of San Francisco affords an example of the way business groups and the boss cooperated. In 1905, the company filed a formal petition asking the city to grant it a franchise (which is a right granted by a government to do something not otherwise legal). In this case, the company wanted to construct a network of telephone systems throughout the city. Knowing that there would be no franchise without a payoff, the company gave Boss Abraham Ruef an attorney's fee of $125,000, payable as a $25,000 retainer and $100,000 when the franchise was obtained. Although Ruef held no elective office, he ran San Francisco politics. He accepted the fee, although he was already employed as an attorney by the Pacific States Telephone and Telegram Company, a rival firm. His legal services to both companies were virtually nonexistent, but the fees were prompted by other considerations.

The franchise had to be approved by the eighteen-member board of supervisors, which was empowered to make such a grant. On March 5, 1906, it approved Home Telephone's franchise by a vote of 13-5. Ruef then was paid $100,000, which represented the balance of his $125,000 payment. Afterward, he went to the office of James L. Gallagher, a member of the board of supervisors. With the shades in the office drawn, Ruef counted out $62,000 to be distributed among the supervisors who had approved the franchise. The payment was complicated by the fact that, of the thirteen members who had voted for it, eight also had taken money from Pacific States. As punishment for their semi-defection, Ruef reduced their share of the graft money, or "boodle," as it was commonly called.

The Urban Elite and Municipal Government: A Transformation

The success of the machine was aided considerably by the withdrawal of many prominent men of affairs from municipal politics. One of the reasons for their indifference to local affairs was that machines gave a seamy appearance to city government, so that socially prominent or well-to-do men with political aspirations were more inclined to seek more prestigious offices on the state or national level. One exception, at least during the early part of his life, was Theodore Roosevelt. In 1881, one year after his graduation from Harvard, Roosevelt shocked his friends by announcing that he wanted to run for office in the New York State legislature. They tried to talk him out of it by arguing that it was run by "saloon-keepers, horse-car conductors, and the like,"[28] an obvious reference to the background of some of the better known machine politicians in the state and in the city. Roosevelt served for three years in the legislature, and for many years thereafter was identified with local politics. He ran unsuccessfully for mayor of New York in 1886, and in 1895 became president of the city's police board. Another privileged young man who ignored the dictum that "nice men don't enter municipal politics" was Boss Abraham Ruef of San Francisco. Unlike Roosevelt, he cast his lot with the machine. Ruef, whose father was a prosperous real estate dealer, decided to participate in municipal politics in 1886. An honor graduate of the University of California in 1883, he received a law degree three years later from the unversity's Hastings College of Law. As a student, he helped to organize a municipal reform club. He subsequently explained his change in attitude by stating that "the people were indifferent, and so I drifted with the machine."[29]

If Roosevelt and Ruef were the exceptions, many of their wealthy kinsmen proved the rule. The ascendancy of the machine coincided with a time when men of wealth, especially businessmen, turned their attention away from the local scene. Where business leaders, along with the commercial aristocracy, had played an important role in urban government prior to the Civil War, their chief concerns in the period that followed were elsewhere. The career of a man like Jay Cooke was indicative of the changes that were taking place in the business community. In 1861, the forty-year-old Cooke opened the private banking house of Jay Cooke and Co. in Philadelphia. A decade later, his firm financed the construction of the Northern Pacific Railway. As banking became institutionalized on a national level and railroads became interstate in operation, Cooke's interests in politics shifted to Washington. By the 1880s, the new businessmen in Philadelphia, like Jay Cooke before them, were engaged in activities far removed from the sphere of municipal politics.

As the upper classes turned away from municipal affairs, there were resultant changes in the socio-economic background of the men who held municipal office. Although municipal politics was not monopolized by "saloon-keepers, horse-car conductors, and the like," the working class origins of many of its officials were apparent. As a result of the boss's stewardship, immigrants were encouraged to work for the machine and were able to climb up the political ladder in a fashion similar to that used by the boss himself. In the 1870s in Providence, Rhode Island, ethnic groups had managed to obtain political office within a relatively short time following their arrival in the city. A comparable process took place in New Haven. Up to the late 1840s, most city officials had been either businessmen or professional men of New England stock. Immigrants started to make inroads on political offices as early as the 1850s, and by 1900 the municipal legislative body had been changed in both ethnic and occupational pattern. The situation in cities governed by the machine was similar, and a significant number of municipal officeholders came from classes that had not served in local government in the past.

This transformation in municipal officeholding might have been applauded as a step in the democratization of the city government, but the nature of the corruption practiced by big city machines made it difficult for various citizens to look with approval at what had transpired. E. L. Godkin, editor of *The Nation* and the New York *Evening Post*, spoke for many members of the upper classes when he wrote in disparaging terms about the background of municipal officials. (See Figure 4.2.) In 1890, the *Evening Post* ran an exposé of the executive committee of Tammany Hall, and in it Godkin alleged that one man was a convicted murderer, another had been indicted for felonious assault, and a substantial number of the others were professional gamblers, former gambling house or "dive" keepers, and liquor dealers.[30] In earlier years, Thomas Nast, whose political cartoons started to appear in *Harper's Weekly* in 1868, used his skill as an artist to comment on machine politicians. Nast turned Tweed and some of his Irish friends into hideous caricatures, causing Tweed to complain to an editor at *Harper's Weekly*: "I don't care a straw for your newspaper articles, my constituents don't know how to read, but they can't help seeing them damned pictures."[31] It was precisely the kind of background to which Tweed referred that caused many of the opponents of boss rule to despair about urban government.

Challenges to the Machines

Boss rule eventually became so repugnant to the upper classes in the community that they staged a comeback in municipal politics. Although these reformers were chided for their anti-immigrant feelings and their antagonism to the working classes, their protest probably was aimed as much at the chicanery of the age as it was at the boss and his followers. There also were other groups in the city who were unhappy about the state of municipal affairs. Businessmen found that the "boodle" was costly to them, and many ultimately broke with the machine and participated in the battle for municipal reform. Ethnic groups, too, had their grievances. In Chicago, Boss John Powers favored his Irish constituents at the expense of the more recently arrived Italian immigrants. Although Italians formed only a small percentage of Chicago's white population in the late 1890s, they had a sizable representation in Powers's ward, and they began to resent his leadership. In 1898, they opposed his machine, re-

Figure 4.2 E. L. Godkin, crusading editor of *The Nation* and the New York *Evening Post*, is shown with other reformers preparing the guillotine for corrupt municipal officials. Godkin holds the weight for the guillotine blade. From *Puck*, June 13, 1894.

garding him as an obstacle to the election of Italian candidates. Their efforts to unseat Powers were unsuccessful, but the antagonism between the Irish and the Italians in his ward remained. By the same token, members of the urban work-

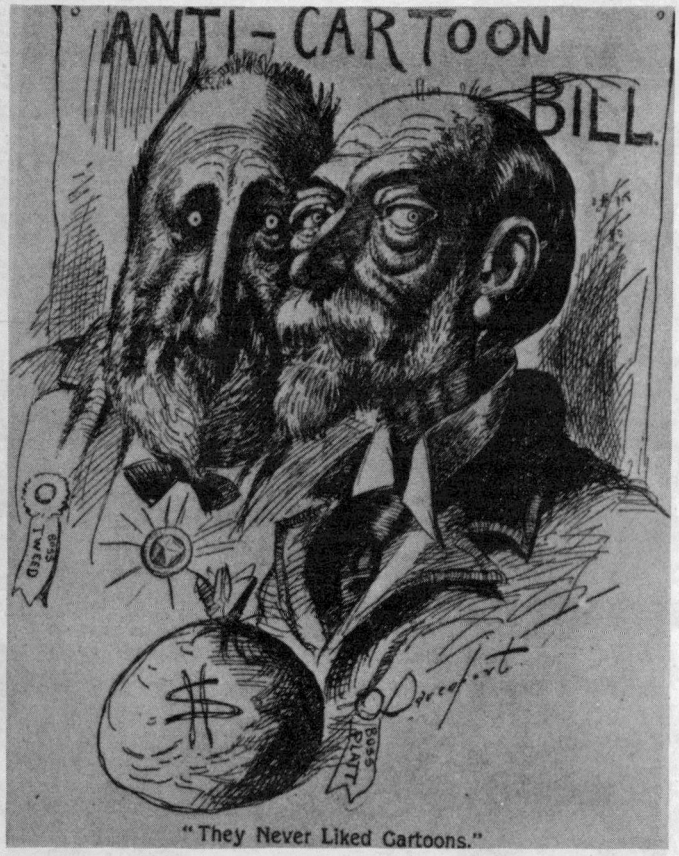

Figure 4.3 The power of the cartoonist's pen in fanning reform movements was acknowledged by Senator Thomas C. Platt who in 1897 presented an anti-cartoon bill to the New York legislature. Cartoonist Homer Davenport likened the Senator to Boss Tweed, using the symbols established by the Nast cartoons—the stickpin and moneybags. From New York *Journal and Advertiser*, April 22, 1897.

GROWING PAINS OF CITY GOVERNMENT 135

ing classes did not give the machine their undivided loyalty. There were workers who found certain attractions in the reform movement, particularly when they realized that they did not always benefit from machine rule. The excessive corruption associated with bossism not only led to an increase in taxes that were imposed upon the propertied classes but also

Figure 4.4 The defeat of Platt's bill inspired this cartoon "There are some who laugh and others who weep," in which Davenport pictured himself laughing while Tweed and Platt wept. From New York *Journal and Advertiser*, April 25, 1897.

resulted in higher fees for public services. As reform groups were fond of stating, the lower and middle classes bore the brunt of the costs that resulted from actions like the selling of utility franchises.

Of greater importance was the fact that the lives of scores of immigrants and poor people were unaffected by the machine. It is unknown exactly what percentage of the city's population availed themselves of the boss's services, but it is obvious that there were numerous persons who passed their lives without any contact with the boss or the machine. The labor movement did not come within the jurisdiction of the machine's largesse, and it was not until the 1930s that unions became active in municipal politics. Blacks were befriended by several urban bosses, but usually only at a time when their numbers in the city led the machine to take notice of their interests and needs. In spite of the machine's activities on behalf of the foreign-born, it did not follow that mobility for immigrant politicians would lead to economic gains for the group as a whole. The Irish gained control of Boston politics in the 1880s, but the condition of Irish people in the city remained bleak. In 1890, two thirds of all Irish immigrants were ordinary unskilled or semiskilled workmen, a figure nearly double that of low income manual workers among all other nationalities. As Stephan Thernstrom has written about the Irish in Boston, their political triumph "was early and decisive," but their economic advancement "was slow to follow."[32]

Toward the latter decades of the nineteenth century, there were waves of discontent within the urban community. The machine was not as invincible as it seemed; municipal politics was ready for a period of readjustment, and aspiring reformers readied to make amends.

5

The Emerging Metropolis

The development of cities was the defining characteristic of the period from 1870 to 1920. The urban network was extended across the continent to the Pacific Coast; America's major cities were transformed into industrial "metropolises," and many of the people in urban areas became big-city dwellers and suburbanites. In the midst of this spectacular burst of urban growth, America was transformed into a nation of city dwellers. Between 1860 and 1920 the total number of Americans living in communities over 2,500 skyrocketed from 6,200,000 (or 19.8 percent of the United States population) to more than 54,000,000 (or 51.2 percent).[1]

Post-Civil War Urbanization

During the 1860s—the Civil War decade—the population drift toward towns and cities accelerated dramatically, as did the diffusion of urban sites all over the nation (outside of the South). More than three and a half million Americans moved into urban communities between 1860 and 1870— an increase of 59.3 percent for the decade. Even though the 1870s was a depression decade, there was a 42.7 percent increase in the urban population, and between 1880 and 1890 more than seven million Americans left farms and villages for cities and towns—a 56.7 percent urban growth rate. But the population migration into cities during the 1890s was even larger—eight million—than the previous decade. Reflecting on these extraordinary migrations, one scholar noted that by 1900 there was no longer "any real question whether the farm and small towns could compete with the . . . city for a major part of the nation's population. The city was not only here to stay . . . it had triumphed."[2]

To grasp the magnitude of the urban changes within this era, it is necessary to subdivide all cities, at least for analytical purposes, into three broad categories: small, medium, and giant.[3] The increase in the number of small cities (with populations ranging from 10,000 to 49,999) and medium-sized cities (50,000 to 249,999 population) was striking. In 1860 there were only 58 small cities the United States, whereas by 1920 there were 608 cities in this category; there were 16 medium-sized cities in 1860—by 1920 there were 119.

More dramatic still was the growth of America's urban giants. In 1860 there were only three cities with a population over 250,000: New York, with 813,600 and adjacent Brooklyn, with 279,122, and Philadelphia, with 565,529. But by 1920 there were twenty-five cities with populations over 250,000. New York, in 1900, had become one of the world's great cities with a population that soared beyond three million. Chicago, the nineteenth-century "shock city," so named because of the speed of its growth, exceeded the million mark in 1890 and by 1920 had almost three million inhabitants. Philadelphia, too, had passed the one-million mark by the turn of the century and had almost two million inhabitants by 1920. The total population in these three giants—10,146,000—almost equaled the combined population of the 608 small cities or the 119 medium-sized cities. Detroit, Cleveland, and St. Louis, meanwhile, had become the fourth, fifth, and sixth largest American cities in 1920 with populations of 993,678, 796,841, and 772,897, respectively, and Boston and Baltimore were the seventh and eighth cities. Although New Orleans slipped from fifth position in 1860 to seventeenth in 1920, its population was close to 400,000.

Moreover, between 1870 and 1920, these twenty-five cities underwent an unprecedented and fascinating change in urban form and structure called "metropolitanization." (See Table 5.1.) Since the functional portions of these cities lay well beyond their legal boundaries, the United States Census Department in 1910 devised the term "metropolitan district" to distinguish them from other American cities. Each metropolitan district—or "metropolis"—was composed of a central city of 200,000 inhabitants and a surrounding ring of smaller cities and towns which had a population density of 150 or more persons per square mile. The combined population of all twenty-five metropolitan districts by 1920 was in excess of 28 million. Eight million of the 28 million people in these districts lived in adjacent suburban cities. In

TABLE 5.1

Population Figures for the 25 Metropolitan Cities by 1920

	Central City	Metropolitan Area
1. New York	5,620,000	7,910,415
2. Chicago	2,701,705	3,178,924
3. Philadelphia	1,823,779	2,407,234
4. Detroit	993,678	1,165,153
5. Cleveland	796,841	925,720
6. St. Louis	772,897	952,012
7. Boston	748,060	1,772,254
8. Baltimore	733,826	787,458
9. Pittsburgh	588,343	1,207,504
10. Los Angeles	576,673	879,008
11. Buffalo	506,775	602,847
12. San Francisco	506,676	891,477
13. Milwaukee	457,147	537,737
14. Washington	437,571	506,588
15. Newark	414,524	included
16. Cincinnati	401,247	606,850
17. New Orleans	387,219	397,915
18. Minneapolis	380,582	629,216
19. Kansas City (Missouri)	324,410	477,354
20. Seattle	315,312	357,950
21. Indianapolis	314,194	339,105
22. Jersey City	298,103	included
23. Rochester	295,750	320,966
24. Portland (Oregon)	258,288	299,882
25. Denver	256,000	264,232
TOTAL	20,909,600	28,130,428

SOURCE: U.S. Bureau of the Census, *Fourteenth Census of the U.S.: 1920* I, *Population* (Washington, D.C., 1921), pp. 63–64, 72, 80, and *Statistical Abstract of the U.S.: 1962* (Washington, D.C., 1962), p. 21.

many cases, these metropolitan districts stretched outward in virtually every direction for 20, 50, or even 300 miles.

By 1920, then, the American people had become city dwellers and the nation was economically dominated by a network of cities at the center of which were twenty-five metropolises.

By 1910, urban dwellers made up 85 percent of the New England population, 70 percent of the Middle Atlantic states, and over 60 percent of the Illinois and California populations. However, the great interior basin between the Great Lakes, the Ohio River, and the Mississippi River was the seedbed for urbanization. The rate of change during this period from rural to urban was greatest in Ohio, Indiana, Illinois, Michigan, and Wisconsin, where mine, mill, and factory towns were mushrooming.

Although southern cities rebounded from the Civil War's devastation, they did not grow or expand at the same rate as did cities in other parts of the nation. During the 1870s and 1880s, railroad and manufacturing were expanded in various parts of the South. Birmingham, Alabama, a new city, was one of the main recipients of this new emphasis, growing to 38,000 between 1870 and 1900 as a result of its steel industry. Atlanta, Nashville, and Louisville, were linked by rail connections and experienced substantial population and economic growth. However, southern cities owed their growth more to the reopening of old trade and commercial ties with urban complexes in the upper-Mississippi and Ohio valleys than to the diversification of the region's economy. By 1920 the south had only nine cities with populations in excess of 100,000, among which were New Orleans, with 387,219, Louisville, 234,891, and Atlanta, 200,616.

Regional cities in the Great Plains, Rocky Mountains, and Pacific Slope—the trans-Mississippi West—grew rapidly during the period from 1860 to 1920.[4] The United States Census of 1880 classified twenty-three trans-Mississippi cities as "important" urban centers. And during the 1880s some of these cities, which were well over 8,000, more than tripled their size. By 1890, Kansas City (Missouri), for example, rose from 60,000 to 132,716, while Omaha, went from 30,518 to 140,452, Minneapolis, from 47,000 to 164,000, Denver, from 35,000 to more than 100,000. San Francisco, meanwhile, had soared upward from 149,473 in 1870 to 233,959 in 1880, and jumped again in 1890 to 298,997. (For urban growth by section between 1870 and 1920, see Figure 5.1.)

The critical factor in the trans-Mississippi West, of course, was the railroad. Between 1860 and 1914, railroad builders laid well over 200,000 miles of track crisscrossing the nation. The first of five transcontinental railroads was completed in 1869, and by 1885 four transcontinentals and their feeder lines bound all major regional cities together into a national urban network stretching from the Atlantic to the Pacific Coast—a continental urban system under the influence of the northeastern and midwestern giants, New York, Philadelphia, Boston, Chicago, Baltimore, St. Louis, and Cincinnati (see Map 5.1.).

The Great Plains Cities and Towns

The Great Plains extended from the Mississippi on the east to the Rocky Mountains on the west, from the Gulf of Mexico to the south and Hudson's Bay in the north. In 1853 Jesup W. Scott, a townsite booster, hopefully predicted that on the Central Plains "will grow up the highest aggrega-

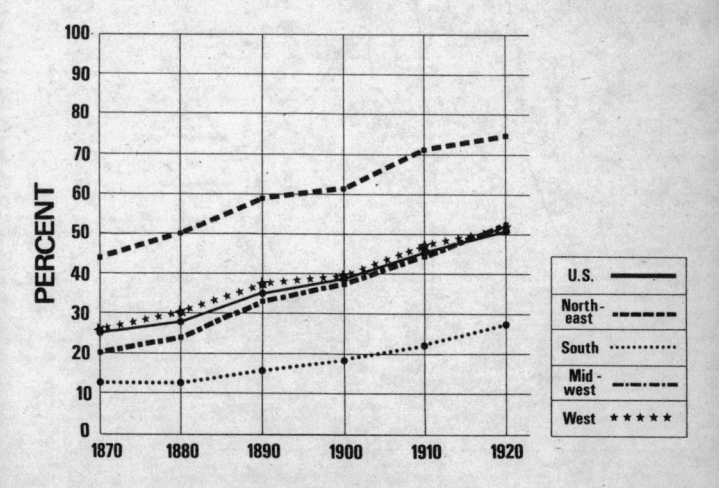

Figure 5.1 Urban Growth by Section: Percent of Population Living in Urban Centers 1870–1920

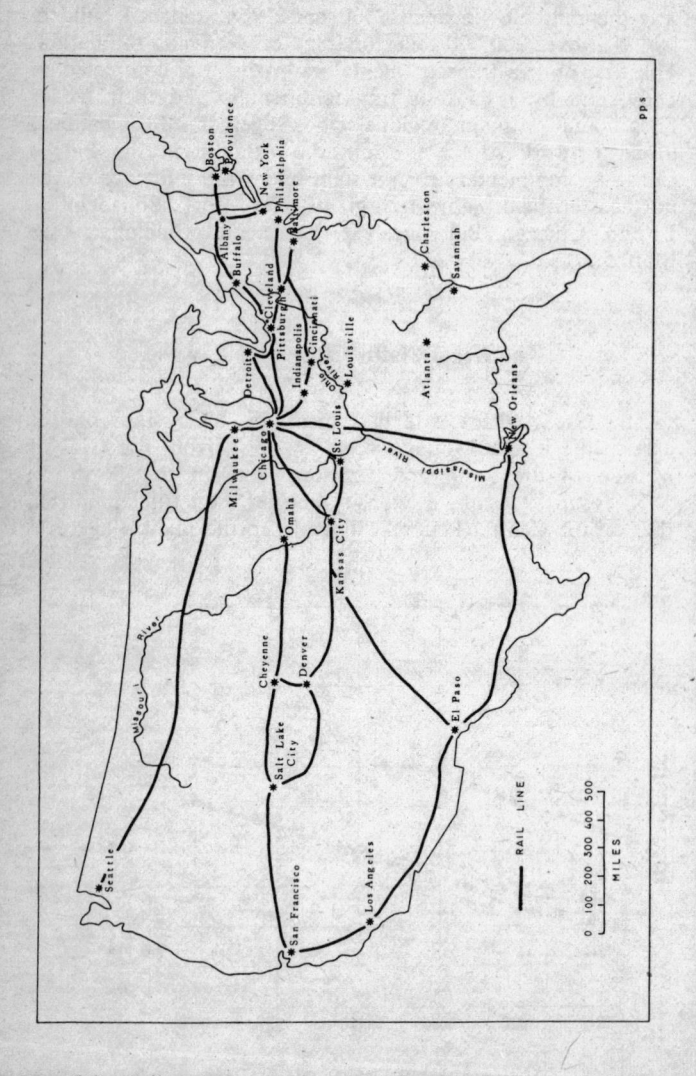

Map 5.1 Railroad Trunk Lines Forming the Continental Urban Network, mid-1880s

tions of people in the world by 1900 and will contain one or more cities numbering ten millions."[5] While that did not come to pass, Josiah Strong, an Ohio Congregational minister, more accurately noted the developments taking place in the West in 1885. The city, he wrote, "stamps the country, instead of the country stamping the city. It is the cities and towns which will frame the state constitutions, make laws, create public opinion, establish social usages, and fix standards."[6]

The history of the plains, then, is largely the history of its towns—its major cities, cattle towns, mining camps, and company towns. There was a basic sameness to the western plains town. Ignoring the terrain, Westerners adapted the identical block or gridiron pattern for their towns. According to historian Robert V. Hine, "Everywhere the same false fronts for dry goods store and post office, saloon and livery stable, church and schoolhouse. From the Mississippi to the Pacific, the towns were like little cornhills—some tall, some short, some with more ears and kernels than others, but from a distance indistinguishable."[7]

Agricultural settlement was quite slow in the Great Plains because of the semi-arid nature of much of the region. Building a successful city in the Great Plains seemed not only to require effective transportation links but also an unusual degree of community vigor and activity. Those towns and cities that did emerge, however, functioned as regional commercial centers which organized their narrow hinterlands, gathering and processing agricultural goods and minerals for transfer into the Midwest and distributing finished manufactured goods. Largely as a result of the transcontinental railroad lines, some towns—Kansas City (Missouri), Omaha, and Denver—rapidly developed into major regional cities, which economically and culturally dominated the Great Plains.

Situated to the southwest of Chicago, at the junction of the Missouri and Kansas rivers, Kansas City, Missouri, had a strategic geographic location. The town was founded in the late 1830s and early 1840s as a supply base for local settlers and those moving farther west. The river trade established with St. Louis and St. Joseph, facilitated its growth, but it was the skillful promotion of railroads that accounted for the city's standing as a major regional center. The rivalry between Kansas City and Leavenworth ended dramatically when Kansas City built the first bridge over the Missouri

River and brought in the transcontinental line; Leavenworth had acted too slowly.[8]

An emerging center for meat packing, Kansas City was heavily involved with the cattle towns in the Kansas territory. After the Civil War, packers in meat-hungry towns in the upper-Mississippi Valley and Atlantic Coast were willing to pay up to $40 a head for Texas longhorn cattle. Hundreds of thousands of cattle were moved north from Texas along the Shawnee, Chisholm, Western, and other trails to cattle towns in Kansas and Missouri.

At one time or another between 1867 and 1885, five central Kansas agricultural towns (Abilene, Ellsworth, Wichita, Caldwell, and Dodge City) functioned as collecting points for cattle on the "long drive." According to historian Robert R. Dykstra, these Kansas towns fully expected to make agriculture their long-range economic base and regarded the cattle trade money as bonus money.[9] Nonetheless, entrepreneurial plans and promotional schemes were employed first to attract the Texas cattlemen and then to keep the trade from moving to competing towns. During the early 1870s, the rivalry between Wichita and Ellsworth for the Texas trade reached a white-heat intensity.

As the termini of the trails that carried cattle from the lower Great Plains to packing houses farther east, the cattle towns occupied a strategic spot. Railroads were extended westward from St. Louis, Kansas City, Chicago, and other packing centers to towns in central Kansas and western Missouri as well—among them, Dodge City on the Santa Fe, Abilene on the Kansas Pacific, and Sedalia on the Missouri Pacific. The railroads also built facilities in the towns, providing jobs; banks moved in, as did a constant flow of settlers.

Dykstra deemphasized the violence in these towns, suggesting instead that even during cattle season they were relatively peaceful places. Between 1867 and 1885, the years covered by his study, there were forty-five killings, which averages out to three a year, less than one per year per town. Dodge City, with the highest murder rate, had an average of only one homicide per year![10] Far more significant than any rowdyness during cattle season, however, was the community sponsorship of schools, churches, newspapers, political parties, and libraries, among other trappings of urban life, which quickly gave these towns (whose principal economic activity was servicing the surrounding farmers) the setttled appearance and life-styles of small eastern and midwestern cities.

However, once the long drive ended, in the 1880s, and the cattle industry shifted from Texas to the northern Great Plains territories of Nevada, Montana, and the Dakotas, only Wichita continued to grow, emerging in the twentieth century as the largest city in Kansas. It did so by converting from cattle to flour milling, lumber, farm machinery, stove manufacturing, and brickmaking, as befit its location in an expanding wheat farm region.

Farther up the Missouri River lay the "Gate City to the West," Omaha, Nebraska. Before the advent of the railroad, Omaha was a regional center locally distributing goods brought upriver from St. Louis. In 1854, Iowa businessmen from across the river in Council Bluffs set up the town on the western side of the Missouri. Omaha was the territorial capital until 1867, when Nebraska came into the Union as a state. However, it was the discovery of gold in Colorado in 1859 that established Omaha, as it became the major regional outfitter for miners headed toward Pikes Peak.

As the most prominent town in the territory, Omaha was the logical choice for the eastern terminus of the transcontinental railroad as it passed through Nebraska on the way to California. Even before the connection was made, however, two regional lines reached the city, in 1867 and 1868—the Chicago and Northwestern and the Chicago, Rock Island, and Pacific lines. These connections, together with its location on the gigantic transcontinental, ensured the city's rapid growth.

By 1884, Omaha had the largest linseed oil mill in the country and the third largest distillery. During that decade, local brewers challenged Milwaukee and Cincinnati as the nation's beer-producing capital.[11] Omaha and Kansas City had become important midwestern railroad terminals with large hinterlands.

Denver also owed its initial spurt of growth to the Pikes Peak gold rush of 1859. The discovery of gold at Cherry Creek in Colorado led to the founding of mining towns in outlying areas. Mining camps and towns sprang up all over the West—in Wyoming, Montana, Colorado, Utah, Arizona, New Mexico, and California. Among the cities that began as mining towns, but succeeded after the mines petered out or the mining companies pulled up stakes and left were Denver, Reno, El Paso, Santa Fe and Albuquerque.

The development of mining camps tended to follow the same general pattern between the 1850s and 1890s.[12] First there was the gold, silver, or copper strike, then the mad rush to stake a claim, the growth of the camp and its resulting problems. On the heels of the miners, whose backbreaking labor was motivated by the hope of striking it rich, came the merchant and his goods, the saloon owner and his whiskey, and prostitutes. Gold and silver united them, for everyone had a stake in the camp and everyone wanted it to prosper. Besides the wealth of the mines, determined by the quality and depth of the vein, the town's survival was enhanced by securing a railroad connection or stagecoach line. The degree of urbanization was indicative of the people's effort to insure their camp's survival—they brought in newspaper editors to "boost" the town, schools, churches, theaters, libraries and other aspects of civilization to the frontier; soon life in these camps began to resemble that of small eastern cities.

Because the nearby mountain passes were too high and treacherous, Denver was bypassed by the Union Pacific Railroad, which chose Cheyenne, the capital and commercial center of the Wyoming Territory. Despite this major setback, Denver's determined promoters and businessmen put up capital to build a 106-mile spur line to Cheyenne, and in June, of 1870, Denver was linked with the transcontinental railroad.[13] There was a rush to complete this spur in order to force the Kansas Pacific, which was building west from Kansas City, to come through Denver. Denver promoters then ran a railroad line, the Denver and Rio Grande (completed in 1883), into the mineral areas to the south. These lines gave Denver commercial and regional hegemony. With a population of 35,629, by 1880, Denver was the largest commercial and industrial city between Kansas City and San Francisco.

Significantly, the forces of industrialization did not come to Denver via the railroad. They were brought to the city in the 1870s by men who had become rich through mining enterprises in Leadville and other Rocky Mountain mining towns. Searching for outlets for their accumulated wealth, these men gravitated to Denver because of its proximity to the coal fields, and they set up smelting furnace complexes.

On the fast-moving, rapidly growing and changing Great Plains frontier, the saloon initially was the preeminent institution, serving as an all-purpose community center. For example, during the period between 1858 to 1876, Denver saloons doubled as hotels, restaurants, bakeries, churches, hospitals, banks (keeping money and valuables as well as advancing local credit), information centers, and government buildings. Thus the saloon and its keeper offered patrons considerably more than draft beer, hard liquor, and premises for gambling, prostitution, and gunfights.

"Long before city halls, county courthouses and statehouses reached the frontier," historian Thomas J. Noel has observed, "pioneers met in saloon halls to institute local government." In 1864, for instance, when the Cherry Creek flood washed away the "shack labeled City Hall," Denver's Apollo Hall was rented by the city as a substitute center of municipal government. More interesting still, saloons not only housed government, to a large extent they helped finance it. Taverns were "numerous and thriving and considered a social nuisance," so they were heavily taxed to pay for the expanding city government functions. In the mid-1870s the quarterly saloon licensing fee of $100 brought into the Denver city treasury upward of $35,000.[14] Robert Dykstra, in his study of contemporary cattle towns in Kansas, also pointed out how these communities used license fees charged tavernkeepers, gamblers, and prostitutes to finance the local police, town police chief (or city marshals as they were often called), and municipal courts.[15]

As soon as community resources made it possible, emerging Great Plains towns and cities, whether cattle towns, mining camp towns, or railroad terminal towns, constructed public buildings, churches, schools, libraries, hospitals, civic clubs, and other places of culture and entertainment. And government, banks, and other business firms moved into buildings specifically designed for these purposes. The saloon was thus eclipsed as the town's principal institution once the frontier phase ended.

Yet another characteristic feature of early Great Plains urban growth was the creation of railroad towns and company-owned towns. Not only did cities build railroads, but railroads also built western towns for specific purposes. Railroad companies secured massive land grants along their rights-of-way from the federal government to help finance the cost of the construction. Following the example set by the Illinois Central Railroad in the 1850s, the transcontinental developers set up land companies that speculated in townsite promotion as well as selling land to farmers. The companies widely advertised their "new western cities," although they were little more than block or grid plans designated on maps at various locations alongside the railroad track. Most of these towns underwent an initial spurt of growth, but without an agricultural hinterland or mine to service they rapidly became ghost towns.

Prospective settlers and townsite promoters closely followed railroad surveyors across the prairie and into the mountains. An observer in Dakota during the 1870s depicted this fascinating process:

> Language cannot describe the rapidity with which these communities are built up. You may stand ankle deep in the short grass of the uninhabited wilderness; next month a mixed train will glide over the waste and stop at some point where the railroad had decided to locate a town. Men, women, and children will jump out of the cars, and their chattels will be tumbled after them. The courage and faith of these pioneers are something extraordinary.[16]

Cheyenne is an example of a railroad town that slowly gained a foothold and survived. Cheyenne was founded by the Union Pacific Railroad in 1867 as one of a number of terminal towns along the line of the first transcontinental railroad. Cheyenne's strategic location, at the base of the Rocky Mountains, seemed so promising that the *Cheyenne Daily Leader* predicted in 1870 that the community would become a "commercial metropolis of a scope larger than France, England, and Holland combined."[17] But hardly anyone lived outside Cheyenne, and despite vigorous promotional efforts, the community leaders were unable to create an agricultural hinterland to service.

Company-owned towns were another significant aspect of western urban history.[18] Besides mining and railroad terminal towns, the Union Pacific Railroad Company set up company-owned coal mining towns all over the Rocky Mountain territory to produce coal for railroad use and sale to the public. In 1868, Rock Springs became a coal town, railroad center, and cow town, controlled in almost every way by the Union Pacific Company. Before 1890 other coal mine towns were created in Almy and Dava, Wyoming; in Northrop, Erie, Louisville, Baldwin, and Como, Colorado; and in Pleasant Valley and Grass Creek, Utah. But little came of these communities unless alternate economic activities developed.

On the lower Great Plains, southeast of Denver, a number of Texas towns—Galveston, Houston, Austin, and San Antonio—rose to the position of regional cities by the 1860s.[19]

All of these cities began as military posts under the Spanish in the 1700s; within the walled quadrangles were the barracks, stores, shops, and stables of the garrison. Thereafter houses and farms sprang up outside the walls and soon came to resemble civilian settlements. These communities were the focal points around which Texas flourished, particularly after the region gained its independence from Mexico in the 1830s.

These Texas towns furnished goods (corn, flour, pork, whiskey, salt, coffee, and molasses) obtained from New Orleans gulf coast steamers to local cotton and sugar planters and wool producers. Commerce rather than agriculture or industry dominated these communities, which vigorously vied with one another for markets. After carpenters and laborers, merchants composed the largest occupational groups in these small Texas towns. In 1860, San Antonio with 8,000, Galveston with 7,000, Houston with 5,000, and Austin with about 4,000 were ready to grow, but the population of Texas remained small until the twentieth century. As late as 1890, Houston had a population of only 27,557, San Antonio 37,673, and newcomer Dallas had 38,067.

The Western Seaports

Far more consequential, however, were the urban developments beyond the Great Plains and Rocky Mountains in the Pacific states of California, Oregon, and Washington where a series of significant coastal seaports had emerged, in some cases before the Civil War decade. San Francisco and Los Angeles in California, Portland in Oregon, and Seattle and Tacoma in Washington were seaports as well as western termini of transcontinental railroads. But it is San Francisco and Los Angeles that had the most spectacular growth.

Founded in 1776 by Franciscan monks while California was part of the Spanish empire, San Francisco was still a tiny outpost of 200 people and fifty houses seventy years later. San Francisco owed its urban birth to the discovery of gold at Sutter's Fort on January 24, 1848, and to its natural harbor.[20]

Because the population of San Francisco ballooned upward from 5,000 in 1849 to 34,766 in 1850, reaching 56,802 in 1860, and 149,473 in 1870, midwestern manufacturers were eager to capture the market via railroad connections. The link was provided in 1869, with the completion of the transcontinental. From the 1850s onward, speculators planned the city on a gridiron or block system, projecting streets straight through the hills surrounding the port. Railroad connections brought industry and even larger waves of migrants, and the city was rapidly changed from a maritime commercial center catering to miners into an industrial city. By 1880 the population of San Francisco had skyrocketed to more than 233,959.

Unlike San Francisco, Los Angeles, another old Spanish town, did not become an important city until the turn of the twentieth century. Although destined to become one of the principal twentieth-century American metropolises, Los Angeles grew quite slowly between 1850 and 1885, from 1,610 to 20,000. Los Angeles' growth after 1885 resulted from railroad connections and industrialization. In 1876 the Southern Pacific came to the city and linked Los Angeles with northern California and the East, but it was the Atchison, Topeka, and Santa Fe that provided a direct connection in 1887 with the Midwest and the Atlantic seaboard.

The climate, available land, good transportation, and promotional efforts help account, not only for the heavy migration from the Midwest but also for the rush of manufacturers to the city. Between 1890 and 1900, Los Angeles' population soared from 50,395 to 170,298, and it jumped to 250,000 by 1910. In the era from 1890 to 1920, residential subdivision practices and electric streetcar lines helped create what has come to be the characteristic Los Angeles form—a city without a very clearly defined central business district and with miles of suburban developments.[21]

Metropolitan District Growth and Economy

The shape and character of the modern American metropolis were cast in the forty-year period between 1870 and 1910—apparently as a by-product of railroads, technological innovations, and urban imperialism. The national network of cities brought together by the transcontinental railroads linked millions upon millions of city dwellers, creating an enormous urban-based domestic market in America.[22] Stimulated by the prospect of national distribution, and of profits on a comparable scale, giant corporations quickly developed, locating their plants and headquarters in the most favorable sites for regional and national operations—the central core cities of evolving metropolitan districts. From these major urban centers, they drew smaller cities and towns in the most remote parts of their regions into the metropolitan economic orbit, acquiring, as they did so, local businesses and distributing to their residents new kinds of products and services. But it was these newly emerging urban constellations themselves which were, because of their densely concentrated populations, the basic markets for virtually every American industry and product.

In addition, an amazing series of technological innovations applied simultaneously to urban construction, transportation, and communication seemed to propel the growth and outward reach of the major American cities, giving rise, well before 1920, to the characteristic but nonetheless quite revolutionary metropolitan district form—the central core city plus suburban city pattern. Thus, cities of 200,000 at the center of metropolitan districts (to use the 1910 Census Department definition) grew geographically larger and more complex, and just beyond their city limits thick rings of industrial and residential suburbs sprouted. The principal sources of central city strength were, of course, the jobs, industries, and economic opportunities provided to city residents and suburban commuters and the wide range of specialized goods and services distributed to the surrounding cities and countryside. Among the most significant of these were the mass transit lines, electric cables, gas pipes, telephone wires, and water lines—the utilities that enabled the metropolitan districts to function as viable economic units developed first within the central core cities and then extended outward into the suburbs.

These twenty-five metropolitan districts—with a combined population in excess of 28 million people (in 1920)—were the financial, industrial, and commercial centers of their specific regions and collectively of the nation. In great measure, this was the result of traditional urban imperialism. Although they were not always in agreement, businessmen and municipal officials did cooperate closely to extend the economic power of their cities, particularly if they were metropolitan core cities. The Kansas City park commissioners made this abundantly clear, for instance, when, in 1893, they advised municipal leaders of the *other* purpose of parks:

To become the metropolis, that is the center, of a large and prosperous territory that contains a large population the [central] city must supply, to a degree materially exceeding other rival cities, all the results of modern progress and of modern civilization. The city must be the center of the sum total of the thought and the activities of the people residing within the territory which the city aspires to dominate. The city must be as well the social center, if she desires to become, without successful rival, the business center . . .[23]

America's evolving metropolitan cities were geographically expanding throughout the nineteenth century, reaching outward like octopi in all directions for more land to develop—and control. Between the 1840s and 1870s vacant city land was swiftly settled, filled in with houses and businesses, and significant numbers of people began moving beyond the city limits into nearby suburban areas. Before the advent of rapid transit systems, this central city overflow resulted in the creation of industrial and residential communities within a three-mile radius of these major cities. However, once these adjacent areas were economically developed, central city leaders systematically began to make them part of their city, apparently convinced that the city's continued prosperity was dependent upon continuous geographical and physical expansion. The regularity of this growth pattern prompted historian Kenneth Jackson to conclude that suburbanization in America "was and is a function of urban growth." Indeed, Jackson has persuasively argued that there would now be no great cities in the United States if annexation (the addition of unincorporated land to the central city) or consolidation (the absorption of one municipal government by an adjacent one) had not taken place during the nineteenth century.[24]

The first of the major nineteenth-century expansions took place in 1854 when Philadelphia absorbed several independent suburban communities, among which were Southwark, Kensington, and Moyamensing, extending the physical boundaries of the city from 2 to 129 square miles. Chicago, in 1875, was surrounded by more than fifty contiguous suburbs, many of which were made part of the city in 1889 through a political consolidation that expanded the city to 133 square miles. And New York climaxed the process of geographical expansion through consolidation, in 1898, of Brooklyn, one of the nation's largest cities, Queens, Staten Island, and part of the Bronx, thereby increasing the population of Greater New

THE EMERGING METROPOLIS 153

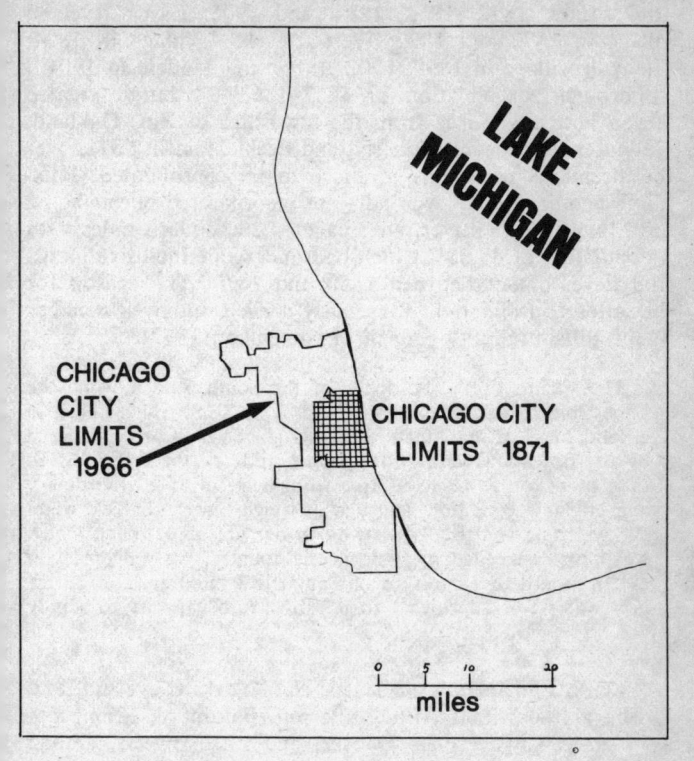

Map 5.2 The Geographical Expansion of Chicago from 1871 to 1966

York by more than 1,000,000 and extended its boundaries from 40 to 300 square miles.

Cleveland's and Pittsburgh's pattern of growth, though less dramatic, was far more characteristic of the nineteenth-century process of urban geographical expansion. Even before its incorporation as a city, in 1836, Cleveland's leaders began annexing unoccupied land as well as consolidating adjacent communities, nibbling away until it swallowed them entirely. Through this method, Cleveland reached its twentieth-century city size in 1910. Cleveland consolidated the city of Ohio in 1854, and annexed parts of Brooklyn township in 1867, 1872, 1890, 1894, and 1904; parts of Newburgh township in

1867, 1869, 1872, 1873, 1894, and 1905; East Cleveland village in 1872 and 1892; West Cleveland village in 1894; Glenville village in 1898, 1902, 1905; and Lindale in 1904.[25]

Through consolidation in 1867–1868 Pittsburgh created eleven new city wards from the townships of Pitt, Oakland, Collins, Lawrenceville, Liberty, and Peeble, and in 1872, over the strenuous objections of those to be consolidated, Pittsburgh acquired the eleven adjacent incorporated boroughs on the Monongahela River, an area of 4,200 square miles with a population of 38,685, which had undergone intensive industrial development between 1850 and 1870. The reason for the latter consolidation was clearly spelled out by a member of the Pittsburgh city council in November, 1872:

> The wealth of the boroughs of the South Side it would be impossible to calculate. From Ormsby to Temperanceville it is a solid mass of manufactures. Your glass works are numbered by the fifties and your [iron] rolling mills by the dozen. More than that, you come to us free from debt, in an extraordinary and enviable condition, and one in which I wish that we were. We welcome you to all we own—to our fire department, which we think is excelled by none in the country; we welcome you to our Board of Health, to our municipal building, and to our new water works, which I trust will have a capacity to supply you all . . .[26]

As with Philadelphia, Chicago, New York, Cleveland, and Pittsburgh, so with St. Louis, Boston, Baltimore, Minneapolis, Kansas City, Dallas, Denver, and Los Angeles, among others. Interestingly, because most central cities acquired and developed vast new tracts of land, even those with sizable populations and industry, the overall density of their populations actually began to drop off (although their total populations increased simultaneously). For example, Chicago, between 1880 and 1890, saw a drop of considerable proportion in its population density because of its increased land area—from 14,314.5 persons per square mile to 6,343.4. The same could be seen in other aggressively expanding central cities.

By annexing unincorporated areas or consolidating adjacent municipalities, major cities sought to increase their land areas, population, wealth, and tax bases. Cities like Pittsburgh could extend desirable and costly urban services to these "new" city areas—which people sought but were at that time unable to afford to develop on their own—and then force new big city dwellers to subsidize continued civic improvements.

Thus, the major cities strengthened themselves, when they could, at the expense of the neighboring suburban regions. When advances in technology made it possible for adjacent suburban communities to obtain services without becoming part of the major cities (well before the 1920s), the process of annexation and consolidation all but ended. Metropolitan city leaders found themselves unable to persuade residents in surrounding communities of the advantages to be gained in becoming part of their cities—nor could they persuade state legislatures to force annexation or consolidation over the storm of objections from these small suburban town dwellers. Suburban communities from that time to this have jealously guarded their political independence of the feared central cities.

The eighth largest metropolitan district in 1920 was Baltimore, and in most ways it reflects the "metropolitanizing" process that was destined to characterize twentieth-century American urbanization. The city of Baltimore, which dominated the district and for which it was named, covered 31.5 square miles, while the surrounding district included industrial and residential suburbs extending outward for about 295 square miles. Baltimore accounted for 83 percent of the district's 787,458 population, 68 percent of the value of products, 92.7 percent of the manufacturing establishments, and 86.9 percent of the wage earners.[27]

From the 1880s, Baltimore's firms competed with New York for the western and southern markets. One third of Baltimore's output went to the South, one fourth to the Midwest, and one third to New York and New England. Baltimore was served by five railroads directly, two to the West—the B.&O. and Pennsylvania Railroad—and three local lines. Yet in contrast to New York, Chicago, Philadelphia, and other cities, Baltimore grew slowly between 1899 and 1914; during this period, the number of her manufacturing establishments rose from 2,352 to 2,698, or 14 percent, and the average number of wage earners increased from 71,648 to 84,937, or 16.2 percent. More significant than the 66 percent increase in the value of products, from $177 million to almost $314 million, was the 57.6 percent increase in the value added by manufactures, from about $68 million to $113 million, clearly suggesting that Baltimore was an industrial city.

Although, like the other twenty-four metropolises, Baltimore was a multipurpose center, ready-made clothing was its major specialty, or export industry—that is, the product directed toward other markets throughout the nation—and all of the men's and boys' clothing was produced entirely within the bounds of the city proper. Other export industries —copper, tin, and sheet-iron ware products, fertilizers, beer and distilled liquors, meat slaughtering and packing—were located outside the city limits within satellite suburban cities.

During the period from 1870 to 1920, the metropolitan district economy was characterized by export or basic industries directed toward other markets and by local market activities (sometimes referred to as "housekeeping" functions) directed chiefly toward the local population. (See Figure 5.2.) Each metropolitan district thus provided for a large proportion of its own needs, generating a vast array of services and products for local—districtwide—consumption. Although this figure cannot be pinpointed precisely for that time, in all probability about 40 to 50 percent of all the workers and industries within the district were engaged in the production of goods and services for export, while the other half provided the housing, foods, transportation, education, and other services that made the export sector possible.

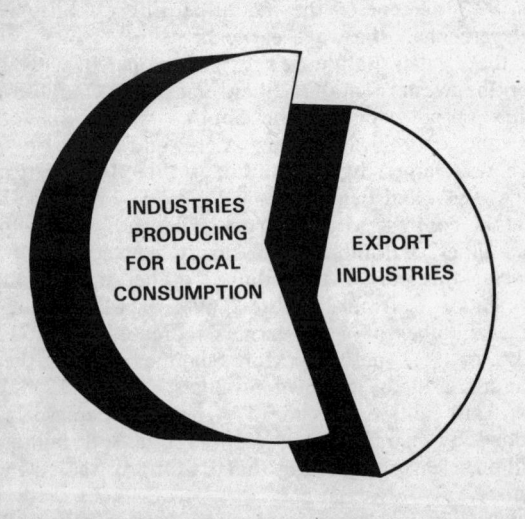

Figure 5.2 American Metropolitan District Growth: 1920

Industrial Transformations

Nine tenths of industrial production occurred in urban factories located within America's twenty-five principal cities or in immediately adjacent industrial satellite cities within their metropolitan districts. Because the railroads created national and large regional markets, companies within the major American cities were able to diversify their industrial activities, and in small adjacent cities they were able to specialize. By 1900, as Sam Bass Warner, Jr., explained, "the sorting out and clustering of specialty manufacturing in specific cities was largely completed and each specialty was increasingly located at its best site and from this single base or cluster of bases sold its products throughout the nation."[28] Well before 1920, then, the shift within the American economy from a "city-organized agricultural and commercial base to an urban-industrial base" had been completed.[29]

Clearly, as in the case of Baltimore, industry outstripped commerce as the chief source of urban growth in the major cities between 1870 and 1900. With nearly 11 percent of the nation's manufacturing workers, New York City by 1900 was America's foremost manufacturing center followed by Chicago, Philadelphia, Cincinnati, Pittsburgh, and Milwaukee. Thus, the roster of manufacturing centers included seven northeastern cities which had attained national prominence before the industrialization of manufacturing—New York, Philadelphia, Boston, Baltimore, Cincinnati, St. Louis, and Chicago—and five new centers encircled by these established cities—Pittsburgh, Buffalo, Cleveland, Detroit, and Milwaukee.

Within the metropolitan districts of these major cities were clusters of smaller cities which were either industrial suburbs or residential suburbs. Thus the metropolitan districts combined the productivity of urban and adjacent suburban mills, factories, and commercial cities. Workers and factories within these employing suburban cities generally produced components or semifinished goods whose use depended on demand for the finished products fabricated in the central city of the district of which they were economically a part. Not infrequently, industrial suburbs also produced finished commodities designed for national or regional distribution.

Clearly, then, the economic vitality of the satellite processing and manufacturing cities was dependent upon the vitality of the metropolitan cities—which provided capital for investment and also markets—as well as upon the strength of the national economy.

Such smaller communities, largely in the Northeast and Midwest, included Albany which made shirts; Troy, shirt collars; Schenectady, electric appliances; New Bedford and Fall River, cotton goods; Lowell, carpets; Lynn and Haverhill, shoes; Waltham, watches; Bridgeport, corsets, brass, and machine tools; Dayton, cash registers; Columbus, railroad cars; Toledo, glass and iron foundries; Youngstown steel; Grand Rapids, furniture; Portland, lumber, foundries, machine shops, and wooden shipbuilding. After 1910, with the rapid development of the automobile a host of cities specialized in car production and parts, such as Detroit and Akron. Central cities in the Northeast and Midwest were thus surrounded by rings of industrial cities which were economically related but usually politically independent.

In the 1870s and 1880s, with the completion of the continental transportation network, nationwide industrial corporations developed and swiftly took command of consumer goods industries (tobacco, canned foods, sugar, textiles, whiskey, cottonseed oil, linseed oil, and lead production, among others).[30] By the 1890s, they had gained a major foothold in the industries making components, semifinished goods, or machinery for the use of producers (rather than of goods for urban consumers or farmers). Among the most significant of the nationwide corporations by the 1890s were A.&P., American Tobacco, American Sugar Refining, Armour and Company (meat packers), Kodak, National Biscuit, Proctor and Gamble, Swift and Company (meat packers), Standard Oil, United Fruit, and United States Steel. Many of these companies pioneered in the production and distribution of new consumer items designed basically for urban dwellers, such as cameras, breakfast cereals, and canned meats.

Urban consumers were increasingly provided with a host of new standardized products sold through chain stores scattered all over the nation as well as through mail-order companies. In 1859, the first modest store in what was to become the Great Atlantic and Pacific Tea Company, or A.&P., was opened in New York City; by 1912, there were 500 stores in the chain, and by 1915, over 1,000. Each of these stores, with their distinctive red-and-gold facades that became a familiar feature within America's cities, sold a wide range of grocery and other allied food products.[31] Drug and cigar stores and other chains like Woolworth's (which was begun as a five-and-ten-cent store in Lancaster, Pennsylvania, in 1879, by Frank W. Woolworth) sprouted all over the nation, also becoming commonplace features of American urban life.

Richard Warren Sears and Aaron Montgomery Ward both pioneered in the nationwide mail-order business, providing the consuming public with a wide range of standardized merchandise, such as clothes, furniture, watches, sewing machines, guns, baby carriages, musical instruments, toys, and the like. Ward in 1872 and Sears in 1886 began their mail-order operations in Chicago, the nation's railroad capital. Both companies used merchandise catalogues that contained vivid descriptions and pictures of their line of products; by 1884, Ward's catalogue numbered 240 pages and contained almost 10,000 items, while the Sears Roebuck catalogue in 1894 exceeded 500 pages. Indeed, by 1903, Sears had to set up his own printing plant to turn out the catalogue.[32] Low prices for standardized products, large volume, rapid turnover of merchandise, and extensive advertising of products were the bases of the mail-order business, which wrought a veritable revolution in consumer purchasing in America. Not only were small town dwellers and even rural residents provided with standardized products, somewhat narrowing the standard-of-living gap between large and small cities and towns, but these companies' catalogues helped familiarize Americans in the pre-radio and -television era with the wide range of easily obtainable American products, whetting consumer appetite and also stimulating further economic productivity.

Major Business Innovations and Their Effects

Nationwide distribution required significant innovations in business operations which in turn had a direct impact upon the economy and upon city life. Many of the nation's industrial corporations were "vertically integrated": that is, the corporation owned everything needed, from the sources of raw materials (sugar and banana plantations, cattle ranches, oil wells, coal and iron mines) to transportation facilities (steamship lines, pipelines, railroad spur lines), production facilities (refineries, factories, steel mills, distilleries), and marketing facilities (warehouses, wholesale distribution agencies, and retail stores). By the turn of the twentieth century, then, the consumer's goods and producer's goods industries were fundamentally organized to service the needs of the nation's city dwellers, wherever they were situated.

Because they controlled much of the nation's productive capacity—through ownership of factories and control of financing and marketing, the corporation (in particular, the industrial corporation) established itself as the "basic unit" in the American economy.[33] Not only were most of America's major industries dominated by a few large firms which emerged through mergers, consolidations, and reorganizations, but all large companies, whether industrial corporation, chain store, or mail-order house, that provided goods and services nationally were organized and administered along centralized, functionally specialized, and bureaucratic lines. Thus, in addition to factory workers, corporations required large numbers of well-trained, educated, professional managers, administrators, and sales personnel. Also needed were thousands and thousands of trained clerical personnel. Almost singlehandedly, these companies created a new occupational category in America—the white collar, urban-dwelling service worker.

The overall significance of these developments were reflected in America's changing occupational structure. By 1880 only one half of the American population was working in agriculture, forestry, fishing, or mining (the extractive industries); the other half was divided between trade, commerce, manufacturing, and service industries. However, only two fifths of the nation's workers were engaged in extractive industries by 1900, while the remaining three fifths were employed in manufacturing, traditional mercantile pursuits, and service industries. (See Table 5.2.)

Clearly, manufacturing was the most important urban growth industry in the late nineteenth and early twentieth centuries. But the proportion of the labor force in metropolitan districts employed in service occupations was rising steadily between 1870 and 1920. Obviously, the largest proportionate increase of any service category was that of clerk (secretaries, stenographers, telephone operators, store clerks) in commercial and financial firms, government work, and the professions. Large numbers of white collar clerks were required to maintain the vast billing and distribution operations

TABLE 5.2

Distribution of Workers by Industry, 1870–1920*

Year: Total Workers	Extractive Industries (Agriculture, Forestry and Fisheries, Mining)	Manufacturing and Construction	Service Industries (Trade, Transport, Finance, Education, Profession, Government, Domestic Service, Personal Service)
1870 12,920,000	6,690,000	3,000,000	3,820,000
1880 17,390,000	9,015,000	4,000,000	5,400,000
1890 23,740,000	10,650,000	8,720,000	6,190,000
1900 29,070,000	11,680,000	8,000,000	11,780,000
1910 36,730,000	12,640,000	10,530,000	12,660,000
1920 41,610,000	12,630,000	13,050,000	15,550,000

*Because not all industries are listed, the figures do not add up to the total number of workers.

SOURCE: U.S. Bureau of the Census, *Historical Statistics of the U.S., Colonial Times to 1957* (Washington, D.C., 1960), p. 74.

of nationwide corporations, mail-order companies, and chain stores, as well as banks, insurance companies, department stores, telephone and electric power companies, and other retail and wholesale operations within these cities. Secondly, the increasing complexity of the cities required large numbers of public service workers or government civil servants (which included unskilled laborers, semiskilled guards and watchmen, and skilled policemen, firemen, officials, inspectors, and teachers). Among the service sectors that grew most rapidly were transportation, public utilities, clerical, professions, and municipal government—many of whom were engaged in providing those housekeeping or local market services without which these cities could not have operated.

Another direct implication for American urban life must be mentioned here as well. The specialized business elites emerging within America's major cities during the period from 1870 to 1920 were drawn from diverse geographical origins, had virtually nationwide economic links, and demonstrated little real interest in exercising a civic role characteristic of the urban elites during earlier periods. Thus, American cities were increasingly shaped—and the conditions of urban life determined—by distant corporate leaders, chain-store executives, bankers, and factory owners and managers, as well as real estate promoters and lawyers, who decided the location of wholesale distribution facilities, large warehouses, massive construction projects, freight yards, factories, railroad spur lines, mass transit systems, and electric power systems, among other crucial things. Previously, most of the decisions affecting the economic life of a community were made by local businessmen, who, though principally interested in private profit, nonetheless had some sense of identification with and concern for the cities in which they and their families lived.

City and Metropolis Expansion

Obviously, neither the large city nor the metropolis could have existed without the technological capabilities for handling the needs—feeding, clothing, sheltering, transporting, and providing jobs—of mass populations. From the late 1870s onward, the physical building of cities—central cities and suburban communities—was a significant generative force within the American economy. Prodigious quantities of iron, steel, coal, oil, copper wire, lead pipe, concrete, and lumber, among other major materials, were needed in these mushrooming cities to build and pave miles of streets, construct office, factory, and residential buildings, mass transit systems, lighting, heating, water supply and sewage disposal facilities, telephone and telegraph systems, and central electric power plants. As valuable central city land was taken over or opened up for new purposes, industries, businesses, and homes geographically shifted to vacant, low-density, inexpensive areas within major cities or just beyond their legal limits in adjacent suburban sites.

City officials busily allocated municipal resources in a thoroughly unplanned, uncoordinated, haphazard, and sometimes corrupt fashion to provide an array of public facilities and services, but each street opened, each city service provided, each transportation line franchised, each electric power station licensed, each development which would cumulatively result in the evolution of the metropolitan district, was improvised, one step at a time. One reflection of the commitment to promote city growth—and inadvertently technological innovation—was the extraordinary increase in municipal indebtedness, which rose from $200 million in 1860 to $725 million by 1880, more than three times the amount of state indebtedness. By 1902, that figure had soared beyond $1.5 billion. The largest payments were for the construction of city halls, schools, courts, jails, streets, bridges, police and fire protection departments, and interest on municipal debts.[34] At the same time, private businessmen in a similar uncoordinated fashion busied themselves with the construction of office buildings, skyscrapers, and residential buildings, mass transit systems, electric power plants and electric-related products and services for urban dwellers.

Housing the millions of new urban dwellers was a monumental undertaking. During the *entire decade* of the 1860s, residential construction was valued at $1,300,000,000, but the *annual* expenditures in 1900 alone were valued at $1,946,000,000. The construction industry, extending as it did into every city and metropolis, provided employment for hundreds of thousands throughout the nation in steel, lumber, cement, transportation, and other fields. Indeed, 63 percent of the construction industry in 1900 was located in 209 cities, according to economic historian Edward Kirkland, and construction expenditures on farms accounted for less than 10 percent of the nation's total.[35] Much of this city construction was devoted to tenements and fashionable apartment houses (as we will discuss in a later chapter).

Among the most significant of the technological innovations influencing city appearance and growth was the office building and skyscraper. Between 1850 and 1880, many cast-iron framed buildings were constructed for use as warehouses, department stores, offices and public buildings, and hotels;

however, few were taller than six stories. Construction of large, compact buildings for business and industry allowed the centralization of office procedures, and large nationwide companies, especially insurance firms, concentrated their activities in a few central city locations. By the mid-1880s, with the widespread introduction of steel frames, electric elevator systems, and steam heating, the true skyscraper came into existence; during the 1890s in Chicago, New York, and Philadelphia, buildings of thirteen or more stories multiplied five- and tenfold, adding to the multitude of wonders to be found in large and, ultimately, in medium-sized cities all over the nation. Chicago is credited with the first skyscraper, the Home Insurance Office Building, constructed between 1883 and 1885. New York's showplace building, the twenty-one-story Fuller Building, commonly called the Flatiron Building because of its unique triangular shape, was completed in 1902, and remained "the skyscraper" until across town the forty-seven-story Singer Building was finished in 1908. It was New York's sixty-story Woolworth Tower, completed in 1913, that remained for some twenty years the world's tallest building.

Electric Power Systems

The adaptation of electric power to city communication, lighting, and transit was one of the most revolutionary of the technological innovations between 1870 and 1900. The demand for telephones, city lighting, and mass transit facilities explains the incredibly rapid growth of electric power companies, and the initial high cost of installation of these systems explains why they were developed first in America's cities. Few inventions were as immediately popular as the telephone; it quickly became an essential business tool. Less than two years after the invention of the telephone in 1876, a company in New Haven had set up the first commercial switchboard (see Figure 5.3); two years later, more than eighty-five cities had telephone lines and switchboard exchanges. At this time, more than 35,000 miles of telephone lines had been strung over American city streets, and there were 148 telephone companies attempting to cope with the insatiable demand for phones and line connections for business and private homes. New York and Boston were connected by phone wires in 1877, and the whole country was crisscrossed by phone lines in 1900. There were more than two million phone company subscribers in 1902, and the number grew dramatically every year thereafter.[36]

Electric lights were used to illuminate Wanamaker's Philadelphia department store in 1878; at about the same time, Cleveland and San Francisco were installing electric street lights to replace gas and kerosene lamps. In 1880, Wabash, Indiana, became the first city entirely lighted by electricity; Denver leaders commissioned the development of electric lighting facilities soon thereafter. Thomas Edison's new incandescent light bulb, invented in 1880, rapidly became available

LIST OF SUBSCRIBERS.
New Haven District Telephone Company.

OFFICE 219 CHAPEL STREET.

February 21, 1878.

Residences.	Stores, Factories, &c.
Rev. JOHN E. TODD.	O. A. DORMAN.
J. B. CARRINGTON.	STONE & CHIDSEY.
H. B. BIGELOW.	NEW HAVEN FLOUR CO. State St.
C. W. SCRANTON.	" " " Cong. ave.
GEORGE W. COY.	" " " Grand St.
G. L. FERRIS.	" " " Fair Haven.
H. P. FROST.	ENGLISH & MERSICK.
M. F. TYLER.	NEW HAVEN FOLDING CHAIR CO.
I. H. BROMLEY.	H. HOOKER & CO.
GEO. E. THOMPSON.	W. A. ENSIGN & SON.
WALTER LEWIS.	H. B. BIGELOW & CO.
	C. COWLES & CO.
Physicians.	C. S. MERSICK & CO.
Dr. E. L. R. THOMPSON.	SPENCER & MATTHEWS.
Dr. A. E. WINCHELL.	PAUL ROESSLER.
Dr. C. S. THOMSON, Fair Haven.	E. S. WHEELER & CO.
	ROLLING MILL CO.
Dentists.	APOTHECARIES HALL.
Dr. E. S. GAYLORD.	E. A GESSNER.
Dr. R. F. BURWELL.	AMERICAN TEA CO.
Miscellaneous.	*Meat & Fish Markets.*
REGISTER PUBLISHING CO.	W. H. HITCHINGS, City Market.
POLICE OFFICE.	GEO. E. LUM, " "
POST OFFICE.	A. FOOTE & CO.
MERCANTILE CLUB.	STRONG, HART & CO.
QUINNIPIAC CLUB.	
F. V. McDONALD, Yale News.	*Hack and Boarding Stables.*
SMEDLEY BROS. & CO.	CRUTTENDEN & CARTER.
M. F. TYLER, Law Chambers.	BARKER & RANSOM.

Office open from 6 A. M. to 2 A. M.
After March 1st, this Office will be open all night.

Figure 5.3 The New Haven Telephone Directory, 1878

for household and office use, and this spurred the demand for expansion of electric power for private use. Electric service was sold to the public after 1879 in San Francisco. The first power plant was built in New York City in 1882, and in that year there were some thirty-eight central electric power stations in the United States. During the mid-1890s the development of high voltage electric cables made it possible for power companies to transmit electricity from the central power plants throughout cities and, most significantly, miles away to suburban factories and homes as well, making it possible for manufacturers to move away from central cities in search of the most efficient, economical sites for production.[37] By the end of the century, there were nearly 3,000 electric power stations spread all over the nation.

Mass Transit Systems

The spinal cord of the modern city is mass transit. So great was the need for mass transit facilities during the mid-nineteenth century that cities experimented with various kinds of systems, ranging from horsedrawn carriages and stagecoaches or omnibuses to horse-drawn streetcars, elevated railways and railroads, electric trolleys, and underground railways. Horse- or mule-drawn streetcar lines (employing cars running on metal rails set into the street) were introduced in New York during the 1850s, and quickly spread to Boston, Philadelphia, Baltimore, Chicago, Cincinnati, and Pittsburgh in the 1860s. By 1860, Philadelphia had laid out more than 145 miles of street railway track.

But these lines were slow (four to six miles an hour), expensive, and uncomfortable, and the animals were balky. Author Mark Twain vividly described the nature of urban mass transit in the 1860s.

> You cannot ride unless you are willing to go in a packed omnibus [a horsedrawn coach] that labors, and plunges, and struggles along at the rate of three miles in four hours and a half, always getting left behind by fast walkers, and always apparently hopelessly tangled up with vehicles that are trying to get to some place or other and can't. Or if you can stomach it, you can ride in a horse-car [street railway] and stand up for three-quarters of an hour, in the midst of a file of men that extends from front to rear (seats all crammed, of course)— or you can take one of the platforms, if you please, but they

are so crowded you will have to hang on by your eye-lashes and your toenails.[38]

Nonetheless, there were 525 streetcar lines with 18,000 cars in over 300 cities by the mid-1880s, and they carried approximately 1.2 billion passengers a year.

Chicago, Boston, and Brooklyn followed New York's example in 1871 and constructed elevated railroad lines (a few cars pulled by small steam locomotives on elevated platforms made of steel girders). New York opened a second elevated line—the Sixth Avenue—in 1878. But these proved smoky, dangerous, and extremely expensive to construct and maintain. Meanwhile, San Francisco, as well as several midwestern cities, constructed cable car lines, using cars pulled by endless cables on massive reels set into the streets. However, transportation within American cities was slow and basically inadequate through the 1880s, and most people still walked to work or to market, while wagons and horses were used for making deliveries.

The problem of moving large numbers of people through the streets to work and home was ultimately solved by the use of electricity. Supplied with electric current from overhead wires, the electric streetcar or trolley was introduced in Richmond, Virginia, in 1887, and revolutionized mass transit and the walking or pedestrian city. The trolley was cheaper, cleaner, more efficient, and faster than the horse car; electric lines could run fifteen to eighteen miles an hour and were unaffected by weather conditions. Within a year, twenty-five trolley companies were operating, and by 1902 more than two billion passengers were carried over 22,000 miles of track; by 1907 this had been increased to 34,000 miles. "Els" or elevated railroads were quickly redesigned to run on electric current in Chicago (1892), Boston (1894), and Philadelphia (1905).

But even as surface and elevated lines were electrified, Boston and New York were constructing underground "subway" lines to handle their monumental transportation needs. Boston's one-and-a-half-mile electric subway—essentially a trolley system under the city's streets—was completed between 1895 and 1897. The first of New York's several subways was finished in 1904, traversing Manhattan from City Hall on the island's southern tip to 145th Street in the north. New York, thus, had trolleys on the streets, els over the streets, and subways under the streets to transport hundreds of thousands of workers to work and home as well as enabling people to shop in distant parts of the city.

Between 1890 and 1920, while major cities were developing mass transit facilities, private transit companies all over the Northeast and Midwest were constructing railway lines connecting these cities and their suburbs. Interurbans, as they were called, were little more than oversized electric streetcars running between two or more cities or towns on their own tracks and rights-of-way. There was an interurban building "craze" during the early 1900s, especially in Ohio, Indiana, Illinois, and Missouri, when it was realized that high-speed travel (up to sixty miles an hour) between cities and outlying territories would make living in small suburban communities practical for many urban workers. In 1897, nearly 1,000 miles of interurban track were in operation, by 1905 nearly 8,000, and by 1915, 15,000.[39]

Electric interurban lines reached their peak in 1920, transporting suburban commuters efficiently, economically, and swiftly over almost 40,000 miles of track. Less than five years later, however, most of the companies were bankrupt and the lines abandoned as Americans gave their hearts to a newer method of transportation, the automobile.

UTILITY COMPANIES, FRANCHISES, AND MUNICIPAL REGULATION

Wondrous as the new technologies were, some of the shady, fast-buck, even corrupt methods used by municipal gas, electric power, telephone companies, streetcar lines, and their willing allies in city government to secure licenses and set rates for service prompted the call for control of these essential utilities by public agencies.

Although utilities were extremely costly to develop, they were also highly profitable for investors—over $300 million was invested in municipal gas works, $250 million in electric lighting plants, and $2 billion in electric street railways around 1900.[40] To develop these systems, private companies first obtained franchises from city governments which conferred upon them monopoly status in return for which the company stipulated the duration of the license or lease, the fees to be paid to the city, and the level of service to be provided. The municipal franchise was the basic method of regulating utilities, but few cities or their leaders either truly understood or, in many cases, cared what they were signing away; for instance, Buffalo and Albany streetcar companies were granted 999 and 1,000-year leases.

Before the twentieth century, as historian David Nord has explained, when most of the major franchises were arranged, the public utility lawyers drafted the franchises and submitted them to "bewildered—if not bought—city aldermen for approval."[41] Cities, moreover, did not have the facilities to carry out the detailed, day-to-day supervision of these utilities' operations, and not until well into the new century would they possess the expertise necessary to make careful examinations of company books, methods of raising investment capital, accounting practices, rate-making procedures, and service levels so as to ensure reasonable rate charges.

Like other major corporations of the day, public utility companies succumbed quickly to large-scale corporate consolidation, and some companies developed into utility empires. This trend was partly in response to high investment costs, to make more effective use of newer technology, and also because larger operations opened up the possibility of cheaper rates for consumers. But fundamentally the concentration of control over far-flung utility companies in different cities resulted from the impulse toward empire-building on the part of syndicates and individuals. Thus, urban dwellers found themselves at the mercy of greedy and/or corrupt manipulators like Charles T. Yerkes, who commanded a vast midwestern street railway combine, William Collins Whitney, whose New York City and Philadelphia-based syndicate controlled street railways in at least 100 cities and towns from Maine to Pennsylvania, or Samuel Insull, who pyramided a Chicago electric company into a utility empire of electric, gas, and transit companies in 5,000 communities spread over thirty-two states by the early 1920s.[42] Chicago Mayor Carter H. Harrison (1897–1905; 1911–1915) might well have been referring to all cities when he wrote in 1914 that "in the good old days Chicago had no [utility] regulation. The corporations carried their extortions as far as they dared without running the risk of being lynched."[43]

Several solutions were worked out during the first twenty years of the century to reform and control the utilities industries.[44] Public ownership was one method. The ease with which cities at the turn of the century were able to float municipal bonds enabled some cities to purchase utility companies outright or develop their own. In 1896, less than 400 municipally owned electric plants existed in the United States, but by 1906 that number had increased to more than 1,250.[45] However, more than 80 percent of the municipally owned electric plants were in smaller cities, with populations of less than 5,000, and here the motive seemed less the desire to regulate irresponsible companies than to develop electric power systems. The most popular device for exercising control over utilities was the regulatory commission, either a state agency or a city commission, staffed with professionals, which was to oversee private utility companies and enforce honest, reasonable standards in rate-making and service operation.

Whatever the problems created by corporate manipulators, it is nonetheless clear that innovations in transportation and communication made the giant city and its metropolitan district a possibility and a reality. As one scholar accurately noted, "It is hard to say whether the [electric] trolley produced the metropolis or vice versa. In any event, we may date the transformation of most American cities from the stage of simple urbanism to complex metropolitanism in the first or second decade following the introduction of trolleys."[46]

Well before 1910, every major American city had its mass transit network, consisting of electric trolleys, elevated railways, subways and/or cable cars, which allowed the population of these cities to grow astronomically and the cities to expand over vast geographical areas without fragmenting into smaller units or losing their traditional identities. Most of these inner-city transit networks were linked with electric interurban railways or commuter railroads that radiated outward into adjacent residential and industrial cities. As an example, the February, 1898, *Harper's Weekly* reported that the number of people who commuted to New York City was greater than the total population of Cincinnati: 100,000 came over the Brooklyn Bridge (completed in 1883) or by ferry boat from neighboring Brooklyn, another 10,000 by ferry from New Jersey, and 118,000 arrived on trains at Grand Central Station from suburban communities in Westchester and Connecticut. Thus, like "beads on a string," suburban communities grew up along—and were attached to—the commuter and interurban lines.

Suburban Residential Communities

Ultimately of far greater significance than the spread of factories and "company towns" on the outskirts of central cities was the massive exodus of city dwellers into suburban residential communities in the late nineteenth and early twentieth centuries. The typical suburbanite was a middle class city resident who sought to escape the noise, soot, and spreading poverty of the central city in an idealized, rural environment blending the best of the city and country—a place in which a simpler, more pleasant life-style in a more natural setting might be enjoyed, while at the same time retaining the economic, cultural, and technological benefits of the big modern city.

Promoters of a Chicago suburban development, on the northern shore of Lake Michigan in 1873, appealed to the underlying hopes and drives of all suburban migrants, then and now.

> The great cities that are building now all have their suburban windows at which nature may be seen in her main expressions —in her verdue and flowers; in her expanse of water and landscape; and in her hills and valleys—and these spots attract to them cultured people, with their elegant homes and elaborate and costly adornment. . . . [These natural advantages] have been enhanced by such improvements in building and adornment as are peculiar to Chicago, and . . . there is no city that surpasses ours in these respects.[47]

However, only those urban dwellers with incomes sufficient to afford the cost of housing, living, and commuting were liberated from the densely populated inner or central cities, as Sam Bass Warner, Jr., has demonstrated in his pioneering study of Boston's "streetcar suburbs." He found that Boston's adjacent suburban communities during the nineteenth century were rigidly segregated into three economic groups—the wealthy (5 percent), the central middle class (15 percent), and lower middle class (consisting of another 20 to 30 percent). Fully half of Boston's population was virtually left out of the suburban way of life between the 1880s and 1900s —this was due to the high housing and living costs and also to exclusionary laws in the suburbs, not to the expense of commuting on streetcars.[48]

This important distinction was noticed by **Graham Romeyn Taylor** in 1915, when he wrote his early study of industrial or employing suburbs:

> The suburbanite who leaves business behind at nightfall for the cool green rim of the city would think the world had gone topsy-turvy if at five-thirty he rushed out of a factory set in a landscape of open fields and wooded hillsides, scrambled for a seat in a street car or grimy train and clattered back to the region of brick and pavement, of soot and noise and jostle. *Yet this is the daily routine for many thousands of factory workers.*[49] [Italics added.]

Streets in the residential suburbs outlying Boston were laid out along the familiar grid pattern and each lot had some small street frontage, resulting in a suburban style of single-family houses "arranged in such a way as to produce for the public the gratifying view of a prosperous street." House lots, though small (generally 50 feet by 100 feet), allowed sufficient space for a garden, a few trees, and a place for children to play in safety. Significantly, the houses in such middle class communities were basically quite similar in design and style along each of these streets, and each house incorporated virtually identical features. Apparently this was the product of market conditions rather than of municipal building regulations or even primitive zoning legislation. The tendency of the individual builder-contractor to construct what his neighbors had built—or what he perceived as what the largely conformist middle class buyers wished in suburban housing—accounts for the similarity of lot size, street design, and housing design.[50]

Communities either too small or financially unable to create their own public improvements and utilities (gas, water, lighting, electric power, and transit networks) willingly voted to consolidate with Boston, as had Roxbury in 1868, Dorchester in 1870, Charleston, Brighton, and West Roxbury in 1873. But by the 1880s, all of Boston's suburbs resisted absorption by the central city; on the one hand, this was an indication of spreading concern that their social enclaves would be undermined by affiliation with Boston and, on the other, the self-sufficiency was made increasingly possible because of the rapid extension of private utility company services and transportation lines.[51]

Evidence for other metropolitan districts is still unavailable, but it is highly likely that the situation just described was basically typical of conditions throughout the Northeast and Midwest. Of course, there were some exceptions to this pattern. Historian Clay McShane, for example, suggests that the electrification of street railways had only a limited effect upon Milwaukee's metropolitanization. Rather than the trolley, he found that it was the automobile that fundamentally altered the city's residential patterns; the car, not the streetcar, freed the working classes, industry, and commerce from the necessity of central city location.[52]

Boston's suburbs were typical of northeastern and midwestern patterns of metropolitanization, but across the continent Los Angeles pioneered another variation of the process, one that would increasingly characterize twentieth-century cities. By 1920 waves of migrants to sunny California had transformed Los Angeles into a city of 577,000, the center of a metropolitan population approaching one million. Los Angeles was the product of a unique combination of streetcar lines, real estate promoters, subdivision practices, and the "exceptional character" of the city's population. Unlike the "impoverished and insecure European immigrants" then pouring into eastern and midwestern cities, "who, in their attempt to find work and fellowship were confined to . . . teeming tenements and crowded ghettos," Robert Fogelson argues, in his study of Los Angeles between 1850 and 1930, most newcomers were relatively well-off native Americans who possessed "adequate resources and marketable skills" and "a conception of the good community . . . embodied in single-family houses, located on large lots, surrounded by landscaped lawns, and isolated from business activities."[53]

The availability of land, water, and streetcar lines, which developed faster than population dispersal, allowed Los Angeles residents to spread out not only within the city but also well beyond the city limits, creating homes in suburban settings. These vast stretches of suburban subdivisions were held together less by a central business district than by streetcars; the automobile only reinforced this basic pattern and made the city's geographical expansion even more rapid during the 1920s.

In 1900, the automobile scarcely seemed capable of challenging the supremacy of streetcars, interurbans, and commuter railroads for metropolitan district passenger traffic, yet by the mid-1920s the car had apparently toppled not only the

TABLE 5.3
Motor Vehicle Registrations, 1900–1930*

Year	Passenger Cars	Trucks and Buses	Total Registrations	Total Population	Ratio of Cars to People
1900	8,000		8,000	76,994,000	1:9,499
1910	458,000	10,000	469,000	91,972,000	1:201
1920	8,132,522	1,108,000	9,239,000	105,710,620	1:13.0
1930	23,035,000	3,715,000	26,750,000	122,775,046	1:5.3

*Based on information contained in U.S. Bureau of the Census, *Statistical Abstract of the U.S.: 1961* (Washington, D.C. 1961), Table 756.

commuter railroads but also the interurbans, many of which were all but abandoned, their companies in bankruptcy. At the turn of the century, the car was regarded as a rich man's plaything and barely 8,000 automobiles were registered in America, an ownership ratio of one car for every 10,000 Americans (see Table 5.3). However, by 1906, Henry Ford's adaptation of mass production techniques (assembly line production employing interchangeable parts) to automobile construction soon made it possible for Americans to obtain relatively low-priced personal cars, and by 1913 there were more than one million automobiles in use.[54]

Widespread adoption of the automobile between 1910 and 1920 accelerated the suburbanization of the middle class and the outward migration of businesses and employment opportunities, a process already well under way. By 1920, there were more than 8,000,000 cars registered, a ratio of one car for every thirteen Americans, and, just as significant, there were more than 1,100,000 truck and buses operating on the nation's expanding system of roads. The suburbanized middle class was first attracted to the car for work and leisure because of its comfort, convenience, and cost, and thus it was at the outskirts of the central cities that the automobile and truck first began to shape urban life. Ultimately, the car, bus, and truck would intensify the division between the central cities and their suburban communities, but at the outset, the car seems only to have reinforced the urbanization pattern that had already been well defined between 1880 and 1910. (See Figure 5.4 for equivalent patterns in Great Britain, Germany, and France.)

Americans transformed their society between 1870 and 1920. Railroads bound the continent together, major corporations took command of the national economy, and wondrous new technologies made possible the evolution of giant metropolitan complexes which dominated the life of whole regions of the country. Not only was America an urban nation by 1920, it was fast becoming a metropolitan nation as well. Americans had proved themselves marvelous builders, but now they had to come to grips with the social results of these extraordinary changes.

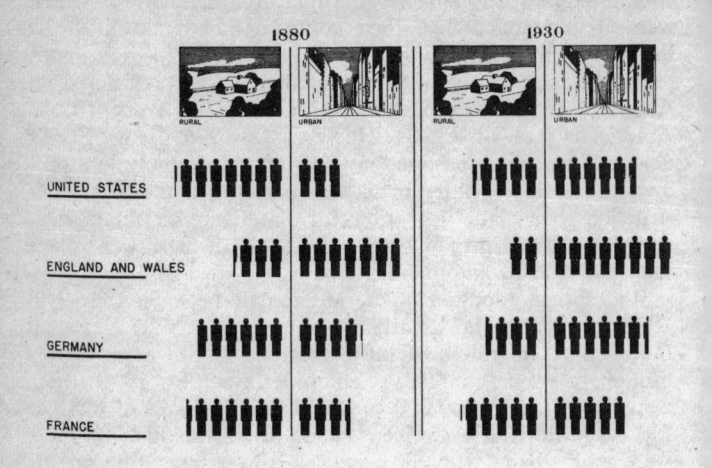

Figure 5.4 Comparison of Urban Population Shift in United States and Europe Between 1880 and 1930

6

Continuing Patterns of Community Development

Between 1870 and 1920, there was a massive increase in the number, size, and influence of America's cities. According to the U.S. Census, the number of cities rose from 663 to 2,722 while the overall urban population went from just under 10 million at the start of the period to slightly more than 54 million at its close; for the first time in its history, the nation was more than half urban. During the same period, cities with populations in excess of 250,000 increased in number from seven to twenty-five, and their share of the nation's population went from slightly over 8 percent to roughly 20 percent.

While in 1870 no American city contained a million people, fifty years later, New York had 5.6 million, Philadelphia 1.8 million, and Chicago 2.7 million. Chicago's record in this era is perhaps the most extraordinary instance of sustained growth in American urban history. Already a major city of 300,000 in 1870, its population in 1920 represented a ninefold increase. A few of the lesser cities also grew at as rapid a clip. The population of Atlanta multiplied ten times during this fifty-year period, and that of Detroit twelve times.

Every federal census, save that of 1880, indicated that more than half the population increase in the preceding decade had taken place in urban areas. Although the number of urban dwellers had more than quintupled from 1870 to 1920, the rural population had not even doubled, moving only from 28 million to 51 million. (See Figure 6.1) Moreover, the decline in the population of many rural areas, beginning with New England before the Civil War, had now spread to other regions. Between 1910 and 1920, there was a net loss of population in the rural districts of three geographic regions and fifteen states.

As of 1920, however, the majority of Americans did not

yet live in large cities. It should be borne in mind that nearly 30 percent of the "urban" population of that year was to be found in places with populations of under 25,000. Thus, 64 percent of the American people were dwelling either in the smaller towns and cities or in rural areas. Although by the 1920s rural and small-town America was thoroughly alarmed by the cosmopolitan character and growing influence of the major cities, it retained sufficient numerical superiority in that decade to sustain policies such as prohibition and discriminatory immigration quotas, to which the great majority of big-city residents were adamantly opposed.

Some of the urban increase in this era was due to the reclassification from rural to urban of localities that had either been absorbed by the expansion of neighboring cities or whose populations had risen above 2,500. Between 1880 and 1910, for the first time natural increase (the surplus of birth over deaths) within urban areas contributed significantly to urban population growth. This trend was the result of lower urban death rates due to improved sanitation and other public health measures and to higher birthrates among the recent migrants from the rural districts of America and Europe. From 1910 to 1940, however, there appears to have been little if any natural increase in the nation's cities because birthrates in urban areas had declined even faster than mortality rates.

As in previous periods, migration was the most important factor in urban growth during this era. Whether within the nation or from abroad, the main migratory movements had proceeded from low wage to high wage areas and from the less developed and rural areas to the more developed and urban. As always, it was largely the young who migrated, and in the earliest waves of newcomers, men were solidly in the majority.

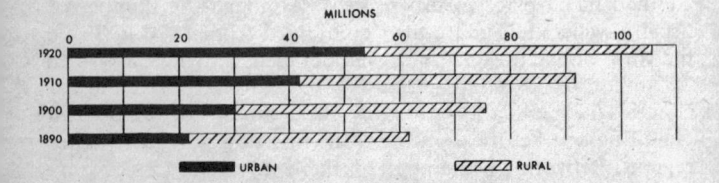

Figure 6.1 The Increase in Urban and Rural Populations in the United States: 1890–1920

Urban Migration

As has been recently pointed out by Stephan Thernstrom and Peter Knights, the migrations *into and out of* the nation's cities and towns were far larger than the net gains in population would indicate. In each major city, the hundreds of thousands (or millions in the very largest ones) of arrivals were all but counterbalanced by the hundreds of thousands who were moving out. In the 1880s alone, contend Thernstrom and Knights, the turnover of Boston's population was more than four times as large as the city's population at the start of the decade.[1]

The great majority of those who emigrated from the cities had entered them very shortly before. In his study of geographic and social mobility in Omaha, Howard Chudacoff found that of those families and individuals who migrated out of that city from 1900 to 1905, more than 90 percent were not listed in the city's directory for 1893 and, therefore, were probably not yet living there.[2] Urban transients, both in Omaha and in other cities, tended to be made up disproportionately of the young and of those who had not yet acquired any substantial stake in society, especially the unskilled, the foreign-born, and blacks.

Because it threatened to bring to a city more artisans of a particular type than could profitably be employed there, geographic mobility posed a constant threat to the status and income of skilled workers. The various attempts to establish national craft unions, beginning with the typographers in 1850, were in large part motivated by the need of the artisans to exert some control over the mobility of those who worked in their trade. After the Civil War, the labor press attempted to deal with this problem by informing unemployed or discontented workers where they might find the best market for their services. Unemployed craftsmen were frequently loaned or given sums of money by their unions with which to seek work in other localities.

Many employment agencies were established in this period in both the private and public sectors, with the private ones playing by far the more significant role. Private labor agencies provided employers with workers en masse and assumed even greater importance to their clients in periods of labor conflict, when they would be called upon to supply strikebreakers. By the end of the period, if not before, labor turnover had become extremely rapid. In the 105 industrial plants for which he examined the employment data for the period from 1912 to 1915, economist Sumner Slichter found an average turnover rate of nearly 100 percent.[3] Apparently, in prosperous years at least, many workers were voluntarily quitting their jobs because better ones had become available.

It has been estimated that about one third of the urban population in 1910 had formerly resided in America's rural districts. As earlier, the urban-ward exodus of the farmers was in large part due to the continuing transformation of modern agriculture. The utilization of new machines and the opening of new land farther to the west, as in the antebellum era, added greatly to the productivity of America's farms, but they also substantially increased the amount of capital needed to begin a new farm and at the same time undermined the competitive position of many of the cultivators of older eastern farmland. The impact of these trends was heightened by the growing involvement of the nation's farmers with the world market, bringing them into competition with farmers from other lands. Thus, whether an Alabama or Iowa farmer prospered depended increasingly on impersonal economic forces and on the actions of those businesses, such as banks and railroads, upon which he was forced to rely. Under these conditions many farmers who were lacking in capital, fertile land, or business skill were unable to earn a decent livelihood from their farms and so migrated to nearby towns; often, they moved again within a few years to larger and more distant cities.

To many for whom life on the farm meant drudgery, privation, and boredom, settlement in the city seemed a welcome deliverance. One Massachusetts city dweller, in recalling his former life on the farm, put it this way: "Hard work and no holidays, no books, no young company. 'Go to bed, John, hard day's work tomorrow.' 'Get up, John, it is 'most five. How lazy you are getting.' "[4] Then as always, however, the single most crucial factor in attracting newcomers was the prospect of a better livelihood. The expansion of industry had created many new jobs for unskilled workers and many employers were eager to hire boys from the farm because they knew English and were ethnically similar to themselves. For these "buckwheats," as one of Andrew Carnegie's foremen called them, advancement was usually more rapid than it was for blacks and the foreign-born.

Blacks, who throughout this period were concentrated primarily in the rural South, also contributed to urban growth. According to the United States Census, only 13.4 percent of blacks were urban in 1870; by 1920, this figure had risen to 34 percent. Like other rural Southerners who had migrated to urban areas, the majority of these black newcomers were from nearby districts, either from within the same state or from neighboring ones. In 1890, blacks comprised over 40 percent of the population in such leading cities within the region as Richmond and Atlanta. After 1900, the rate of growth in the black population of southern cities lagged behind that of the region's urban whites. In the latter year, one southern black in every four was classified by the census as urban, as compared with 29 percent of the region's whites.

The migration of blacks to the North, which had begun to gather momentum after 1890, was caused by a combination of pushes and pulls. The passage of harshly discriminatory laws throughout the South certainly contributed to the movement, but the most important factors were economic: poor conditions on the southern farms as opposed to opportunities for unskilled black workers in the North. During World War I, black migration to the North was greatly accelerated, due partially to floods and the boll weevil epidemic which beset southern farmers. However, the principal factor was the war itself, which caused unskilled labor to be in great demand while sharply narrowing the flow of immigration from Europe. From 1870 to 1910, fewer than 300,000 blacks left the South, while from 1910 to 1920, more than 500,000 did so.

In the northern states as of 1920, more than 85 percent of the black population was dwelling in urban areas, with much of it concentrated in the larger cities. In the World War I decade the black population of Chicago had risen from 44,000 to 109,000, that of New York from 91,000 to 152,000, while Philadelphia's rose from 85,000 to 135,000. By 1920, well over a third of the black population of the North was to be found in just six cities: New York, Chicago, Philadelphia, Detroit, Cleveland, and Pittsburgh.

Largely unskilled and flagrantly victimized by discrimination, the great majority of urban blacks of both sexes were employed in some form of domestic and personal service, with a sizable minority among the men toiling as laborers or in other forms of unskilled work. Even immigrants were often granted better opportunities than were blacks. It was only in World War I, with millions of men in the armed forces and immigration sharply down, that a high percentage of the blacks in the northern cities were employed in factories, most of which had kept their doors closed to them in the past. So little were most black men paid that the proportion of their wives and children who worked was far higher than among whites.

In every city where there were appreciable numbers of blacks, most of them were relegated to the oldest and most dilapidated housing, for which they were invariably charged more rent than was paid by whites for equivalent housing. Down to about 1900, however, the districts of black residence also contained many white families. Thereafter, as the black population rose rapidly in various cities, segregation was increasingly imposed and with far greater rigidity than it had ever been enforced against foreign-born whites. The Negro quarter, or "ghetto," became increasingly congested, since even middle class and wealthy blacks were usually unable to buy or rent homes outside it. Adding to the squalor of these neighborhoods was the practice of many big-city mayors and police chiefs of confining the local vice districts within them.

As usual, the blacks, along with other nonwhite groups like the Chinese, were more severely harassed than were the white ethnics. In 1882, the Chinese became the first people ever to be barred from settling in the United States. After Reconstruction, the South made second-class citizens of its blacks, depriving virtually all of them of the vote and legally requiring the separation of the races. Even in the North, where by 1880 the segregation statutes of an earlier era were largely defunct, public opinion in the early twentieth century became increasingly hostile to all social contact between the races. By 1900, all the more fashionable hotels and restaurants in northern cities, and even many of the churches, were again, as in the antebellum era, denying admission to blacks. Finally, the rapid increase in the black population of northern cities during the First World War and the resulting competition between the blue collar element in both races for available housing and jobs culminated in the riots of 1919 in which white mobs in several cities attacked many blacks and the blacks retaliated with mob violence of their own. The worst of these outbreaks took place in Chicago where twenty-three blacks and fifteen whites were killed and 3,000 families, mainly black, were left homeless.

Patterns of Adjustment Among the Foreign-Born

In all but the southern cities, blacks were greatly outnumbered by the growing hordes of foreign-born whites. Between 1870 and 1920, the number of foreign-born in American cities rose by more than 7 million, attaining in the latter year a total of 10.5 million. This net increase was the outcome of immigration on a scale more massive than ever before. In the three decades prior to 1880, an average of 220,000 immigrants arrived annually in the United States, but in the four decades that followed, immigration would average more than half a million each year.

In the 1890s, there was a shift in the sources of supply, with most immigrants after 1894 coming from Italy and

Figure 6.2 Immigrants landing at the Castle Garden reception center in New York City in 1878. From *Frank Leslie's Illustrated Newspaper*, November 23, 1877.

eastern Europe rather than from Great Britain, Germany, and Scandinavia, which had formerly supplied the great majority. Between 1900 and 1910, this "new immigration" accounted for 81 percent of all new arrivals. In general, many of the same pushes and pulls that had earlier set in motion multitudes of Germans and Irish, as well as millions from the American countryside, lay behind the influx from southern and eastern Europe. The latter regions were then undergoing the same economic and social transformations that had begun earlier in northern and western Europe and the United States. Once again, great multitudes of peasants and smaller groups of artisans and traders were displaced by economic change, and they attempted to salvage their fortunes through migration. Other factors were the heavy demand for labor in America and the greater speed and safety of the Atlantic crossing after 1860, due to the introduction of the ocean-going steamship.

Not all who came over remained here permanently. The improvement of ocean transport also led to a great increase in the number of those who returned. Many skilled workers now shuttled regularly across the Atlantic, settling temporarily on whichever side wages were highest and conditions best. Even among the unskilled, a substantial percentage, especially among those from Italy and Greece, had come to America only to accumulate money, returning home once they had done so.

As always, the foreign-born were more prone than native Americans to settle in cities. In 1920, 72 percent of those of foreign birth or parentage were dwelling in urban areas, but among people of native parentage, the urban percentage was only 41 percent. The disparity was even more marked in the major cities. Thus, the dozen cities with populations of more than 500,000 in 1920 contained 35 percent of the nation's foreign-born, 27 percent of those of mixed or foreign parentage, but only 8 percent of those of entirely native parentage.

New York continued to serve as the port of entry for the great majority of immigrants, while Boston, Baltimore, and San Francisco attracted small but still significant segments of the immigrant traffic. As a result of the extension and improvement of the national railway network and of the facilities and institutions attending to their needs, the foreign-born had greater mobility than ever before. In addition, there were employment agencies and labor bureaus that specialized in supplying employers with cheap immigrant labor. As a result, immigrants became, according to immigration historian Maldwyn Jones, "a kind of mobile reserve force which could be concentrated wherever the demand summoned them."[5]

Most of the new arrivals would move on from the ports of entry to the cities and towns of the hinterlands. Thus, many who had entered the country by way of Boston went to the

TABLE 6.1
Foreign-Stock Whites in Largest Cities: 1920

CITY	TOTAL POPULATION	FOREIGN-BORN WHITES Number	(%)	NATIVE WHITE FOREIGN OR MIXED PARENTAGE Number	(%)
New York	5,620,048	1,991,547	35.4	2,303,082	41.0
Chicago	2,701,705	805,482	29.8	1,140,816	42.2
Philadelphia	1,823,779	397,927	21.8	591,471	32.4
Detroit	993,678	289,297	29.1	348,771	35.1
Cleveland	796,841	239,538	30.1	310,241	38.9
St. Louis	772,897	103,239	13.4	239,894	31.0
Boston	748,060	238,919	31.9	309,755	41.4
Baltimore	733,826	83,911	11.4	162,839	22.2
Pittsburgh	588,343	120,266	20.4	213,465	36.3
Los Angeles	576,673	112,057	19.4	140,349	24.3
Buffalo	506,775	121,530	24.0	215,377	42.5
San Francisco	506,676	140,200	27.7	182,643	36.0
Milwaukee	457,157	110,068	24.1	213,911	46.8
Washington	437,571	28,548	6.5	58,824	13.4
Newark	414,524	117,003	28.2	166,807	40.2
Cincinnati	401,247	42,827	10.7	121,665	30.3
New Orleans	387,219	25,992	6.7	69,283	17.9
Minneapolis	380,582	88,032	23.1	155,155	40.8
Kansas City, Mo.	324,410	27,320	8.4	57,063	17.6
Seattle	315,312	73,875	23.4	89,004	28.2
Indianapolis	314,194	16,958	5.4	43,156	13.7

SOURCE: *Statistical Abstract of the U.S.: 1929* (Washington, D.C., 1929), pp. 46–49, and U.S. Bureau of the Census, *Fourteenth Census of the U.S.: 1920*.

industrial cities of New England, while various New Jersey cities absorbed some of the overflow from New York. Other immigrants headed for the commercial and industrial centers of the Midwest. By 1910, the share of the population that was of foreign stock (immigrants and their children) comprised 74 percent of residents in Detroit, 75 percent in Cleveland and exceeded 75 percent in both Milwaukee and Chicago.

In that year, nearly half of the foreign-born were in the Northeast and about a third were in the North Central states. Outside of these two regions, which comprised the nation's industrial heartland, immigrants contributed significantly to urban growth in only three states: Texas, California, and Washington. The South continued to hold little appeal for most immigrants. Even in such old and established southern urban centers as St. Louis, New Orleans, and Baltimore, each of which had once attracted immigrants in great numbers, the foreign-born now made up less than a fifth of the population, and in New Orleans, less than 10 percent.

The largest cities became increasingly diverse in their ethnic composition. As of 1890, the Germans and Irish were either the most numerous or the second most numerous immigrant groups in every major American city, with the exception of Minneapolis, where Swedes were first, and Boston and Detroit, where Canadians were second. By 1920, however, both the largest and the second largest foreign-born groups in America's major cities were ofttimes from the nations of southern and eastern Europe. In that year, Russians were the most numerous foreign-born element in New York, Philadelphia, and Pittsburgh, while in Newark the lead was held by the Italians and in Chicago and Buffalo by the Poles.

Despite the increased mobility of the period, the continuing flow of immigration brought about the largest concentrations of particular immigrant groups in American history. By 1910, New York, which had long contained more Irishmen than Dublin, had more Hungarians than Budapest and, with more than half of the nation's Jewish population, was the most Jewish city in the world. In that year, Chicago had more Swedes than any city but Stockholm, more Poles than all but two cities in Poland, and the world's third largest concentration of Czechs.

Immigrants from a particular village or town would often settle in the same neighborhood or even on the same block and, on occasion, even in the same apartment house. "People

TABLE 6.2
Dominant Nationalities Among Foreign-Born Whites in Cities Having, in 1920, over 250,000 Inhabitants: 1920 and 1910

CITY	1920 First	1920 Second	1910 First	1910 Second
Baltimore	Russians	Germans	Germans	Russians
Boston	Irish	Canadians	Irish	Canadians
Buffalo	Poles	Germans	Germans	Canadians
Chicago	Poles	Germans	Germans	Austrians
Cincinnati	Germans	Russians	Austrians	Hungarians
Cleveland	Poles	Hungarians	Germans	Germans
Detroit	Canadians	Poles	Germans	Canadians
Jersey City	Italians	Irish	Germans	Irish
Los Angeles	Mexicans	Canadians	Germans	Canadians
Milwaukee	Germans	Poles	Germans	Russians
Minneapolis	Swedes	Norwegians	Swedes	Norwegians
New Orleans	Italians	Germans	Italians	Germans
New York	Russians	Italians	Russians	Italians
Newark	Italians	Russians	Germans	Russians
Philadelphia	Russians	Irish	Russians	Irish
Pittsburgh	Germans	Poles	Germans	Russians
St. Louis	Germans	Russians	Germans	Irish
San Francisco	Italians	Germans	Germans	Russians
Washington	Russians	Irish	Irish	Germans

from the same town," writes sociologist William F. Whyte of Boston's Italians, "settled together, formed mutual aid societies and each year celebrated the Festa of their patron saint, as they had in Italy."[6] Frequently, the small enclaves of a given nationality were located near one another and together comprised a larger neighborhood, known by such nicknames as New Greece, Little Italy, Bohemia, and so on. In a few of these districts, such as Philadelphia's Little Italy or the Jewish areas on New York's Lower East Side, the overwhelming majority of residents belonged to the dominant group. In most immigrant areas, however, there were few blocks or even buildings that were solidly of one nationality. In his study of Omaha, admittedly one of the less congested urban centers, Howard Chudacoff found that there was very little segregation of immigrant groups. "With but a very few exceptions," he writes, "the regions most densely occupied by a single nationality housed only a small fraction of that particular group."[7]

As the great majority of immigrants were unskilled, knew little or no English, and were totally unfamiliar with American life, they had no choice but to accept whatever work they could get, no matter how onerous, insecure, or poorly paid. Frequently, they were taken in hand by labor contractors, or *padrones*, who were of the same nationality and frequently from the same village or town. This man, who had often arranged their passage to America, would find lodgings and jobs for the immigrants in his charge, and their wages would be turned over to him. In their ignorance of American conditions, the immigrants would live where he told them to, take whatever jobs he obtained for them, and would meekly accept whatever pay this "boss" saw fit to give them. In effect, the *padrone* functioned as an intermediary between many recently arrived foreigners and American life, siphoning off a large portion of their earnings as the price for his "services."

There was also a distinct tendency for immigrants of a given region or nation to be concentrated within certain industries, frequently finding work in shops and factories where relatives and old acquaintances were already employed. Thus, the cigar-making trade in New York and Chicago was dominated by Czechs and Germans, and the shoe-blacking jobs in New York were preempted first by Negroes and Italians, and later by Greeks. In a number of highly mechanized industries like shipbuilding and textile manufacture, the original labor force, made up predominantly of skilled

British workers, was increasingly displaced by unskilled newcomers, initially from Canada and Ireland, but after 1890, from southern and eastern Europe.

While most immigrants were paid more than they could have earned in their homelands, it was frequently necessary nevertheless for their wives and children to work. In the sweatshops of the major cities, whole families would labor through virtually all of their waking hours, producing cigars, articles of clothing, or other commodities. Hours were nearly as long in the factories where unskilled immigrants were employed. In the blast furnaces of Pittsburgh, unskilled workers, most of them Slavic immigrants, would put in a standard seven-day workweek of eighty-four hours.

As has generally been the case in America, the class structure of the period was reinforced by ethnicity. The great majority of those holding the lowest jobs and dwelling in the poorest housing in the cities of this era were immigrants and blacks. In 1909, nearly two thirds of all workers in twenty-one major industries were immigrants or blacks, and if we include the children of immigrants, the "foreign" proportion of the labor force in these industries approaches 80 percent. Frequently, the immigrant's progress was impeded by prejudice, as in the case of the Slavic steel workers who, on applying for promotion, were told "that is not a hunky's job and you can't have it."[8]

Nativism and Restrictionism

While it is probably true, as some scholars have recently maintained, that anti-foreign attitudes have always been widely held in America, it was not until the 1890s, with the emergence of the anti-Catholic American Protective Association and of the drive to restrict immigration, that these prejudices again found expression in major social movements. As in the antebellum period, the foreign-born were again blamed for crime, pauperism, and slums. "It is not abject poverty which causes such nasty and cheap living," editorialized one Chicago newspaper in 1887, "it is simply an imported habit from Italy."[9] As in the past, native white Protestants attempted periodically to impose the strict observances of the Puritan Sabbath upon the predominantly Catholic immigrants. What was new about the nativism of the late nineteenth and

Figure 6.3 This 1888 *Harper's Weekly* cartoon, entitled "The Last Yankee," exemplifies the nativism of many Americans of the period who felt that the arrival of new ethnic groups threatened the nation with "mongrelization."

early twentieth centuries was its demand that immigration be sharply curtailed or even prohibited altogether, and the argument of many of its spokesmen that the "new immigration" was biologically inferior to the old. (See Figure 6.3.) "The new immigrants," declared the Massachusetts Institute of Technology's president Frederick Amassa Walker in 1891, "are beaten men from beaten races."[10]

With the foreign-born taking most of the hardest, worst-paying jobs, additional opportunities were created for the native-born whites. Many of them now moved up to jobs that were more highly skilled or that entailed the supervision of other workers, while others shed their blue collars altogether to become clerks and, in rare instances, even entered the professions. While native-stock whites were, by far, the most upwardly mobile, the foreign-born and their families also scored some gains. There was continual turnover in the shops and factories with the most recent arrivals taking the lowliest jobs while those who had preceded them graduated to skilled and white collar work. Although less often than among the sons of the old-stock families, the sons of the immigrants frequently obtained jobs with more pay and higher status than those for which their fathers had been compelled to settle.

Some of the immigrant groups advanced at a notably faster rate than others ostensibly because of cultural factors. For example, the urban background, business experience, and industrial skills of many German and of most Jewish immigrants stood them in good stead in urban America. On the other hand, the peasant background of the great majority of immigrants from Sicily or Poland left them with little preparation for life in Chicago or New York. It has been argued by various sociologists, most recently by Nathan Glazer and Daniel Moynihan in *Beyond the Melting Pot,* that the Roman Catholic church has often impeded upward mobility among its followers by stressing in its teachings the relative unimportance of worldly success and the acceptance of one's lot in life.[11]

The most successful businessmen in the immigrant communities were among their most socially mobile and influential members. In each national group, there were men who, beginning as peddlers or petty contractors, had managed to accumulate substantial property and wealth. A good many of these had risen by exploiting those who had just arrived in America (the "greenhorns" as they were called) as thoroughly as they themselves had once been exploited. Thus, in the "Pig Market" of New York, a sort of informal labor exchange in the district around Essex and Hester streets, contractors would obtain as many "greenhorn" workers as they needed, and would then proceed to overwork and underpay them. Moreover, aspiring professionals and businessmen among the foreign-born obtained much of their patronage from their fellow immigrants. Finally, the particular culture of each group generated certain opportunities for profit. For example, the natural desire of each nationality for the foods and dishes of the homeland, what the writer Edward Steiner has termed the "patriotism of the stomach," assured a market for the restaurants, groceries, and food products manufacturers of each national group.[12]

Among urban blacks, there was hardly any social mobility. In Atlanta, at the turn of the century, only about half of the white labor force, whether native or foreign-born, were blue collar workers, but 97 percent of the blacks were in this category. The absence of social mobility among blacks may have been due partially to the rural backgrounds of the great majority or to obscure cultural factors, but it was mostly due to the prejudice and discriminatory acts of the white majority. The argument of some authorities that today's urban blacks are behind economically simply because they are the latest of the "immigrant groups" is disproved, argues Stephan Thernstrom, by the fact that until recently, even among black families who had persisted in a particular city for generations, there had been little upward mobility.[13]

Aside from the blacks, there has been no permanent proletariat in American cities. For many unskilled workers, and to an even greater extent for their sons, there was movement up the social ladder, though generally at a pace of one short step per generation. According to several historical studies of social mobility in such American cities as Boston, Norristown (Pennsylvania), and Philadelphia, it was more than twice as common for blue collar workers to enter the middle class as it was for white collar workers to "skid" down to the proletariat.[14]

On the whole, the condition of the labor force improved greatly in this period. Although the disparity between the wealthy and the other social elements widened, the purchasing power of the masses also increased. According to the most recent students of this subject, "real" wages or purchasing power among manufacturing workers rose on the average by about 50 percent between 1860 and 1890 and by another 37 percent in the quarter century that followed.[15] Among unionized craft workers in 1900, the standard work day was generally nine hours, and in a few instances, eight hours. The average workweek for all nonagricultural workers, which had stood at sixty-six hours in 1860, had been cut to fifty-seven hours by 1890 and to forty-eight by 1920. Finally, the extent and harshness of child labor was reduced somewhat during the first two decades of the twentieth century, thereby permitting a higher proportion of working class children to go on with their education.

Suburban Growth

In general, the higher a family rose in income and status, the farther it was likely to recede from the city's central core. The tendency of those who prospered to move farther out was encouraged by economic development in the central districts, the arrival of fresh waves of impoverished newcomers, and by the improvements made in the speed of urban transit. People of means were continuing to vacate old dwellings and moving either to peripheral areas within the city or to recently developed suburbs. Middle income families had then moved into the areas abandoned by the rich, and their dwellings and neighborhoods were, in turn, inherited by the poorer segments of the working class, consisting in large part of the families which had arrived most recently. "This system of residential mobility," write historians Mayer and Wade, "permitted the gradual incorporation of all kinds of people into American life and the city became the staging ground for the upward movement of successive groups of newcomers."[16]

In the nineteenth century, urban families changed residences more frequently than they do today. In Boston during the 1880s, according to Thernstrom and Knights,[17] an average of 30 percent of the city's families established a new address each year. In New York and in a good many other cities, most leases would expire on May first; and on that date the streets would always be clogged with moving vans bearing to new addresses the worldly possessions of innumerable families. "People are always moving," observed one European visitor to New York, in the 1920s, "the only permanent addresses are those of banks."[18]

With the core districts in the major cities suffering increasingly from industrial blight and becoming ever more crowded with the foreign-born, many skilled and white collar workers fled from them to the "zone of emergence." This was generally an area just outside of the tenement district, which had recently become accessible to the lower middle classes through the extension and electrification of streetcar service and the construction in certain cities of elevated railways. (See Figure 6.4.) The houses in these areas, many of which were owned by the families who lived in them, were larger and more comfortable than those in the central districts.

By the 1890s, the zone of emergence tended to contain both a sprinkling of the less successful old-stock Americans and the upwardly mobile families of old immigrant stock, most of whom were of German, Irish, or Scandinavian descent. For both of these elements, it was crucial that they

Figure 6.4 Steam-powered cable cars, such as this one in the Pittsburgh area, were another important form of intracity and interurban transit in the 1880s, and were used in many of the larger cities, including New York, Chicago, and, of course, San Francisco. From *The Street Railway Journal*, 1888.

avoid identification with, and therefore the proximity of, the most recently arrived immigrants, especially those from eastern and southern Europe. These newcomers were unwelcome for a time in the zone of emergence, in part because its residents tended to blame them for the deterioration of their old neighborhoods, and also because they seemed to threaten their own status and hard-won respectability.

As one might expect, many of the newcomers responded in kind to the suspicion and disdain of the established groups. However, despite the mutual hostility between the two groups, it was usually only a decade or two before the more prosperous families among Poles, Italians, and other peoples of the "New Immigration" were invading the zone of emergence. Once settled there, many would purchase homes which to them, as to their predecessors, symbolized their newfound respectability and seemed to secure their position within American society.

As new ethnic groups entered these "inner suburbs," many who had previously settled in them moved away. For decades to come, the great majority of people who changed neighborhoods would continue to cleave to their ethnic group, but as the process of invasion and succession was repeated over the years, each nationality, except for the "colored" minorities, tended to become somewhat less concentrated within special districts. Thus, residential patterns among whites came in the twentieth century to be based somewhat less upon ethnic differences and increasingly on distinctions of income and social class.

After 1890, the urban middle class took advantage of the new media of transport, including in certain cities after 1900 the subway, to follow the well-to-do to the periphery and to the suburban areas beyond. As these areas became less exclusive, they were abandoned by the rich, who now moved even farther out. When, for example, the elevated railways and the subway made New York's outer boroughs fully accessible to the middle class, the wealthy who had settled earlier in these areas moved to Long Island, Westchester, Yonkers, and even Connecticut. Through such expansion, the dimensions of metropolitan areas were increased quite dramatically. The radius from the center of Boston to the outer edge of its metropolitan area increased from two or three miles in 1850 to about ten miles in 1900. Such an increase would result in a more than tenfold multiplication in the potential area of metropolitan Boston.

Prior to 1910, it was typical for suburbs to eventually become legally incorporated within the central cities. The most famous instance was the creation of Greater New York in January, 1898, a little over three years after the referendum in which a majority of the residents in Long Island City and in each of the five boroughs had voted to become legally a part of an enlarged New York. As early as the 1880s, however, there had been suburbs, notably some of those near Boston, that declined formal annexation by central cities. Even in the 1894 referendum in New York City, the suburbs of Flushing and Mount Vernon, among others, voted against becoming part of Greater New York. After 1910, annexation by central cities was increasingly rejected by middle and upper class suburbs which were determined to avoid the high taxes and appalling environmental and social problems of the central cities.

The unwillingness of many suburbs to affiliate legally with the central cities reflected the increasing fragmentation of the American metropolis. After 1870, the revolutionary improvements made in urban transportation and the growing inequality in incomes had helped to increase the physical distance within the metropolis between income groups and to some extent between ethnic and religious groups as well. By 1920, the residential segments of the major metropolitan areas consisted more than ever of distinctive enclaves based in part on ethnicity, but above all, on social class and level of income.

Residential segregation was sometimes reinforced by such devices as real estate covenants, a provision in the deed of each purchaser of land in which he pledged that he would not construct any multiple dwelling units nor any single-family homes worth less than a stipulated sum. There were also covenants of another type, explicitly requiring a homeowner not to sell to Jews, blacks, or Orientals. More commonly, realty agents would help in maintaining segregation by showing homes only in certain parts of town to blacks or people who were Jewish or noticeably "foreign."

Urban Tenements and Housing Reform

Another important development of the period after 1870 was the emergence of the modern apartment house which appeared first in some of the older urban districts and had then spread rapidly into uptown areas. An apartment building differs from a tenement house in possessing more of the amenities needed for urban living. These early apartments, which were exclusively for the rich, often included parlors and quarters for the servants.

The first American apartment house, the Stuyvesant, was built on Eighteenth Street in New York City in 1869. It was designed by Richard Morris Hunt, a leading American architect, who drew many of his ideas from the apartment houses that he had seen while studying in France. Apartments were known for a time as "French flats," not only because of their origins and popularity in France, but also because housing more than one family under a single roof struck many as subversive of morality and as somehow un-American. Nevertheless, by the 1880s many apartment houses were being constructed in New York and Chicago, signaling, as Mayer and Wade have put it, "a more intensive use of land and acceptance of a new kind of urban living."[19]

The suburbs and the better central city neighborhoods remained, of course, beyond the reach of the poor, the black, and the great majority of recently arrived migrants who, as in the past, could only afford the cheapest housing which was usually crowded, unhealthy, and located in deteriorating neighborhoods. Wherever level land was abundant and cheap, notably in the newer cities of the South and West, virtually every family, no matter how poor, dwelt by itself in a rented wooden house or cottage. Even in such important metropolitan centers as Milwaukee, Detroit, and Cleveland, around 1910, more than 95 percent of the working class families were residing in such cottages, which usually had neither cellars nor bathtubs and were heated only by coal stoves.

By 1900, most of the nation's leading cities had slum or tenement districts. In St. Louis and Chicago, the poorer working class families were housed in very cramped cottages on narrow lots or in two- or three-story wooden flats, holding from two to six families. In Philadelphia and Baltimore, one- and two-story row houses were still being built, but in the black and immigrant districts, there were now two or more families on each floor.

In New York, which had the worst slums of any American city, builders after 1880 had supplanted the old barrack type of design with a new type of tenement which was called the dumbbell because it was narrower at the center than at the front or back. On either side, there was an indentation of two and one half feet so that when two such buildings were placed together, there was a five-foot-wide airshaft between them. Hailed at first by reformers as a significant stride toward better housing for the poor, the dumbbell was also popular with landlords as it permitted them to crowd more people than ever before onto a standard housing lot of 25 by 100 feet. These buildings were generally constructed to five or six stories, with four cramped apartments on each floor.

The tenement districts suffered greatly from overcrowding. By 1900, there were 90,000 tenement buildings in New York City, and the Jewish quarter on the city's Lower East Side had become the most crowded of all urban districts outside of the Orient. The working class districts of other cities were also becoming more crowded as additional cottages were constructed on lots that already contained housing, and the existing tenement houses were subdivided to provide more but smaller apartments. Adding to the congestion was the practice followed by many already overcrowded families of permitting friends and relatives to lodge with them.

Most of the working class dwellings of this era were neither comfortable nor healthy. In the dumbbell tenements, only one room in each apartment had direct access to the air and sunlight of the street or rear courtyard. The remainder, including many of the rooms in which people slept, obtained their only ventilation and natural light from the airshaft, with the result that sunlight seldom penetrated to the bedrooms of the apartments on the lower floors. Poor urban families of this period often had to share the same toilet facilities, and bathtubs remained a luxury until after World War I. In 1904, the Housing Problem Committee of the Cleveland Chamber of Commerce reported instances of eight slum families sharing a single toilet and claimed that 99 percent of the people in the tenement districts visited by the members of the committee were "absolutely without respectable provision for bathing purposes."[20]

By the late nineteenth century, urban housing problems had come increasingly to the attention of reform activists and the public at large. At that time model tenements had been constructed in various cities by philanthropic reformers like New York's Alfred T. White. Under the banner of "philanthropy plus five percent," these idealists attempted to demonstrate, sometimes with success, that with effective management, the construction and rental of clean and comfortable dwellings for the working class could be made to yield a reasonable profit.

Another approach to the tenement house problem was to regulate such buildings by law. From time to time, the housing codes of various cities had been added to and strengthened in order to attack those conditions in the tenements that seemed to endanger the health and safety of the community. Despite the adoption of measures in various cities that required improved ventilation and indoor privies in the tenements, the slum problem seemed only to get worse. Since 1867, New York City had passed many housing ordinances. Yet, according to the Tenement House Commission of 1900, the city's housing situation was worse than it had been in 1850.

In 1901, due in part to the crusading journalism of Jacob Riis and to the work of Robert De Forrest and Lawrence Veiller, chairman and secretary, respectively, of the Tenement House Commission, the New York State legislature enacted the nation's first truly comprehensive housing law. This measure set minimum requirements for every tenement building that would thereafter be constructed in the cities of New York, Rochester, and Buffalo and also required that certain standards be met in the existing tenement buildings. The new law required that much more space be left between buildings than the five-foot-wide airshaft allowed for in dumbbell tenements. It further specified that in both new and existing tenements, every room was to have direct access to outside air. In both new and old buildings, each apartment was to have access to a fire escape, and of the new structures, those above five stories were to be completely fireproof, while those of five stories or less were to have fireproof staircases. Finally, this measure also provided that every apartment in the new buildings must have its own water closet and its own sink with running water.

In the ensuing decade, comprehensive housing laws, in many cases modeled after that of New York, were adopted in several other eastern states as well as in the cities of Chicago, Boston, Cleveland, San Francisco, and Baltimore. Paradoxically, such measures, by adding to the cost of tenement construction, may have made it more difficult for the poor to obtain housing at rents they could afford. On the other hand, the quality of urban housing was sometimes improved by such laws. Thus, from 1909 to 1914 in the borough of Brooklyn, the number of windowless rooms was cut from 60,000 to about 500.

Other Environmental Safeguards

The prevention and control of destructive fires remained a basic urban problem. The nation's annual dollar loss from this source had doubled between 1878 and 1892. Thereafter the annual totals had fluctuated, but the figure for 1920 had been nearly twice as high as that for 1915. It is undeniable, however, that these losses would have been far worse had it not been for basic improvements in the methods used to fight and to prevent fires. Fire departments were becoming more professional and had ever more sophisticated equipment at their disposal, such as the mechanical ladder truck and the alarm telegraph. Moreover, the increasing use in building of such fire-resistant materials as steel and concrete and the growing strictness after 1900 of urban building codes had served to mitigate the problem.

Gains were also made in dealing with other aspects of the urban environment. When telegraph and utility wires had been strung overhead in such profusion that they had threatened in certain parts of the city to turn day into twilight, several of the larger municipalities, starting with New York in the 1880s, had begun to place their wiring underground. In 1880, the great majority of urban streets were so poorly paved that they would turn to mud whenever it rained. (See Figure 6.5.) By 1900, some headway had been made. Washington and Buffalo were regarded by the experts as the best paved cities in the world, and Boston and New York were not far behind. Though far from universally applied, such durable substances as brick, macadam, and asphalt had come into increasing use after 1900. "Street paving," noted political scientist Charles Zueblin in 1916, "has advanced more in twenty years than it did in [the previous] twenty hundred."[21]

Harder pavements had greatly improved the chances of keeping the streets of the cities clean. Where, prior to 1895, the cleaning of the streets had been left to private enterprise in virtually all of the cities, the trend thereafter was to make it in large part a governmental responsibility. It was in that year that Colonel George E. Waring, a noted sanitary engi-

CONTINUING PATTERNS OF COMMUNITY DEVELOPMENT 201

neer, was appointed Commissioner of Street Cleaning in New York City in the reform administration of Mayor William Strong. Under Waring, the city was cleaned as never before. He established a 2,500-man "army" of sweepers whom he organized in brigades and dressed in white uniforms, from which their collective nickname, "White Wings", was derived. Waring did everything possible to attract the notice of New

Figure 6.5 An unpaved and garbage-littered street in New York's Fourth Ward in 1881.

Yorkers, even enlisting the aid of the city's schoolchildren in keeping the city clean. Waring actually gave New Yorkers clean streets, an accomplishment that left contemporaries aghast and led to the emulation of his quasi-military system by other cities.

Another program that had an important bearing on the health and well-being of urban residents in many cities was the construction of growing numbers of parks and playgrounds. As of 1870, there were only three well-developed parks in America, but by the century's close, virtually every major city had at least one. After 1890, park acreage in many cities had been greatly increased. Boston and Chicago, for example, had developed notable systems in which the major parks were linked with residential areas by broad, tree-lined boulevards. After 1900, in several cities, including Kansas City and Cleveland, parks commissions had functioned as planning agencies and had attempted to assure that parts of the land in the as-yet uncrowded portions of these cities would be maintained as "breathing spaces" in which urban residents could take refuge from the congestion and hubbub of the city.

The first public playground was established in Boston in 1898, and thereafter much municipal parkland was utilized for this purpose. In 1906, the Playground Association of America was organized, and by 1910, 150 cities had public playgrounds. Within five years this figure had almost tripled.

Although by 1880 a number of cities had permanent boards of health with considerable power, sanitary arrangements even in these cities were still woefully inadequate. By 1875, more than 100 cities had sanitary sewers, but in most of them, the sewage was still poured into the nearest body of water. By 1880 there were waterworks systems in 600 cities, yet many urban residences were still without sanitary bathrooms and running water, particularly in the tenement districts of the big cities. As a result, the death rate in America's major cities had declined only slightly, if at all, from the peak mortality rate of the 1850s.

The acceptance of the germ theory of disease in American medical circles during the late 1880s gave added impetus to the various drives to extend and improve urban systems of water supply and waste disposal. From 1880 to 1910, the number of waterworks had increased from 600 to nearly 5,000, about three fifths of them municipally owned. In 1880, water filtration programs existed in only a handful of cities and on a very small scale, reaching little more than 1 percent of the urban public, but by 1914, these programs had grown so much that 40 percent of the nation's urban residents were drinking filtered water.

The new science of bacteriology had made it abundantly clear that the proper handling and disposal of human wastes was absolutely critical to the prevention of typhoid and other devastating diseases. Such considerations speeded the construction and expansion of sewers in American cities. Thus, in the first decade of the twentieth century, New Orleans and Baltimore had built sanitary sewers, while New York and Chicago were each extending their sewer systems to a length of 2,000 miles.

Public Health and Welfare

Between 1880 and 1920, there was a huge increase in the size and scope of the public health programs in America's cities. According to urban historians Charles Glaab and A. Theodore Brown, between 1900 and 1907, there was a 600 percent increase in spending on public health by cities with over 50,000 people.[22] The National Association for Public Health, which had been founded in 1872, contributed to the trend by coordinating and mobilizing the nation's public health professionals. The new awareness of the bacterial sources of many diseases had also lent encouragement to the movement to sanitize the cities and had helped to gain public support for such coercive measures as the compulsory vaccination of schoolchildren and the new laws requiring commercial dairies to pasteurize their milk. Public health, remarked Charles Beard, had become "the gateway to revolutionary change."[23] The sheer size and complexity of urban health problems in an industrial society had served to increase the discretionary powers of health officials who, in order to protect the public, were often granted, or had assumed, the authority to close restaurants they regarded as unsanitary and to order demolished the buildings they considered unsafe.

The public was also provided in this period with many new medical facilities and programs. The number of hospitals had multiplied twentyfold between 1860 and 1910. While most of this increase had been in the private and charitable sectors, there were also 164 municipal hospitals and 574 public dispensaries by 1910. By that year, the visiting nurse system that had been pioneered by Lillian Wald at New York's Henry Street Settlement had been widely adopted by municipal governments. By the 1900s, nurses and even doctors were increasingly employed by urban school systems. In 1914, more than 750 public school systems had programs of some sort for the medical inspection of their pupils. By then, too, dental clinics for children, most of them conducted free of charge, existed in over 130 cities; and at least 33 municipalities were maintaining their own psychological clinics.

As a result of these and other improvements, the death rates in American cities had declined. Between 1865 and 1889, the combined average mortality rate for New York, Philadelphia, Boston, and New Orleans had stood at 25.7 per 1,000, but in the quarter century that followed, the combined annual average for mortality in the same four cities was only 18.7 per 1,000. Infant mortality also declined. In New York City, for example, deaths among babies less than a year old had gone from over one in four in 1885 to fewer than one out of every ten by 1915.

The Drive to Combat Poverty

The well-being of the cities in this era was also threatened by the problem of poverty which, despite the gains scored by many individuals and families, was more severe than ever. In addition to the growing population of those, like the elderly and the disabled, who were simply unable to provide for themselves, there were in all the large cities hundreds and even thousands of transients and vagrants who frequented the dives and hangouts of the most run-down districts. In addition, there were the hundreds of thousands of unskilled workers who, while usually hard-working and able-bodied, earned too little to do much more than barely survive. Unable to accumulate much in savings, they were left destitute by any prolonged period of unemployment or ill health. Virtually all unskilled workers, according to the writer Robert Hunter, hovered near the poverty line, and were pushed onto the charity rolls by any personal setback.[24]

Every economic downturn put hundreds of thousands out of work. Thus, a Department of Labor survey of fifteen cities in the spring of 1915 revealed that about 12 percent of their wage-earning populations were unemployed and another 16 percent were working part-time. Even in prosperous times, many unskilled workers were unemployed in the winter months and would, of necessity, move with their families to the local almshouse. "Unemployment," wrote political scientist William B. Munro, in 1916, "runs up and down like the temperature of a New England autumn."[25]

In addition, many a working class family was forced into dependence upon charity by the death or disability of its breadwinner, often as the result of industrial accident. In 1913, for example, there were over one million such accidents and more than 25,000 fatalities.

As always, growing poverty fostered vice and crime. In New York City below 14th Street, there were as of 1890 nearly forty saloons for every church. Of the nation's eighteen largest cities in 1880, not one had fewer than 100 brothels. By the early 1900s the surreptitious traffic in prostitution, gambling, and drugs was becoming increasingly profitable and well organized. In Chicago around 1910, the profits from organized vice and "white slavery" were estimated at $15 million per year.

In spite of the fact that police departments in the cities were generally growing much faster than their populations, law and order seemed to many city dwellers to be perpetually on the verge of breaking down. Historians are uncertain about whether urban crime rates rose after 1870, but, with the vast increase in the population of urban areas, we can at least be sure that the *number* of crimes committed in them *did* increase. Then, as now, moreover, the United States had a far higher rate of crime than any European country. As in the antebellum era, hoodlums and criminals abounded in the larger cities, but they were now more numerous, better organized, and, in some instances, more professional. Juvenile delinquency was rampant, especially among the children of slum dwellers and immigrants. While less common than in the preceding period, violent clashes between ethnic groups still occurred occasionally, as in the anti-Italian riots in New Orleans in 1891 and the anti-Chinese outbreaks in San Francisco in the 1870s. Finally, a good many labor disputes after 1870 were accompanied by riots, looting, and sabotage, causing many middle and upper class people to view the working classes as a standing menace to civilization. (See Figure 6.6)

The magnitude of urban social problems had contributed to a growing sense of social crisis and had helped to generate

Figure 6.6 In the great railroad strike of 1877, violence broke out in several cities, among them Pittsburgh where the looting and burning of a railroad car is shown here. From *The History of the Great Riots* by E. W. Martin.

the extraordinary expansion of charitable and reformist activity of the late nineteenth and early twentieth centuries. As early as 1878, Philadelphia had over 800 charitable and benevolent institutions, and in 1891, New York City had nearly 700 such organizations, excluding those that were of a religious character. In a book published in 1883, Professor William Graham Sumner of Yale, a leading proponent of *laissez-faire* observed with annoyance that there seemed to be "an unlimited supply of reformers, philanthropists, humanitarians, and would-be managers of society in general."[26]

The sheer size and diversity of charitable activity in this era led many to suspect that private benevolence and public assistance were being abused, were encouraging pauperism, and were, in general, doing society more harm than good. In 1877, a permanent, citywide organization was founded in Buffalo for the purpose of organizing and integrating the work performed by that city's charitable organizations. This body, which was known as the Charity Organization Society, had been modeled after a similar institution in London, and was, in turn, quickly imitated in other American cities. Charity Organization Societies existed in 25 cities by 1883, and in 138 cities by 1900.

In order to prevent duplication and waste, each COS maintained a central registry in which were kept the case histories of all who had ever received or even applied for assistance from charitable organizations in that city. The ultimate goal of such activity was, in the words of the New York branch, "to lift the poor above want by helping them to help themselves."[27] In their determination to discourage pauperism, they extended assistance only to those whom they judged worthy of help. Able-bodied men who sought charity were frequently required to prove their sincerity by chopping wood in the wood yard maintained for the purpose. Initially, the COS had regarded the moral failings of the poor as the true source of their poverty, but by the early twentieth century, they were placing most of the blame upon social conditions. Social work historian Robert Bremner attributes this change of heart to the organization's narrowly factual case-history approach which, he maintains resulted in a more objective assessment of the causes of failure and want.[28]

Where the Charity Organization Society sought to aid individuals and families, the settlement house movement, which had emerged in the 1880s, attempted to improve conditions in entire neighborhoods. The settlements consisted of idealistic young college graduates living as a group in a slum district where they tried to be of service to the residents of the area.

The settlement idea, like so many social innovations, had developed initially in England, beginning with London's Toynbee Hall in 1883. In 1887, Stanton Coit, who in the previous year had resided briefly at Toynbee Hall, established the first American settlement, the Neighborhood Guild, on New York's Lower East Side. Two years later, in Chicago,

Jane Addams, a recent graduate of an Illinois seminary, established Hull-House, the most celebrated of all the settlements. By 1900, according to Blake McKelvey, there were more than 100 settlements, with nearly 500 staff members and housing about 700 residents.[29]

In trying to bridge the gap between the lower classes and the rest of society, they supplied their neighborhoods with a variety of services. Through lectures and classes on such subjects as domestic science and civics, settlement workers attempted to impart practical skills and middle class values to the poor and the immigrants. They were particularly active in fostering clubs of all sorts and supplied them with space for their meetings. Settlements also pioneered by creating such programs as workrooms for the unemployed, free nursing programs for the poor, and the provision of free bathhouses. Frequently, these and other programs that had originated in the settlements were undertaken later by the municipality on a citywide basis.

Finally, settlements also functioned, in the words of Jacob Riis, "as fulcrums for the lever of reform."[30] Their staff members and residents gathered much useful data and produced many informative articles and books. They agitated in their communities for more and better public services and contributed significantly to such national reform movements as the drive against child labor.

WELFARE MEASURES—PUBLIC AND PRIVATE

After 1880, growing numbers of Protestant ministers became deeply involved with urban social problems. By that time, many churches had followed their upper and middle class members into new and "better" neighborhoods, thereby abandoning the congested working class districts. Some of the remaining ministers in the poorer areas, aroused by the indifference to the church of many working class Protestants and by the unchecked vice and crime in these neighborhoods, sought to win over the local Protestants by transforming their houses of worship into institutional churches. These supplied their congregants with a number of free services, including lectures, reading rooms, kindergartens, and homes for the needy.

There emerged in these years a theology known as the Social Gospel which stressed the responsibility of Christians, and of all good men, for the well-being, material as well as spiritual, of their fellow men. In seeking to bridge the gulf between urban workingmen and the churches, Social Gospel ministers, such as Washington Gladden of Columbus, Ohio, and Walter Rauschenbush of Rochester, New York, combined the institutional church with the advocacy of the rights of labor.

Where the Social Gospel diverged most fundamentally from such previous forms of Protestant social action as the YMCA (1851) and the Salvation Army (imported from England in 1879) was in its insistence that virtue could only flourish if social conditions were favorable. They therefore called for the rejection of the Social Darwinist philosophy of unbridled competition and for the reconstruction of society to allow for greater cooperation and a measure of collectivism.

The Roman Catholic churches and Jewish synagogues had always in a sense been "institutional," in providing a wide range of services within their respective communities. Not until the 1890s, however, did the Roman Catholic Church participate significantly in movements for social reform. By the early 1900s, most Catholics appear to have favored temperance legislation and protective labor legislation, especially the minimum wage. Many Jews were also participating actively in movements for social reform. Rabbis of the Reform persuasion, like New York's Stephen Wise, became pillars of the liberal community and leading advocates of reformist and welfare measures.

Like private philanthropy and the churches, municipal governments had also become increasingly active in the field of social welfare. "The new era in public charity," wrote Charles Zueblin in 1916, "is marked by the extension of welfare work beyond the former dreams of charity workers!"[31] Beginning with Kansas City in 1908, departments of public welfare were established in a number of cities for the purpose of coordinating their social service functions with those of the private sector. Many city governments, especially those with "progressive" administrations, now supplied their residents with day nurseries for working mothers, lodging houses for the destitute, bathhouses, employment agencies, and municipal stores. Finally, in many cities concerts, dances, and other forms of amusement were furnished by the municipality, for which little or nothing was charged.

These local measures were supplemented by the new social legislation adopted by the states. By 1914, labor below a minimum age, generally fourteen, had been prohibited in every state but one, and children were also excluded in many states from night work and dangerous occupations. By 1917, there were minimum wage laws for women in thirty-nine states, and twenty of the states were providing pensions for widowed mothers. As of 1917, Workmen's Compensation laws had been adopted in forty states, providing in general that employers must purchase insurance against injury to their workmen and that an injured employee was to be compensated in proportion to the seriousness of his injury.

After 1900 there was a notable quickening of the pace of reform in virtually every aspect of municipal affairs. The areas of public health and social reform were increasingly characterized after 1900 by professionalism and specialization as well as by a growing willingness to deal with urban problems through governmental action. In each problem area there had emerged by 1910, a nationwide association of professionals in the field. These included the National Housing Association, the American Association for Labor Legislation, the Committee of 100 on National Health, and the National Child Labor Committee. Each of these organizations served as a clearing house for new ideas and represented its particular membership before governmental bodies.

These trends have been linked by historians with the emergence of a new middle class who, it is argued, had sought through such activities to win the adoption of their reforms and to add to their own status and power. "The heart of progressivism," writes historian Robert Wiebe, "was the ambition of the middle class to fulfill its destiny through bureaucratic means."[32]

Public Education

Of all the social programs in urban areas, it was the public schools that were the most ambitious and comprehensive. After 1870, the school year was lengthened and the proportion of school-age children who were enrolled had increased. As urban schools became larger and more elaborate, their pupils were classified by grade on the basis of age.

Urban school systems were greatly extended in these years. Over the entire period from 1890 to 1918, public high schools were constructed in the United States at the rate of more than one per day. By 1910, there were over 10,000, with a total student population of more than a million and a half. In 1873, the public school system of St. Louis, under the leadership of School Superintendent William T. Harris, became the first in the nation to establish kindergartens. By the early 1900s this innovation had become established in urban areas throughout most of the nation.

By the 1890s the traditional methods and curricula of the schools were beginning to change. Certain schools were already placing less emphasis upon the study of the classics while adding to courses in such areas as American history, the sciences, and civics. Finally, various high schools were starting to supplement their academic offerings with vocational training and domestic science.

These trends had all accelerated in the early decades of the twentieth century as critics from many quarters joined forces to demand that the schools become more practical, more useful, and less remote from everyday life. The emerging movement for progressive education assailed traditional forms of instruction, not only for their almost entirely academic content, but also because of their emphasis on memorization and rote-learning.

According to John Dewey, a professor of philosophy at Columbia from 1904 to 1930 and the leading theorist of progressive education, the proper function of the schools in the twentieth century was to promote the "social efficiency" of their pupils. This could best be done, he maintained, by helping students acquire not merely academic skills but also technical ones. More than this, Dewey wanted the schools to enable the student to acquire the practical knowledge of how things work that, prior to the rise of the factory and the city, had been imparted by the home, the farm, and the shop. The schools should, he wrote, draw closer to life by becoming "active with occupations that reflect the life of the larger society and permeated throughout with the spirit of art, history, and science."[33] Due in part to Dewey's influence, the trends in public education toward vocational training and a less mechanical approach to learning would continue to gather force.

Ethnic Organizations and Divisions

Despite the rapid extension of municipal services, the all-encompassing community envisaged by socialists and by such progressives as Dewey found few supporters. Instead,

American city dwellers had continued to seek companionship and solutions to their problems in private organizations which now proliferated more rapidly than in the past. For many, perhaps most, city dwellers, the extraordinary mobility of American urban life had deprived traditional institutions and neighborhood relationships of much of their meaning. As a result, the purely voluntary forms of group life, those which are based solely on individual preference, now took on added significance. A man could be a Republican or a member of the Elks Club, regardless of whether he lived in Cincinnati or Los Angeles. Many new social clubs were now organized, ranging from upper class athletic clubs and ancestor-worshipping fraternities, like the Sons and Daughters of the American Revolution, to the lodges and fraternal orders favored by the masses.

Lodges such as the Masons and Odd Fellows were primarily social in purpose, while fraternal orders like the Woodmen and Maccabbees were established to supply insurance to the membership. Eventually, this distinction became blurred as organizations of each type took on some of the functions of the other. As of 1905, the lodges and mutual aid societies are believed to have had over five million members, and by 1920, they had twice that figure, the great majority belonging to their urban branches. Many clergymen were suspicious of these organizations, which were often secretive about their meetings and seemed to attract many who had either ceased to belong to churches or who were attending only rarely.

Social clubs of this era tended to be segregated according to class, race, ethnic group, and, to a lesser degree, by sex. Most men of immigrant stock belonged solely to the clubs of their national group. Particularly rigid were the rules against black membership in the clubs and lodges that had been established by whites. Black men and women responded by creating lodges of their own, including several, such as the Negro Masons, which were the exact counterparts of lodges in the white world. Although women figured as auxiliary participants in male-dominated lodges and clubs, they were also establishing organizations of their own. By 1900, the Federation of Women's Clubs, which was to play a large role in the reform movements of the day, had 100,000 members; by 1914, it had over a million.

The increasingly diverse character of the immigrant population and the growing importance of private organizations in social life were reflected in the amazing number and variety of the foreign-speaking lodges and social clubs. As in the past, such organizations were based originally on the village and regional origins of their members, but as they became increasingly conscious of belonging to a "national" group, many of these clubs and mutual aid societies joined forces on the basis of a common "nationality," both within particular cities and throughout the United States. "I never realized I was an Albanian," said one immigrant, "until my brother came home from America in 1909. He belonged to an Albanian society over here."[34]

As of 1905, both the Polish National Alliance and the Sons of Italy had more than 100,000 members who were scattered through many cities and states. In many instances, the foreign-born also developed their own financial institutions, as there was usually no one in American banks who could speak their language or knew their problems. To cite one example, by 1915, there were 227 building-and-loan associations for Czech immigrants.

The influx of migrants and immigrants brought more linguistic and cultural diversity to American cities than ever before. According to Bayrd Still, a historian of Milwaukee, the German influence in that city resulted in some public buildings reminiscent of Strasbourg and Nuremberg.[35] Virtually every foreign-speaking element had its own newspapers, which sought to help their readers adapt to American life; some attained sizable circulations. Perhaps the most striking of all such publications was the *Jewish Daily Forward* in New York City, which, under the tough-minded editorship of Abraham Cahan, had at its peak in 1916 a circulation of over 200,000. The *Forward* combined American style sensationalism and stories on Jewish life in both the old country and the new, with educational material of a high order. Finally, most immigrant groups had their own entertainers and theatrical groups.

As the members of a given ethnic group became more assimilated and successful and moved ever farther from their old neighborhoods, their special institutions would disintegrate. Thus, after 1900, the Ancient Order of Hibernians, the leading Irish fraternal order, went rapidly into a decline. By this time too, the upper and middle class elements in the German community of many cities were more active in American organizations than they were in German ones. As their institutions decayed, all that remained to mark off a particular ethnic group from other white Americans was its lingering sense of group identity and the continuing tendency of many in the group to form new ethnic concentrations by residing near one another.

As a result of the large-scale migrations from eastern Europe and Italy, eastern Catholics and Orthodox Jews became numerically significant in American cities for the first time. Most of the newcomers, however, were Roman Catholics, and they demanded priests of their nationality and churches of their own. After meeting with some initial resistance, these demands were generally conceded by the hierarchy in America. In so doing, the Church was acting in accordance with the pluralist patterns of American society. In all four of the major faiths, people of diverse ethnic backgrounds, who often differed significantly in social and religious outlook, were learning to draw together on matters of common concern and were beginning to form a common culture. Through such interactions, but especially through intermarriage, contend sociologists like Will Herberg, ethnic identifications were gradually absorbed within a wider religious identity.[36]

Among the more assimilated members produced by the various ethnic communities there were, typically, several who, in retaining some of their ties to the group, came to function as links between it and the wider American world. Professionals of foreign stock, who derived much of their clientele from their own group, often performed this function as did the foreign-speaking labor leaders and politicians who, as organizers of, and liaisons to, the foreign-born, became useful to such American entities as the American Federation of Labor and Tammany Hall. In turn, their prestige within their communities permitted these go-betweens to exert a measure of influence over politics and public affairs.

In spite of the efforts of ethnic community leaders, mistrust of the foreign-born deepened in the early decades of the twentieth century. Immigration totals now soared to record levels, averaging more than a million per year over the entire decade from 1905 to 1914, more than four fifths of it from southern and eastern Europe. In the wake of this influx, many localities inaugurated large-scale programs of Americanization which called upon immigrants to forsake their old ways and adopt forthwith all aspects of the "American way of life."

In 1907, Congress appointed the Dillingham Commission to investigate all facets of the immigration question. In its final report, the Commission declared, and purported to "scientifically" prove, that newcomers from southern and eastern Europe were, in virtually every respect, "inferior" to the northern and western Europeans who had formerly comprised the great majority of immigrants. The "new" immigrants were said to be less skilled and literate, and more prone to poor health, indigency, radicalism, and crime. It is now well established that the commission's methodology was faulty and that it unconsciously manipulated its data so as to arrive at preconceived conclusions.[37]

The reserved attitude that many immigrants initially had toward America's involvement in the First World War reinforced the tendency among old-stock Americans to regard the foreign-born as of doubtful loyalty and dangerously prone to radicalism. As a result, the programs of Americanization that had been developed in the early 1900s were greatly expanded. The public's fear of the foreigner and of radicalism was intensified by the Bolshevik Revolution in Russia in November, 1917, and by the postwar militancy of organized labor. In many cities, there were antiradical riots, and the civil liberties of socialists and other radicals were severely curbed.

Though the Red Scare was largely over by the end of 1920, the movement to restrict immigration continued to gather strength. The quota system adopted by Congress in 1921 was insufficiently restrictive to satisfy the foes of immigration. Three years later, the restrictionist movement reached its climax with the adoption by Congress of the National Origins Act. This law set an annual limit of 150,000 on all immigration from outside the Western Hemisphere. Another of its provisions set yearly immigration quotas for each European nation on the basis of its estimated proportion of the nation's white population in 1920, thereby reducing immigration from Southern and eastern Europe to a virtual trickle. The law also excluded virtually all Orientals from emigrating to the United States.

As we have seen, the urban populations of this era were divided by color, ethnic group, religion, and social class. What cohesion there was among them came from their common involvement with the city and with the local and national systems of political and economic life. The remarkable geographic and social mobility of the period was accompanied by the unprecedentedly rapid proliferation of social and civic clubs and by the emergence of a powerful trade union movement. The socialist ideal of a comprehensive community based on complete social equality mustered little support. In America's cities, as in the nation generally, the "common good" would be sought not in the main through sweeping government programs but by piecemeal and gradualist activity in both the public and private sectors.

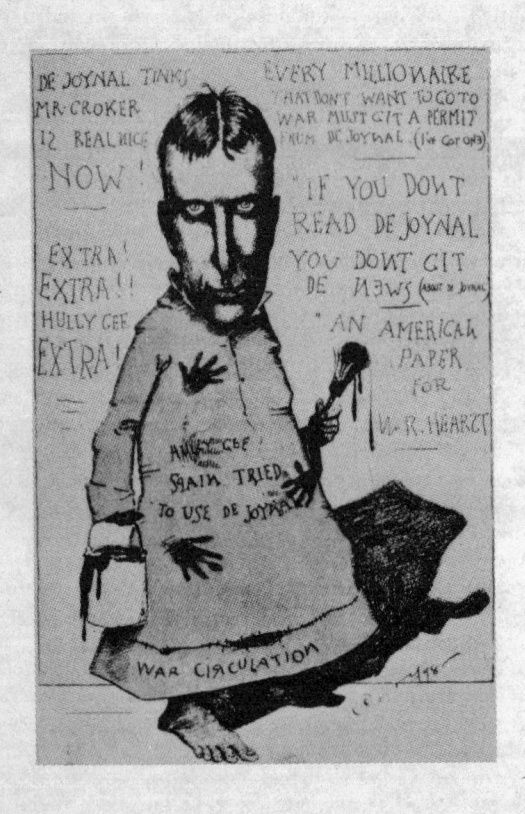

Figure 6.7 The influence of newspapers on the urban masses increased greatly after 1880. Publishers like William Randolph Hearst, caricatured here, built huge circulations in a number of cities by resorting to sensationalistic techniques that came to be known as "yellow journalism."

7

A Taste of Reform

"I did not know much about municipal government in those days . . ." reminisced progressive reformer Brand Whitlock, in commenting on his attitude in the early 1890s. "But the fact that we knew nothing about it in those days," he added, "was not unusual; nobody knew much about it except that Mr. James Bryce had said that it was the most conspicuous failure of the American Commonwealth, and we quoted this observation so often that one might have supposed we were proud of this distinction."[1] By the end of the decade, Whitlock's interests and commitments had changed, and he became immersed in urban reform. He served as an adviser to Samuel M. "Golden Rule" Jones, the reform Democratic mayor of Toledo, made use of his legal training by helping to win a major lawsuit restoring Toledo's police to the mayor's control, and went on to serve four terms as mayor following the death of Jones in 1904.

The Progressive Era

Whitlock's eventual concern for urban politics was by no means unique, as scores of citizens from all over the country joined in the battle for municipal reform. This quest for municipal reform was part of the Progressive period in American history, lasting from approximately 1901 to 1917, in which a concerted effort was made on the national, state, and local levels to improve the structure of the government, abolish corruption, and end the abuses of special privilege on the part of the business community. What was distinctive about municipal progressivism was that it antedated both state and national progressivism, and that it represented the largest-scale movement for urban reform in the history of the United States.

The motivations that led citizens like Whitlock to turn their focus to city politics were varied as well as obvious in terms of the pervasiveness of the corruption on the municipal scene. A substantial number of progressives were upper and middle class Protestants who came from a professional or business background. They were shocked by the dishonesty associated with boss rule and disturbed at what appeared to them to be the emergence of a new breed of urban politician. Some progressives also were products of what Richard Hofstadter has suggested was the Yankee Protestant tradition, which implied that politics should be run on the basis of disinterested activity and not on the personal and material terms practiced by the machines. Other reformers could be classified as the zealous optimists depicted by Arthur Mann in his study of social reform in Boston during the last two decades of the nineteenth century. Their civic consciousness was aroused by the urban conditions they deemed to be detrimental to their society, and they had faith in the ability of society to right itself. The businessmen in the progressive ranks, many of whom came from the managerial class that started to emerge during the late nineteenth century, may have sought, as Robert H. Wiebe and Samuel P. Hays have indicated, to make the city efficient via a network of institutional changes, and were less concerned about questions of municipal purity. The working classes, while not in the forefront of the movement, supported many of the reforms enacted during the period, and were regarded by J. Joseph Huthmacher as playing a significant role in the enactment of progressive legislation. As a result, municipal progressivism can be viewed as a movement that accommodated an amalgam of interests.[2]

State Commissions and Civic Organizations for Reform

The first concerted attempts at American municipal reform began in the early 1870s. Much of the impetus for this interest came from the Tweed Ring scandals, which prompted political leaders to give serious consideration to the conduct of city affairs. This civic awakening was sporadic and its accomplishments were limited, but it generated a mood in the country that was sympathetic to reform. It also helped lead to the creation by state authorities of investigative committees to study municipal administration.

Among the more notable of these state commissions was the ten-member Tilden Commission of New York, set up by Governor Samuel J. Tilden in 1876. It was headed by William M. Evarts, and its members included several prominent attorneys, journalists, and civic leaders. In 1877, the Tilden Commission issued its report and called for the ratification of a series of constitutional amendments aimed at strengthening the framework of New York City's government. The most controversial part of the proposals was a section calling for the establishment of a new municipal body, the members of which were to be elected by the city's taxpayers. The argument behind it was that only citizens who paid property taxes had a direct stake in fiscal responsibility, while those who did not were prone to favor reckless spending schemes on the part of municipalities. Nevertheless, this section was deemed by its critics to be an attack on universal suffrage. The amendments were defeated in the state legislature in 1878, and the criticism of the section apparently served as a warning to those who were involved in this early stage of municipal reform. Whatever their misgivings about the ability of the non-propertied classes to participate in local government, reformers abandoned the idea of property qualifications for voting.

A further indication of the growing concern for municipal problems was the proliferation of civic organizations. In 1863, a group known as the Citizens' Association was established in New York under the leadership of Peter Cooper, who had achieved fame as the inventor of the first steam locomotive built in the United States. The Citizens' Association was made up predominantly of lawyers and merchants, and it supported the principle of nonpartisanship in municipal government. Although the formation of this association antedated the disclosures about the Tweed Ring, most of the leading civic organizations in New York and in other cities came into existence during the following decade as a result of the indignation over the corruption of Boss Tweed and his cohorts.

The New York Council of Political Reform was formed in 1871 and was dedicated to driving the Tweed Ring from power.* That same year, the Citizens' Municipal Reform Association was organized in Philadelphia. It worked to modify registry and election laws and to effect changes in the state constitution limiting the control of the legislature over the city. The Citizens' Association of Chicago was started by businessman Franklin MacVeagh in 1874. Its goals included arousing interest in municipal legislation and administration, promoting projects for reform, investigating the police department, keeping the public advised about civic problems, and calling attention to the needs of sanitation. Another Chicago organization, the Union League Club, was founded in 1879 and dealt with a variety of local problems, including municipal government.

Several of the newly created organizations focused only obliquely on the question of municipal government, and there were clubs that were chiefly interested in the general area of civic betterment. Anthony Comstock, an active member of the Young Men's Christian Association, founded the Society for the Suppression of Vice in 1873 in New York. Four years later, the Society for the Prevention of Crime was established in New York. The latter society received national attention in the 1890s when it became indirectly involved in politics. It was at this time that the Reverend Charles H. Parkhurst, its president, exposed the close ties that Tammy Hall had with organized crime. Among the other activities in which groups of citizens across the nation participated were drawing up tenement house ordinances, opening settlement houses, and drafting plans for parks. However, many individuals eventually started to blame the plight of the city on the inadequacy of the local government, particularly after Bryce's indictment of municipal government reminded them of the magnitude of the problem. In the words of one settlement house worker, "I never go into a tenement without longing for a better city government."[3]

By the 1880s and 1890s, the momentum for improving city government had increased, and by 1894 there were over eighty local reform organizations in existence. More than thirty groups had been formed in 1894 alone, including New York's

---

*The council was one of the many reform organizations that flourished in New York during the 1870s. It played an important role in the victory of anti-Tammany candidates in 1871, although Tweed survived the landslide and managed to be reelected to the state senate. The demise of Tammany was only temporary, however, and it came back to power within three years of its defeat.

Citizens' Union, which scrutinized legislation and recommended candidates for municipal office. The rapid growth of these organizations in the 1890s and their widespread efforts to end corruption in municipal government have prompted several historians and political scientists to pinpoint the decade as the "great era of reform," and the beginning of the "civic renaissance."[4]

The National Municipal League

In 1894, the Municipal League of Philadelphia and the City Club of New York took the lead in sponsoring the first nationwide meeting of local reformers—a group that was the forerunner of the National Municipal League. Its meeting was held in Philadelphia in January and was attended by 150 delegates and invited guests, many of whom were lawyers, journalists, clergymen, and government officials. Horace E. Deming, who made one of the speeches to the delegates, echoed the sentiments of many members of the audience when he referred to the urgency of the need for municipal reform. "The majority of the people of this country," he said, "will soon live in our cities. . . . If our cities are left impure, of what avail is a national government? We shall not have one very long. If we make our municipalities pure, the future of our institutions is assured."[5] At the conclusion of the conference, a resolution was passed calling for the establishment of a permanent league, and in May the National Municipal League was officially launched. Its first president was attorney James C. Carter, president of the City Club of New York, who had earlier served as a member of the Tilden Commission. By the following year, there were 180 branches of the league scattered in various sections of the country, and in 1896, over 80 more branches were founded.

Although the National Municipal League members were united in their belief that municipal government was corrupt, they—and reformers throughout the United States—were divided on how to tackle the problem. Some were of the opinion that the election of honest officials was all that was needed to improve conditions. Carl Schurz had told the delegates assembled at Philadelphia that "there is not a municipal government in this country, on whatever pattern organized, which will not work well when administered by honest, public-spirited, capable, and well-trained men. On the other hand, the best form of municipal government will work badly when administered by bunglers or knaves. . . ."[6] Other reformers disputed this reasoning and argued that the election of honest officials would be meaningless without the addition of structural changes in the framework of the government. There also was support for the sentiment expressed by *The Outlook* in 1894 after the Philadelphia conference had adjourned; the magazine observed that "the vigorous municipal spirit manifested made the conference an event of public importance. The only limitation to its usefulness was its failure to consider the social reform measures in which the working class organizations are concerned."[7] In view of the controversy, the league initially begged off formulating a definite program for reform.

In 1899, members of the National Municipal League adopted a municipal program, which is sometimes referred to as the first Model City Charter in the United States. Among the reforms advocated were home rule for cities; greater responsibility for the mayor; adoption of civil service; separation of city from state elections; secret ballot; and restrictions upon the unlimited duration of city franchises. The proposals were well received by municipal reform organizations, but the demands of the social reformers would have to await another forum.

Other Boosts to Urban Reform

The founding of organizations like the National Municipal League indicated a growing awareness of the need to understand the problems connected with the growth of the city in America—an awareness that was felt in scholarly and academic circles as well. In 1894, the University of Pennsylvania created the first American lectureship in municipal government. A number of textbooks on urban affairs were published during the course of the decade of the 1890s, and authors like Alfred R. Conkling, Thomas C. Devlin, Frank Goodnow, William H. Tolman, Adna F. Weber, and Delos F. Wilcox made significant contributions to the field. In 1900, the National Municipal League made a survey of the study of municipal government in colleges and universities and reported that out of 222 schools queried, 42 gave courses in the subject.

Another survey was made by the league in 1912. Replies from 172 institutions indicated that instruction in municipal government was being offered in 64 schools. By 1916, the number had increased to 95. Among the educators who offered pioneer work in the study of American government were Andrew D. White at Cornell; Woodrow Wilson at Princeton; Theodore D. Woolsey at Yale; A. Lawrence Lowell at Harvard; and Edmund H. James at the University of Pennsylvania.

In addition to studies being undertaken by colleges and universities, research in municipal affairs was encouraged with the founding of the Bureau of Municipal Research in 1906 in New York. It was the first such bureau to be established in the United States. Within a decade, similar bureaus were set up in other cities throughout the country. These bureaus were privately financed and focused much of their research on the problems of finance and administration.

The reform movement also was given a forward thrust by the appearance in 1904 of *The Shame of the Cities* by Lincoln Steffens. Steffens's articles had appeared initially in *McClure's Magazine,* a publication founded by S. S. McClure in 1893. It was a leading periodical in the field of muckraking, or protest, journalism. The muckrakers concerned themselves with exposing corruption in political life, and, quite naturally, some of their interest turned toward the cities. In 1901, three leading muckraking journals ran exposés on misconduct in New York politics. *McClure's Magazine* ran a three-part series, beginning in April, on the connection between the New York police and criminal elements in the city, and the November issues of *Cosmopolitan* and *Everybody's Magazine* featured stories about graft in New York politics.

Steffens began his famed articles in October, 1902. Earlier, when he first had been given the assignment, he told his friend Brand Whitlock that "I'm going to do a series of articles for the magazine on municipal government." When Whitlock asked: "And what do you know about municipal government?" Steffens replied, "Nothing. That's why I'm going to write about it."[8] Steffens learned quickly; his travels took him to several cities, notably St. Louis, Cleveland, New York, Chicago, Philadelphia, and Pittsburgh. The gloomy picture he presented of the extent of graft and corruption created a topic for discussion and aroused considerable interest in his stories. Ironically, James Bryce, who had helped to set so much of the protest in motion, regarded Steffens's book with "mingled feelings of admiration for the vigor and directness with which he tells his story and of regret to have such a story told."[9] The American public, on the other hand, seemingly took Steffens to heart. In the aftermath of the 1905 victories for reform candidates, Joseph W. Folk, the newly elected governor of Missouri, wrote to Steffens: "You started the revolution."[10]

The Success of Municipal Progressivism

The "revolution" had actually been in existence for many years prior to the appearance of *The Shame of the Cities*, as various civic organizations and reform clubs had mobilized their forces to lead an attack against boss rule in American city government. As a result, many of the nation's largest cities had experienced a sweeping wave of reform. Boston's reform mayor, Edwin U. Curtis, was elected in 1894. Following his victory, he named a board of commissioners to supervise the electric railway system, initiated changes in the financing of the public schools, and placed each city department under a commission. In New York, Republican William L. Strong was elected mayor in 1894 on a reformist slate with bipartisan support. Strong was a firm advocate of civil service reform, and two of his appointees, Street Commissioner George E. Waring, Jr., and Police Commissioner Theodore Roosevelt, revitalized their departments and made significant improvements in the areas of health and public safety. James D. Phelan was elected mayor of San Francisco in 1897, and pledged that his administration would support lower taxes, as well as a charter that would provide for municipal ownership of the street railways, water service, and the gas and electric utilities. Two years after his election, a new charter was adopted. It included a provision permitting the city to own and operate all utilities, and another provision which restricted the conditions under which franchises were to be granted in the future. St. Louis, in 1901, elected a reform mayor, after Circuit Attorney Joseph W. Folk had exposed the corruption practiced by boss Edward R. Butler, who had dominated city politics since 1882. Folk's popularity in bringing the scandals to light led to his election as governor in 1905. Los Angeles, whose population grew dramatically from 50,000 in 1890 to 102,000 in 1900, experienced a reform movement at the beginning of the twentieth century. In 1909, a progressive administration came into office under Mayor George Alexander as a consensus was reached in the city about the need to improve municipal administration.

Reform in Chicago

A more detailed look at municipal progressivism in the city of Chicago provides a clearer picture of the reform process and the kinds of individuals and groups that participated in it. Chicago had chosen a nonpartisan municipal administration after its great fire in 1871, but by the 1890s, as one historian later noted, there was "ample justification for Bryce's generalization that the government of cities was 'the one conspicuous failure of the United States.' "[11] An important event that contributed to altering the situation took place in 1892, with the celebration of the World's Columbian Exposition. The Exposition, which was held in Chicago, marked the four hundredth anniversary of Columbus's voyages to the New World and featured displays, lectures, and exhibits. Amid the festivities, residents of Chicago were reminded that conditions in their city were a far cry from the concept of progress being heralded at the Exposition. The Exposition also brought to the city English writer W. T. Stead, who became disturbed over the conditions he had seen in the course of his stay. At a meeting he called in Chicago in November, 1893, he spoke about the need for a religious and civic revival—a topic he later explored in his book, *If Christ Came to Chicago* (1894).

While the populace of Chicago had a chance to ponder Stead's indictment, civic groups were busy at work. One of the most important was the Municipal Voters' League, a nonpartisan group consisting primarily of Chicago business leaders and professional men. In 1896, it appointed a committee to investigate the activities of the board of aldermen. (See Figure 7.1.) Using methods that by this date had become standard procedure for many reformers, it studied the political situation in each ward in the city, conducted a house-to-house canvas, published its findings, and distributed circulars. Its secretary, Walter L. Fisher, had a knack for knowing what type of candidates could win, understood the needs of each of Chicago's thirty-four wards, and kept tabs on aldermen to see if they were serving the interests of reform. When Steffens

[Illustration: Cartoon captioned "COURIER FROM THE FRONT — 'They're routed the Old Guard, General!'"]

Figure 7.1 "Campaigning with Bathhouse John" mocked the antics of "Bathhouse John" Coughlin and Michael (Hinky-Dink) Kenna, notoriously corrupt aldermen from Chicago's First Ward. Here they are seen being routed by the forces of reform. From Chicago *Record Herald*, March 20, 1902.

visited the city, he wrote that Chicago's "political reform, politically conducted, has produced reform politicians working for the reform of the city with the methods of politics. They do everything that a politician does, except buy votes and sell them. They play politics in the interest of the city."[12]

In the 1896 election, the league charged that fifty-seven of Chicago's sixty-eight aldermen were "thieves." Of the total, thirty-four were up for reelection that year. As a result of the league's intensive campaign, all but six of the aldermen were defeated in their bid for reelection. Within four years, the league had a clear majority in the city council. It was then able to force Chicago streetcar magnate Charles T. Yerkes to sell his holdings to the city. Yerkes had previously bribed the legislature to pass bills granting him franchises for periods up to 100 years without any payment to the city. The termination of the Yerkes's franchises marked the culmination of a policy that actually had first been put into effect in 1888 when Chicago began to revise its system of granting franchises. More franchises were issued in 1888 than in any other previous year, and they all contained a provision requiring financial compensation to the city for the privilege of obtaining the franchise. Another stipulation specified that the city would receive a percentage of the gross earnings from the franchise companies. This reform, which was put into practice elsewhere in urban America, ended one of the long-time abuses associated with machine politics.

Settlement houses in Chicago also played a role in the reform movement. The settlement houses, which were first opened in the United States in the mid-1880s, represented an attempt to help immigrants adjust to American life. They offered instruction in English, served as a neighborhood recreation center, and provided community services in matters relating to health and education. Although not all settlement house workers took an interest in politics, those who did could make use of their standing in the community by attempting to influence local affairs. Chicago Commons, a settlement house founded in 1894 by University of Chicago faculty member Graham Taylor, was located in the city's Seventeenth Ward. Taylor and his associates investigated the records of candidates, gathered statistics, exerted pressure on local officials, and worked closely with the Municipal Voters' League. In 1897, the ward elected James Walsh, a member of Chicago Commons, as an alderman and for nearly two decades thereafter, Chicago Commons continued its vigorous campaigns and was able to control the election for aldermen in the ward.

Hull-House, Chicago's other famed settlement house, decided to take the plunge into municipal politics at the behest of its founder, Jane Addams. Hull-House was located in Chicago's Nineteenth Ward, which was controlled by Alderman John Powers. Three attempts were made—in 1895, 1896, 1898 —to elect reform aldermen, but all these efforts were unsuccessful, as Powers proved to be too popular with his constituents. "I may not be the sort of man the reformers like," Powers admitted, "but I am what my people like, and neither Hull-House nor all the reformers in town can turn them against me."[13]

Miss Addams later gave up her quest to reform local politics and directed her energies toward state and national reform. It can be argued that her efforts might have produced more fruitful results had she understood the ethnic tensions in the ward between the Irish and the Italians, and had she sought to enlist the support of the latter in her battle against Powers. But the socially prominent Miss Addams, who herself chided other upper class progressives for being too occupied "with a concern for the better method of administration, rather than with the ultimate purpose of securing the welfare of the people,"[14] was not always able to relate to the immigrant groups whom Hull-House hoped to aid. In her writings, she referred to the South Italian immigrants as a "primitive people" who were childlike in their understanding of politics.[15] It was this kind of attitude, evidenced in some of the best-intentioned reformers like Jane Addams, that would leave municipal progressives open to the accusation that they were not sufficiently committed to working with the lower classes. Nevertheless, it was this same group of reformers that made a concerted effort, both through politics and individual endeavor, to grapple with slums, factory regulation, poverty, and other social problems of the Progressive era.

Maverick and Radical Progressives

Progressivism also produced its maverick and radical reformers—those who believed that neither the Democratic nor Republican version of reform went far enough in the direction of improving the condition of the city residents. A few mavericks, like Tom L. Johnson of Cleveland and Samuel M. Jones of Toledo, were among the most famous of all municipal progressives, although they were more atypical of, than akin to, other urban reformers.

More militant than the maverick progressives were various labor groups and Socialists, who made a strong showing on the local level during the Progressive era. Henry George, whose *Progress and Poverty* (1879) was one of the first major attacks on late-nineteenth-century American society, ran as an independent for mayor of New York in 1886. George received heavy support from labor groups and polled 68,000 votes. Although he lost to Democrat Abram S. Hewitt, he ran 8,000 votes ahead of Theodore Roosevelt, the Republican nominee. George ran again in 1897, but died in the middle of the campaign.

San Francisco experienced its own brand of municipal radicalism in 1901, when Boss Abraham Ruef helped to organize the Union Labor Party. Capitalizing on labor discontent in the area, the party scored an immediate victory with the election of Eugene R. Schmitz as mayor. However, the party's rise came to a dramatic halt in 1907, when Schmitz was removed as mayor after having been found guilty of extortion. (See Figure 7.2.)

In 1911, Socialist party tickets were triumphant in thirty-three cities and towns, among them Berkeley and Oakland, in California, and Butte, Montana. Two years earlier in Los Angeles, where the labor situation was tense, Socialist Fred Wheeler narrowly lost the mayoralty election, even though he was virtually unknown and had little money to spend on the campaign. In 1911, Joe Harriman, the Socialist party candidate for mayor, polled a plurality of votes in the three-cornered primary, but was subsequently defeated in the election by a Republican running with the support of the local reform organization. Milwaukee had two Socialist mayors during the heyday of progressivism, and one of them, Daniel W. Hoan, proved to be one of the most durable of all elected officials. Despite attacks on his socialist views, Hoan held office until 1940.

The first influential maverick was Detroit's Hazen Pingree, who was described by Henry Demarest Lloyd in 1897 as "the best Mayor America ever has produced."[16] Pingree looked askance at enforcing the Sunday saloon-closing laws, tolerated prostitution as a "necessary evil," and stated that his kind of religion was "divide and help your neighbor."[17] Born in Maine in 1840, he was one of eight children in a farm family that had experienced economic hardship. He went to Detroit in 1865 to better his opportunities and, within a few years, became a leading shoe manufacturer and a respected businessman. In 1889, several of his business friends prevailed upon him to run for mayor on the Republican ticket, and he was elected.

Although Pingree had given little indication during the

Figure 7.2 The Wasp of San Francisco led a campaign against Boss Ruef (right) and his puppet mayor, Eugene R. Schmitz. From *The Wasp*, December 1, 1906.

campaign about his views on specific issues, he came to be regarded as a radical during the eight years that he served as mayor. He forced gas and telephone companies to reduce their prices, and established a municipal electric plant after he determined that the city was paying a private utility a price he deemed too high. In 1894, he launched a campaign against the Citizens' Company, Detroit's local street railway company, which was controlled by Tom L. Johnson.* In an at-

---

*At this stage of his career, Johnson was a successful businessman, and had not yet turned to municipal reform.

tempt to provide the city with better service at a lower rate, Pingree helped to obtain a franchise for a competitor company, the Detroit Railway Company. In 1895, this company began its operation at three cents a ride, with Mayor Pingree piloting the first car up the tracks. The following year, however, Pingree appeared to suffer a major setback when the Detroit Railway Company merged with Johnson's company. Pingree refused to be undone by Johnson, and was able to force the Citizens' Company to lower its rate by threatening political reprisals. By 1899, the three-cent fare was in effect on approximately one third of the street railway mileage in Detroit.

Pingree's record in other areas was equally successful; he encouraged the construction of schools, parks, and a free public bath. During the Panic of 1893, he set aside public land for the unemployed to use as gardens, which became known as Pingree's Potato Patches. He was popular enough to be elected governor of Michigan in 1896, and he attempted to keep his job as mayor while serving as governor. A state court ruled against him, and he relinquished the mayoral office in 1897.

It was about Samuel M. "Golden Rule" Jones of Toledo that Frederick C. Howe remarked, "Everybody was against him except the workers and the underworld."[18] Jones was born in North Wales in 1846 and came to the United States when he was three years old. He made money in the oil business, although he would later say, "I have simply taken advantage of opportunities offered by an unfair social system and gained what the world calls success."[19] He was first elected mayor of Toledo in 1897, having received the Republican nomination for the office after a deadlock had developed at their convention.

Jones favored municipal ownership of public utilities which, like most of the other reforms he advocated, made him controversial. His tolerant attitude toward vice aroused the ire of Toledo's clergy, who also considered him to be too friendly to saloonkeepers. When Jones issued an order prohibiting policemen from using clubs, several clergymen brought another Sam Jones to Toledo. This man, the Reverend Sam Jones, told an audience: "I am for the Golden Rule myself, up to a certain point, and then I want to take the shotgun and the club."[20] Mayor Jones sought renomination in 1899, but the Republicans refused to support him. He then ran for governor on a no-party platform, but lost. In 1901 and 1903 he ran as an independent for mayor and was reelected both times. He died in office in 1904, after having accomplished reforms which included the establishment of a merit system in the police department, an eight-hour day for policemen, introduction of kindergartens and public playgrounds, setting up lodging houses for tramps, and the regulation of utility companies. (The morning after his death, the stock of a street railway company went up twenty-four points.) In 1905, Brand Whitlock, one of Jones' advisers and close friends, became mayor.

Like Pingree and Jones, Cleveland's Tom L. Johnson came from a humble background, but had acquired considerable wealth in business. Born in Kentucky in 1854, his initial financial successes came when he went to work for the Louisville Street Railroad and invented the first fare box for coins. With the money he made from his invention, he invested in steelworks and in street railway systems. His ethics as a businessman were not above reproach, and as a streetcar magnate he was often accused of taking advantage of the public by charging excessive rates. He eventually became converted to the reform ideology of Henry George, shared the faith of the progressives in the American city, and when Frederick C. Howe's book, *The City: The Hope of Democracy*, was published in 1905, he sent a copy of it to every member of the Ohio legislature.

Johnson, a Democrat who frequently was at odds with his own party, served as mayor of Cleveland from 1901 to 1909, and embarked on a series of far-reaching reforms. Although he failed in an attempt to obtain municipal ownership of the street railways, he secured the reassessment of property values, initiated a three-cent fare for the streetcar system, established a building code, created a forestry department for the protection of the city's trees, improved the paving on several hundred miles of streets, and built bathhouses and comfort stations. Unlike the more traditional progressive reformers, he took a broad view of the function of the city government. According to Johnson, "Good sanitary conditions, public parks, pure water, playgrounds for children and well paved streets are the best kind of investments; while the absence of them entails not only heavy pecuniary loss, but operates to the moral and physical demoralization of the city's inhabitants."[21] Johnson's measures evoked criticism, and he was defeated for reelection in 1909. Nevertheless, in the opinion of Lincoln Steffens, he was the "best mayor of the best-governed city in America."[22]

Milwaukee's Daniel W. Hoan was a Socialist, but in some respects he was less of a maverick than either Johnson, Jones, or Pingree. He was the second socialist to be elected mayor of Milwaukee, the first being Emil Seidel, who was elected in 1910. Under Seidel, Milwaukee became the first large city to be controlled by the Socialist party. As was later the case with Hoan, Seidel's victory was attributable to the support given the socialists by the city's trade union movement and the large number of German residents, in addition to the candidate's appeal to disenchanted Republicans and Democrats who had become disgusted with the failure of either of the major parties to provide Milwaukee with effective leadership. Hoan, a lawyer who had worked his way through college, was first elected mayor in 1916, and he held office until 1940. His initial success at the polls is particularly striking in view of the fact that he served at a time when the Socialist party was under sharp attack because of its opposition to American entry into World War I. Part of his popularity was due to his ability to give Milwaukee what one historian has called "Yankeefied Socialism."[23] His administration stressed municipal solvency and community safety and order, and his approach to municipal ownership was more cautious than committed. During Hoan's twenty-four years in office, Milwaukee placed fewer restrictions on public utilities than did cities like Detroit, Cleveland, San Francisco, and New York.

Problems of Reformers

In spite of the victories of mavericks like Hoan, the progressives were sometimes taken aback by the subsequent return of the bosses to power. Ironically, their sweeping movement for reform proved to be only minimally successful in driving machine politicians from office, even though the changing nature and scope of municipal government eventually brought about the demise of many bosses in a later period. Nevertheless, the resultant struggle for power between the reformers and the bosses led to certain modifications in the conduct of machine politics.

The reformers were not always adept in the ways of municipal politics. Editor Charles G. Dana's famed comment in the 1890s about the "infantile blabber of the goo goos"[24] reflected the criticism to which municipal reformers were subjected because of their alleged unrealistic and naïve approach to politics. Even Steffens, whose sympathy for reform was more firmly rooted than Dana's, characterized reform waves as those which "wash the 'best people' into office to make fools of themselves."[25] Novices to party politics and inexperienced in government service, the progressives had to grapple with the baffling complexities of municipal affairs. They frequently failed to perceive that honesty and efficiency had only limited appeal to various segments of the electorate and that their administrations would be subject to criticism due to their failure to provide the kinds of services offered by the machine. Many reformers remained opposed to establishing a permanent reform organization to perpetuate thir goals, and practiced what Theodore J. Lowi has termed "a politics of disintegration."[26] There usually was disagreement among them on what course to pursue. Some were merely content to overthrow the machine without formulating a new program of their own. Several wanted additional structural reforms, and still others voiced concern over the social problems in the city. In Baltimore, for example, the diverse interests that made up the progressive coalition clashed over specific issues. Businessmen wanted city planning but frowned on child labor legislation. Property owners favored the building of parks and playgrounds but vetoed other measures that would have resulted in the enactment of higher taxes.

The voting public responded enthusiastically to the progressives in the early stages of the "civic renaissance," but they tended to grow apathetic when the novelty of reform wore off. The absence of sustained interest on the part of the public, coupled with the inability of the reformers to maintain a solid organization, led to the abatement of the movement for reform. In the wake of the defeat of the New York reformers in 1897 after only three years in office, Jacob Riis commented that the public was "tired of too much virtue."[27] Several years later, in 1903, Steffens was weighing the possibilities of a reform victory in that year's election. "New York has been so far an anti-bad government, anti-Tammany, not a good government town," he wrote, "can it vote, without Tammany in to incite it, for a good mayor?"[28] The "good Mayor" to whom Steffens was referring was incumbent Seth Low, who was defeated for reelection.

Low, who had been a successful businessman before turning to politics, serves as a good illustration of the difficulties faced by a reformer in learning the art of practical politics and in comprehending the priorities of many of his constituents. Elected on a nonpartisan fusion ticket in 1901, he believed that the city should be run according to sound business principles—a technique which he had applied with vigor when he served as mayor of Brooklyn from 1882 to 1885. Although he tried to provide New York with the same type of administration that he had given to Brooklyn, he was less successful. He lowered taxes, improved streets, supported public education, extended the merit system, and generally gave New York an administration that, as Steffens viewed it, was "undeniably one of the best in the whole country." But, as Steffens noted, Low had a talent for making an enemy even when he was agreeing to a request, and he lacked the attractive personality necessary to make the reform movement appealing to the urban citizenry.[29] He was not well liked by the lower classes, many of whom were indifferent to his stress on efficient management for the city. Like scores of reformers, Low may have been successful in doing what he had set out to accomplish, but he was reluctant to tackle the vast amount of social problems besetting the city. Despite his fine accomplishments, he was ousted by Tammany candidate George B. McClellan. Apparently, a majority of New Yorkers preferred the machine.

Modifications in Machine Politics

The machine, even when returned to power during the Progressive era, nevertheless felt the impact of the movement for reform. What resulted were several adaptations on the part of machine politicians, and what appeared to be a new attitude toward municipal reform, at least on the surface. Tammany Hall, by the early twentieth century, tried to change its image, if not its philosophy. George B. McClellan, who had beaten Low in 1903, was a Princeton graduate and represented a new breed of aspiring Tammany politicians. McClellan, like numerous machine candidates in other cities, displayed the kind of political independence that had been unknown in the past. The machines also lent their support to many of the measures enacted into law by the progressives. While the city machines bitterly fought the passage by the state legislatures of measures such as civil service, short ballot, and the commission and council manager plans, they supported proposals like factory legislation, regulation of public utilities, home rule, direct election of United States Senators, and women's suffrage. These measures usually had the wholehearted endorsement of the machine's supporters, and bosses could embrace this aspect of progressivism because it represented no threat to their own vested interests. Home rule, for example, promised to enhance the power the city bosses held over local legislation.

Although bosses did respond to the demands for reform, the difficulty in labeling bosses as "reformers" can be seen by taking a closer look at Tammany Hall during the high tide of municipal progressivism. Tammany's leader during these years was Charles F. Murphy, who served from 1902 until his death in 1924. In addition to putting forth an able leader like McClellan, Murphy offered the city a number of significant concessions to reform, such as subways, a new water system, street repair, and increased police protection. Murphy's influence also extended to the state capitol in Albany, and much of the statewide progressive legislation was pushed through because of his support. This legislation was particularly beneficial to the working classes, for it included the implementation of a system of public employment agencies, a scholarship program for underprivileged youngsters, new safety regulations for industry, a constitutional amendment authorizing compulsory workmen's compensation, and the establishment of a State Factory Investigating Commission to ascertain the conditions that led to the disastrous Triangle Shirtwaist Company fire of 1911.

In other respects, Tammany hardly appeared to have changed at all. Its followers continued to make money at the public's expense, even though several of its leaders used a series of new refinements which made their misconduct harder to detect. Tammany's control of the city government continued until 1933, and during that period it padded city departments with party regulars, violated the civil service law, and wasted huge sums of money through mismanagement of finances. One of its most blatant abuses occurred in the city's Health Department, where a ring of grafters connived to adulterate the city's milk supply and sell food products below the standard established by the department. During one period in the 1920s, 1,200,000 quarts of impure milk were being distributed daily, and some of it was being fed to tubercular children and used in hospitals, homes for the aged, and orphanages.

Structural Changes in Municipal Government

The struggle between reformers and bosses has had the effect of obscuring the fact that an impressive array of structural reforms were enacted during the Progressive era which greatly altered the workings of American municipal government. The most notable achievements included home rule; curtailments on special legislation; delegation of greater authority to the mayor; reduction in the size of the council; substitution of election-at-large for election by wards in the council; the short ballot; separation of city elections from state and national contests; the Australian ballot; direct primary; initiative, referendum, and recall; nonpartisan primary; civil service; and commission and council manager plans. These measures, which were primarily (although not exclusively) the work of reform administrations, corrected many of the weaknesses that had dated back to the nineteenth century and eased the burden of the municipal reformer in the future.

Of all the reforms enacted, few were more important for cities than home rule. It was hoped that the enactment of this measure would remove the stifling hand of the state legislature from the city government and would result in more responsive and effective local government. St. Louis, in 1875, became the first city in the United States to get home rule. In that year, Missouri's new state constitution specified that any city having a population of more than 100,000 could frame its own charter. St. Louis was the only city in the state with a large enough population to qualify, and it promptly took advantage of the opportunity. Its new charter was generally considered to be the best that St. Louis had had.

Missouri's constitutional provision for home rule was adopted by California in 1880. It enacted the same general plan of home rule for cities having a population of more than 100,000, the one eligible city being San Francisco. In the case of San Francisco, however, there was an added provision requiring that its charter, after passage, had to be submitted to the state legislature for approval. After San Francisco adopted home rule, the state of California revised its constitution in 1887 so that cities with more than 10,000 inhabitants were allowed to write their own charter. In 1890, the provision was extended to cities with a population of over 3,000 people.

The "Missouri idea" caught on, and in 1889, the state of Washington passed a constitutional provision giving all cities with a population in excess of 20,000 the right to devise their own charters. Home rule provisions for cities were also enacted by Minnesota, Colorado, Oregon, Oklahoma, and Michigan. The Ohio constitution of 1912, which went into effect on January 1, 1913, contained provisions enabling cities either to frame their own charters or to adopt by local referendum any general or special charter which the state legislature had passed.

The movement for home rule has not been an unqualified success, and many cities at present continue to protest their subservience to the state legislature. Moreover, even as the home rule pattern was enacted, states still did not trust cities to administer local laws. In several states, commissions were appointed to supervise the enforcement of laws at the city level, particularly state liquor laws and state election laws. Despite the fact that between 1870 and 1906 approximately half of the states passed acts forbidding the state legislature to enact special municipal legislation, various ways of getting around these provisions were found. The most common method was to classify cities according to their size; thus, a large city would be put into a class by itself, and special laws would be enacted by the state legislature for it. In 1902, an Ohio Supreme Court declared such a provision to be unconstitutional, but the ruling never gained general acceptance throughout the country.

The demand for increasing the power of the mayor reflected the view that only a strong chief executive could provide the kind of leadership required if a city were to be governed effectively. The potential danger of giving the mayor too much power was offset by the belief that civic protest—which was so common during the Progressive era—would prevent him from becoming a tyrannical figure. Until 1880, mayors had few powers vis-à-vis the council; New York was the only large city where the mayor had control over the council. In most cities, however, the mayor lacked all veto rights, his appointments were subject to the confirmation of the council, and he had a limited role in matters pertaining to health, sanitation, and public safety. An important change occurred by 1900, when cities like Cleveland, Buffalo, Louisville, Indianapolis, Baltimore, and St. Louis extended the authority of the mayor in the city government. Among the changes made in the office of the mayor were the extension of his term, the power to appoint and remove heads of most municipal departments, and the right to veto legislation passed by the council.

As the mayor's power was increased, there was a corresponding decrease in the role of the council in American municipal government. At the end of the Civil War, city councils tended to be large and divided into two bodies. By the end of the 1880s, the size of the council was reduced, many councilmen were elected at large by the residents of the entire city rather than by individual wards or districts, and there was a movement to return to the single-chambered council that had existed in the colonial era. As in earlier periods, the term of service varied from one to four years, but one major change was the movement to provide councilmen with compensation. Until the Progressive period, it was common practice for many local representatives to serve without pay. After the 1920s, it was only in parts of New England, Pennsylvania, and in some southern states that the practice of gratuitous service remained.

The shift to an at-large constituency was aimed at reducing the power of the ward bosses. It was assumed that it would be more difficult for them to secure the election of candidates selected by voters outside their bailiwick. A few municipalities opted for a compromise, so that cities in Ohio, Indiana, and Iowa had a small number of councilmen selected at large, in addition to ward representation. In the large cities that retained the bicameral council, there was a tendency to specify that the smaller council was to be elected from the whole city rather than from districts.

Voting Reforms

The trend toward the unicameral council led to a reduction in the number of candidates seeking municipal office and, indirectly, to the short ballot. The leader of the movement to obtain the short ballot in both municipal and state elections was Richard S. Childs, who in 1908 circulated a privately printed pamphlet, "The Short Ballot." The following year Childs and Woodrow Wilson helped establish the National Short Ballot Organization. The idea gained acceptance in many cities by the end of the Progressive period, particularly in those cities operating under a commission or a council manager plan. The short ballot represented a marked improvement over what Charles A. Beard had dubbed "the ballot's burden," citing as an example the fact that in one election district in Chicago in 1906 the ballot was over two feet long and contained a list of 334 candidates for office.[30]

The separation of city elections from state and national elections was achieved by many smaller cities in the hope that the voter would be free to concentrate his interests on local matters and familiarize himself with candidates and issues. Large cities resisted the proposal, partly because of the additional expense in providing for a separate election and, on occasion, due to the opposition of the state organization which believed that it would be adversely affected by a separate contest. In New York, attempts were made on various occasions to change the date of city elections. From 1834 to 1849, they were held in the spring; from 1850 to 1856, they were made simultaneous with general elections; from 1857 to 1869, they were scheduled for December; and in 1870, they were put back to November.

City elections, regardless of when they were held, were no longer plagued by widespread practices of fraud, thanks to the use of the Australian, or secret, ballot. Introduced for the first time in 1888, the new ballot not only was secret but was also a uniform, officially printed ballot. Previously, various party organizations printed and distributed ballots at the polling places, openly purchased votes, and watched to see that the voter paid his "debt." By the 1890s, the Australian ballot was used by virtually every city in the country.

The changes made in the conduct of elections foreshadowed certain modifications in the conduct of primaries. In 1866, both New York and California attempted to enact primary laws, but it was not until the 1890s that states started to regulate the city primaries. These laws—which were put into effect in approximately two thirds of all the states—provided that nominations for local office were to be made by the voters of the political parties at a specified primary election, on official ballots and under official supervision. It represented another attempt to take the nomination process away from the machine and give it directly to the voters.

The direct primary represented that aspect of progressivism which was designed to return government to the people, and the use of the initiative, referendum, and recall was a further application of that principle, The initiative is a right given to a specified number of voters to propose legislation, either by submission of a measure to the city's legislative body or directly to the electorate. In a referndum, a requisite number of voters may nullify an act passed by the council, while a recall provides voters with the option of dismissing an elected public official. Lincoln and Omaha, Nebraska, adopted the initiative and referendum in 1897, and the following year the South Dakota constitution specifically gave its municipalities the right to enact both types of measures. As a result of the great wave of progressivism on the state level during the first decade of the twentieth century, Oregon, in 1906, Oklahoma, in 1906, and Maine, in 1908, enacted provisions in their constitutions authorizing the use of the initiative and referendum on a citywide basis. In states like Missouri, California, Washington, and Colorado, where home rule provisions already were in effect, many cities adopted the initiative and referendum. The recall was adopted for the first time in Los Angeles in 1903, and the next year, Los Angeles became the first city in the country to recall an elected official.

Another reform, the nonpartisan primary, specified that candidates for office would receive no official party designation. The idea behind it was to provide voters with the opportunity to seek out the best-qualified nominees rather than vote for a candidate with the preferred party designation. In 1907, Des Moines was the first city to adopt the nonpartisan primary. It became widespread in cities operating under the commission form of government, and by the early 1960s it was in force in an estimated 66 percent of American cities with a population in excess of 25,000. At the time the nonpartisan primary came into use, it appeared to represent an improvement in the method of choosing candidates, but its implementation, like several other progressive reforms, can be viewed as having favored the wealthier classes in the community who had the funds necessary to run without an official party endorsement. It also gave rise to nonpartisan elections, which, by the end of the 1960s, were in effect in eleven of the nation's twenty largest cities, having a population of over 50,000.

Civil Service Reform

Civil service was the top priority reform for most progressives, since its introduction would cut into the boss's patronage and replace party workers with a corps of public servants who, on the basis of ability they displayed on a competitive examination, were deemed to be capable of serving the needs of the community. In the case of civil service, Congress helped pave the way for reform with the passage of the Pendleton Act of 1883, which applied the merit system to the federal government. The first states to provide civil service for their larger cities were New York, in 1883, and Massachusetts, in 1884. Louisiana followed suit in 1896, although on a less comprehensive basis, and by 1898 Philadelphia and Chicago were among the cities that had adopted some form of civil service system. By the 1930s, four fifths of the country's municipal employees were under civil service.

During the Progressive period, the administration of civil service varied from city to city, especially since some states feared that local politicians would attempt to make a mockery of the law. In thirty-three cities in Massachusetts, there was no municipal civil service commission. Instead, supervision was entrusted to a state board. In Philadelphia and Chicago, administration was in the hands of a commission appointed by the mayor. While several cities in New York State had a commission appointed by the mayor, it was subordinate to a state commission appointed by the governor. In later years, however, the cities were given greater flexibility by the state legislatures in devising their civil service systems.

Commission and Council Manager Plans

The most innovative of all the progressive reforms were the commission and council manager plans, which represented a new approach to the problem of governing American cities. Both plans emphasized efficiency, nonpartisan politics, and the supervision of city government by experts, usually from business and professional groups. Both tended to flourish in smaller cities, where there was recognition by the business community that a streamlined, efficient, and graft-free municipal administration would reduce taxes and enhance their own economic interests.

Prior to 1900, the commission form had been tried out in Washington, D. C., and in New Orleans, but it was not until the beginning of the twentieth century that the idea attracted serious consideration. In 1900, Galveston was nearly destroyed by a tidal wave, and the corrupt city government was unable to cope with the emergency. The state intervened, changed Galveston's charter, and set up a five-man nonpartisan commission, which had both legislative and executive authority to run the city. The commission, whose first members were a lawyer, a banker, a wholesale merchant, a real estate broker, and an officer of a livestock company, had one commissioner who was designated as mayor and who acted as general manager. Originally, the mayor and two members of the commission were appointed by the governor, and two others were elected by the voters at large. By 1903, however, all the members were made elective, following a ruling by a state court that the appointment by the governor was unconstitutional. Galveston's new government proved so successful—the city was rebuilt in 1906 and one third of its operating expenses were cut—that other cities adopted the plan. It was put into effect elsewhere in Texas, and by 1907 it was in operation in Houston, Dallas, Fort Worth, and El Paso. In 1912, it had been adopted in over 200 cities, including Birmingham, Des Moines, and Oakland.

The council, or city manager plan, was a modification of the commission form of government. Under the plan, full administrative authority is vested in a manager, who is chosen by the commission or city council. Its advocates maintained that the concentration of authority in the manager represented an improvement over the shared responsibility of the commission-type government. The council manager plan was first tried out in Staunton, Virginia, in 1908. Between 1918 and 1923—a time when the Progressive movement was considered to have come to an end—153 cities had adopted the plan. It gained even wider acceptance after World War II as a result of the rapid growth of suburbia. The suburbs, by size and by temperament, looked with favor upon the professional and businesslike approach of the city manager.

The popularity of the manager plan came to overshadow the commission plan, which has been on the decline since the 1930s. Of the three basic types of city government—mayor–

council, commission, and council or city manager—the last is most prevalent in small- to medium-sized cities. Nevertheless, the mayor–council type continues to prevail in very large and very small cities. In 1966, all but three of America's seventeen largest cities were governed under a mayor–council form, as were nearly two thirds of cities with populations ranging from 5,000 to 10,000.

Shifting Currents in Municipal Politics

The impact of these structural changes upon municipal administration was encouraging, and local governments appeared to have changed for the better by the 1920s. In 1921, James Bryce referred to the "active spirit of reform" in the United States, and was favorably impressed by the adoption of the commission and council manager plans.[31] In those cities where boss rule prevailed during the 1920s, further inroads were made into the boss's grip on municipal affairs. The extension of civil service and the restrictions in immigration robbed him of valuable sources of support, as did jobs dispensed by the federal government which began in the New Deal era. With the rise of educational opportunities, people came to have job outlets other than those supplied by the boss. When members of the lower classes acquired property and began to pay taxes on it, they became aware of the fact that they could lose financially as a result of corrupt city machines. Similarly, the assimilation of ethnic groups into American society made the kind of politics practiced by the machine embarrassing to the more successful members of their group. By the end of the 1930s, old-style machine politics went into eclipse.

If the machines became unpopular, latter-day reformers were nevertheless aware of the advantages of the formalized techniques of political warfare. When municipal reformers have been victorious at the polls, it is usually because of their skill in organizing the electorate, canvassing the districts, and getting out the vote. Conversely, some bosses have tried to emulate the reformers. Tammany Hall's Carmine DeSapio, a leading boss in the 1950s, consulted a public relations man in order to change his image. He began to dress conservatively, improved his speech, and became a political lecturer at New York University. Unfortunately for DeSapio, his new image was marred in 1969, when he was found guilty by a federal court of having conspired to bribe a public official. Those bosses and political leaders who survived the rigors of municipal politics found ways to adjust to changing situations.

Thomas J. Pendergast, long-time czar of Kansas City politics, was capable of endorsing reform proposals when the occasion demanded. In 1925, he supported the city's highly popular council manager plan. After the plan went into effect, Pendergast used his influence to elect a pro-Pendergast council, which, by virtue of its reduced size, was easy for him to control. Since the council selected the manager, Pendergast was able to swing the election to Henry F. McElroy, who went on to hold that office for the next fifteen years. When the New Deal came to Kansas City, Pendergast was able to put it to good use as far as his own organization was concerned. His machine was actually strengthened in the process of distributing local jobs, for as one historian wrote, "If a local machine was fortunate enough to win the favor of the powers in Washington, it could continue to direct its community's welfare services—and the national government would pay the bill."[32] The city ticket supported by the Pendergast machine received large majorities for reelection in 1930, 1934, and 1938, but the organization was attacked for allegedly accepting bribes, handing out tax abatements to favored business firms, and protecting vice and illegal gambling in Kansas City. Pendergast fell from power in 1939 when he was sentenced to fifteen months in federal prison for failing to disclose over $1 million in personal income over an eleven-year period.

Frank Hague, who became Jersey City's mayor in 1917, ran one of the most effective political machines in the country during the thirty consecutive years that he served in office. He entered Democratic politics during the Progressive era and built a reputation as a reformer by attacking public utilities, building contractors, narcotics agents, prostitution, and food retailers. Although he originally opposed a commission-type government for Jersey City, he gave it his support when it went into effect in 1911, and he ran successfully for one of the commission posts two years later. His work on the commission helped pave the way for his election as mayor in 1917. From that point on, his progressivism was muted. As mayor, Hague's popularity stemmed from his actions in expanding government services, a move that was costly enough to make Jersey City the highest taxed municipality in the nation. Despite his subsequent endorsement of many New Deal measures, his statement, made in 1937, that "I am the law in Jersey City,"[33] suggested that old-time bossism was riding high in that city during his reign. He became implicated in a major scandal after he left office in 1947; several of his key aides were involved in a lawsuit that accused them of having required city employees to kick back part of their salaries to the Hague machine. Although the suit ultimately was dismissed, Hague's political career was over.

Fiorello H. LaGuardia, New York's mayor from 1933 until his retirement in 1945, was regarded as one of the leading municipal reformers of his era. LaGuardia represented both the old and new approaches to municipal politics. His "machine" combined the professionalized organizational features used by the late-nineteenth-century bosses, while his personal integrity and progressive programs represented the best aspects of urban liberalism. Like many municipal leaders of the New Deal period, he eschewed the provincialism of the earlier bosses and managed to develop a personal style and urbanity that elevated him into the national limelight at a time when control over the cities shifted from the state to the federal government. During the depression, New York received substantial amounts of federal money, and LaGuardia, although elected as mayor on a nonpartisan fusion ticket, campaigned vigorously for Franklin D. Roosevelt. On the local scene, his frequent radio addresses endeared him to the public, while his support of public housing, playgrounds, schools, and health centers won him the backing of large segments of the vote from Italians, Jews, blacks, and labor. Throughout his career, he criticized bossism and politicians, but his talent for seeking out voters and keeping them in his camp created, according to Rexford G. Tugwell, "the paradox of a machine that was anti-machine."[34]

Another prominent New York mayor was John V. Lindsay, who liked to identify himself with the nonpartisanship and reformist zeal of LaGuardia. Lindsay's patrician upbringing and Ivy League background seemed to make him a logical heir-apparent to the upper-class genteel tradition of the Progressive era, but he served at a time when the shifting structure of urban life required reformers to court the kind of constituency that previously had identified with the machine. Elected as a Republican in 1965, he came into office in the midst of a strike by the city's powerful Transport Workers' Union in January, 1966. He worked out a settlement with the union, but the strike cost the city an estimated $1.5 billion in economic losses. For the rest of his eight years in office, Lindsay was largely identified with the cause of the city's burgeoning black population. His popularity with blacks was attributed to his willingness to be responsive to the problems of the ghetto, and to make public assistance available to all residents of the city. The number of welfare recipients increased markedly during Lindsay's administration, and as a *New York Times* article pointed out, in referring to what had occurred in August, 1968, "In One Month, 50,000 Persons Were Added to the City's Welfare Rolls."[35] As a result of his efforts, Lindsay's supporters claimed that he understood the needs of urban America, while his critics accused him of impairing the financial solvency of New York and likened him to a modern-day Boss Tweed. In 1971, Lindsay announced that he was leaving the Republican party and becoming a Democrat. The following year he made an unsuccessful bid to become the Democratic presidential nominee; he returned to the private practice of law when he left office in 1973.

Richard J. Daley, who served as mayor of Chicago from 1955 to 1976, remained in power by offering the type of services previously made available by the machines, albeit in a different setting. He gained the backing of organized labor, in contrast to earlier bosses who tended to rely more on the support of individuals. His public works program provided numerous jobs in Chicago and earned him the goodwill of business contractors, who contributed heavily to his organization. Daley's power further stemmed from his dual position as mayor of Chicago and chairman of the Cook County Democratic Committee. Consequently, Chicago's municipal government and the Democratic party seemed to enjoy a mutual coexistence. In spite of the implementation of the merit system in Chicago, Daley managed to use his appointing power to considerable advantage and provided city jobs to scores of his precinct workers. These close ties between party workers and the city government were well known, and in view of the fact that so many citizens had a personal stake in Chicago's government, journalist Mike Royko quipped that the city's motto was, "Where's mine?"[36] Nevertheless, Chicago had the reputation for being "the city that works." When Daley died in 1976, his passing was regarded by many observers as signifying the end—or the epilogue to the end—of boss rule in American politics.

It remains to be seen if that conclusion is correct, but it

often appears that the country needs another dose of municipal progressivism, even if that movement failed to fulfill the expectations of those ardent citizens who rallied to its banner.

8

The Era of the Metropolis

The development of modern America's cities, like those in other parts of the world, has been characterized in this century by two major trends. First, an ever-larger percentage of the population has come to reside within metropolitan, or urbanized, areas in the vicinity of sizable cities. Second, in spite of this increase in their population, urban areas have tended to become less densely settled as people have moved out into the adjoining suburbs, so that the increase in suburban population has been far more marked than that of the central cities. It is largely this mushrooming of the suburbs that accounts for the impressive increase in the urban population since 1920. In that year's census, the nation's urban residents numbered over 54 million, or just over 51 percent of the population; in 1970, the figure was 149 million, or 73.5 percent of the national population.* (See Figure 8.1.)

Since 1920, the proportion of the American people living in central cities has gradually declined, in spite of the common tendency to describe the United States as "an urban nation." Although there were many cities that grew impressively during the 1920s when the populations of both Detroit and Los Angeles passed the million mark, the growth of central cities slowed after 1930, and since World War II, the majority have declined in both population and power. In 1930, the five central cities with populations of over one million together comprised 12 percent of the American

---

*In censuses prior to 1950, the urban population consisted of all persons living in incorporated towns of 2,500 and in areas classified as urban under special rules relating to population size and density. Since 1950, the Census Bureau has redefined the urban population as comprising all persons living in urbanized areas (central cities of 50,000 or more and the adjoining closely settled areas) and in places of 2,500 or more that are outside of urbanized areas. As a result, the urban population now includes several million more people than it would have under the older definition.

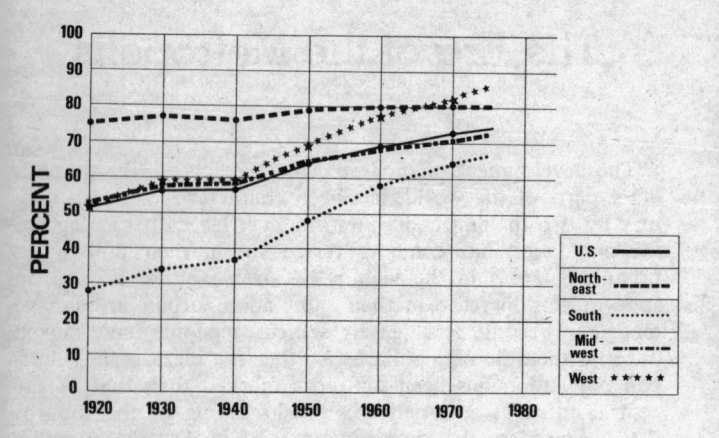

Figure 8.1 Urban Growth by Section, 1920–1970

people, but the combined populations of the six cities in this category in 1970 came to only 9 percent of the nation's population.

These trends have been accompanied and promoted by the emergence of new communications media. The telephone, for example, serves both to connect the central cities with the rest of their metropolitan areas and to link together, via long distance, the metropolitan regions of the nation and of the world. Even more important, perhaps, has been the emergence of new media of culture and popular entertainment: the motion picture, radio, and television. These media have resulted in a pervasive mass culture which serves as something of a bond between individuals, in that most Americans have been entertained and, to a limited degree, educated by the same, or similar, movies and broadcasts. Radio, and especially television, owe some of their vast influence and popularity to the fact that they are so well-suited to the diffused patterns of residence that typify the modern metropolis.

Except for the 1930s, the exodus of rural Americans to the cities has continued as before, a shift now abetted by the rise of large-scale farms and agri-business corporations which, by absorbing an ever-increasing share of the earnings of

American agriculture, have driven multitudes of small farmers from the land. By 1970, fewer than one American out of twenty was employed as a farmer. So massive an abandonment of farming was made possible by the dramatic improvement of farm technology which enabled the nation's remaining farm workers to produce sufficient food and fiber not only to meet the needs of their countrymen but also of many people overseas. The rural exodus, as well as the decline of many urban areas, led to a decrease in population in 41 percent of the nation's counties in the 1920s, in nearly half of the counties in the 1940s, and in more than half in the 1950s and 1960s.

Metropolitan Growth

Of the counties that grew, the great majority were within metropolitan areas. America's cities in the twentieth century have tended increasingly to take the form of the metropolis—an entity in which a relatively large central city is integrated functionally with nearby suburbs and satellite cities, forming a region with the central city as its focal point.

Since 1910, more than half of the nation's population growth has occurred in the metropolitan areas. Between 1920 and 1930, the nation's population increased by about 17 million; the increases in the ninety-six metropolitan districts (as defined by the census in 1930) accounted for over 10 million of this figure. The trend continued, though at a slower pace, in the 1930s in spite of a slackening in the national rate of growth. By 1940, the metropolitan population was tabulated at slightly more than 63 million, roughly 47 percent of the national total.

In the realm of urban affairs, the period between World War II and 1970 has been described as the era of the "exploding metropolis," a time when metropolitan areas mushroomed much as central cities used to. In 1950, the U. S. Census Bureau, in seeking to assess the extent of metropolitan development, introduced the concept of the Standard Metropolitan Area. This is defined as a county or contiguous group of counties which contain at least one city of 50,000 inhabitants plus the adjacent counties with which that city appears socially and economically integrated. In 1950, there were 168 SMAs with over 84 million residents. Twenty years later, 243 SMSAs (the name was changed in 1960 to Standard Metropolitan Statistical Areas) were enumerated by the census, having an overall population of over 139 million.* (See Table 8.1.)

Growth was especially rapid in the largest of the SMASs. In 1950, there were fourteen with over a million people that, taken together, totaled just over 44 million. Two decades later, there were thirty-three SMSAs in this category, totaling just under 81 million people. (See Figure 8.2.) The latter figure represents 56 percent of all metropolitan residents and roughly two fifths of the national population.

In 1975, the Census Bureau reported that, since 1970, metropolitan growth had lagged behind that of the nation as a whole, thereby reversing, at least temporarily, a trend that had persisted for more than a century and a half. The growth of the sizable cities was outstripped in the early 1970s by that of the rural areas and small towns. Over that span, only five of the nation's twenty-one largest metropolitan areas grew faster than the national average.

The modern metropolis has also been characterized by "urban sprawl," the far-flung and rather haphazard outward movement of urban people, businesses and institutions into formerly autonomous small towns and rural vilages. As early as the 1920s, a number of metropolitan districts were expanding well beyond their previous boundaries with the help of the automobile. It was during the suburb-building boom of the late 1940s, that the boundaries of the metropolis were most dramatically extended. As a result, estimates Leo Schnore, the functional boundaries of the metropolis had, on the average, more than doubled between 1940 and 1050.[1] This outward expansion was accompanied by a reduction in the density of settlement. Where America's metropolitan population had averaged 407 residents per square smile in 1950, it averaged only 360 residents per square mile twenty years later.

In certain metropolitan regions, growth and diffusion have brought about extremely long, virtually uninterrupted stretches of urbanized land. This is the phenomenon known as megalopolis, a term coined in 1957 by the French geog-

---

*These figures were not fully comparable since the 1970 total includes areas which were not classified in 1950 as being part of the SMAs. The population in 1950 of the 1970 SMSAs was roughly 94 million.

TABLE 8.1
Number and Total Population of Standard Metropolitan Areas (SMAs) as Divided Between Central Cities and Outer Rings, 1950–1970*

Year	Number of SMAs	Population of SMAs	Percent of U.S. Population in SMAs	Central City Population of SMAs	Percent of U.S. Population in Central City	Ring Population of SMAs	Percent of U.S. Population in Ring
1950	168	84,500,680	56.1	49,413,792	32.8	35,086,888	23.3
1960	212	112,885,178	63.0	58,004,334	32.4	54,880,844	30.6
1970	243	139,418,811	68.6	63,796,943	31.4	75,621,868	37.2

*The data for each year are presented exactly as they appeared in that year's census.

SOURCE: U.S. Bureau of the Census, *Historical Statistics of the U.S.*, Vol. I, p. 39.

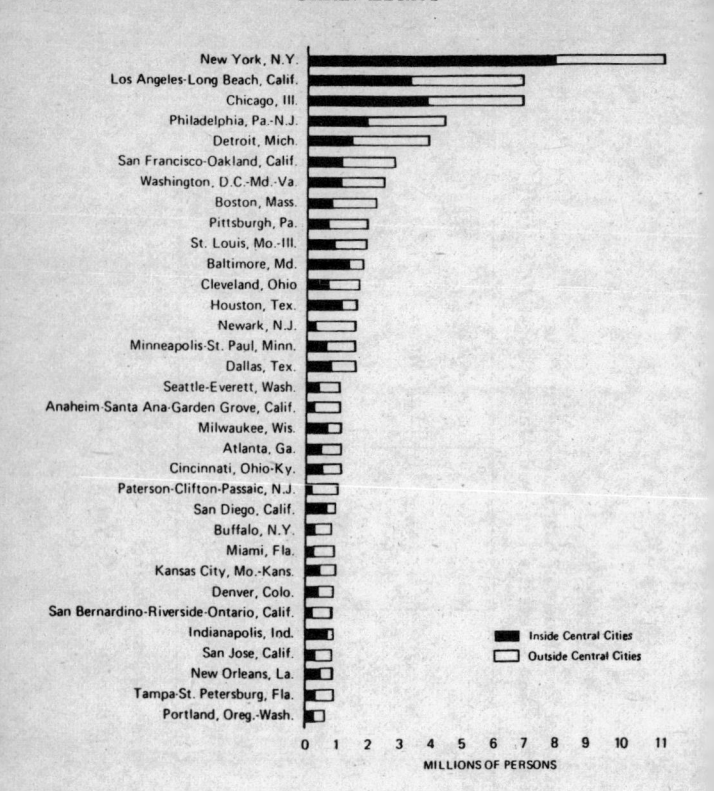

Figure 8.2 Standard Metropolitan Statistical Areas (SMSAs) of One Million Persons or More, Ranked by Size: 1970

SOURCE: Bureau of the Census, *Our Cities and Suburbs* (Washington D.C.: U.S. Government Printing Office, 1973), pp. 3–4.

rapher Jean Gottmann.[2] The most notable and extensive American megalopolis is the one in the Northeast that by 1970 stretched 450 miles from Boston to Washington, D. C., reaching as far inland as Harrisburg, Pennsylvania, some 150 miles from the coast. Other lengthy urban regions are to be found in the Great Lakes region, in Florida, and in California.

By the year 2000, according to a 1972 report by the Presidential Commission on Population and the National Future, these four megalopoli would together contain roughly 187 million people, about 60 percent of the nation's population. By then, this study asserted, there will be approximately twenty-four super-cities, extensive strips of urbanized land, each with a population of a million or more.[3] This trend, which is expected to place great strains upon the available supplies of clean air and water and to pose critical traffic and planning problems for the nation, has led some of the nation's leaders to advocate a policy of channeling urban growth into less congested portions of the country.

The principal factor in the outward movement of contemporary cities and metropolitan areas has been the automobile. By 1930, there were already over 26 million cars and trucks; in 1970 there were more than 90 million. Thanks largely to the automobile, the truck, and the steady improvement of the nation's roads and highways, the new metropolises of the South and West generally lack a well-defined central business district and have limited systems of public transport, or none at all. Such relatively youthful western metropolises as Houston and Phoenix are more spread out and less densely populated than are the major metropolitan areas in the eastern half of the country. Los Angeles was the first city to follow this pattern, and it has frequently been described, for better or for worse, as the prototype of the twentieth-century city. "Nowhere else," writes Robert Fogelson of Los Angeles in the 1920s, "did suburbs extend so far into the countryside and downtown decline so drastically as the center of commerce and industry."[4]

Even in the older, more compact centers, in which there often are elaborate systems of public transport, the automobile has had a decentralizing effect. Thus the New York metropolitan region, estimates the Regional Planning Association, a widely respected, New York-based, private-sector planning body, increased its area from slightly over 5,500 square miles in 1922 to nearly 13,000 square miles in 1965.

The growing nationwide use of the automobile was, in due course, accompanied by the construction of several million miles of roads and highways. As early as the 1920s, Detroit and Los Angeles had begun to plan for superhighways and for highly dispersed patterns of residence. By the 1930s, many of the major cities had installed uniform systems of street lights and traffic signs. Meanwhile, highway engineers had already begun in some places to employ the grade separations (the placing of opposing traffic streams at different height levels), cloverleaf interchanges, and highway dividers that are so common today.

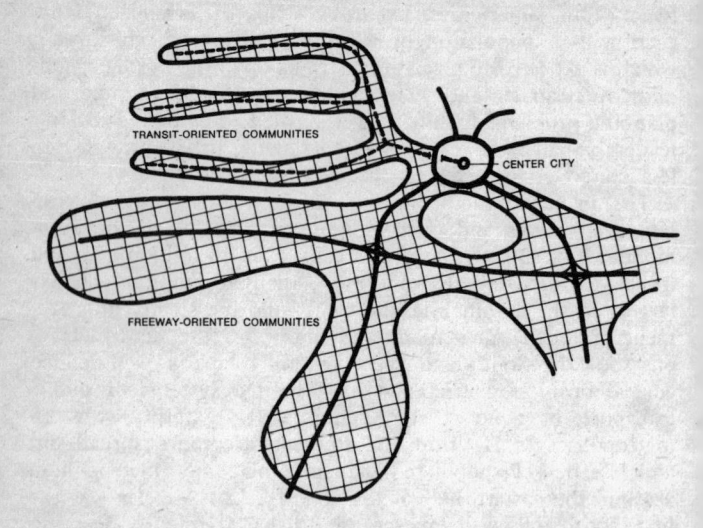

Figure 8.3 Communities where efficient systems of rapid transit exist are more likely to grow in a linear pattern, conforming to transit lines, and to have a more concentrated population (see top, left). In contrast, where systems of transportation are geared primarily to the automobile, communities are more open, with a more widely spaced population (see bottom, right).

SOURCE: *The Freeway in the City: Principles of Planning and Design* (Washington, D.C.: U.S. Government Printing Office, 1966), p. 28.

Since 1945, many multi-lane, limited access expressways (on which cars are allowed to enter only at certain interchanges) have been built both within and between the country's major metropolitan areas. Frequently, the superhighways rim the central cities without going through them and are linked radially by other highways to the central city districts. The Interstate Highway Act of 1956 provided for a nationwide system of toll-free superhighways to be constructed principally at federal expense. Under the program, 41,000 miles of highway were built, providing links between most of the nation's major cities and also other roads that run exclusively within particular metropolitan areas.

In building the new highways, the officials in charge appear not to have concerned themselves particularly with the social consequences of their projects. The sites for the roads were selected on the basis of three criteria: suitability for the movement of traffic, the price of the land, and the extent of community opposition. Most urbanists believe that the new highways are contributing to the continued outward sprawl of the nation's suburbs. "Today," wrote urbanist John Dyckman in 1965, "expressways are opening up a far greater number of new suburban housing developments and shopping centers than the subways and street railways did."[5]

Suburbanization: 1920–1945

Since at least 1910, the portions of metropolitan areas that lie outside of central cities have been growing much more rapidly than the cities themselves. In the 1920s, rapid growth was taking place alongside major cities in innumerable villages and towns, some of which had become sites for specially planned communities. A majority of the cities incorporated from 1921 to 1930 in Michigan and Ohio were located within the metropolitan zones of Detroit and Cleveland, respectively. By 1930, out of a total metropolitan population in excess of 55 million, nearly 17 million, roughly 30 percent, were dwelling outside the central cities. Even in the economically depressed 1930s, suburbia had continued to increase faster than either the central cities or the nation at large. By 1940, another three million had been added to the total of those dwelling in metropolitan areas but outside of the central cities, bringing the suburban share of the metropolitan population to 32 percent. In the metropolitan district of Chicago, to cite one example, the central city population increased by less than 11 percent between 1930 and 1940, whereas the population outside of the central city rose by 44 percent. During the same period, the city of Philadelphia suffered a net loss of 20,000, while the outer portion of its metropolitan zone increased by 372,000.

The process of suburbanization was described in 1925 by Frederick Lewis Allen, a professional writer and editor who was then living in Scarsdale, New York. "The city is growing fast and is swallowing up the surrounding country. When the trains from the city draw in at night, the crowds that swarm down on the platform are nearly half as large again as they were a year ago. The price of land has doubled or tripled in a few years. New houses are springing up everywhere."[6]

Suburbs have traditionally fallen into three major categories. One is the old town or village, sometimes called "the reluctant suburb," which finds itself becoming suburban as a result of the "invasion" of newcomers from the city. Another type is the satellite city which is primarily a center of business and industry but serves also as the place of residence for many of those who work in it. Finally, there is the new community which has been laid out in its entirety by contractors and subdividers.

Until the 1920s, the great majority of suburban residents were still relying on steam railroads and electricity-powered interurban streetcars to convey them to the central city and back. Some notable suburban communities were developed on this basis by such realty and traction magnates as Henry Huntington, the developer of a string of streetcar suburbs on the outskirts of Los Angeles, and the Van Sweringen Brothers, whose new community just outside of Cleveland, Shaker Heights, increased its population in the 1920s by more than 1,000 percent.

Suburbanization in the 1920s was encouraged by the rapid growth of automotive transport. "The automobile," Harold Mayer and Richard Wade observed, "created a whole new suburban world. It now became possible for people to live miles from suburban railway stations and still be able to work downtown."[7]

In the 1920s and 1930s, the majority of the suburban population were upper and upper middle class. Suburban communities, even more than the central cities that had spawned them, tended to be segregated by income and ethnic group. As in the past, suburban growth was also encouraged by the process of "invasion and succession," the flight from their neighborhoods of long-settled groups due to the movement into them of "alien" newcomers. Some scholars have viewed the migration after World War I of the well-to-do to the suburbs as in part the outgrowth of their political and social frustration. From this standpoint, the upper income exodus is seen as an attempt to escape from the jarring diversity and losing power struggles of the big city while re-establishing a homogeneous community in which the status and influence of wealthy and prominent families would be secure.[8]

THE ERA OF THE METROPOLIS 259

Since the early 1900s, many suburban developments have been somewhat influenced by the garden city concept of Ebenezer Howard, the English reformer. In 1898, Howard wrote a book entitled *Tomorrow: The Peaceful Path to Real Reform*, in which he described the ideal community as a fusion between town and countryside which should have permanent boundaries, no more than 32,000 people, and sufficient industry to keep it independent of surrounding localities. As Howard envisaged them, these communities would have abundant parkland and would be surrounded by a permanent greenbelt which would be used both as a farming area and as a recreation ground. All of the city's land was to be owned and its uses controlled by the community at large.

With the partial exceptions of Clarence Stein's Radburn, New Jersey, project of the late 1920s, and the greenbelt communities of the 1930s, no attempt was made in America to carry out all of the features of Howard's plan.* What the garden city movement did accomplish in America, however, was the popularization of the idea that communities could be planned as a whole. The nation's first garden suburb was Forest Hills Gardens in the Borough of Queens in New York City, a project of the Russell Sage Foundation; it was completed in 1911, but proved far too expensive for the working class that Howard had originally sought to assist. Thereafter, many new suburbs were built in which, note Christopher Tunnard and Henry Hope Reed, "the emphasis was on neo-Romantic planning and on greenery."[9]

Another planning concept which influenced the evolution of suburbia was the country club district, developed after 1912 by the Kansas City realtor J. C. Nichols. Nichols's idea was to create a stable middle class community by placing controls on the use of the land and by the formation of a community association. Restrictions on the householder were written into the deeds, including the requirement that the owner not sell his home to blacks. The community association had the task of enforcing the various regulations for the use of the land. It would also see to it that community facilities were maintained and would undertake such public tasks as refuse collection, meeting the expense through assessments on

---

*For discussions of Radburn and the greenbelt towns, respectively, see page 286 of this chapter and pages 343–345 in Chapter 10.

the local property owners. Nichols's system was widely imitated by other real estate developers.

Suburbia Since 1945

After 1945, there was an enormous upsurge in the population of the suburbs. Between 1950 and 1970, the number of people residing in metropolitan areas but outside of central cities went from 35 million to nearly 76 million. As a result, the percentage of the nation dwelling in the outer metropolitan districts increased from 23 to 37 percent, while the share of metropolitan central cities showed a slight decline. Of course, some outer metropolitan districts were not, aside from the census count, truly suburban because they were not integrally linked with the central cities. These were largely offset, however, by the communities which were suburbs of cities of less than 50,000, so that qualitatively the suburban population as of 1970 comprised roughly a third of the national population.

The massive growth of the suburbs since 1945 was due principally to the continuance of generally favorable economic conditions and federal policy. The mass prosperity of the postwar era, with its higher pay and shorter working hours, made it possible for many workers, both working class and white collar, to live farther from their jobs than ever before. The fact that median real income had more than doubled between 1950 and 1975 enabled the majority of American families to afford serviceable cars and to own homes. Suburbanization has been encouraged by the federal government which, through the Federal Housing Administration and GI Bill of Rights, has underwritten the low-interest mortgages of millions of home buyers. The government has also contributed to suburban growth through the construction of thousands of miles of highway which have made additional localities accessible to commuters.

In moving out of the city, the suburbanite sought to retain the economic and cultural advantages of urban life while avoiding its afflictions and resisting its way of life. The suburbs seemed cleaner, quieter, and safer than the city. It should also be noted that many of the new suburbanites had fled from their old central city neighborhoods because the poor and blacks had moved into them. Like those who had earlier fled from the immigrants, the middle income migrants of the postwar era were moving partly because of their prejudice and exaggerated fears, but also because of the genuine problems which inevitably accompany the arrival of impoverished newcomers.

Perhaps the most appealing feature of the suburbs is that they afford middle income families the opportunity to own their own homes, traditionally one of the goals of the average American. The trend to suburban living is reflected in the fact that whereas in 1940 only 44 percent of America's families owned their homes, 64.5 percent were homeowners by 1973.

The appeal of the suburbs also reflects the powerful anti-urban strain in American thought, an offshoot of the agrarian tradition of Thomas Jefferson who viewed cities as inevitably harmful to the moral and political health of the republic. The desire of most Americans for at least a measure of rusticity was demonstrated by the results of a 1973 Gallup Poll which asked a random group where they would most like to live. Of those queried, only 13 percent expressed a desire to live in a city, with the others opting for suburbs, rural villages, or farms.[10] "The suburbanite," writes Janet Roebuck, "makes his own compromise between the rural dreams of Thoreau and the urban realities of IBM."[11]

Undoubtedly, there are aspects of suburban life that are rural in character. Thus, as Daniel Elazar has pointed out, many residents of the suburbs inhabit "plots of land that would look large to a Chinese or Indian farmer."[12] In order to retain their rural flavor, suburban towns often reject proposed improvements such as sewers and sidewalks, which would, according to the residents, add to their tax burden and lend too urban a tone to their communities. In avoiding such citification, they are also seeking to keep out such unwanted features of the central city as apartment houses and the urban poor.

Much of the suburban growth since 1945 has taken place in planned developments like the various Levittowns, starting with the one begun in 1947 on Long Island by builder Abraham Levitt. These communities were at first remarkably homogeneous, containing houses of only one or two types and attracting families that closely resembled one another in age and income. During the 1940s, in some of the new communities in Long Island, outside of New York City, the residents were bunched so closely in age that for several years there were scarcely any children of high-school age.

In recent years, the nation's senior citizens have become increasingly suburban. While it remains true that those over sixty-five make up a higher proportion of the central cities than they do of the suburbs, by the 1970s the disparity was very slight, less than 5 percent. The proportion residing in suburbs has also increased among the unmarried and among childless married couples. The growing diversity of population in suburbia has led to the construction there of many new apartment houses, some of them specifically designed for the elderly. In addition, many new retirement communities have sprung up in Florida, California, and in other warm-weather areas. The oldest retirement community is Sun City, Arizona, which opened in 1960 and had 28,000 residents by 1973.

Historically, blacks have settled in the suburbs far less than have whites. In spite of a rapid increase in the rate of black migration to the suburbs in the late 1960s, by 1970 less than 5 percent of suburbia was black, although blacks accounted for 11 percent of the national population and over 20 percent of the central cities. Nevertheless, by the early 1970s the suburban tide was running strongly enough among blacks, particularly among those in their twenties, to lead some sociologists to forecast a suburban future for the nation's young blacks.

Today, as in the past, most suburbs are racially segregated. In the 1930s and 1940s, many deeds to private homes contained racial covenants, clauses which bound the owners of the houses not to sell to anyone who was not white. In 1948, the Supreme Court, in the case of *Shelley* v. *Kramer*, declared this practice unconstitutional, but segregation still persists throughout most of the nation's metropolitan areas. "Most suburban blacks," wrote urban sociologist John Kramer in 1972, "live in mini-ghettos wedged between the more usual white suburban places."[13]

Decentralization of Business

The growth of residential suburbs has been accompanied and encouraged by the increasing decentralization of economic life. In the nineteenth century, major commercial and industrial firms were, of necessity, anchored near the railroad terminal and the ocean or river docks in the central cities. Whereas the technology and transport of the nineteenth century had promoted the centralization of business and industry, the technological trends of the twentieth century have promoted their dispersion. Thus, the thorough utilization of the telephone has made it possible for business to be conducted with far less personal contact than in the past. Similarly, the growing use of the truck for commercial transport and the airplane for long-distance travel has reduced the dependence of business upon central cities, which can now be bypassed by trucks and which are sometimes farther from the airport than are some of the suburbs.

Deconcentration was also promoted by the fact that the price of land and the level of taxation are almost invariably lower outside of the central city than they are within it. In the field of manufacturing, the tendency to decentralize had resulted, by the first decade of the twentieth century, in the erection of numerous factories in "satellite cities," which as noted earlier, are communities linked closely to and utterly dependent upon nearby central cities. "The metropolitan manufacturing district," wrote Graham Taylor in 1910, "stretches out in belts and flanges from New York into Long Island, Staten Island, and New Jersey, while Eastern Massachusetts is a mosaic of mill towns. In some sections of the South, scarcely a city of any size lacks one or more satellites, thrumming with spindle and shuttle."[14] After World War I, the increasing use of the assembly line in manufacturing, which required larger factories than in the past, led still more employers to the suburbs.

The suburbanization of industry accelerated greatly after 1945. In 1948, the suburban share of manufacturing jobs within SMSAs was 33 percent; by 1963, it was 52 percent. An important factor in the continuing decentralization of industry is that mechanization and automation have reduced the value to industry of unskilled workers who have traditionally congregated in the central cities and whose presence there earlier had been an economic asset.

The dispersion of manufacturing has been followed in turn by the decentralization of wholesaling and retail trade. Thanks to the automobile revolution, it is no longer indispensable for a wholesale merchant to locate in the central city; by 1970, more than a quarter of the jobs in wholesale trade were located in the suburbs.

Retailing was revolutionized by the emergence of the large-scale shopping center in the 1930s. These centers are located in either the outer districts of the central cities or in the suburbs beyond and have parking space for hundreds or even thousands of cars. Although some developers, such as J. C. Nichols, had experimented with shopping centers in the 1920s, it was not until the 1930s when various big-city department stores established suburban branches that the modern shopping center began to evolve. Ultimately, the department stores were grouped in centers with retail outlets of national companies and dozens of smaller retail establishments. Many of these centers now include restaurants, movie theaters, and even churches. By 1971, there were 13,000 shopping centers in the nation, and they had succeeded in diverting a large and growing share of metropolitan retail business from the downtown merchants of the central cities. In that year, shopping centers had roughly half of the retail trade in 21 of the nation's major metropolitan areas.

Of all the economic activities in the central cities, the ones that have tended to remain longest within them are those connected with business management and with the service sector of the economy. In these areas, centrality and the face-to-face contact it permits are still important. The concentration of corporate management and of such service industries as banking and communications is reflected in the high density commercial activity traditionally found in the central business districts of the large cities. In the twelve leading centers of business administration, office space increased by 44 percent between 1950 and 1970. Between 1950 and 1970, gross floor space in Manhattan's central business district increased from 128 million to 226 million square feet.

The skyscraper has been the symbol of the big city in this century. In the 1920s, such buildings were constructed in all the major urban centers. By 1929, there were 377 buildings of twenty stories or more. By then too, construction had already begun in New York City on the two famous structures that were for more than three decades the two tallest buildings in the world: the 77-story (1,046 feet) Chrysler Building and the 102-story (1,250 feet) Empire State Building. Some of the skyscrapers, notably the Empire State, proved unprofitable, and consequently, few tall buildings were constructed in the depression and during World War II. The office building boom of the 1950s and 1960s produced many new multi-story structures, but not until the late 1960s was there much interest in producing buildings of more than sixty stories. The early 1970s witnessed the construction of the 110-story (1,350 feet) World Trade Center in New York City, the 110-story (1,454 feet) Sears Tower in Chicago, and new structures in excess of sixty stories in a number of cities including Dallas, Atlanta, Houston, New Orleans, and Los Angeles.

Despite the office-building boom in the central cities, the suburbs and satellites in many of the older centers of the East and Middle West have since World War II absorbed a growing share of both the managerial and service functions within their respective metropolitan areas. Suburban office parks in places like Carlton (outside St. Louis), or Greenwich, Connecticut, are luring major corporate offices away from the central cities. New York City in the 1970s lost financial firms to New Jersey and corporate headquarters to suburbs in Westchester, Long Island, and Connecticut.

This exodus has occurred for a number of reasons. Undoubtedly, the high taxes and severe social problems of the contemporary central city have played a role. More important has been the high cost of central city space in comparison to the suburbs. Another significant influence on the decision to move has been the desire of company officials to work closer to where they live, so that they can spend more time with their families and avoid a daily round-trip journey that in some instances took as much as four hours. Furthermore, by the 1970s new developments in communications and computer technology were beginning to make it less necessary for many companies to be near the financial, legal, and cultural resources on which they had traditionally relied.

In general, many central cities, especially in the East and Middle West, have been losing jobs while the suburbs have been gaining them. By 1972, the metropolitan suburbs had equaled their central cities as sources of employment. By then too, more than twice as many suburbanites were working in the suburbs as were commuting to central cities, and there was also a swelling tide of reverse commuters, proceeding from central city homes to suburban jobs.

To a considerable extent, even culture, which has traditionally been centered in the big cities, has been decentralized. Concert halls have been built in places like San Rafael outside of San Francisco, and many small cities have their own symphony orchestras. Theaters have proliferated in suburbia, as have a wide variety of restaurants and even singles' bars.

Professional sports have also been suburbanized with the construction of major league athletic stadia in such places as Pontiac, Michigan; Bloomington, Minnesota; Hackensack, New Jersey; and Foxboro, Massachusetts.

With their continued growth and development, many suburbs have ceased to function merely as "bedrooms" for central cities and have come increasingly to resemble the cities from which they sprang. In the suburbs, as in the outermost central city areas, commercial and industrial areas are now to be found interspersed with residential districts. By the 1970s, high-rise office and apartment buildings had begun to emerge in the suburbs. "Suburbia," wrote Louis Masotti in 1973, "is clearly no longer just a family place."[15]

With the suburbs becoming ever more city-like, the political boundaries which separate them from their central cities have become increasingly artificial. While it is true that central cities have a far higher average density than do the suburbs, there are in most of them areas, normally at the periphery, that seem "suburban" in character, consisting of detached, single-family houses, populated in the main by people from the same or from similar ethnic backgrounds, most of whom own their own homes.

The Sun Belt

The most dramatic examples of urban and metropolitan growth in recent decades have occurred in the so-called Sun Belt, the southern and southwestern areas stretching from Virginia to southern California. (See Figure 8.4.) Of the nation's thirteen fastest growing metropolitan areas between 1970 and 1974, eleven were located in Florida, Arizona, and Texas. The growth of these metropolises has been encouraged both by their warm weather and, paradoxically, by the growing use of air conditioning which alleviates the harmful effects of a hot climate without lessening its benefits. The rising urban centers of this region have also benefitted from the fact that, on the whole, their social and environmental problems are not yet as severe as those in the older metropolises to the north and east.

The growth of the Sun Belt metropolises is part of a long-term shift of population and power toward the South and West that is fraught with important consequences for the

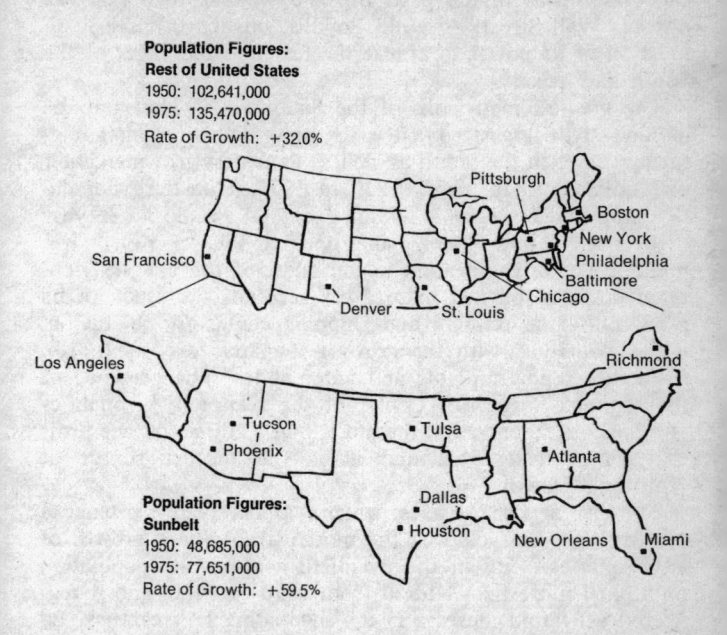

Population Figures:
Rest of United States
1950: 102,641,000
1975: 135,470,000
Rate of Growth: +32.0%

Pittsburgh
Boston
New York
Philadelphia
San Francisco
Baltimore
Denver — St. Louis Chicago

Los Angeles
Richmond
• Tucson
• Tulsa
• Phoenix
• Atlanta
Dallas
Population Figures:
Sunbelt
• Houston
1950: 48,685,000
New Orleans
Miami
1975: 77,651,000
Rate of Growth: +59.5%

Figure 8.4 Population Growth in the Sunbelt Region: 1950–1970

future. According to a 1976 study by the *New York Times*, should the present trend continue, the southern and western states will for the first time have a majority of the seats in the House of Representatives by 1980.[16] In 1976, Governor Ruben Askew of Florida remarked that "the wheel of power is turning, undeniably and unmistakably, toward the South."[17]

The rapid increase in territory and population of the rising urban centers of the South and West is due also to the steady movement into these regions of people, companies, and capital. "During the past few decades," contended Beverly Duncan and Elliot Lieberson in 1970, "we have witnessed the final stages of the inter-regional colonialism which had accompanied the emergence of the national economy."[18] For example, a growing percentage, of the banking activity of the South and West is handled exclusively by regional banking centers rather than being passed along to New York and Chicago, as it was in the past. It is no wonder then that the phrase "Wall Street," the old Populist bugaboo, has lost almost all of its power to arouse the fear and the anger of the South and West.

The greatest metropolis of the Southwest is Houston, the nation's sixth largest city; it is the most diversified manufacturing center in the South as well as its fastest growing center of wholesale trade. From 1920 to 1970, Houston's population multiplied ninefold, attaining a total in the latter year of over 1,200,000 out of a metropolitan total of nearly two million. The city's location in the midst of the nation's richest deposits of oil and natural gas accounts for much of its growth. As the refining and shipping center for its region, it has flourished with the growing demand for fuel to run the nation's power plants and automobiles. The presence of the Manned Spacecraft Center of the National Aeronautics and Space Academy, and the more than 1,200 aerospace firms that have clustered around it, is yet another source of Houston's growth.

The city of Los Angeles, which was barely in existence a century ago, has achieved the most extraordinary growth of any American city in the twentieth century. Its population multiplied more than tenfold from 1890 to 1920, and it registered a fivefold increase in the succeeding half century. By 1970, it ranked third among central cities with a population in excess of 2,800,000, while its metropolitan total of more than seven million was second only to that of New York.

In the 1920s and 1930s, Los Angeles had very little manufacturing, but its thriving extractive and service industries and its glamour as the capital of the movie business made it a magnet for multitudes of newcomers from the Midwest and Southwest. Los Angeles is today more diversified economically than any other western city. Its economic base resembles Houston's in its emphasis upon the oil, electronics, and aerospace industries, but Los Angeles is also an automobile and rubber manufacturing center and still functions, of course, as the capital of the motion picture and television industries.

Since 1940, there have been extensive annexations in many Sun Belt cities. Between that year and 1970, the central city areas of Houston and Dallas grew more than sixfold, that of Mobile approximately tenfold, and that of Phoenix twenty-eight-fold. As Kenneth Jackson has pointed out, the population increases after 1940 in Houston, Phoenix, and some other southern and western cities were due entirely to the incorporation of neighboring areas. Had their boundaries remained where they were in 1940, each of these cities would have lost population.[19] Over the same span there was scarcely any territorial gain in the leading cities of the Northeast and Middle West, nor in such old and established far-western centers as San Francisco.

A major reason for the extensive annexations by the newer metropolitan centers was their eagerness to avoid the predicament of cities farther to the north and east, such as Newark and Cleveland, that are surrounded on all sides by prosperous and well-populated communities that are rather hostile toward them and indifferent to their problems. Consequently, they have sought to annex their suburbs while the latter were themselves still too small and poor to provide a full array of services and, therefore, were usually amenable to the idea. Finally, such cities as Houston, Texas, and Charlotte, North Carolina, have been aided in their expansion by the laws of their respective states which deny to suburban residents any say as to whether their communities shall be annexed by nearby cities.

Decline of the Older Cities

Students of the urbanization process have long contended that the leading metropolises are those which perform a wide array of functions. The great urban centers have tended to combine large-scale manufacturing with extensive activity in interregional commerce as well as in the service trades. A purely industrial city, such as Akron, the dominant center of the nation's tire industry, has been unable to become a leading metropolis because of the narrowness of its economic base. After achieving the highest growth rate of any metropolis in the 1920s, Akron was able to achieve only modest growth thereafter because of the weakness of its commercial and service sectors. Detroit, on the other hand, which had the second fastest rate of growth in the 1920s, has become the nation's fifth ranking metropolitan center, due in part to the growing diversity of its economic base.

Significantly, none of the five metropolises which are now growing most rapidly is in either the northeastern or the north-central region of the country. Over the past quarter of a century, nearly all of the major cities of these regions have failed to achieve significant growth. Thus, both New York and Chicago, still the nation's two largest central cities, have declined slightly since 1950. The decline has been far larger, both absolutely and relatively, in such cities as Boston, Pittsburgh, and St. Louis, each of which has lost more than one fifth of its population since 1950. While it is true that the metropolitan areas surrounding the important eastern and midwestern cities have in most cases continued to grow, the increase in their populations has not been as rapid as in the past, nor has it kept pace with the growth of the burgeoning metropolises of the South and West.

In spite of the fact that the declining cities of the Northeast and Middle West remain the nation's greatest centers of culture, finance, and business management, it is within them, and especially in their oldest neighborhoods, that we find today's urban problems at their worst. A major source of their problems lies in the fact that they have continued to function as magnets for the poor and unskilled, principally blacks from the South and Caribbean and Spanish-speaking immigrants from Latin America. Such newcomers increase the need for public services at a time when the tax base is declining because of the departure of business and the middle class for the suburbs and for other regions. From 1970 to 1974, notes George Sternlieb, the income of those moving into central cities was in aggregate nearly $30 billion less than the income of those moving out.[20] "Twenty years down the road," said a Cleveland official in 1971, "it is perfectly conceivable that the city will be just one great big poorhouse."[21]

Caught between rising social needs and falling tax revenues, the cities have been forced to choose between bleak alternatives. They must either cut back on services, a course likely to injure the well-being of the poor, or raise taxes, which is likely to add to the city's problems by speeding the departure of business and the middle class. It was precisely these conditions which brought New York City to the fiscal crisis of 1975 in which the city was forced into additional borrowing, higher taxation, and extensive cutbacks in services. These conditions have also enabled the suburbs to spend significantly more than the central cities in such areas as education and recreation.

A key aspect of the urban condition, now as in the past, is the shortage of adequate housing for low income families. The migration to the suburbs of middle income and moderate income families after 1945 alleviated the problem somewhat by creating millions of inner-city vacancies which then became available for rental to others. At the same time, however, many formerly livable areas in the central cities were themselves becoming slums. From 1960 to 1965, the percentage of all Los Angeles housing that was classified as "substandard" rose from 18 to 35 percent. In New York City, the number of slum dwelling units increased from 475,000 in 1960 to roughly 800,000 by 1968.

Deterioration has occurred because of many factors. Probably the most important reason is the inadequate earnings of the unskilled. Poverty necessitates overcrowding, which, in turn, promotes decay and blight. The process has been furthered by the advanced age of much of the housing. As of 1970, nearly half of the nation's stock of housing had been built before 1929. Congestion and decay have also been encouraged by federally subsidized urban renewal, which from 1949 to 1967 demolished over a million housing units, at least some of it livable, while providing only a little more than half a million units of public housing. Frequently, owners have been unwilling to make repairs on buildings which might reduce their profits. Finally, the antisocial conduct of a minority among the poor, perhaps embittered by the way society has treated them, has also been a factor at times in the creation of slums, as may be seen by the rapid deterioration of some public housing projects.

The population is rapidly declining in the most impoverished districts of the nation's older big cities as building after building deteriorates and is scrapped by its owner. Hundreds of apartment buildings, row houses, and even private homes have been abandoned each year in New York City, Philadelphia, Detroit, Chicago, St. Louis, and other cities. Landlords abandon buildings in order to escape from the taxes and the mortgage payments. With no heat and no repairs, the regular tenants soon depart, leaving the building to be occupied by vagrant and criminal elements until torn down by the city. "Some blighted areas," Kenneth Jackson has remarked, "are left to the rats, and some are devoid even of rodents."[22]

Since the 1960s, crime, and particularly violent crime, has become the problem of greatest concern to most residents of the major cities. Between 1960 and 1974, according to the FBI, the national rate of violent crime nearly tripled, while that for property crime increased two and one-half times.

Crime in general, and violent crime in particular, tends to occur disproportionately in big cities. Thus, in 1974, in the six cities with populations of over a million, whose residents comprised only 10 percent of the national population, roughly 30 percent of all reported crimes of violence took place. With the crime rate soaring upward, central city residents, particularly the elderly, increasingly tend to remain home at night rather than run the risk of being mugged, robbed, or worse.

While social conditions are, on the whole, better in the suburbs, these areas have increasingly been afflicted with the same maladies as the cities. Hardest hit have been the oldest suburban communities, which are usually those nearest the central cities. Since 1950, the rate of taxation has been rising spectacularly in many suburbs, in some cases doubling and tripling in the course of a single decade. In some of the older suburbs, as in their central cities, population has declined, weakening the tax base. In 1969, the total of suburban residents with incomes below the poverty line was about two thirds of that for the central cities. Housing blight has also emerged in the suburbs where it usually takes the form of rundown cottages and shacks. Moreover, suburban crime rates have been climbing far more rapidly of late than have those of the central cities. During the 1960s, according to FBI crime reports, the rate of serious crime increased 50 percent faster in the suburbs than in the central cities.

In the 1970s, a counter-trend to suburbanization had begun to emerge as a small but growing minority among suburban families migrated to the central cities. The rising cost of all forms of energy, including heating oil and gasoline, and the rapid increase in many suburbs of property taxes had contributed to this trend which could conceivably lead to a revitalization of the central cities.

Environmental Problems

Since World War II, metropolitan areas have also been beset by environmental and physical problems, one of which is the problem of water supply. The nation increased its consumption of water by roughly 50 percent in the 1960s, primarily to meet the expanding requirements of industry. In spite of the fact that municipalities require only about 6 percent of the nation's water supply, many cities and towns have suffered shortages on occasion. Many cities have been compelled to go even farther afield for their water. Thus, San Francisco extended its reservoir system from 25 miles outside of the city in the early 1930s to a distance of 150 miles by 1964. Perhaps the best example is Los Angeles, which, with hardly any rainfall of its own, obtains some of its water from over 300 miles away. Currently under construction is the California Water Project which will, when completed, pump water from rivers in lightly populated northern California some 550 miles to Los Angeles, and over 600 miles to San Diego.

The problem of water supply has been complicated by the growing burden of pollution. Seepage from the septic tanks used in many suburbs has often served to contaminate local streams. Some rivers and lakes are so dirty that people can no longer safely swim in them. By 1965, Lake Erie, after decades of serving as the receptacle for the wastes of twelve American and three Canadian cities, was aproaching the point at which it would no longer be able to support life. In 1965, the states of Michigan, Indiana, Ohio, Pennsylvania, and New York joined with the Public Health Service in launching a long-term program for the cleansing of Lake Erie.

So severe a problem has water pollution become that some urbanists contend that the harm done by the flush toilet to the environment far outweighs the benefits it affords in terms of privacy, comfort, and convenience. As of 1970, an estimated 10 percent of the nation's sewage was dumped untreated into nearby bodies of water, while another 25 percent was given only preliminary treatment. Moreover, over half of the American people are using water that has been used before and then purified through filtration and chlorination. That these methods are effective is clearly demonstrated by the virtual disappearance of diseases traceable to infected water, including those one-time scourges, cholera and typhoid. However, the day may come when existing methods of purifying water will no longer be effective against the new industrial substances, some of which dissolve very slowly, if at all.

Another severe problem is air pollution. It has been claimed that merely to breathe the air in New York City is as damaging to health as smoking two packs of cigarettes a day. On occasion in certain cities, notably New York and Los Angeles, pollution becomes intolerable as a result of what is called a temperature inversion, in which warm air rises above the layer of cold air, thereby trapping the remaining warm air below. Since the now unmoving air is polluted, many people become ill. In New York City, an inversion took place in 1953 which killed at least 170 people, and another occurred ten years later which caused about 400 deaths.

Virtually all our air pollution has come about through the use of the fossil fuels on which we rely for the bulk of our energy supply. Experts believe that about 60 percent of all atmospheric pollution as of the 1970s is caused by automobile emissions. Other important sources of dirty air are incinerators and smokestacks, especially those of factories and public utilities. Forty times as much electricity was being generated in 1970 as fifty years before, 80 percent of it through the burning of natural gas, coal, and other fossil fuels. Roughly a tenth of all the fuel burned enters the atmosphere as pollution.

Down through the years, local governments have passed measures from time to time against pollution from such sources as incinerators, trash burners, and smokestacks. It was not until the 1960s, however, that a substantial segment of the public became aroused and a powerful environmentalist movement began to emerge. The relative affluence of most Americans has made many of them less willing than in the past to sacrifice the environment in the interests of economic growth. By 1973, there were at least 2,000 environmental organizations in the United States. Due in large measure to their agitation, laws have been passed at all levels of government requiring the application of antipollution devices to automobiles and factories. Thanks to the mounting intensity of the nationwide campaign against pollution during the 1970s, literally hundreds of private companies, including such corporate giants as United States Steel, the Allied Chemical Corporation, and the Ford Motor Company, were taken to court and frequently were indicted and fined.

The federal government has been particularly active in the environmental field. In 1969, Congress enacted the Environmental Quality Act, under which federal agencies are required to file environmental impact statements on all federally assisted projects, a procedure which has resulted in the cancellation of some of them. The following year, President Richard M. Nixon established the Environmental Protection Agency, assigning it the responsibility of setting and enforcing mandatory standards of pollution control in the localities and states. By the end of 1975, the EPA was the nation's largest regulatory agency, with more than 9,000 employees, nearly half of them stationed away from Washington. The agency's areas of responsibility include air and water pollution, pesticides, solid waste, and noise.

During its first seven years, the EPA mainly devoted itself to carrying out the Clean Air Act of 1970 and the Water Pollution Control Act of 1972. These statutes set national standards of quality for air and water, provided for large-scale programs to combat pollution, and set the deadlines for achieving the program's goals. By the end of 1975, the EPA had issued approximately 10,000 enforcement orders to states, localities, and private businesses, roughly 1,000 of them in the area of air pollution, 5,000 on water pollution, and some 4,000 about pesticides.

However, in spite of all this activity, most of the environmental deadlines have not been met. Moreover, the enforcement work of EPA has on dozens of occasions been challenged in the courts, and the loud protests against the agency's rulings voiced by people who have been adversely affected by them have in a number of instances led Congress to rescind EPA policies, particularly in the areas of air pollution and traffic control.

The deadline initially set by Congress in 1970 for states and cities to meet the national standards of air quality was May 31, 1975. In its attempts to implement these standards, the EPA has exacted many changes from state and local governments. For example, in overseeing the air pollution programs of the states, EPA has often ordered states to require the use of cleaner (but more expensive) types of fuel, both by municipalities and in the private sector. In 1971 when there was an air pollution crisis in Birmingham, the EPA ordered twenty-three factories to shut down until the crisis was over.

The activities of the agency have been especially extensive in the area of traffic control. In 1975, it ordered the state and city of New York to implement a plan for reducing daily traffic into Manhattan by 10 percent and also required the imposition by mid-1977 of tolls on the eleven bridges across the Harlem and East rivers. In 1973, the EPA had directed nine cities, including Chicago, Boston, and Los Angeles, to levy special taxes on motorists who commuted to the central cities or who parked on their streets, but this measure was dropped in less than a year due to local and congressional opposition. For a time, the agency attempted to screen every proposal for the construction of shopping centers, apartment and office buildings, parking lots, highways, and airports, in order to regulate pollution from automobiles. So vociferous was the opposition to this policy in Congress and among real estate developers, municipal officials, and other local groups that in the middle of 1975 the agency abandoned it, except where highways and airports were concerned.

Congress and the state and federal environmental authorities have also sought to reduce automobile pollution at its source by requiring the nation's car manufacturers to annually scale down, step by step, the amounts of harmful gases emitted by their automobiles. The Clean Air Act of 1970 required car manufacturers to cut the 1970 emission levels of key pollutants by an average of 90 percent as of 1975. The evident inability of the industry to meet this deadline resulted in 1974 in its extension to 1977 and subsequently to 1978. After these postponements, however, the industry had, on the whole, succeeded (up to the end of 1976) in reducing pollution to the levels required by law.

The federal government has also dealt on a massive scale with the problem of water pollution. In the Water Pollution Control Act of 1972, authorization was provided for the expenditure of $18 billion for the construction of sewage treatment plants and for the cleansing of the nation's lakes, rivers, and streams. The act also required every discharger of fluid waste, whether a private firm or a municipality, to obtain a permit from the EPA which would be issued only if the polluter was either in compliance with federal clean water standards or was implementing the corrective program devised for it by the EPA. The same legislation required every polluter of water to install by 1977, "the best practicable pollution control equipment" and by 1983, "the best available equipment." By the beginning of 1977, even though the nation's waters were somewhat cleaner than when the program had begun, it was clear that many, if not most, of the offending cities, states, and business firms would be unable to meet the federal deadline.

Action has also been taken on other aspects of the environment. By 1975, the federal government had begun to set standards in the areas of solid waste, chemical pollution, and noise pollution. It has been estimated that between 1974 and 1983, Washington will have spent over $200 billion on environmental improvement, and over the same decade total expenditure on the environment, including that of private enterprise and local government, will come to well over $300 billion.

Environmental controversies are often highly complex, with at least some merit on both sides of the issue. Government agencies that deal with these issues often have the thankless and difficult task of reconciling the requirements of economic growth with the promotion of a healthy environment. Often, EPA and other environmental agencies have been the target of simultaneous attack—accused by business of doing too much, thereby injuring the economy, and by environmentalists of doing too little, and thus failing to protect the public. Although environmental officials have often retreated, or been forced to retreat by elected officials, their efforts during the 1970s resulted in somewhat cleaner air and water for many of the nation's metropolitan areas.

Traffic and Transit

In the post-World War II era, certain problems of metropolitan areas have been severely worsened by the widespread use of the automobile, which by the 1970s accounted in urban areas for approximately 90 percent of all travel and over 80 percent of all trips to work. These vehicles contribute significantly to the noise and, as we have seen, to the pollution of the central cities. Worst of all its effects are the traffic jams which daily clog many of the nation's highways and central business districts, some of which were originally laid out in the era of the horse. Traffic congestion, not only causes the annual loss of billions of dollars but also inflicts much wear and tear upon commuters.

In seeking to alleviate the crush, more and more miles of expressway have been built. In some cases, however, improved highways have brought only temporary relief. Within less than a decade of its opening in 1955, New York City's Long Island Expressway was derisively referred to as the "world's longest parking lot." Even in the Houston Metropolitan Area, which contains 200 miles of high-quality freeways and is perhaps the most automobile-oriented metropolis in the country, extension and improvement of the highways have not kept pace with the increase in traffic. "Traffic jams have multiplied," noted a 1973 article in *Business Week* magazine, "and for many Houston commuters, a relatively easy one-half hour drive to work has become an ordeal of one or two hours."[23] Defenders of the automobile contend, however, that without the superhighways, traffic jams would be still worse and insist that if new highways are equipped with sufficient lanes, they can permanently improve the movement of traffic in their respective areas.[24]

Cities have made intermittent efforts to accommodate the automobile. Starting in the 1920s, they have widened their streets and have established sophisticated systems of traffic control, such as timed traffic lights. Through traffic has been expedited and linked to local streets by means of tunnels, overpasses, and underpasses, many of them constructed with federal funds. In order to clear a path for traffic, restrictions have been placed on parking in the street. At the same time, city governments have added to available parking through municipal garages and parking lots.

There has been a decline in the ridership on public systems of transportation, due in part to the growing use of the automobile, that has left them financially undermined. This, in combination with their rising costs, especially in the labor area, has forced the transit lines to raise fares and skimp on maintenance, thereby losing still more of their riders. The interurban and intracity streetcars had gone out of existence in most metropolitan areas by 1950 and by 1975 were virtually extinct. Though heavily subsidized by the federal government, as of the 1970s most commuter railroads were in bad shape both physically and financially. The remaining media of collective transit, the buses and subways, have also suffered sharp declines in ridership. The national average of daily users of public transit declined from its all-time peak of over 23 million in 1946 to 5.3 million in 1975.

In the 1960s, many cities, hoping to alleviate traffic snarls and perhaps to staunch the outward flow of residents, began to plan for new transit lines and in some cases for the construction of whole new systems of rapid transit. Work was begun on metropolis-wide subway systems in the San Francisco–Oakland area and in and around Washington, D. C. In 1972, the BART (Bay Area Rapid Transit) system began operations in the San Francisco–Oakland region, but its ridership up to 1976 fell far short of expectations and its revenues were paying only one third of its operating costs.

BART's failure is symptomatic of the limitations inherent in mass transit. For one thing, population has become too dispersed in most metropolitan areas for commuting to be provided for easily or conveniently through trains and buses. Rapid transit is also, in its way, rather wasteful. Transportation experts estimate that, on the average, about 80 percent of the volume of traffic on public transit is concentrated in only twenty hours of the week. In these "rush hours," more trains and facilities must be used and kept in working order than are needed at other times. This results in the underutilization of equipment and in high operating costs relative to the car. Moreover, as many urban experts acknowledge, the train and the bus can never match the automobile in privacy and flexibility and are usually inferior to it in speed.

Despite the failings of mass transit, many programs have been adopted at every level of government, seeking either to promote public transportation or to discourage the use of private cars. Due largely to the energy crisis and to growing concern over air pollution, in 1974 Congress adopted and the President signed into law a measure providing subsidies for six years to mass transit at a rate of $2 billion per year, to be paid for out of the federal tax on gasoline. Some critics of the automobile have urged that private passenger cars be barred altogether from major business districts, but this has never actually been done. Various cities have experimented with some success with shopping malls that can be entered only on foot. To much, and possibly a majority, of the public, however, traffic jams and carbon monoxide pollution are of little moment. In a referendum held in the Houston area in 1973, the voters rejected a proposed extension of the city's bus lines by a margin of over three to one. Under the proposed plan, the new buses were to have been paid for by a levy on automobiles, taxing each car-owner in direct proportion to the size of his vehicle. "We still like cars," explained the mayor of one of Houston's suburbs, "and even more, we like those pickup trucks with the gunracks."[25]

City Planning

The persistent social and environmental ills of the metropolitan cities have led to a variety of planning movements. In the first decade or so of the twentieth century, the dominant planning approach was known as the City Beautiful, a concept which had first emerged at the architectural exhibit of the Chicago World's Fair of 1893. The exhibit's temporary buildings were all in either the classical or the Renaissance style and were so grouped as to convey an impression of order, harmony, and unity.

The fair had demonstrated to many the possibilities of city planning for the promotion of beauty and civic grandeur. "This temporary world of stuff and plaster," Tunnard and Reed have written, "changed the taste of a nation."[26] As a result, there emerged in most of the nation's major cities a City Beautiful movement in which innumerable museums, libraries, and other public buildings were built on a monumental scale and in the classical style of the Greeks and the Renaissance. In dozens of cities after 1900, the new public buildings were grouped to form civic centers, some of them designed by such leading planners as Frederick Law Olmsted, Jr., and John Nolen.

The outstanding figure of the City Beautiful movement was Daniel Burnham, a leading Chicago architect, who had been in charge of the architectural exhibit at the 1893 fair. He had also participated prominently in the revival and partial implementation of the original plan for Washington D. C., by the French-born engineer and veteran of the American Revolutionary War, Charles L'Enfant. Burnham later devised comprehensive plans for San Francisco (1905) and Chicago (1909), in both of which, unlike the usual City Beautiful plan, he devoted considerable attention to transportation. His San Francisco design was for the most part scrapped after the 1906 earthquake, but his plan for Chicago was followed in later years and has had a continuing effect on the development of that city.

Burnham also illustrated the shortcomings of the City Beautiful, for he, like its other advocates and planners, largely ignored the social problems of the cities, especially the problem of the slums. In criticizing this movement in 1907, industrialist Richard Crane observed, "I would not put money into boulevards and statues and fine bridges and elaborate buildings until the immediate surroundings of the poor are made better and decenter."[27]

The City Beautiful was also criticized by architects and theorists of the Functionalist school, whose intellectual leader was Louis Sullivan of Chicago, one of the nation's most prominent architects and the man who is generally credited by historians with being the greatest single influence on the development of the modern skyscraper. The Functionalists argued that the cities could best be beautified not by reviving the building styles of previous eras, which they regarded as increasingly irrelevant to contemporary needs, but by responding in new and imaginative ways to the economic and social forces and to the technological imperatives and possibilities of the industrial age. "Thus," wrote Sullivan scornfully of the classical revival, "architecture died in the land of the free and the home of the brave, in a land declaring its fervid democracy . . . its unique daring, enterprise, and progress. Thus did the virus of a culture, snobbish and alien to the land, perform its work of disintegration; and thus ever works the pallid academic mind."[28]

Interest in city planning rose rapidly in the early 1900s, an era of crusading journalism and extensive reform. In 1909, a city planning exhibit was presented in New York City, and the First National Conference on City Planning was held in Washington, D. C. The first city planning commission was appointed in Hartford in 1907. By 1920, there were nearly 300 such commissions and more than 700 a decade later.

In this period, urban planning, whose first practitioners had been architects and landscape designers, began to evolve into a specialized profession. With the vogue of "science" in the administration of business and government, there emerged a growing body of planners who had been trained in the new disciplines of scientific management and public administration. In 1917, a professional association was organized, the American City Planning Institute, known today as the American Institute of Planners.

The newer planners turned increasingly away from the City Beautiful approach, with its emphasis on the aesthetic and the monumental, in favor of a new concept, the City Functional, or City Efficient, which stressed efficiency and convenience. A key element in this kind of planning was the improvement and channeling of transportation. A famous example of the efficiency-oriented transportation planning that was emerging at this time can be seen in the career of Robert Moses, who has been called "the great expediter." The recipient in 1914 of an earned doctorate in Public Administration from Columbia University, Moses was for more than forty years the initiator and administrator of a wide variety of public works in New York City and its environs, including highways, tunnels, and recreation areas, which have had a tremendous cumulative impact upon the developmen of the region. Social reformers have been critical of Moses and the type of planning he represents, arguing that such planning ignores the human element, plunging blindly ahead regardless of the social and environmental consequences.

A major tool of the City Functional planners was zoning: the placing of controls on the use of the land, a type of planning first developed in Germany. The object of zoning was to maintain the character of urban districts and, in particular, to protect residential areas and high-toned commercial districts from the invasion of skyscrapers, factories, and low income housing. Five American cities had limited forms of zoning by 1915. The most extensively zoned city up to then was Los Angeles, which in 1909 had enacted an ordinance designating seven industrial districts and reserving nearly all of the city's remaining area for residential use.

In 1916, New York City adopted the first comprehensive zoning ordinance in the United States. The measure's prime movers were property owners threatened by a loss of amenity and money due to the construction of tall buildings and garment factories, respectively, in exclusive residential areas and fashionable business districts. The new ordinance divided the whole city into districts, classified as either residential, commercial, or industrial. Permissible building heights were to vary, depending on the width of the adjoining street and the nature of the district. The 1916 ordinance was widely imitated by other cities. In 1930, there were 985 cities with zoning of some kind. By the 1970s, Houston was the only major city in the nation with no form of zoning at all.

Zoning was conservative in that it accepted and tried to protect most of the existing uses of the land. For that reason, it was usually supported by businessmen who regarded most other forms of planning as unwarranted intrusions by the state into matters that were properly the province of private enterprise. As a method of planning, however, zoning is quite limited, for it is largely incapable of dealing with bad uses of city land that have been inherited from the past. It also provided little relief from such persistent urban problems as traffic congestion and the shortage of housing.

Many suburbs have zoning ordinances, the object of which is to so control and limit growth as to preserve property values while maintaining the essential character and homogeneity of the community. In many towns, a limit has been placed on the number of apartment houses that may be constructed while others have simply prohibited the construction of any but one-family houses. Many suburbs have stipulated a minimum area for building lots and have set a price below which no house in the community may be purchased. Through these and other regulations and restrictions, contractors are discouraged or altogether prevented from constructing dwellings suitable for low income families, who, in many metropolitan areas, are disproportionately black or Spanish-speaking. It was estimated in 1969 that 90 percent of the population in the New York Metropolitan Area lacked access to the greater part of its land area.

Exclusionary zoning has been challenged by profit-seeking contractors who want greater freedom to build houses, as well as by civil rights and other liberal organizations attempting to integrate the suburbs and obtain better housing for the poor. The federal government has at times attempted to construct low-cost public housing in suburban communities but has usually met with stiff resistance. "Observers in the suburbs," wrote a *New York Times* reporter in 1969, "say that there is no more emotional issue than zoning, not only because there are racial overtones, but also and perhaps more compelling because apartment buildings mean that the city and all its problems have come a little closer."[29] In 1976, the question of "opening up the suburbs" figured briefly in the presidential campaign and was the subject of a decision by the United States Supreme Court. In *Hills* v. *Gautreaux*, the high court ruled that the federal courts could order the location of low-income public housing in suburbs where government policy in the past had contributed to segregation.

Regional Planning

In the twentieth century, planners and civic leaders have increasingly concluded that planning could not be effective if confined to central cities but must embrace whole metropolitan regions. A distinctive and rather utopian approach to regional planning was that developed by the Regional Planning Association of America, a coalition of architects, planners, and social critics that was founded in 1923. The RPAA, which included such figures as Lewis Mumford, Clarence Stein, and Henry Wright, envisaged a city that would be regional in extent but would make room for communities of every type and size. The association denounced both metropolitan centralization and suburban diffusion as destructive of community and amenity and considered such planning efforts as the City Beautiful and zoning as merely cosmetic attempts to make atrocious social arrangements somewhat more tolerable.

Most regional planning efforts, however, were much less radical than the RPAA. During the 1920s, public planning agencies were established on a countywide basis in the vicinity of Los Angeles, Milwaukee, and Washington, and other cities. Regional planning studies were also carried out by private bodies in such cities as New York, Chicago, and San Francisco. In 1929, New York's Regional Plan Association issued the first volume of its comprehensive plan for the future of the region. Paul Windels, formerly president of the association, pointed out in 1964 that many of the proposals in the 1929 plan were later carried out, including four bridges, three tunnels, eleven expressways and parkways, five parks, and four airports.[30] Though such regional plans have at times been influential, none has yet been able to definitively control the development of a region.

Since the 1960s, the federal government has sought to encourage coordinated metropolitan planning. Various programs, especially in the areas of transportation, housing, and community development, now require the submission of a metropolitan plan before a locality can receive funds. In 1967, Congress enacted the Demonstration Cities and Metropolitan Development Act, which stipulated that all applications for federal grants in selected areas of policy must first be reviewed by the federally recognized regional planning agency. The following year, 171 such agencies were designated officially by the Bureau of the Budget.

During the 1960s and 1970s, comprehensive long-range plans, focusing principally on the areas of transportation and land use, were drawn up for a number of metropolitan areas. One such was the "wedges and corridors" scheme for Washington, D. C., known as the Year 2000 Plan. Drafted in 1965, this plan called for the funneling of all growth in the Washington–Baltimore area within six equidistant corridors, extending outward, like the spokes of a wheel, from the center of the nation's capital. The wedges of land between the corridors were to be used exclusively for recreation and farming. (See Figure 8.5.) This scheme proved unworkable in practice and has largely been shelved. Another notable plan was that adopted by the region planning board for

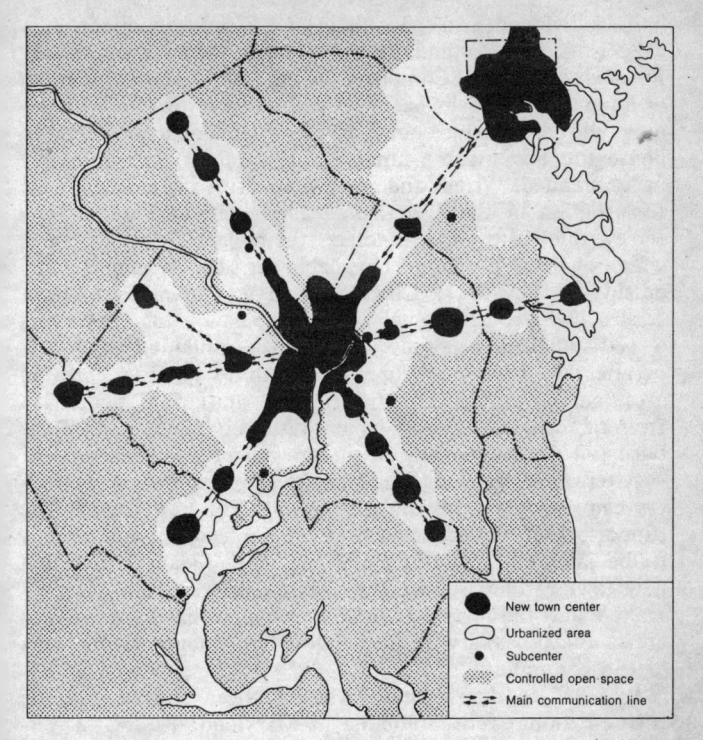

Figure 8.5 The Year 2000 Plan—the "Wedges and Corridors" Scheme for Washington, D.C.

SOURCE: Maryland–National Capital Park and Planning Commission, p. 20.

Nassau and Suffolk counties in Long Island, just outside of New York City. This provided for the extension of the highway system, required all new housing to be constructed in clusters rather than in separate tracts, and called for the preservation of virtually all existing open space, where necessary, through the purchase of land by one of the counties.

Inspired in part by the garden city concept of Ebenezer Howard and by the planned communities constructed by the federal government during World War I, the Regional Planning Association of America advocated the planning of new communities which would be large in scale but low in density. In 1924, the City Housing Corporation, a New York-based, limited dividend firm, gave Stein and Wright an opportunity to construct a community on a seventy-acre tract in the Borough of Queens. Completed in 1928, their new community of Sunnyside Gardens has been praised by critics for its planning and architecture, but its rents remained too high to house the low income families for whom it had originally been intended. Wright and Stein were also responsible for the construction of the even more experimental Radburn, New Jersey, dubbed by its promoters "the city of the motor age," which by 1929 had houses available for sale. Seventeen miles outside of New York City, Radburn was intended to be a garden city or "new town" with a population of 25,000 and a self-sufficient economy. The town contained such experimental features as super-blocks thirty to fifty acres in area, curved streets, and the rigid separation of pedestrian from motor traffic. For all its innovations in civic design, Radburn failed economically in the great depression.

After 1950, growing numbers of planners and civic leaders came to advocate the establishment of new towns. The supporters of this policy saw it as a means of eliminating traffic jams and pollution, and the more idealistic felt that new towns would reduce the distance between the decision-makers and the people at large and hoped that it would also create the possibility of meaningful ties among all members of the community.

By 1967, a dozen new towns had been started, but the furthest along were Columbia in Maryland, Reston in Virginia, and Litchfield Park in Arizona, all of them financed by business corporations. In all three communities, auto traffic was separated from pedestrian and the land was divided into centers, each of which was given over exclusively to certain forms of activity. Thus, the "town center" contained business and cultural activities, the "neighborhood centers" held the high schools and shopping centers, and the "villages" had the playgrounds and grocery stores.

In 1968 and 1970, laws were passed providing federal loans to developers of new towns and communities who would undertake to provide housing for all income groups. Such bargains were struck between the government and the developers of fifteen new towns. As things have turned out, however, there are few low income families in these communities. In 1975, the Department of Housing and Urban Development decided to extend aid to no new towns other than those it was already assisting.

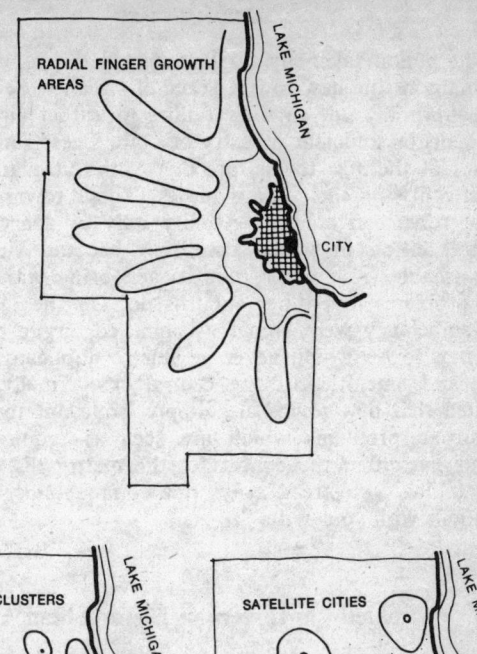

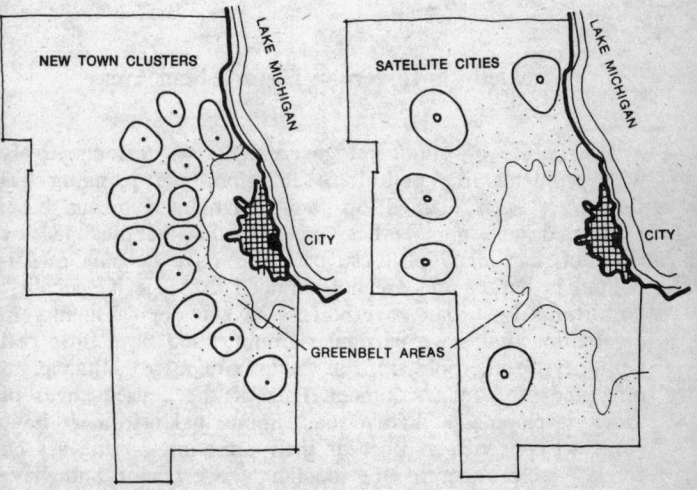

Figure 8.6 Three possible regional development plans: Radial Finger Growth Areas; New Town Clusters: Satellite Cities.

The Finger Plan calls for mass transit that would produce corridors of growth along the transit lines. Expressways would move around and between the fingers.

In the New Town Cluster Plan, cluster centers would be connected with each other and the center city by mass transit but would also have an interconnected system of expressways.

The action taken by HUD reflected the setbacks suffered by many of the new towns, some of which were on the verge of bankruptcy due to their failure to attract either sufficient residents or sufficient industry or both. These failures, say the critics of the new towns, are due to the utopianism and impracticality of such communities. These towns, their argument runs, can achieve viability only by locating near the central cities, in which case they become virtually indistinguishable from other suburbs and bring with them all of the problems that other suburbs do. On the other hand, if self-sufficiency were somehow achieved, argue these writers, the new towns would never be able to duplicate the best culture and amenities of the central city. Finally, some have argued that new towns are simply irrelevant to the solution of urban problems which are seen as requiring attention primarily within the context of the metropolis. "It is rather like taking a mistress," says one commentator, "to improve relations with your wife."[31]

Problems in Governing Metropolitan Areas

The failure of municipal governments to deal effectively with problems like pollution, sanitation, and planning has sometimes been blamed on their fragmented power base. Municipal governments have been further handicapped by the fact that many of these problems have become metropolitan in nature and are not confined to a specific locality. Unfortunately, urban governments have enough difficulty in combatting their own particular troubles and have little real authority to take bold steps in the area of metropolitan planning and area redevelopment. One of the consequences of these developments is that many municipal reformers have come to concentrate most of their attention on the search for a viable form of metropolitan government and have

---

The Satellite Plan calls for major self-sufficient cities surrounded by greenbelts. Expressways would interconnect the satellite cities and rapid transit systems would link all the centers to one another and to the central core.

SOURCE: *The Freeway in the City: Principles of Planning and Design* (Washington, D.C.: U.S. Government Printing Office, 1966), p. 26.

tended to push the perennial quest for honesty in municipal government into the background.

While there is some dispute among government experts as to whether the best solution lies in the establishment of metropolitan government—a single-purpose government with authority to govern an entire metropolitan region—there is more agreement over the point that the number of local governments has become burdensome. This contention is hardly a new one. As early as 1931, the National Municipal League's Committee on Constructive Economy in State and Local Governments reported that "the United States is cursed with too many local governments."[32]

At that time, it was generally agreed that most municipal governments were well run and efficient—a situation that does not appear to exist in the present period. In more recent years, the zealousness with which small units of local government guard their own autonomy frequently has been regarded as one of the major obstructions to effective municipal and metropolitan action. The modernization of sewage disposal facilities, for example, can be totally ineffective if outlying areas resist participating in any proposed changes. By the same token, industrial suburbs can contribute to the air pollution of their neighboring counties without running the risk of being subject to adequate regulation.

During the last several decades, the number of local governments has continued to grow at a rapid rate. As of 1972, the Census of Governments listed 78,268 units of local governments, such as counties, municipalities, townships, school districts, and special districts. Many of these units overlap within the confines of a given metropolitan area. It is ironic that, in spite of the existence of all these units of government, there is usually no one central body to resolve the more urgent regional questions. If it is conceded that the modern metropolitan community is beset by difficulties that would tax the capacity of even the most efficient type of government, it is also likely that metropolitan fragmentation compounds the problem. As Daniel R. Grant has argued, "the structure of local government is perhaps ten percent of the problem, if a figure must be picked, but it is an important ten percent."[33]

Efforts have been made to achieve a more efficient governmental organization as a consequence of annexation, already discussed in Chapter 5 and elsewhere in this chapter, or through consolidation—the joining of existing governments, such as city and county, into one governmental unit. Nevertheless, there is substantial opposition to proposals of this type. Suburbanites view them with disdain because they fear they will be forced to pay additional taxes to revitalize inner city areas, and will lose control over their schools and their zoning regulations. To local officials, annexation or consolidation means a loss of jobs. Other citizens have misgivings about the dangers of super-government. Central cities presumably would benefit from integrated government as a way of relieving their financial burden, but residents do not always see it that way. Minority groups, who are now becoming a force in politics in several large cities, often view these plans as a threat to their hard-fought political ascendancy. Instead, they talk about decentralization and community control.

The legal ramifications with respect to consolidation can be complicated. In many states, laws affecting county lines cannot become effective unless submitted to a vote of the people in the counties affected. Various states also have requirements providing that a consolidation of two or more counties, or the division or the abolition of a county, can only be achieved with a separate referendum held in each of the counties involved. Paradoxically, home rule charters, which had been won by American municipalities in the late nineteenth and early twentieth centuries after considerable agitation, have been invoked on innumerable occasions to block any attempts at general governmental reorganization. It is interesting to note that the two best-known examples of metropolitan government outside the United States—Greater London and Metropolitan Toronto—were both achieved by an Act of Parliament and without the requirement of a popular referendum.

The record of the consolidation movement in the twentieth century has been marred by repeated failures to achieve its goal. In the late 1920s, Pittsburgh and Allegheny County appeared to be on the verge of establishing a metropolitan federation. Such a federation, of course, would have entailed a loss of autonomy to the 123 cities and towns in Allegheny County, and opposition to the plan developed. As a result, the rural-controlled state legislature specified that the plan must receive a majority vote in Allegheny County and a two-thirds vote in a majority of municipalities in the county regardless of size, before it could be ratified. Although the total vote was two to one in favor of the federation, the plan obtained a two-thirds majority in only fifty of the sixty-two municipalities needed to win, and was defeated in 1929. Previously, similar efforts at consolidation had failed in 1923 in Seattle and in St. Louis in 1926.

While relatively little attention was focused on consolidation during the depression, the issue flared up again in the mid-1940s. In 1944 in Boston, a Harvard professor won a local contest after speaking about the need to consolidate the governments of the sixty-six cities and towns encompassing the metropolitan area. However, the plan floundered in Boston, although proponents of consolidation achieved one notable victory in 1947 in Louisiana with the merger of Baton Rouge and East Baton Rouge Parish. Elsewhere, in cities like Birmingham, Houston, and Seattle, consolidation was defeated.

Consolidation in Miami had been blocked by home rule advocates from the surrounding towns on four separate occasions prior to 1957, when the city was successful in establishing a metropolitan government for Miami and Dade County. Under the plan, autonomy was guaranteed to all municipalities, but certain common functions were given to the new metropolitan government. Other cities in which consolidation was adopted in the 1960s and 1970s were Nashville, Tennessee; Jacksonville, Florida; Indianapolis, Indiana; Columbia, Georgia; Carson City, Nevada; Juneau and Sitka, Alaska; Suffolk, Virginia; and Lexington, Kentucky.

These governmental reorganizations did not prove to be an unqualified success, as was initially the case in Miami where the suburbs sometimes blocked the implementation of traffic, sanitation, tax, and zoning plans. One city in which it apparently has worked out very well is Jacksonville, which put consolidation into effect in 1967. Its newly created government was given substantial power, and it used it effectively. Thanks to the efforts of Mayor Hans Tanzler, a massive antipollution drive was begun. In addition, the city replaced sewer lines, upgraded schools, built health centers, and installed over 16,000 street lights.

Although consolidating metropolitan government appeals to various political scientists as one of the most satisfactory solutions to integrating the services and functions of urban America, there are several other approaches. In 1958, voters in Seattle, who had earlier frowned on the idea of consolidation, approved the creation of the Municipality of Metropolitan

Seattle. It was authorized to handle all sewage disposal for the region. At the time that it was set up, there were over 130 different units of government within the region, and it was obvious that little would be accomplished if the matter were entrusted to each unit on an individual basis. The municipality has been largely successful in dealing with sewage pollution. It constructed four new treatment plants, and by 1970 pollution on Lake Washington and Puget Sound had been halted. Theoretically, if the voters of the metropolitan area are so willing, the powers of the "Metro" could be expanded to include matters like transit, air-quality control, or land-use planning, enabling it to be an important factor in regional planning.

Another interesting experiment was Metro Council in Minneapolis and St. Paul, or the Twin Cities Metropolitan Council, established in 1968. The Twin Cities, which are only fifteen miles apart, traditionally had been bitter rivals, but they came to share problems that were common to many metropolitan areas: polluted air from the industrial districts was spreading to the confines of suburbia, urban sprawl was threatening open space and land that environmentalists wanted to earmark for parks, and transportation systems rapidly were becoming outmoded. The real crisis, however, arose over sewage pollution, which was imperiling the lakes and rivers in the area, as well as the underground water reserves. After the degree of this pollution had reached alarming proportions, it was apparent that unified action was needed, particularly in view of the fact that adequate sewage disposal systems were costly if undertaken on a piecemeal and city–suburb basis.

Metro Council was designed as a sanitary district, although it received authorization to handle certain specific problems within its jurisdiction. Since its enactment, it has proven to be remarkably effective in areas like sewage disposal, airports, and health. Its success can be attributed, in part, to the civic spirit and sense of community which seemingly permeated Minneapolis and St. Paul, and the overall feasibility of implementing such a project in medium-sized cities. Another advantage that worked to its benefit was the provision by the state legislature that it would have its own funding, thereby helping it to function as a regional body, free from the dictates of local authorities.

In spite of some success in coordinating metropolitan services, the picture is far from encouraging. Regardless of what is achieved in the area of metropolitan reorganization, corruption still remains a major shortcoming in municipal affairs. To cite one example, Christopher Norwood's *About Paterson: The Making and Unmaking of an American City* (1974) depicts this small city as allegedly being victimized by its influence-peddling officials; it is run, according to the author, by banks, contractors, realtors, organized crime, and county prosecutors. Although writers like Norwood have attempted to arouse public ire over what they consider to be a distressing situation, it remains to be seen how much they will accomplish. While the picture is not always as bleak as they depict, municipal corruption—as opposed to federal corruption—may be harder to tackle due to the fact that the press and citizens' groups generally play a more active role in serving as a watchdog on national affairs.

One hopeful sign in the upgrading of urban affairs is that the federal government has come to the aid of municipalities by giving them substantial funds to grapple with environmental and social concerns at the same time that the states have shown more interest in municipal matters. States have encouraged studies about governmental problems in metropolitan areas, often undertaken with the backing of local and national foundations. Beginning in the 1960s, there was a consensus that the states should have some kind of agency for local affairs, and many such agencies were established. States also encouraged the formation of Councils of Governments (COGs), which usually consist of a council of elected officials from city, town, and county governments. To date, the COGs have not completely justified their existence, for they lack authority to put their proposals into operation. A more successful endeavor was undertaken by Georgia in the mid-1960s. It set up eighteen economic development districts, which function as regional planning and development agencies. State officials distribute federal and state moneys through them, rather than through Georgia's 159 county governments. These special districts have had the effect of eliminating waste and the duplication of services, and have provided for the orderly growth and development of the areas involved.

Another dramatic attempt to solve urban problems was the formation of the Urban Development Corporation in New York State in 1968. It was a super-agency designed to take forceful action in the field of housing in substandard areas as a way of combatting the repeated defeats of housing bond issues and the lack of initiative on the part of local government officials to make effective use of existing housing programs. The Urban Development Corporation was organized as a public corporation with authority to set aside local laws, ordinances, zoning codes, charters, and construction regulations. It was hailed as a bold experiment, but soon ran into trouble with respect to some of the construction that it undertook. In February, 1975, it defaulted on a loan and on $100 million in bond-anticipation notes. New York State subsequently made efforts to reorganize the Urban Development Corporation, but its default reminded many people of the difficulties involved in finding solutions to problems of this magnitude.

The Future of the Cities

The problems stemming from the rise of the twentieth-century metropolitan city have prompted several important critics to ponder the consequences of urban growth and its effects on the populace. The results of their thinking on this subject have been varied, ranging from attempts to undermine the city, efforts to transcend it, and discourse on how to learn to live with it. Yet, in terms of the increasing preference of Americans for life outside the central cities, it is not altogether surprising that the views of a substantial number of contemporary writers express an anti-urban bias. To some exextent, they may be following an old American tradition. Thomas Jefferson, one of the first Americans to comment on the quality of urban life, called cities "sores on the body politic." Although Jefferson's adverse comments were directed at European rather than American cities, he feared that the spread of commercial centers in the United States would be a disruptive influence on the life of the Republic. This type of thinking has never completely disappeared from American values, but it has taken on different forms and concepts in more recent times.[34]

Lewis Mumford, who was one of America's foremost urban scholars and writers, was also one of the modern city's most vocal critics. His conception of the form that a city should take resembled the garden city idea of Ebenezer Howard, and he was an ardent exponent of urban decentralization and regional planning. In the course of his long and distinguished career, Mumford wrote several books, including *The Culture of Cities* (1938) and *The City in History* (1961). The earlier work contained a study of the rise of urbanization throughout the world, and in it the author lamented the decline of the relatively small and culturally sophisticated medieval cities. After their decline, Mumford found little to console himself in terms of what was to follow. He termed the next period the Paleotechnic Age, beginning around the twelfth century, in which both community and culture were dispersed by the rise of capitalism and technology. The Paleotechnic Age, in turn, was superseded by the Neotechnic Megalopolis, or super-city of skyscrapers, sprawl, and mechanization. Nevertheless, Mumford hoped that the future would bring the Biotechnic Age, whereby man would restore human values to his urban society and build a decentralized city.

By the time that *The City in History* appeared in 1961, Mumford foresaw the possibility that urban civilization would destroy itself. "War," he wrote, "was one of the 'lethal genes' transmitted by the city from century to century, always doing damage but never yet widely enough to bring civilization itself to an end. That period of tolerance is now over."[35] After megalopolis, Mumford envisioned the appearance of Tyrannopolis, followed by Necropolis, the city of death. This bleak view was modified somewhat by Mumford's contention that there could be an alternative solution. He cited the new towns and greenbelts which had been established around London and Stockholm as proof that mankind could devise other options to overcome the perils of an overspecialized and dehumanizing urban society.

While Mumford's preference for the decentralized and smaller-scale city remains a popular idea in terms of what has been advocated by various regional planning associations, government agencies, and private developers, his ideas about the suburbs seemingly run counter to the thinking of the vast number of people who live there. He viewed suburbs as culturally deprived entites. Mumford stated this view categorically in an article written in 1921 entitled "The Wilderness of Suburbia,"[36] and it represented a consistent aspect of his later thinking as well.

The quality of urban life is not nearly as distressing to certain urbanologists as it was to Mumford. Writer Jane Jacobs has argued in favor of preserving city neighborhoods and against imposing limitations of size on cities, views which she set forth in her book, *The Death and Life of Great American*

Cities (1961). She found vibrancy and excitement in city living, and felt that some of the older, crowded city neighborhoods were a decided improvement over the superstructures associated with the megapolis. To Jacobs, the ethnic enclaves within the city fostered a spirit of community, and she pointed out that the crime was lowest in areas of high-density living where people were out on the streets.

Several of Jane Jacobs's assertions about the advantages of densely populated cities were spelled out further by Jonathan Freedman in *Crowding and Behavior: The Psychology of High-Density Living* (1975). Freedman maintained that he could come up with little evidence to substantiate the assumption that crowded living conditions are conducive to antisocial behavior. Instead, he came to the opposite conclusion. Whatever the nostalgic pull of the countryside. Freedman believed that the cultural amenities of life, as well as the everyday necessities such as education, health care, transportation, and waste disposal, are those which can be most efficiently utilized by a concentrated population base. Accordingly, he looked to the well-designed and high-density city to supply mankind with its basic human and spiritual needs.

Even if we accept the premise that the future of the world lies in perfecting its urban components, it nevertheless can be stated that city problems are easier to define than to solve. Unfortunately, the world has not yet learned to live in harmony with itself, let alone its cities. In January, 1976, the *New York Times* surveyed nine major world cities, notably Acapulco, Mexico; Addis Ababa, Ethiopia; Calcutta, India; London, England; Paris, France; Rome, Italy; Moscow, U.S.S.R.; Hong Kong, China; and Saõ Paulo, Brazil. Several of the cities lacked such rudimentary needs as pure water and sanitary sewers. In Saõ Paulo, more than one half of its streets were unpaved, and its burgeoning populace far outdistanced improvements made in water and sewage facilities, schools, medical services and transit. Acapulco, once considered to be the haven for the international jet set, went bankrupt during the summer of 1975. On the basis of its survey, the *Times* alluded to many of the difficulties that New Yorkers were facing and reminded its readers that "misery loves company."[37]

Although it is clear that there are no international boundaries to urban problems, American cities have produced several positive results in learning to solve some of the dilemmas faced by other metropolitan communities in the world. In spite of viable alternatives to the giant city—the growth of the suburbs, the development of planned communities, the blueprints advocated by urban planners and regional planning associations—metropolitan cities offer too many attractions to render them obsolete, in this country or elsewhere. The quest for the Heavenly City, however, still remains elusive.

9

Black Urbanites in a Changing City

In Irving Kristol's frequently cited article for the *New York Times* in 1966 entitled, "The Negro Today Is Like the Immigrant Yesterday," he expressed the view that the native-born black urbanite, as a newcomer to the city, was experiencing the same kind of difficulties that beset the foreign-born white immigrant in the past.[1] Not all observers have come to share Kristol's opinion, however. Although many black urban dwellers have continued to make significant gains since the time that the Kristol article appeared, the pros and cons of the issue can still be argued.

In several respects, it is somewhat misleading to refer to the black as a "newcomer" to the city, even though the term is essentially correct if viewed by the fact that a significant portion of the nation's black population first took up residence in cities in comparatively recent years. In terms of the twentieth century, a closer look at population figures reveals that sizable numbers of blacks already lived in cities as of the 1920s, and during these years, as well as in succeeding periods, they generally faced prejudice and discrimination.

The first mass movement of black people to American cities, which dates back to World War I, generated a response which served to make them strangers in their own land. While foreign-born migrants have been subjected to some similar abuses, they were not necessarily discriminated against to the same extent. Black workers in the decade of the 1920s had only limited job opportunities in comparison to native white and immigrant workers of comparable skills and training, and the depression of the 1930s proved to be particularly disastrous to black urbanites.

In the period beginning in the 1940s, which has seen the main thrust of the black urban migration, the demand for unskilled workers has been diminished, placing blacks at an

TABLE 9.1

Urban-Rural Distribution of Black Population and Total Black Population: 1880–1970

Year	Total Black Population	Urban (%)	Rural (%)
1880*	6,580,793	12.9	87.1
1890*	7,488,676	17.6	82.4
1900*	8,833,994	20.5	79.5
1910	9,827,763	27.4	72.6
1920	10,463,131	34.0	66.0
1930	11,891,143	43.7	56.3
1940	12,865,518	48.6	51.4
1950	15,042,286	62.4	37.6
1960	18,871,831	73.2	26.8
1970	22,580,289	81.3	18.7

SOURCE: U.S. Bureau of the Census.

*Definition modified to exclude population in incorporated places and New England towns in the 2,500 to 3,900 range.

even greater disadvantage than the immigrants of the nineteenth and early twentieth centuries. In addition, the sheer magnitude of this migration has had the effect of aggravating their situation in terms of separating them more sharply from contact with the rest of urban society than has been the pattern for their white immigrant predecessors. As demographer Philip M. Hauser has pointed out, American cities had experienced huge increments of population during periods of heavy European immigration, but none of the earlier migrations brought in so many persons of one ethnic or racial stock over so short a span of time. Between 1940 and 1960, the black population of central cities in metropolitan areas of 1,000,000 or more increased by 4,230,000 persons, or 59.7 percent of their total population in 1960.[2]

The black urban population continued to grow during the 1970s, and various cities are becoming largely populated by black people. As more and more blacks move into urban areas, the question remains whether the disparity between them and other members of the community is disappearing, abating, or increasing. It further remains to be seen whether the upward mobility experienced by certain segments of the black population will eventually be characteristic of the group as a whole, as was the case with the immigrants.

Migration Patterns: 1918–1930

In spite of the large-scale anti-black riots of 1919, the migration of black people to the urban North accelerated. While the ending of World War I initially resulted in layoffs and cutbacks in industry, the long-range economic view appeared favorable. The demand for black labor continued as Americans entered what at the time was believed to be the "prosperity decade." The war also produced a dramatic about-face with respect to immigration policy. A combination of factors, including anti-foreign sentiment, pressure from labor unions, and a feeling of postwar isolationism, resulted in the passage of laws that vastly restricted the number of immigrants allowed to enter the United States. As a result, the work formerly done by immigrants had to be filled by other sources, and black workers once again had opportunities for jobs in American industry.

In Chicago, the ten years between the First World War and the onset of the depression gave rise to an enormous increase in that city's industrial output, resulting in the hiring of an additional 328,000 workers. Of this total, an estimated 64,000 black men and women from the South were added to the labor force. It was at this time that Detroit's Ford Motor Company, incorporated in 1903, started its own steel and glassmaking operations. Although in its early years, Ford did not have a policy of discrimination toward blacks, the company's foremen, who were white, hired workers from their own ethnic groups. Consequently, Ford did not employ its first black until 1914. By the 1920s, the expanding Ford Motor Company had replaced Packard as the largest employer of blacks in the automobile industry.

The pattern of migration for black urbanites in the decade of the 1920s was geared toward a few specific cities. Although some rural blacks migrated to the urban South, it was the northern city that received the largest number of black migrants. In the North, however, only a handful of cities were selected for migration, while blacks tended to ignore the West altogether. As of 1930, of the seven cities with more than 100,000 blacks—New York, Philadelphia, Baltimore, Washington, Detroit, Chicago, and New Orleans—only one was located in the South; the West was not represented at all.

In 1930, there were as few as 130,000 black people living in the entire western portion of the country. Movement to the West increased by 21.1 percent during the depression, although as of 1940 only 2.2 percent of all black people lived west of the Mississippi River.* Interestingly, black writer James Weldon Johnson found San Francisco a desirable place for blacks; in 1905, referring to San Francisco, he wrote: "With respect to the Negro race, I found it a freer city than New

TABLE 9.2

Black Population: Distribution by Regions, 1790–1970

	South (%)	Northeast (%)	North Central (%)	West (%)
1790	91	9	—	—
1800	92	8	—	—
1810	92	7	1	—
1820	93	6	1	—
1830	93	5	2	—
1840	92	5	3	—
1850	92	4	4	—
1860	92	4	4	—
1870	91	4	5	—
1880	90	4	6	—
1890	90	4	6	—
1900	90	4	6	—
1910	89	5	6	—
1920	85	7	7	1
1930	79	9	11	1
1940	77	11	11	1
1950	68	13	15	4
1960	60	16	18	6
1970	53	19	20	8

SOURCE: U.S. Bureau of the Census.
*These figures for the West also include the North Central region.

York."[3] Nevertheless, it was not until the period after World War II that black Americans would flock in large numbers to cities like Los Angeles and San Francisco, despite competition from Orientals and Mexican Americans.

In the North, most black migrants went to New York, Chicago, Philadelphia, and Detroit, where they had already concentrated in large numbers prior to 1920. Other smaller industrial cities like Buffalo, Cleveland, and Gary also received numerous groups of black migrants. There was enough industrial activity in other northern cities to encourage migration, but black people, like the foreign-born in past decades, preferred to live in large northern cities already peopled by members of their own group. In addition, there were other factors that influenced their choices. To pull black people toward specific areas, labor agents from the large northern urban centers were active in the South, and black newspapers, like the Chicago *Defender*, which had a large circulation in the South, told readers stories about local job opportunities that awaited the black migrants.

Although there was some black migration to southern cities in the 1920s, these cities proved to be more attractive to rural southern whites. At the same time, blacks migrated in greater numbers to the urban North than did southern whites. Whereas many rural white Southerners regarded the North with uncertainty, to blacks in the decade of the 1920s, the South—whether rural or urban—remained primarily an area of injustice. In 1930, the percentage of all southern-born blacks residing in the northern states located east of the Mississippi River was double the percentage of southern-born whites who lived there.

The blacks who lived in the urban South or who migrated there worked largely in domestic or personal service, but faced increasing competition from white workers throughout the decade of the 1920s. In many southern cities, blacks were being pushed out of jobs formerly monopolized by them. By 1930, white workers had replaced thousands of black men and women as waiters, waitresses, and elevator operators in hotels, restaurants, and boarding houses. Equally discouraging, according to Gunnar Myrdal in his study, *An American Dilemma* (1944), was the fact that "Negroes, in most cases, failed to get any appreciable share in jobs whenever new lines of production were opened up. Negro workers, therefore, are likely to be found in stagnating or retrogressing industries. . . . When there were technical innovations, making work less strenuous, less dirty, and generally more attractive, this often implied a redefinition of the occupations from 'Negro jobs' to 'white man's work.' "[4] As Myrdal further pointed out, the use of women in industry, which occurred in all sections of the United States both during and after World War I, led to special problems in the South. The southern code placed a taboo upon white women and black men working together, giving southern factory owners another excuse for discharging black workers.[5]

The North offered no panacea, particularly since many of the black rural migrants lacked the skills needed by industry. While there was upward mobility in industry, even for unskilled white workers, mobility for black workers was very limited.

In Chicago after the war, approximately 10,000 black workers were displaced from clerical and industrial jobs that they had formerly held due to a wartime shortage of white labor, and there was a correspondingly sharp rise in the already large numbers of black migrants engaged in domestic and personal services. Black men were able to retain their unskilled and semiskilled jobs in the steel and meat-packing industries, but the more skilled black workers skidded downward economically at the same time that many white blue-collar workers were moving into white collar positions. Chicago's black women workers were categorized in a similar fashion. Nearly all of the black women who sought employment went into either domestic or semiskilled work. While 40 percent of white women workers in the 1920s secured clerical jobs, only 5 percent of black women performed this kind of work. Conceivably, few migrant black women from the South were trained for such occupations, but black women already in the city were not upgraded for these positions either. This situation led St. Clair Drake and Horace R. Cayton in their study of Chicago entitled *Black Metropolis* (1945) to state that Chicago's blacks, as of 1930, may have bettered their economic condition after fifteen years of urbanization during a period of industrial expansion, but "they had not made the kind of rapid progress which white European immigrants had made in an equal period between 1895 and 1910."[6]

A similar assessment of the labor market was reached by Myrdal as to the overall job opportunities in the North for blacks during this decade. He found that most of the increase in black employment occurred in nonmanufacturing work, so that "even in the North, the Negro remained confined to certain jobs—either those where he had earlier acquired something of a traditional position or where he managed to gain a foothold during the extraordinary labor market crisis of the First World War."[7]

Discriminatory Practices

The mass migration of blacks made them the most segregated group in the community. Philadelphia blacks, as of 1920, were less segregated than Russian, Roumanian, Italian, and Hungarian immigrants, but by 1930 they became the group with the highest segregation index in that city. As of 1920 in Boston, Chicago, and Cleveland, blacks replaced Italians as the people with the greatest degree of residential segregation. Prior to the migration of the war period, over 50 percent of Chicago's blacks lived outside the black belt. However, as soon as sizable numbers of blacks poured into the city there were efforts to restrict them to the ghetto district. By 1930, three fourths of all residential property in the city was bound by restrictive covenants barring the sale of homes to blacks. In New York's Harlem, the white population—most of whom were first- and second-generation immigrants—moved to the Bronx, Brooklyn, and Queens as the black migration reached huge proportions. Between 1920 and 1930, 118,792 white people left Harlem, and 87,417 in-migrant blacks entered. In 1930, 72 percent of Manhattan's black population were residents of Harlem.[8]

Segregated facilities went hand in hand with inferior housing. A report issued by the Commission on Negro Housing, which was set up by President Herbert Hoover in 1931, charged that in virtually every large city where the black population was numerous, blacks occupied the oldest and most dilapidated housing available. Its findings with respect to several cities were discouraging. According to the commission, Kansas City, Missouri, was notable in providing above-average housing for the middle classes and large parts of the working class, but had inferior accommodations for blacks. Elizabeth, New Jersey, like many other northern cities, had no new houses built for occupancy by black tenants, and many of the older houses occupied by blacks were "unfit for human habitation." In Albany, New York, the houses where black residents lived "do not represent what the city approves according to its Building Ordinance, but it does represent what Albany tolerates and offers to the increasing Negro population group."[9]

Immigrant groups also had their ghettos and they were subjected to the same kinds of inferior facilities, but their enclaves differed from the twentieth-century black ghetto in certain respects. First, the immigrant ghetto in most cities throughout the nineteenth and twentieth centuries was neither permanent nor enduring. Second, immigrant ghettos produced their own businesses and helped to promote the beginnings of an ethnic entrepreneurial class. In the black ghetto, where most of the residents were American citizens, they were not as sufficiently motivated to create their own institutions as a way of preserving their past. Third, many black ghettos, unlike the immigrant ghettos, were not as bound together by the ties that resulted from a shared historical, religious, or cultural tradition. Immigrants, whatever their handicaps, never had to overcome what psychiatrists Abram Kardiner and Lionel Ovesey have termed "the mark of oppression"—the stigma of having been relegated to an inferior caste position.[10]

It should be kept in mind, however, that blacks were not the only group to feel the onus of discrimination during the postwar years. For much of the decade of the 1920s, Catholics and Jews were also the objects of intimidation and abuse. The Ku Klux Klan, which had been given the *coup de grace* in terms of effective legislation directed against it by Congress in the 1870s, was revived in 1915 and grew rapidly in the period thereafter. It not only prospered in the small southern towns, but in large cities throughout the country. Historian Kenneth T. Jackson has estimated that of the over 2,000,000 members who joined the Klan between 1915 and 1944, at least 50 percent resided in metropolitan areas of more than 50,000 persons. He singled out Chicago, Indianapolis, Dayton, Portland, Youngstown, Denver, and Dallas as the main centers for Klan activity.[11]

Klan members were mostly Protestant blue-collar workers who were in direct economic competition with white ethnics and black workers. Their tactics ranged from an attack by the Dallas Klan in 1921 on a black bellboy at a hotel because of his so-called associations with white women to an attempt in 1922 to force Atlanta's board of education into dismissing Catholic teachers.

Paradoxically, the major riot of the decade—the Tulsa

Race Riot of 1921—was not the work of the Klan. The riot broke out after a black man had been arrested on charges of rape brought by a white woman. Fearing that the man might be lynched, a group of blacks brought arms to the jail to protect him. Fighting broke out at the jail and spread to other parts of the city. When the riot was over, thirty people had been killed. The Klan, although not involved in the riot, took advantage of the unrest that it caused in the community and embarked on a series of night raids and assaults.

Despite the appearance of the Klan and the resurgence of nativism that accompanied it, its prominence was relatively short-lived. By 1925, the Klan had reached its peak, and it declined in the years that followed. It never recovered its popularity following the arrest in 1925 of Indiana Klan leader David C. Stephenson, who was later convicted of assaulting and causing the death of Madge Oberholtzer, a twenty-eight-year-old secretary. In the cities, many of its tactics not only angered the local populace but had the effect of uniting the very groups it sought to harass. When disgruntled Klansmen and enterprising citizens helped publish lists of Klan members—as was the case in Chicago in 1922 and Buffalo in 1924—many ethnic groups retaliated by staging boycotts against the businessmen who were so named.

Certain segments of the black community were far from immobilized by the difficulties that black people encountered, but their achievements were limited. Politically, the black voter had some bargaining power, both in the North and in the South. Several machines courted the votes of the blacks as eagerly as they had done with the immigrants. Boss Edward R. Crump of Memphis, who controlled the city's most influential political machine from 1909 until the 1940s, sought the support of the black voters and had a reputation for being fair to the black community in matters relating to civil rights. In those southern cities ruled by machines, blacks in the 1930s generally fared much better than they did in other parts of the South. They were often able to obtain paved streets and schools in their neighborhoods, and were not subjected to discriminatory practices in their dealings with the city administration, law enforcement officials, and the courts. This kind of treatment represented a marked contrast with what blacks had experienced in the rural South, where they were denied the right to vote and were generally treated as pariahs in southern society.

In New York, five blacks were elected to the state legislature in the 1920s, and Democratic Mayors John E. Hylan and James J. Walker were regular visitors to Harlem. Chicago sent the first black representative to Congress, when Oscar DePriest, a Republican, was elected to the House of Representatives in 1928. Chicago's Republican mayor, William Hale Thompson, who served from 1915 to 1922, and from 1927 to 1931, relied heavily on the black vote. His Democratic opponents used the song "Bye-Bye Blackbird" in an attempt to defeat Thompson, claiming that hordes of blacks would leave the South immediately and invade Chicago if he were elected. During Thompson's last term in office, he appointed several black attorneys to high-ranking positions in the city government.

In spite of this activity in municipal affairs, black political involvement after World War I made little dent in the overall economic status of the urban black. Educator Ralph Bunche even argued that the *quid pro quo* for the black vote in the machine-dominated city was protection for the black underworld that flourished in the ghetto, and the awarding of minor administrative jobs for the Negro politicians who marshaled the black vote.[12]

Black Organizations

The Urban League was founded in 1910 by a group of black and white citizens in order to deal with the problems arising from black migration to the cities. Many of its early members, like sociologists Eugene Kinckle and Charles S. Johnson, were also active in the National Association for the Advancement of Colored People, which had been organized the previous year. To some extent, the Urban League functioned like the settlement houses that had been established by social workers to help the foreign-born adjust to city living. By 1925, the Urban League had formed forty-two local leagues, but like the settlement houses, they were faced with a wide variety of problems and limited resources. At times, the overwhelming burdens that beset the black migrant would cause league members to despair of the urban experience. In 1922, James J. Hubert, executive secretary of the New York Urban League, made the following statement:

> Many students of the race problem in America have looked to urbanization and northern migration as one possible solution. But in deserting the country for the city, the Negro appears merely to have jumped from the frying pan into the fire.... Urbanization has accentuated the growing conviction that, regardless of efforts, the Negro finds it increasingly difficult to "make it on the level"; that he cannot beat the color line; that the barrier of race has condemned him to the lower level of life.[13]

A majority of black migrants had no regrets over their decision to leave the South, but many became particularly sympathetic to the arguments of black leaders like Marcus Garvey and W. D. Fard, who tried to give them a spiritual uplift in the midst of their travail. While immigrant spokesmen were inclined to enunciate the ideology of the melting pot, Garvey and Fard spoke about the virtues of separateness. Their philosophy ran counter to the beliefs of both the NAACP and the Urban League, but they managed to gain an important hearing.

Garvey, a native of the West Indies, founded the Universal Negro Improvement Association in Jamaica in 1914, and in 1916 set up a chapter in New York. He later established branches in other cities, and the organization flourished. Stressing racial pride and speaking about the glories of ancient black civilizations, he attempted to launch a back-to-Africa campaign among American blacks. Within a few years, he became the head of the largest mass movement of blacks in the United States, with varying estimates that Garvey had from 100,000 to 4,000,000 followers. In 1923, he was found guilty of using the mails to defraud the public on the promotion of stock for the UNIA. After serving time in prison, he had his sentence commuted by President Calvin Coolidge in 1927, but was deported. He was unsuccessful in his attempts to keep the movement alive following his deportation, and he died in relative obscurity in London in 1940.

W. D. Fard, an itinerant peddler, made his appearance around 1930 in Paradise Valley, a black ghetto in Detroit. He claimed to be divine, preached a religion in which the white man was the creation of the devil, and, like Garvey, told black people of their greatness. Fard disappeared in 1934, but one of his followers, a Georgia migrant by the name of Robert Poole, started a similar movement in Chicago. Poole changed his name to Elijah Muhamad and became head of the Black Muslims. In the 1950s, there was renewed interest in the movement, and the Black Muslims became identified with the doctrine of separatism for all black Americans.

Depression Decade

During the depression of the 1930s, urban white and black families shared a similar plight, but there were differences in their respective situations. According to black writer George S. Schuyler, "the reason why the Depression didn't have the impact on the Negroes that it had on the whites was that the Negroes had been in the Depression all the time."[14] In the South, there was a change in the migratory pattern of black rural dwellers. As conditions in the rural South continued to decline, large numbers of southern blacks went to the urban South. They went there in far greater numbers than did rural whites. This movement represented a shift from previous decades, when the black population of the urban South had declined. Once again, however, the rural white Southerner in the southern city was at an advantage vis-à-vis his black counterpart. The southern white male labor force in the urban South increased at about the same rate as did the white population, but, in spite of the increase of the black population, there was a decline in the percentage of black workers in the total male labor force.

There was a substantial gap between white and black family income throughout the cities in the South. In Atlanta, between 1935 and 1936, the median family income for blacks was $632, while the median white family income was $1,876. In Columbia, South Carolina, and Mobile, Alabama, the median white family income exceeded black family income during the same period by over 30 percent.

Black migration to the North was not as high during the 1930s as it had been from 1915 to 1930, but it continued despite the absence of employment opportunities. It also kept up at a time when the white population temporarily halted its movement to the cities. One major attraction that the North had for black people during these years was that it was easier to get relief than in the South, where discrimination was frequently shown in the distribution of public assistance.

Local residents in the North often voiced complaints about the swelling relief rolls. Tension was especially high in Chicago, as the black population grew by an additional 43,000 in the 1930s, due to the birth rate and migration. In 1930, when four out of every ten persons on relief in Chicago were blacks, the Illinois legislature passed a three-year residency requirement for relief recipients in an effort to stop the movement of indigent migrants.

For those blacks who were able to find work, some unskilled jobs opened up again in several cities when white workers abandoned them to take jobs in various New Deal agencies.* Previously, many blacks had been replaced in their menial jobs by white workers, who were forced by the depression to take any jobs they could find. As in other periods, the black traditionally was the last to be hired and the first to be fired. Despite some job openings, the rate of black unemployment was exceedingly high. As of 1940, 33.1 percent of black males in Philadelphia were out of work (compared to 15.4 percent for white males), in New York, the figure was 20.1 percent (compared to 15.2 percent for whites), and in St. Louis, the black male unemployment rate was 19.6 percent (compared to 10.5 percent for whites).

Some of these high unemployment figures for blacks are noteworthy in view of the fact that blacks were not necessarily less qualified than whites. In 1940, Boston's blacks were nearly as well educated as the average white residents of the city. The median school years completed for blacks was about 93 percent of the median for the total population, but blacks were underrepresented in all occupational levels except unskilled labor and service work.

Tensions between blacks and whites ran high in this uncertain period. In Chicago in 1929 and 1930, a black newspaper, the *Whip*, founded in 1919, began a campaign urging blacks to boycott white businesses in the ghetto which would not employ black workers. "Don't spend your money where

---

*Ironically, the New Deal, which helped bring the black voters into the Democratic party, discriminated against black workers even as it improved their overall opportunities for work and public assistance. The National Recovery Administration codes in the steel, tobacco, and laundry industries provided for lower minimum wages for black workers. In industries where there was no discrimination in the minimum wage, employers were prone to fire black men and hire white workers rather than pay the black man a "white man's wages." Another New Deal agency, the Civilian Conservation Corps, which many young black men joined, set up segregated facilities for them.

you can't work," was its slogan. Initially, the campaign was successful, and many black men and women were able to secure employment. However, the *Whip*'s efforts incurred the wrath of its business advertisers, and it ceased publication in 1932.

Similar attempts, frequently with the help of local Urban Leagues, were made in cities like Pittsburgh and Cleveland, and several times blacks were able to find jobs in previously all-white establishments. In Harlem, the Reverend Adam Clayton Powell, Jr., gained recognition as a spokesman for the black community by leading picket lines, organizing boycotts, and planning marches to enable black people to get jobs in the community. He also helped to organize the Greater New York Coordinating Committtee for Unemployment, which was set up in 1938. One of its major accomplishments resulted from a demonstration that it staged at the 1939 New York World's Fair. As a consequence, it was able to get the World's Fair to revise its decision to hire blacks only in menial and unskilled jobs.

Evictions because of inability to pay their rent was a recurring problem for blacks. Although this was a situation also faced by countless whites, the Communist party made a special effort to go to the aid of blacks, and did its best to engineer clashes with the police in order to dramatize the issue. Most blacks were thankful for the help that they received, and in Chicago it was not unusual for a mother to shout to her children, "Run quick and find the Reds!" when an eviction notice arrived.

In 1931, one of these incidents in Chicago nearly led to a riot. Over 2,000 people left a meeting of Unemployed Councils, a group set up with the blessings of the Communists. They proceeded to go to the black belt in order to stage a protest outside a house where a black woman had just been evicted. The police were summoned, fighting broke out, and three blacks were killed. City officials then hurriedly met with black leaders and were told that reforms were necessary if a communist revolution or a race riot were to be averted. After this confrontation, the Renter's Court temporarily held back eviction orders, and state and local authorities formulated plans for providing relief.

An equally tense Harlem faced a crisis situation that resulted in the Harlem Riot of 1935. It started after a black youngster was caught stealing a knife from a neighborhood store. Although he escaped, rumors quickly spread through the ghetto that he had been killed, and an angry mob started breaking store windows and looting their contents. When the riot was over, three blacks lay dead, and property damage was estimated at $2 million. At the behest of New York's Mayor Fiorello H. LaGuardia, black sociologist E. Franklin Frazier headed a committee to investigate the riot; he urged the city to take measures to relieve poverty in the ghetto.

Initially, the depression did not lead labor unions to alter their policy of exclusionism toward blacks. Although labor unions had proved to be a refuge for the immigrants, a large portion of the American working class held on to its anti-black bias. A major breakthrough, however, was the founding in 1938 of the Congress of Industrial Organizations, a national central body of industrial unions, which included both skilled and unskilled workers. Unlike the older and more exclusive American Federation of Labor, the CIO was committed to a policy of nondiscrimination. By 1940, there were over 2,000,000 black workers in the CIO; the CIO also represented an important step forward for scores of unskilled white workers who had been excluded from the labor movement in the past. Other unions that accepted blacks without discrimination during these years included the United Mine Workers and the International Ladies' Garment Workers Union.

In earlier years, black leaders sometimes justified the use of black strikebreakers on the grounds that it was the only way in which black workers could find jobs. Chicago's black strikebreakers in the 1920s gained entry into jobs in the packing, steel, and garment factories, all of which had previously been closed to them. In these instances, several unions were forced to accept black workers in order to prevent their continued use as "scabs." Nevertheless, the entry of blacks into unions was often bitterly contested. In Detroit, the leadership of the United Automobile Workers was committed to equal employment opportunities for black workers throughout the 1930s, but there was no guarantee that the rank-and-file union members would cooperate in enforcing it. In spite of the policy of the UAW leaders, white union workers at the plant level, who were dependent upon the votes of many southern and immigrant workers for reelection, discriminated against blacks.

The strain of the depression years also helped to foster the growth of the Black Legion, an organization that bore a resemblance to the Ku Klux Klan of the 1920s. Its original founders had been members of the Klan, who dyed their robes black and formed a separate organization. The Black Legion had a sizable following in Detroit and in parts of the Midwest from 1931 to 1936, and a membership estimated as high as 300,000 people. Like the Klan, it was not only anti-black, but anti-Jewish and anti-Catholic as well. Its enemies also included radicals, communists, or anyone branded as a "foreigner."

The Black Legion drew support from three main groups and endeavored to offer them financial assistance during a time of economic difficulty. Its supporters included many southern migrants of Anglo-Saxon stock, members of the working classes who were unhappy and insecure in their blue collar jobs, and a coterie of men of middle class origins who had lowered their socio-economic status by accepting factory work or menial jobs from New Deal agencies. It extended welfare benefits to needy members and established an employment agency, although its prevailing mood was one of anger. The Black Legion took out its frustration through violence and murder, and, in the process, made the Klan of the 1920s look pallid by comparison. Eventually, thirteen of its members received life sentences for murder, and thirty-seven more were sentenced to prison terms of up to twenty years for terrorist activities.

World War II and the Postwar Era

The American nation began to recover from the depression around 1940, and the beginning of World War II further encouraged black migration to the cities, mostly from the rural South. The decade from 1940 to 1950 produced a greater urbanization of the black population than had any preceding decade. While many northern cities continued to receive large numbers of black migrants, cities like Los Angeles, San Francisco, Portland, and Seattle also gained a substantial portion of blacks. In Los Angeles, the black population increased from 63,774 to 171,209 between 1940 and 1950.

In addition to the black population, the postwar period witnessed the increased urbanization of several ethnic and native American groups. Immigrants from Japan and China, like other persons of foreign birth, were more urbanized than the American population at large. The American Indians also showed a tendency toward rapid urbanization, although at the end of the decade only 16.3 percent lived in cities. Rural white migrants from Appalachia—a region in the southeastern United States that encompasses states including Kentucky, Tennessee, and West Virginia—left their economically depressed areas and headed for Cincinnati, Detroit, Chicago, and other northern cities. Mexican Americans, or Chicanos, and Puerto Ricans also became visible as urban dwellers. This latter group became even more numerous in the decade of the 1950s, when the "new" immigration consisted of Mexicans, Puerto Ricans, and South Americans. By the 1960s, New York, Philadelphia, and Boston had a distinctive Puerto Rican population. Mexican Americans, usually employed as unskilled laborers in the cities of the West Coast, were the most poorly educated members of the country's population, and in the 1950s became the only ethnic group in which there was no appreciable gain in socio-economic status between the first and second generations.

Although black urbanites did raise their status during World War II, they once again ran afoul of discriminatory practices. Unlike what happened during World War I, when there was a labor shortage, the entry of the United States into the Second World War occurred at a time when the depression had produced a surplus of workers. Therefore, black workers quickly learned that they would have to wait their turn until the available supply of white workers had been tapped.

When the federal government first started its defense buildup in the early part of 1940, black workers were able to obtain only the lowest-paying jobs. As a result, the shortage of desirable work temporarily halted the urban black influx, and throughout much of 1941 the number of white in-migrants to northern and southern cities exceeded the number of black in-migrants. At this point, the early war boom provided more of an impetus for white migrants to flock to cities.

One early deterrent had to do with the fact that blacks were discriminated against in defense work. When the federal government took no steps to end the discrimination, several black leaders decided to act. Therefore, in January, 1941, black leader A. Philip Randolph, president of the Brotherhood of Sleeping Car Porters, threatened to send disgruntled black citizens on a march to Washington to demand equal employment opportunities in defense jobs. The march never took place because in June, 1941, President Franklin D. Roosevelt, rather than risk a mass demonstration in the nation's capital, set up the Fair Employment Practices Commission ending all discrimination in defense contracts.

Discrimination did not end altogether in spite of the enactment of the FEPC, and in many cities, notably Detroit, defense work continued to net blacks lower pay. In nondefense work, black workers did not always receive equal pay for equal work. Nevertheless, job opportunities did widen, and the black population in urban areas grew markedly.

While the black population made important economic gains in these early war years, the year 1943 proved to be a bitter one in several cities across the nation. Race riots broke out in Detroit, New York, and in Beaumont, Texas, and various skirmishes developed in Newark, Philadelphia, and Los Angeles. Unlike the riots of 1919 when whites assaulted blacks, many of these riots were initiated by blacks. In cities where there was no major riot, an element of luck entered the picture. Chicago escaped a riot chiefly because there was no mass movement into the city of southern white workers with strong anti-black prejudice, as was the case in Detroit. Moreover, there was no outward expansion of the black belt into the neighboring white areas, the labor scene was relatively calm, and the large black minority was better able to absorb newcomers than was the case in the small community of World War I days. In addition, Chicago's mayor was sufficiently concerned about the riots in other cities to set up an eleven-member Committee on Race Relations as a vehicle for easing racial unrest.

Detroit's riot of 1943 was the most serious of all the various disturbances. The city's black community had many grievances, and there was smoldering resentment becase the FEPC order was not being enforced. Detroit had 185 war plants, but fifty-five of them refused to hire black workers—an open violation of the provisions of the FEPC. Blacks were disturbed at losing out in their bid for better jobs to large numbers of southern migrants who sought to take advantage of economic opportunities in Detroit's booming defense industry. Detroit's second-generation black population was particularly bitter at the second-class status that was imposed upon them, since many of them were better educated than this group of newcomers. Therefore, the riot did not come as a surprise to those who were watching the scene with interest. After doing a story on Detroit in August, 1942, nearly a year before the riot broke out, *Life* magazine concluded that "Detroit Is Dynamite," and that it "can either blow up Hitler or it can blow up the United States."[15]

The Detroit riot began on June 20, 1943, when fighting broke out in the morning between white and black people on a bridge leading to Belle Island, a popular recreational facility. Within a few hours, the police broke up the fighting. While there were some injuries, no one was seriously hurt. Later that night in the Paradise Valley ghetto, rumors circulated that white people had started the attack and that a black woman and her baby had been thrown off the bridge and killed. These stories set off an attack, mostly on the part of black youths, on the white-owned ghetto stores. The police were summoned, and later there was an invasion of white rioters amid reports that blacks were raping white women and killing the police. At this point, President Roosevelt authorized the sending of federal troops to Detroit. The riot was quelled, but over thirty people had been killed.

Other cities were experiencing trouble, especially in the area of equal employment opportunities. In Washington—which in the 1920s was described by Howard Professor Kelly Miller as the "social capital of the Negro race"[16]—there was a dispute involving what was frequently referred to as the FEPC's most conspicuous failure. The controversy stemmed from the refusal of the Capital Transit Company to hire black men as streetcar conductors. Capital Transit was publicly owned but was subject to the jurisdiction of the FEPC because it was chartered by Congress. The company managed to ignore FEPC directives for three years, beginning in 1942. By 1945, with the ending of the war, the FEPC was no longer in existence, and Capital Transit successfully avoided punitive action for its violation of the law. On the whole, however, the FEPC did a commendable job in ending discrimination, even though attempts to thwart the upgrading of blacks continued. Philadelphia faced a disruption in its public transportation system in August, 1944, as white workers opposed the upgrading of black workers to motormen. It took three weeks and the calling out of federal troops before order was restored.

In spite of the turbulence associated with the World War II period, by the end of the 1940s blacks—like other urban dwellers—had improved their levels of income. The wage gap between white and black workers had narrowed, and the war provided economic opportunities for most Americans. However, whites made more gains than blacks, so that the difference in living standards between the two groups was magnified. Between 1940 and 1950, over 2,000,000 whites left central cities, usually for residential areas on the fringes of the outer city or for the suburbs. Blacks, on the other hand, continued to pour into the inner cities, and over 1,300,000 nonwhite in-migrants entered the cities during the same period. A black resident of Newark recalled that growing up there in the 1930s and 1940s meant living in a neighborhood where there were fellow blacks, as well as immigrant groups. "Before the war," he said, "we were *all* poor. As kids we wore the same kind of shoes, you know, welfare shoes. . . . After the war, everything changed. The white people made money and moved. The black people remained poor and stayed."[17]

Population Patterns: 1950–1960

Although not all white persons "made money and moved,"* a substantial number continued to leave during the 1950s. In only two of the nation's ten largest cities—Los Angeles and Houston—did the white population rise during the 1950s. In the other eight—New York, Chicago, Philadelphia, Detroit, Baltimore, Cleveland, Washington, and St. Louis—the nonwhite population grew by 1,400,000, as contrasted to a decline in the white population of 2,100,000. Significantly, the drop in the white population came at a time when the white population in the United States was increasing, and the net loss of white people in these cities was substantially greater than the actual numbers would indicate. The figures for these ten cities were representative of the general population move-

---

*In actuality, many cities contained a high percentage of poor whites and poor blacks. In 1960, 21.6 percent of Detroit's total population of 1,670,144 had incomes of less than $3,000 per year. Of this number, 204,820 were nonwhites and 156,528 were white. In Newark, where the total population in 1960 was 405,220, 22.2 percent of the population made less than $3,000 annually. The white population in this category numbered 41,851, as compared to 48,098 for the nonwhite population. In New Haven, which had a total population of 152,048 in 1960, the number of whites earning less than $3,000 per year—22,233—was greater than the number of nonwhites—9,021—in this classification. Altogether, 20.6 percent of the city's population earned less than $3,000 per year.

ment taking place in other cities throughout the country. From 1950 to 1960, black population in inner cities grew by 3,300,000, and the white population dropped by 2,000,000.

Throughout the 1950s, black people continued to leave the South. Los Angeles was one of the cities that had a sharp increase in its black migrants, most of whom came from Texas, Louisiana, Mississippi, Arkansas, and Alabama. Between 1955 and 1960, over 50 percent of New York's nonwhite migrants came from North Carolina, South Carolina, Virginia, Georgia, and Alabama, and 60 percent of Chicago's nonwhite migrants, during the same period, came from Mississippi, Tennessee, Arkansas, Alabama, and Louisiana.

Those members of the black community that had the economic means to participate in the movement to the suburbs encountered obstacles in doing so, even though the Supreme Court, in *Shelley* v. *Kraemer* (1948), declared that restrictive covenants forbidding the sale of property to blacks were not enforceable in the courts. Local communities found ways of keeping the suburbs predominantly white, usually through the use of zoning ordinances. In the 1960s, about 800,000 black people did move to the suburbs, but they moved to mostly black areas.

As inner-city blacks attempted to move outside the ghetto into other parts of the city, where vacancies occurred with greater frequency due to the white exodus, they often met with fierce opposition. When the black belt expanded in Chicago, black citizens were greeted with bombings, mob harassments, and property damage to their homes. In 1957, eighty-five such incidents were reported to the police, although the number declined the following year. It was in the zone of emergence, the area between the ghetto and the more affluent outer residential fringes of the city, that many of these clashes occurred. However, it was impossible to stem the tide of this advance. Once black people were successful in moving into a previously all-white neighborhood, many whites fled. The result was often a predominantly black neighborhood, as opposed to a mixed one.

One inner city area in Detroit—the Twelfth Street neighborhood—offers a striking illustration of the changes that took place in some urban neighborhoods in the 1950s. As Robert Conot pointed out in his study of Detroit, there was suddenly a surplus of housing in the area as many white people moved away, and the rents became more reasonable than they had been in the past. Both blacks and lower-class whites from surrounding areas sought to take advantage of these reasonable prices. Between 1955 and 1960, one elementary school in the neighborhood was changed from an essentially Jewish to a black school. In 1955, 80 percent of the parents were businessmen, professionals, white collar workers, and skilled tradesmen. No family was on welfare, and 90 percent of the children had both parents in the home. As of 1960, 45 percent of the parents were unskilled laborers, nearly 20 percent were on welfare, and 40 percent of the children had only one parent in the home.

Before long, the school was experiencing difficulties. As long as children from problem homes constituted a relatively minor percentage of the enrollment, they seemed to benefit from the school's better facilities, and an atmosphere that stressed scholastic achievement. However, by the time the proportion of the problem students reached one third, the quality of education in the school started to decline. The white parents generally had two reactions: first, to enroll their children in private schools; second, to move away from the area.[18]

Although the northern cities in the 1950s were spared the violence that was to flare up during the next decade, both the urban and rural South witnessed massive demonstrations and protests. Montgomery, Alabama, was the scene of the famous boycott of the city's buses led by Dr. Martin Luther King, Jr., in 1955 and 1956, which ended in victory when the Supreme Court declared that Alabama's state and local ordinances requiring segregation on buses were unconstitutional.

The Montgomery boycott marked the beginning of a protest movement that would spread throughout the South in an attempt to end segregated facilities. The civil rights movement was given an added boost earlier in 1954, when the Supreme Court in *Brown* v. *Board of Education* outlawed segregation in public schools, and later called for total compliance "with all deliberate speed." The South fought the order, while the northern housing pattern made *de facto* segregation a way of life. In the next decade, however, some boards of education began to bus students from various parts of the community, including the all-white suburbs, in order to achieve school desegregation, and Berkeley, California, in 1968, became the first city to desegregate its public school system in this way.*

---

*The controversy over busing has become a heated issue, and its legality is still in question. In 1973, the Supreme Court, in a four-

Population Patterns: 1960–1970

In the decade between 1960 and 1970, the black population of urban centers accelerated at an even faster rate, and cities like Newark, Washington, Atlanta, and East St. Louis had a majority of black residents. Between 1960 and 1970, all cities with a black population of over 100,000 except Birmingham experienced a further increase in black dwellers. In Washington, D.C., blacks comprised 71.7 percent of the total population as compared with 53.9 percent in 1960. Atlanta also witnessed a major growth in the decade, going from 38.2 percent black to 51.3 percent black.

The population in the large cities became more diversified ethnically than it had been in the recent past. A liberalized immigration law passed by Congress in 1965 brought more immigrants to the United States between 1965 and 1975 than at any other period since the massive migration between 1880 and 1924. In the ten years between 1965 and 1975, an estimated 400,000 legal immigrants and an undetermined number of illegal immigrants have settled in cities like New York, Boston, Chicago, Cleveland, Miami, Los Angeles, and San Francisco. Beginning in 1965, approximately 25,000 Italian immigrants entered the United States each year, nearly one third of them going to New York. Spanish or Hispanic Americans (the term generally includes Mexicans, Puerto Ricans, Cubans, and persons from Central and South America) have also made New York their home, and they made up one sixth of its total population in 1970. About 100,000 Mexican Americans resided in Los Angeles as of 1970, and 40,000 of them settled in Chicago. In Miami, in 1970, about 42 percent of the population was of Cuban background.

A significant change with regard to black migrants was discernible in the decade of the 1960s, in that they were more apt to come from other metropolitan areas than from the rural portions of the country. In 1960, only 20 percent of the nonwhite population of the American metropolitan areas consisted of persons born on farms. It has been suggested by Charles Tilly that even if every single one of the approxi-

---

to-four decision, permitted a lower court decision to stand which outlawed the busing of schoolchildren in Virginia across city-suburban lines.

mately 200,000 black farmers living on American farms in 1960 had moved to a metropolitan area by 1965, the black rural migrants would still constitute a minority among other black migrants.[19] Accordingly, as the components of the black migration have changed from an economically disadvantaged rural segment to a more prosperous metropolitan population, the in-migrants are more apt to be younger in age and to come from a higher social and economic group than the black people already living in the cities.

In addition to migration, the black urban population has grown substantially because of a rising birth rate. Since World War II, black death rates have fallen at a much faster rate than those for whites, while black fertility rates are much higher than those for nonblacks. Given these figures, it is estimated that the black urban population—as well as the black population in general—will continue to grow rapidly in future decades.

In spite of the rising status of the black newcomers and the more diversified nature of the urban population, black people continued to be the most segregated urban group in the United States in 1960. While the segregation index for foreign-born groups has declined in most cities in the forty-year period from 1910 to 1950, changes within this perod for blacks, as Stanley Lieberson has written, "indicate that Negroes and immigrant groups have moved in opposite directions, i.e., declining segregation for immigrants and increasing segregation for Negroes."[20]

Another study of residential segregation, this one for Chicago in the early 1960s made by Karl E. and Alma F. Taeuber, concluded that segregation for black people has remained at a high level, despite their considerable social and economic advancement. For example, it was higher than that for Puerto Rican and Mexican American groups that are less well off economically than blacks. The Taeubers also found that, in 1960, even in cities like Los Angeles and San Francisco where there were a substantial number of Hispanic Americans and Orientals, blacks were the most segregated group. On the basis of their findings for the urban black population in the United States as of 1960, the Taeubers wrote:

> A high degree of residential segregation is universal in American cities. Whether a city is a metropolitan center or a suburb; whether it is in the North or South; whether the Negro population is large or small—in every case, white and Negro house-

holds are highly segregated from each other. Negroes are more segregated residentially than are Orientals, Puerto Ricans, or any nationality group. In fact, Negroes are by far the most residentially segregated minority group in recent American history.[21]

As the ghetto was perpetuating itself rather than dispersing, it became associated with problems like drugs, crime, broken families, and juvenile delinquency. Indeed, the statistics for most black ghettos are staggering when measured against the rest of the community. (See Figures 9.1 and 9.2.) A study of a Minneapolis ghetto in 1960 revealed that the delinquency rate was more than twice that for any other area in the city. There were similar findings that year for Cleveland's predominantly black Hough area. A St. Louis ghetto in 1961, which was 60 percent black, had a delinquency rate three times that of the rest of the city. However disturbing these statistics are, it is the contention of black psychologist Kenneth B. Clark that they reveal only part of the story. "One of the paradoxes in attempting to understand the problem of juvenile delinquency in a ghetto," wrote Clark, "is not so

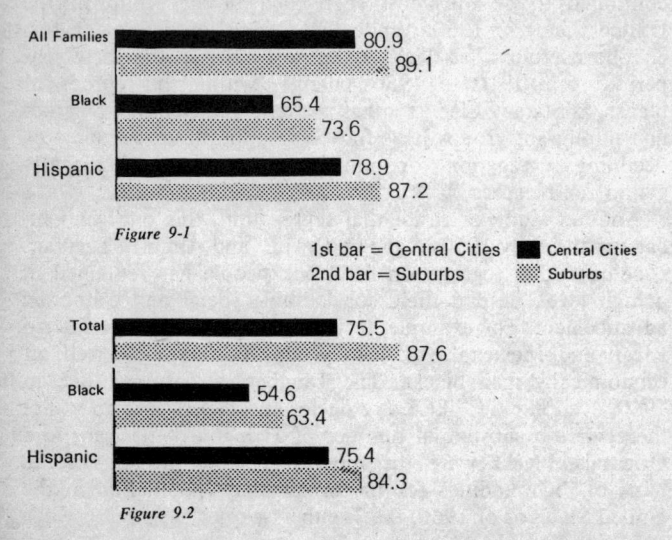

All Families: 80.9 / 89.1
Black: 65.4 / 73.6
Hispanic: 78.9 / 87.2

Figure 9-1

1st bar = Central Cities ■ Central Cities
2nd bar = Suburbs ▒ Suburbs

Total: 75.5 / 87.6
Black: 54.6 / 63.4
Hispanic: 75.4 / 84.3

Figure 9.2

Figure 9-1 Percentage of Metropolitan Families That Are Husband-Wife Families: 1970
Figure 9.2 Percentage of Children Under 18 Years Living with Both Parents: 1970

much the obvious facts of the disproportionately high rate when compared with the rest of a city, but that even in a community of such obvious pathology, so many—more than 90 percent of the youth population in most ghettos—do *not* come in direct conflict with the law."[22]

On the other hand, it cannot be denied that social disorder is a reality of life in the black ghetto.* One statistic that is often cited to explain this problem is the absence of male-dominated households. Black males have traditionally found it harder to secure employment than white males, causing many of them to desert their families. In the 1960s, the percentage of black families headed by females was more than double the figure for whites, and in 1974, 35 percent of all black families were headed by women, as opposed to 28 percent in 1970.

Faced with the hardships of broken homes and scarcity of employment, many blacks have sought public assistance. While the problem of poverty has been mitigated to a certain extent by welfare payments, food stamp programs and aid to families with dependent children—which represent the kind of continuing assistance that was not available to immigrants or disadvantaged groups in the past—it remains one of the most pressing of all urban problems.

Demonstrations and Riots in the 1960s

The 1960s produced the greatest amount of violence in American cities since the race riots of 1919. Consequently, it is often forgotten that the decade began with peaceful demonstrations. On February 1, 1960, four black college freshmen sat down at a lunch counter in Greensboro, North

---

*The great fear of social disorder in these areas has made many Americans oblivious to some of the anxieties faced by the majority of law-abiding citizens who reside in ghettos. A Gallup poll conducted between June 27 and June 30, 1975, which was based on interviews with 1,558 adults living in cities with a population of at least 500,000 persons, indicated that a substantially higher percentage of nonwhites than whites were fearful in their neighborhoods at night. Nonwhites and people in lower income levels felt that crime in their cities was a bigger problem than either the unemployment or high prices that so many Americans complained about during that year.

Carolina, to register their protest at the refusal of the owner to serve black customers. Within six weeks, the "sit-in" caught on across the South and spread to Atlanta, Jackson, Nashville, and about sixty other southern cities. These demonstrations were successful, and by September, 1961, restaurants in 188 southern border cities had ended racial segregation.

In April, 1963, marches and demonstrations in Birmingham —regarded by some black leaders as the nation's most segregated city—were aimed at ending discrimination in employment and segregation in public facilities. Police Commissioner Eugene Connor authorized the use of police dogs and fire hoses against the marchers, and a widely circulated photograph showing a Birmingham police dog leaping at the throat of a black youngster helped to win public sympathy for the protesters.

There seemed to be other indications of a shift in the attitude of the country, for on August 28, 1963, an estimated 200,000 black and white citizens marched in Washington on behalf of the civil rights movement. However, the nation was startled three weeks later, on September 15, when a black church in Birmingham was bombed, and four children were killed. Although peaceful demonstrations by black people continued, the next few years were marked by riots and further violence.

The race riots of 1964 began in Harlem, followed by outbursts in Rochester, several cities in New Jersey, and in Philadelphia.* The fighting in Harlem broke out on July 18 after the fatal shooting two days earlier of a black adolescent by an off-duty white policeman. Several nights of looting and violence followed, which spread to the Bedford-Stuyvesant ghetto in Brooklyn and other areas around New York City. A week later, Rochester had a riot over alleged police brutality toward a black man arrested for molesting a black woman. Similar disturbances erupted in three New Jersey cities, Jersey City, Elizabeth, and Paterson, during the first two weeks in

---

*The summer riots of 1964 antedated the passage of the Civil Rights Act of 1964, signed on July 2. It outlawed discrimination in public accommodations, prohibited discrimination in voter registration, and authorized the withholding of public funds from schools and hospitals that practiced discrimination. Ironically, to many residents of the ghettos, the Civil Rights Act of 1964 may have acted as a catalyst in releasing deep-seated hatred and discontent.

August. The last of the summer riots occurred in Philadelphia on August 28 after a black police officer used force to arrest another black.

The Watts riot in Los Angeles in August, 1965, was accompanied by cries of "Burn, baby, burn!" It broke out following the arrest of a black motorist by a white policeman, and for six days there were riots, lootings, and burnings. By the time 4,700 United States paratroopers and 8,000 National Guardsmen had restored order, forty-three people had been killed and property damage was estimated at as much as $250 million. The intensity of the Watts riot and the vast amount of publicity that it received prompted an investigation as to its cause, authorized by California Governor Edmund P. Brown under the direction of John A. McCone, former Central Intelligence Agency head. The McCone Commission warned that if the breach between white and black people continued, more serious fighting would erupt in the future.

In 1966, there were over twenty other racial outbursts, and 1967 brought serious riots to areas like Newark and Detroit, as well as to other cities. Although the Newark riot was not unexpected (in spite of the fact that the federal government had spent more per capita on anti-poverty efforts there than in any other large northern city), Detroit, with its respected city government and urban renewal programs, appeared to be a city where much progress had been made. Further disturbances occurred in 1968, notably in Chicago, Cincinnati, and Washington after the assassination of Dr. King in Memphis on April 4. The King assassination came three years after the death of black leader Malcolm X, who was murdered in New York in February, 1965, apparently by three fellow Black Muslims.

After the 1967 riots, there was a feeling in Washington and on the part of many civil rights leaders that a full-scale investigation of the riots was in order. Consequently, on July 29, President Lyndon B. Johnson appointed the National Advisory Commission on Civil Disorders, headed by Illinois Governor Otto Kerner,* to conduct an investigation on the reasons for the riots. Seven months later, the Kerner Commission issued its report.

The commission compiled a composite profile of the typical

---

*Governor Kerner subsequently had difficulty with the law. In 1973, he was convicted on charges of mail fraud and spent seven months in prison.

1967 rioter, based on data gathered from the riots. According to the commission findings, the rioter was a young, unmarried male between the ages of fifteen and twenty-four, who tended to be a life-long resident of the city in which he rioted. He was somewhat better educated than the average inner-city black, but, if employed, was more likely to be working in a menial or low status job. He felt that he deserved a better job, and that he was barred from achieving it, not because of lack of training, ability, or ambition, but because of discrimination by employers.[23]

To remedy the situation, the Kerner Commission called for massive spending by the federal government to wipe out poverty, slum conditions, and economic discrimination. Its warnings were stern; it noted that "our nation is moving towards two societies, one black, one white—separate and unequal." The most controversial parts of the report were its statements that "white racism is essentially responsible for the explosive mixture which was accumulating in our cities since the end of World War II," and "what white Americans have never fully understood—but what the Negro can never forget —is that white society is deeply implicated in the ghetto. White institutions created it, white institutions maintain it, and white society condones it."[24]

Cities in Transition

After the Kerner Commission's report, significant political developments took place which affected the black urban population. The late 1960s and the early and mid-1970s brought important gains in political power to the black community. In 1974, cities like Los Angeles, Detroit, Washington, Atlanta, Newark, Cincinnati, Gary, Dayton, and Grand Rapids all had black mayors, and altogether there were twenty-six black mayors heading cities with populations ranging from 25,000 to over 1,000,000. Interestingly, in over one half of these cities, blacks were a distinct minority. At the same time, many of these cities were wracked by internal problems stemming from inner-city decay and the loss of a tax base because of the increasing number of white people who had moved out to settle in the suburbs.

Since many of the black mayors preside over potentially explosive urban areas, it is pure conjecture to predict how well they will be able to handle some of the problems that have plagued their white predecessors. Carl B. Stokes, who was elected mayor of Cleveland in 1967 and 1969, did not seek reelection in 1971. During his administration, there was trouble over school integration, and racial tension remained high. Coleman R. Young, elected Detroit's mayor in 1973, was credited with handling a riot in the city in July, 1975, in such a way that a near disaster was averted. Young rushed to Livernois-Fenkell section of Detroit when fighting broke out, and spent the whole night trying to calm the mob. He summoned over 600 police, armed with nightsticks, tear gas, and riot helmets, but gave orders that "the use of fatal force [is] prohibited unless . . . life is endangered."[25] After two days of fighting, two men were dead, and one hundred persons were arrested, but it was a minor skirmish in comparison to the bloody 1967 riot.

The amount of violence decreased by the mid-1970s, but the troubled cities faced additional crises. Conflicts continued, this time mostly between inner-city blacks and white ethnic groups. Confrontations occurred over low income housing in a largely Italian area of Newark, Jewish groups in New York protested that the quota system guaranteeing black students a certain number of places in the City University of New York represented racism in reverse, and during the 1974–1975 school year, Boston's lower-income predominantly Catholic population fought a court edict ordering the busing of black ghetto children in order to achieve school desegregation. Although a survey conducted by pollster Louis Harris in March, 1970, for the Urban League indicated that the white urban ethnics were more apt to favor desegregation than white urban Protestants—a view which was confirmed by a similar study published in 1971 by Angus Campbell—[26] the actions manifested appeared to belie the findings.

Black Urbanites: A Perspective

If the overall picture fluctuated considerably during these years, there also were strong indications that various members of the black community had vastly improved their socioeconomic position and were experiencing the same kind of upward mobility that traditionally had been available to most groups in American society. Their mobility was partly a consequence of the expanded activities of the federal government, particularly in the early and mid-1960s, in seeking to end discrimination in jobs and in housing, and in offering financial assistance to black youngsters to continue their education.

Several examples illustrate the gains manifested by black urbanites in the 1970s. Middle class black families were able to join the exodus to suburbia, and move to neighborhoods that had been barred to them in the past. In Los Angeles, the black suburban population totaled 8.4 percent in 1970, as compared to 4.7 percent in 1960, and 2.9 percent in 1950. In Chicago, blacks accounted for 2.9 percent of the suburban population in 1950, 3.1 percent in 1960, and 3.5 percent in 1970. Among the factors contributing to this movement to suburbia was rising family income; in 1974 the median black family income was $7,800, an increase of 7.4 percent over 1973. Education also played a part in the ability of blacks to improve their status. Between 1970 and 1974, enrollment of blacks in colleges rose by 56 percent, against a gain in white enrollment of 15 percent. Equally impressive has been the growing number of minority workers recruited by private industry and local, state, and federal governments. As of mid-1975, blacks, Hispanics, and other members of minority groups held 19.1 percent of all government jobs in New York State. While these figures do not alter the fact that substantial inequities still exist—in 1975 the median income of all black families in the nation was 62 percent of the median income of white families—the picture has undergone several significant modifications.

Another factor that may affect the status of blacks is the presence of sizable numbers of Hispanics in the urban community. Their estimated population in 1975 has ranged from 11.2 million to nearly 20 million,* indicating that another large-scale migration is in progress. As was the case in the 1930s when the movement of blacks to northern cities received scant notice, many segments of the public have been unaware of the scale of this migration.

Hispanics have tended to concentrate in urban centers, and the 1970 census estimated that 83 percent live in cities. Although 60 percent of all Hispanics live in the five southwestern

---

*The Census Bureau, which accounted for 11.2 million Hispanics in 1975, also estimated that there are at least 8 million illegal aliens in the United States. Even when this latter figure is omitted, Hispanics still comprise 5.3 percent of the total national population.

states of Arizona, California, Colorado, New Mexico, and Texas, their migration has encompassed other areas as well. By the mid-1970s, Chicanos were more numerous than Indians in Utah, Cubans were found in substantial numbers in Elizabeth, New Jersey, and Puerto Ricans in Chicago outnumbered white ethnics in neighborhoods that had previously been predominantly occupied by Czechs, Poles, and Lithuanians. In general, Hispanics have tended to fare better economically than blacks, but considerably worse than whites (See Figure 9.3.) A federal census report for 1975 indicated that nearly 27 percent of Hispanics were below the federally defined poverty level of $5,500 for an urban family of four, compared to 9.7 percent for whites and 31.3 percent for blacks.

There are conflicting views on the magnitude of the "crisis" confronting the present-day black urbanites. In 1963, Nathan Glazer and Daniel P. Moynihan argued in *Beyond the Melting Pot* that the protest movement was entering an era of diminishing returns. In calling upon the black community to take the initiative in solving the dilemmas of the ghetto, they wrote that "one can detect the need for a period of self-examination and self-help."[27] Subsequently, Moynihan, in March, 1965, when serving as Assistant Secretary of Labor, prepared a report in which he wrote about the problems besetting the black family. In it, while citing illegitimacy rates, welfare studies, and figures on broken homes, he praised the federal government's attempts to end poverty and called upon the black community to join the effort to achieve that end.[28] Moynihan later served as an adviser to President Richard M. Nixon, and, repeating a theme that was stressed in *Beyond the Melting Pot*, urged an attitude of "benign neglect" on the question of race.

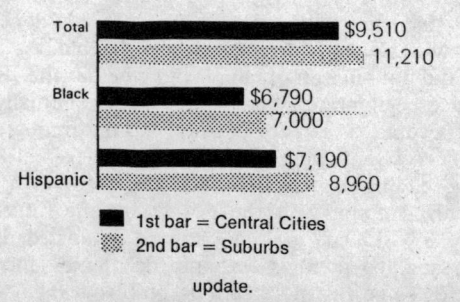

Total: $9,510 / 11,210
Black: $6,790 / 7,000
Hispanic: $7,190 / 8,960

1st bar = Central Cities
2nd bar = Suburbs

update.

Figure 9.3 Median Income of Metropolitan Families: 1969

Political scientist Edward C. Banfield, in *The Unheavenly City* (1970) and *The Unheavenly City Revisited* (1973), stated that the degree of the urban crisis—both generally and with respect to blacks—has been overstated, and that one of the basic difficulties is that actual accomplishment has not kept pace with the rising expectations as to what can be achieved. He regarded the black as being disadvantaged in much the same way as is the Puerto Rican and the Mexican: namely, in being the last of the immigrants to reach the city from a backward rural area. Nevertheless, Banfield stated that "like earlier immigrants, the Negro has reason to believe that his children will have increases of opportunity even greater than his." Banfield discounted race prejudice as a factor in the treatment of blacks, arguing that "much of what appears (especially to Negroes) as race prejudice is really *class* prejudice, or at any rate, class antipathy." He offered the view that had it not been for the flood of European immigration in earlier years and had the black worker been allowed to enter the urban labor markets, "there is no reason to suppose that he would not have long since been fully assimilated into the working, middle, and upper classes."[29]

Historian Stephan Thernstrom, whose studies of social mobility have added an important dimension to the study of urban history, discounted the theory that views black problems in terms of the fact that they are the last of the "immigrants." In his study of Boston during the years 1870 to 1970, Thernstrom concluded that black urbanites, whether migrants from the South or natives of Boston or of other metropolitan areas, simply did not experience the same kind of upward mobility that was characteristic of European immigrants, even those of peasant origin. He conceded that blacks experienced upward mobility in Boston in the period after World War II, but prior to that time "the only group that could be considered a truly permanent proletariat was the blacks. . . ."[30] Although he did not offer an opinion as to whether the changes that took place beginning in the 1940s would eventually lead the black to become, as Kristol put it, "like the immigrant of yesterday," Thernstrom suggested that mobility for all Americans may be ending as the United States becomes a fully-fledged urbanized country in the not-too-distant future and the supply of low-skilled rural migrants is exhausted. If that be the case—and the point is certainly debatable—the cities might be in for some far more serious problems than writers like Kristol ever envisioned.

10

Dilemmas of Urban Policy

Since the time of the New Deal, the federal government has come to play an increasingly active role in urban affairs, a role that has overshadowed what has been done by the states and cities, both jointly and on an individual basis. As a result, the dimensions of what has come to be regarded as the urban crisis—decaying inner cities, inadequate facilities, overcrowded schools, traffic congestion, noise, pollution, sprawl, and fragmented government—have been viewed largely from the perspective of what action the national government should take in this area. Yet as many observers of urban affairs point out, both the cities and the states are instrumental in shaping urban policy. Depending upon the magnitude of the problem, some of their own spheres of activity can be just as significant as those embarked on by Washington.

The efforts of all levels of government to come to grips with the problems of urban America in areas like poverty, housing, crime, and education have intensified over the years, particularly on the federal level. In spite of the vast sums of money that have been spent, the legislation that has been enacted, the projects that have been undertaken, and the recommendations that have been made, many of the problems refuse to go away. The persistence with which they continue not only leads to inconveniences in city living but to perennial skepticism as to what can be done.

The urban crisis is regarded by most Americans as a major source of national concern, and there is a certain amount of cynicism as to whether or not the problem can be solved. The inability of various cities and states to deal effectively with the crisis has caused repeated frustration, and the federal government's handling of urban problems generally has received as much criticism as praise. Even those who are willing to argue that the crisis can be resolved nevertheless take the position that the federal government has failed to perceive its complexity and has therefore adopted a series of makeshift and piecemeal solutions.

A Nation of Cities: The 1920s

The federal government's awareness of municipal problems was slow to evolve, for it was the states that traditionally had formulated policy with respect to the cities. By 1920, however, the United States had become a nation of cities; the census of that year revealed that for the first time in the country's history more Americans were living in cities than in rural areas. (See Table 10.1.) Hence, the decade represented a watershed mark in American development, even if few were aware of its long-range implications. As before, cities continued to dominate the economic life of the country. In 1929, 64.7 percent of all the country's industrial establishments, 74 percent of all industrial wage earners, and 80.7 percent of all salaried officers and employers were concentrated in the 155 counties that contained the larger industrial cities. (See Figure 10.1.) Yet just when the cities were surging forward and determining the direction in which the country would move, it sometimes seemed that this impressive growth merely reinforced the deep-seated anti-urban feelings of certain segments of the American public. It was not coincidental that Warren G. Harding, whose election in 1920 made him the first President to head an urban nation, came into office proclaiming that "there is more happiness in the American village than any other place on the face of the earth."[1] While sentiments of this type abounded, the amount of constructive activity in American cities in the 1920s indicated that the municipalities were engaged in learning how to cope with their newly found responsibilities.

During the era of "normalcy," city governments were generally praised for the determination that they showed in trying to solve municipal problems. As the progressive movement lost much of its momentum on the national and state levels, it continued to flourish locally in the commission and city manager plans as well as other structural reforms undertaken by municipalities. The educational and welfare activities of the cities increased, and, as in the past, municipalities proved to be energetic in meeting emergency situations. Communities

TABLE 10.1

Total and Urban Population of the United States: 1790–1970

Year	Total Population	Percent Increase over Preceding Census	Urban Population	Percent Increase over Preceding Census	Percent of Total Population Urban	Rural
1790	3,929,214		201,655		5.1	94.9
1800	5,308,483	35.1	322,371	59.9	6.1	93.9
1810	7,239,881	36.4	525,459	63.0	7.3	92.7
1820	9,638,453	33.1	693,255	31.9	7.2	92.8
1830	12,866,020	33.5	1,127,247	62.6	8.8	91.2
1840	17,069,453	32.7	1,845,055	63.7	10.8	89.2
1850	23,191,876	35.9	3,543,716	92.1	15.3	84.7
1860	31,443,321	35.6	6,216,518	75.4	19.8	80.2
1870	38,558,371	22.6	9,902,361	59.3	25.7	74.3
1880	50,189,209	30.2	14,129,735	42.7	28.2	71.8
1890	62,979,766	25.5	22,106,265	56.5	35.1	64.9
1900	76,212,168	21.0	30,214,832	36.7	39.6	60.4
1910	92,228,496	21.0	42,064,001	39.2	45.6	54.4
1920	106,021,537	15.0	54,253,282	29.0	51.2	48.8
1930	123,202,624	16.2	69,160,599	27.5	56.1	43.9
1940	132,164,569	7.3	74,705,338	8.0	56.5	43.5
1950*	151,325,798	14.5	96,846,817	29.6	59.6	40.4
1960*	179,323,175	18.5	125,268,750	29.3	69.9	30.1
1970*	203,211,926	13.3	149,324,930	19.2	73.5	26.5

SOURCE: U. S. Bureau of the Census.

*New urban definition includes those persons living in unincorporated parts of urbanized areas.

like St. Louis, Denver, Louisville, Boston, Bridgeport, and Baltimore set up public works projects in 1919 to provide work for returning servicemen and discharged war workers. Detroit's Mayor James Couzens, who had played a prominent role in the development of the Ford Motor Company prior to his election as mayor in 1916, helped to expand the city's activities to such an extent that he managed to spend a total of $243 million in his first three years in office, a sharp con-

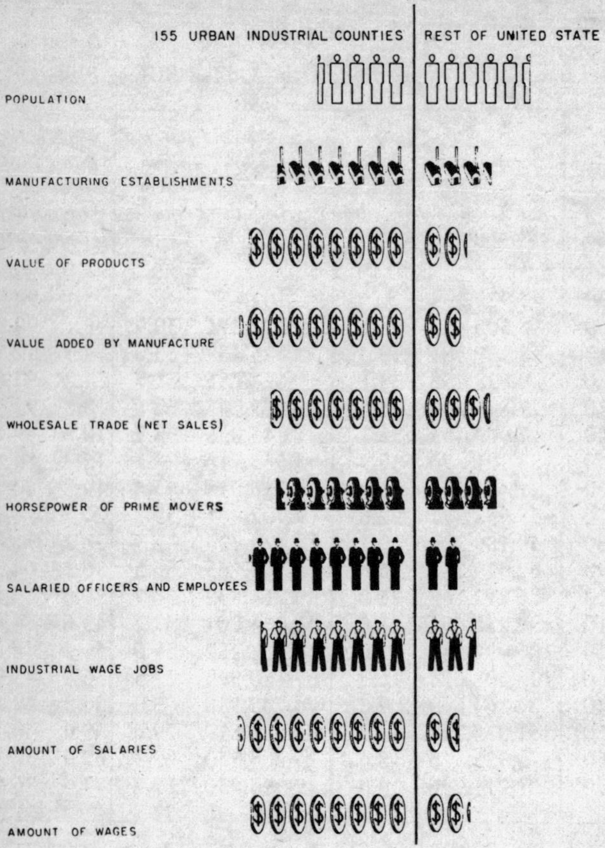

Figure 10.1 Urban Industrial Concentrations: 1929*
*Each figure represents 10 percent.

trast to the annual tax budget of $6.3 million during the preceding decade. A few years later, he established a public works program in an effort to counter the effects of the business recession of the early 1920s. The cities started organizing in other areas, as never before, and an unprecedented amount of information on urban life became available in the form of books, studies, and statistical compilations. Old established city clubs directed their attention to community endeavors, and in many cities new clubs and municipal leagues were founded.

Several important municipal associations can trace their origins to the 1920s, among them the American Municipal Association (later called the National League of Cities) which was created in 1924 as a federation of state leagues of municipalities. It proved to be an effective pressure group in the 1930s, when it was influential in getting the federal government to respond to the problems of urban dwellers. The formation of city planning commissions predated the 1920s, but during that decade they began to experiment with zoning and regional planning. New York, Boston, Cleveland, San Francisco, and Chicago had active regional planning associations, and in Philadelphia, one such association raised $60,000 in 1926 to engage a staff to make a preliminary survey of the mutual problems affecting residents within the metropolitan area. On occasion, there was talk of enlisting the federal government's involvement in municipal affairs, albeit in a limited way. At a 1924 meeting of the National Municipal League, one speaker, Professor William Anderson of the University of Minnesota, dealt with this subject. Although he made few references to financial assistance, he called for the expansion of administrative services, such as harbor improvements and postal services, which benefited municipalities.[2]

Throughout the 1920s, the federal government had an essentially *laissez-faire* approach to the cities, although it recognized a need to function in some kind of coordinative capacity. In 1927, when Secretary of Commerce Herbert C. Hoover was asked by the periodical *The American City* to enumerate the activities of his department that related to municipalities, he mentioned the services offered by its advisory committees on building codes, city planning, and zoning, among others, and stressed the part played by the federal government as a coordinator of information about cities. In noting the advantages of limited federal involvement, he stated: "Uniformity is promoted where it is desirable, while on the other hand the way is left entirely free for the local experimentation and progressive development which are so fruitful, and so firmly engrained in the American tradition."[3] His opinion on the role of the federal government with respect to the cities remained unchanged when he was elected President in 1928. In his memoirs, his only mention of urban problems was a notation of the fact that he helped municipalities in the Los Angeles area obtain a loan from the Reconstruction Finance Corporation for the construction of a gigantic aqueduct system to bring water from the Colorado River. However, as political scientists Robert H. Connery and Richard H. Leach have pointed out, Hoover's comments "indicate he was more impressed by the engineering aspects of the undertaking than he was by its implications for metropolitan development."[4]

The one area of activity involving the federal government and the cities at this time was an indirect one, and it pertained to housing. The federal government, consistent with the position that it had maintained in the 1920s, sold to private individuals the public housing that it had built during World War I. The housing program, which involved the construction of over 15,000 dwelling units, had been reluctantly authorized by Congress in June, 1918—only five months before the Armistice—as a result of a shortage of homes near war plants and navy yards. In the wake of charges that the program smacked of socialism, Congress had appropriated funds on condition that the housing would be sold at the end of the war. Dwelling units were built for skilled workers at seventy-nine project sites in the country, with construction under the supervision of two federal agencies, the Emergency Fleet Corporation and the United States Housing Corporation. Since the housing was built for workers who were commanding a good salary, it was at least on a par with private housing and, at times, was even imaginative and bold in its design and concepts. When the federal government again ventured into the field of public housing, as it did in the 1930s, the kind of housing that it built in cities was a far cry from what it had completed during the First World War.

Cities and the Depression: 1929–1932

Following the stock market crash of 1929 and the economic decline known as the great depression, cities attempted to respond in a way that was in keeping with their heightened activities throughout the 1920s. During the earliest stages of the depression, it was the municipal government rather than the federal or state governments that assumed responsibility for providing for the needs of the local populace. They were aided in their efforts by private charities, citizens' groups, and local organizations. The nature of the involvement varied from community to community, but a spirit of cooperation helped to mitigate the full impact of the economic losses. In 1929, Cincinnati's city manager set up subcommittees to study public works, temporary employment, job training and placement, and when the more devastating effects of the depression were felt, cities like Boston and Indianapolis financed similar studies. After Frank Murphy became mayor of Detroit in 1930, he asked local banker Hall Roosevelt, uncle of Eleanor Roosevelt, to become chairman of an unemployment committee established by the mayor. Murphy also set up a municipal employment bureau, at which 112,000 applicants registered for work in the first seven months of its operation. Shortly thereafter Roosevelt asked some of the city's business leaders to hire the unemployed, and 24,000 additional workers were hired. Nevertheless, unemployment continued to mount, and Murphy was obliged to divert millions of dollars from other city funds for relief.

Private charities endeavored to do their share in providing aid to the needy, and their funds augmented what cities were expending on relief. Until the mid-1930s, all government welfare activities were amply supplemented by contributions from various private agencies, and in the first four years of the depression there was a more than fivefold increase in contributions received from private funds for direct cash assistance to persons in need. These contributions came at a time of hardship, but the concept of charity seemingly was deeply rooted in the American people. Throughout the country, community chests played a key part in these fund-raising endeavors, and they grew in number from 49 in 1922 with a budget of less than $24 million to 397 in 1933 with a budget in excess of $77 million. Their success in raising money prompted the comment made in 1930 by Allen T. Burns, director of the American Association of Community Chests and Councils, that "while stocks crashed, the community chests did not."[5] However, private sources eventually proved unequal to the task, and by 1935 relief in urban areas was supplied almost entirely out of public funds.

Many cities were driven to the brink of bankruptcy in trying to meet the problem of relief. Per capita expenditures for public welfare in cities over 200,000 increased more than fourfold between 1928 and 1933. During 1932, total expenditures by urban governments amounted to $4.25 billion, or one third of the total government expenditures of the country, and it represented a sum greater than federal, state, or local nonurban expenditures of that year. Yet in spite of these expenditures, the cities did not have enough funds at their disposal for public welfare. In Philadelphia during 1932, one out of every five families had to be rejected for relief because the city ran out of funds. Although $5 million had been allocated to Philadelphia's unemployment relief by the United Fund, a local charity, it had been used up in four months. Philadelphia's private charities, which ordinarily had helped 5,000 families, were offering assistance to 54,532 by the beginning of 1932.

As the proportion of people in the need of relief continued to mount, cities looked around for new sources of revenue. Property taxes, which in the past had been used to meet municipal expenditures, were hopelessly inadequate, particularly since many property holders were already in arrears. The public angrily protested any proposed increases in local taxes, and cities soon discovered that it was almost impossible to borrow money, either from private sources or through the sale of municipal bonds. As a result, public assistance was cut back, municipal services were curtailed, employees were dismissed, and salary cuts were made. Fortunately, some aid was forthcoming. By the end of 1931, most state governments had appropriated funds for additional relief, with New York, under the leadership of Governor Franklin D. Roosevelt, being the first state to provide substantial funds for this purpose. Nevertheless, 600 cities and towns had defaulted on their debts as the year 1932 drew to a close, and committees of bankers had assumed control of the local administration in cities including Detroit, Philadelphia, Rochester, and Chicago.

The day for active federal involvement in municipal affairs had not yet arrived as of 1932. The federal government's expenditures to local governments that year amounted to $10 million—in contrast to state payments in the amount of $801 million—and nearly all of the former sum was earmarked for the District of Columbia. Despite the enactment of certain significant measures by the Hoover administration—expenditures for public works were increased, the Reconstruction Finance Corporation was set up in 1932 to make loans to business, and the Home Loan Act of 1932 provided mortgage relief for persons in danger of losing their homes—the President clung to his belief that voluntary cooperation was the best way to bring about economic recovery. In 1931, he was instrumental in initiating a community chest drive in 174 cities across the nation, and two years later led a campaign for the formation of Citizens' Councils in various cities to prevail upon the public to pay its delinquent taxes.

One of Hoover's chief aides, Walter S. Gifford, who in 1931 became chairman of the President's Organization on Unemployment Relief, presumably spoke for the administration when he wrote a magazine article in February, 1932, entitled, "Cities, Counties, States Can Handle the Situation." In it he maintained that federal involvement in the area of relief would encourage local units of government to slough off their responsibility.[6] Whether or not this article won him any adherents, he had nonetheless suffered a serious setback the preceding month when, in testifying before a United States Senate Committee on Unemployment, Gifford revealed that he had no figures on the extent of unemployment, did not know how many families were on relief, and gave the impression that the administration was unaware of the effect of the depression on those people who were unable to find work. When he was requested by one of the Senators on the committee to file whatever reports about unemployment and relief he had received from governors, local relief associations, and his own staff, he replied: "I have none, Senator."[7] Revelations of this type did not endear the administration to the public, and in the 1932 presidential election Hoover was soundly beaten by Franklin D. Roosevelt, his Democratic opponent. Roosevelt captured over 57 percent of the popular vote, and ran ahead of Hoover in 91 of the 106 cities in the nation with a population of over 100,000.

New Deal Housing Programs

When Roosevelt first took office, critics of urban living could find some solace in the fact that the cities were feeling the depression more keenly than the rest of the country. Between 1933 and 1935, about three fifths to three fourths of the total relief population was urban, and the per capita expenditures for relief were almost twice as great in 1934 in the most urbanized states. As of 1935, one fifth of the total relief load was concentrated in the ten largest cities. These sobering statistics had an effect on the migratory patterns of the American people, as many of them decided to forsake the city in favor of the farm. By 1935, the number of persons living on farms had increased by two million over the 1930 figures. This trend was reversed during the later years of the decade, but for the decade as a whole the city recorded less than half the gains it had registered during the 1920s.

To the credit of his administration, Roosevelt made a concerted effort to alleviate the plight of the cities. In the process, he not only brought a new deal to the American people, but a new deal with respect to the federal-city relationship. The federal government went to the aid of cities, providing jobs, furnishing relief, and constructing homes. Yet it is also ironic that its most vigorous social planning venture, the Tennessee Valley Authority,* was aimed at rural—not urban—America. By the same token, its most imaginative housing program was undertaken in the greenbelt towns on the fringes of metropolitan areas. Roosevelt, who had grown up in the secluded rural beauty of Hyde Park in New York State, listed his occupation as "farmer" upon becoming President, and in an address delivered on June 20, 1921, before the Berkshire Bankers' Association, on "The Danger of Big Cities," he had expressed the view that the "growth of cities while the country population stands still will eventually bring disaster to the United States."[8] His election triumph in the big cities was in contrast with the sentiment expressed at the 1932 Democratic convention, where he had been opposed by many of the city machines and had drawn his heaviest support from agricultural states. As President, however, Roosevelt demonstrated his concern for both rural and urban Americans, but whether the New Deal harnessed its energies most effectively for the big city is debatable.

One New Deal agency that addressed itself to the problems in the cities was the Housing Division of the Public Works Administration (PWA). The division was set up by PWA Administrator Harold L. Ickes in June, 1933, with power to make loans to limited dividend corporations (firms which agreed to limit their profits) for the construction of homes. It also had power to buy and build projects on its own. At the time that it was established, the housing industry in the United States had come to a virtual standstill, and much of the older housing was inadequate. While the Housing Division

---

*The Tennessee Valley Authority came into existence in 1933. Initially, it was engaged in both regional and social planning for the area, which included parts of seven states with a population of two million people, and covered about 80,000 square miles.

recognized the need for new construction, its first priority was to give employment to workers. It began a program of slum clearance, but it did so primarily to relieve the unemployment crisis.

The Housing Division undertook much of the new construction itself after encountering difficulty in finding acceptable limited dividend corporations. By the time the program ended in November, 1937, it had sponsored forty-nine projects in thirty-six cities and had built over 21,000 dwelling units for some 87,000 persons. The rents in these projects averaged $26 per month, and, like other government-sponsored projects that would be built in the coming years, they met the needs of manual and white collar workers rather than those of poor families. Unlike some of the projects that were constructed under government auspices in later years, they may have been too well built. Construction costs averaged $1,700 per room, thanks to Ickes' "mania for durability."

Prior to its demise, the Housing Division ran into some difficulty over its acquisition of private property for its projects. It had seized private property under the right of eminent domain—the right of government to take property for public use, provided that the owner is given fair compensation for it. A resident of Louisville, whose property Ickes sought for a housing project, brought suit to stop the government from obtaining his land, and in 1935 a federal district judge, in *United States* v. *Certain Lands in City of Louisville* ruled against the government. The court stated that while the federal government could acquire land for its own use, eminent domain did not entitle it to seize such property in order to build public housing. The federal government never appealed the decision, and during the next year the Housing Division was forced to build only on vacant land. Meanwhile, state courts took a more lenient view regarding the right of agencies created by state governments to engage in this type of activity. In *New York City Housing Authority* v. *Muller* (1936), the New York Court of Appeals held that the right of local authorities to acquire land for public use was a proper exercise of the state's police power. Accordingly, when a new federal housing program was enacted in 1937, it was framed in a way that was meant to accommodate the views theretofore expressed by the lower courts.

The Wagner Steagall National Housing Act, or the National Housing Act of 1937, set up the United States Housing Authority (USHA), which was a public corporation operating out of the Department of the Interior. The USHA had an initial appropriation of $500 million (later increased to $800 million) and was authorized to give or lend to local public housing authorities up to 90 percent of the costs of clearing a slum and developing it as a project for low income families. In contrast to what had been done under the PWA, the projects were to be built, owned, and maintained by local agencies, which were to be established under state law. To be eligible for public housing, families could not have an income in excess of $1,150, in keeping with the government's estimate in 1936 that 63 percent of urban families earned less than $1,500 per year.

The National Housing Act of 1937 was supported by Roosevelt chiefly because he regarded it as a measure that would give a boost to the construction industry, for nearly one third of the nation's jobless had worked in the building industry. Thus, while the act described the shortage of housing for low income families as injurious to the nation and declared that the elimination of slums was a national goal, the language did not entirely reflect the thinking of the administration.

In the beginning, the activities of the USHA gave rise to much praise. The construction was welcome, for in addition to providing jobs and stimulating industry it made needed housing available to many people who had been unable to afford decent living quarters. Within one year after the passage of the act, the USHA had contracted with twenty-eight cities to spend $154 million for over 30,000 dwelling units. By the end of 1938, there were projects underway in 142 cities, and the intensification of the program the next year led Nathan Strauss, administrator of the USHA, to say: "In 1939, for the first time in a hundred years, the slums of America ceased growing and began to shrink."[9] Black families also were aided by the government's housing program, and during Roosevelt's presidency almost one third—or approximately 47,500 units—of federally sponsored housing was occupied by blacks. Commenting on this aspect of the program, Gunnar Myrdal said in 1944 that the USHA gave black people "a better deal than has any other major federal public welfare agency."[10] In later years, however, some of the remarks about the New Deal's public housing policies became more critical. William E. Leuchtenburg, in his study of the New Deal published in 1963, wrote that the federal housing venture, like many other New Deal operations, "was notable more because it created new precedents for government action than for the dimensions of its achievements. Measured by needs, or by the potentialities, Roosevelt's public housing program could make only modest claim."[11]

Since the depression, the government has continued to finance the building of public housing, and by the early 1970s there were over one million units available for occupancy. Black people moved into government projects in relatively large numbers during these years, and at present more than one half of the families in public housing are black. Many of the tenants in these projects are on relief, although the National Housing Act of 1937 originally specified that relief families were ineligible for public housing. As to the location of public housing, there has been a tendency to build it in the least affluent sections of the city, creating additional ghettos within the inner city. In the 1960s, the Commission on Civil Rights stated that of the 750,000 public housing units built by city housing authorities in the twenty-four largest cities, Cincinnati had the only ones built outside the central city.

To many critics of public housing, their design is unimaginative, and the multi-story structures inject a bleak and impersonal tone into city living. Writing in this vein, Lewis Mumford referred to them as "high rise slabs."[12] In addition to drastic changes in design, one of the other suggestions repeatedly made by urban planners is that government housing consist of both low and high density units, and that it be located in the suburbs as well as in metropolitan areas.[13] There are also planners who believe that the government should embark on a massive housing program to provide homes for lower and middle income families, a concept that was not seriously considered by Roosevelt or his successors in office. They cite the fact that in spite of all the talk about public housing, it represents only about 1 percent of the country's housing stock, and only 1 percent of the population lives in it.

More to Roosevelt's liking than the building of public housing in the cities was the building of greenbelt towns near the suburbs. The construction of these towns was entrusted to the Resettlement Agency, set up in 1935. Rexford G. Tugwell, the Undersecretary of Agriculture, became director of the project. The program was designed to build several rural-industrial communities on the outskirts of crowded cities, and the term "greenbelt" was applied because each town was to be surrounded by a broad girdle of park and farmland.

Tugwell's goals included the building of attractive low-income housing to enable city residents to move to the suburbs. He envisioned a type of design that would serve as a model for both private builders and public housing authorities. The greenbelts also included provisions for the building of parks and playgrounds, and several sections were set aside for gardens for the benefit of those tenants who wanted to supplement their own incomes by raising fruits and vegetables. Other sections of the land were allotted to full-time farmers, who, it was assumed, could bring their produce to market simply by crossing their own fields.

Three greenbelt towns were constructed—Greenbelt, Maryland, seven miles from Washington, D.C.; Greenhills, near Cincinnati; and Greendale, outside of Milwaukee. Each town accommodated from 500 to 800 families. They were carefully planned, located close to employment, and were ready for occupancy in 1937 and 1938. As in public housing, an upper limit was set for income; in this case it was $2,200 a year. Upon the completion of the program, the government specified that it would transfer the ownership to a local public agency.*

These communities generated much excitement, and they proved to be a favorite attraction for foreign visitors. From the government's viewpoint, they had been very expensive to construct, with the cost of many units amounting to between $15,000 and $16,000. In 1952, the government sold most of the land, houses, and buildings in the towns, and the great experiment was abandoned.

Interestingly, in justifying the program in 1936, the Resettlement Administration had called attention to the great strides made in public housing in Europe. It noted that Holland, with a population smaller than metropolitan New York, had built ten times as much public housing as existed in the entire United States, Germany had provided homes for 2.5 million low income families, while England had spent $3 billion on housing during the 1920s. (See Figure 10.2.) But,

---

*In spite of its pledge to transfer ownership, the government did encounter some legal difficulties as a result of the greenbelt program. In 1936, a federal court injunction prevented Tugwell from proceeding with Greenbrook, one of the projected greenbelt towns, which was to be built in New Jersey. The case was *Township of Franklin* v. *Tugwell*, 85 F2nd 208, and, accordingly, the plans for Greenbrook were abandoned. The adverse decision further convinced government authorities that federally built public housing, as opposed to federally sponsored public housing, would be struck down by the courts.

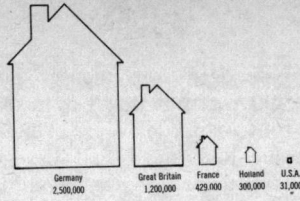

Figure 10.2 A Comparison of the Number of Homes Built with State Aid in Europe and the United States: 1918 to 1934

contrary to the expectations of the Resettlement Administration, in the field of public housing Europe and the United States went their separate ways.

The greenbelt town was just one example of the planned community built under the New Deal. When the National Industrial Recovery Act (NIRA) was passed in 1933, an omnibus bill was included which provided for setting up subsistence homesteads. The program was justified on the grounds that these homesteads, located in rural areas, would create a better balance in population between rural and urban America. It was also hoped that whenever possible, industry would be encouraged to relocate in these areas. Louis Howe, one of Roosevelt's closest advisers, referring to the projected program in a radio address in 1933, said that it "might be the answer to urban congestion."[14]

The New Deal built ninety-nine subsistence homesteads. The most famous one was Arthurdale, located in West Virginia, which became a favorite project of First Lady Eleanor Roosevelt. Like her husband, she felt that rural life was superior to urban living. While she acknowledged in 1930 that cities were absorbing and stimulating because of "the variety of human existence" to be found in them, she wrote that she "would rather live where trees and flowers and space and quiet give me peace."[15] Mrs. Roosevelt viewed Arthurdale as a laboratory for all new communities, and was active in planning its operations.

By November, 1933, the first families started to move there. Many of the men had worked as miners and farmers, but had been out of work because of the depression. The program operated on the premise that they would be able to earn their living farming the land or working in local industry, and they were given thirty years to repay the government for their homes. Despite Mrs. Roosevelt's repeated efforts, Arthurdale had difficulty in attracting industry to the area, and only one third of the community's labor force was able to find work in private industry during the decade. Her desire to see the homesteaders enjoy modern conveniences pushed the costs well above the $1,000 per unit that her husband had anticipated. The unit costs at Arthurdale were over $16,000, making it the most expensive homestead that the government had built. The entire subsistence program eventually was abandoned; it had cost over $108 million.

The mounting costs involved in the building of the subsistence homesteads turned many people against government housing—a feeling that was reinforced by the greenbelt program. The *Saturday Evening Post* ran an article about Arthurdale in 1934; in it, the author cited the program as an example of New Deal bungling and an object lesson as to what happens in a planned economy.[16]

Federal Aid to Urban Dwellers and Municipalities

Other New Deal agencies, while not specifically designed to deal with municipal problems, were nevertheless of aid to urban dwellers. In June, 1933, Congress established the Home Owners Loan Corporation to help homeowners get loans at low interest rates in order to keep their homes and make repairs. When it stopped making loans in 1936, it had already assumed about one sixth of all urban home mortgage indebtedness. An Emergency Housing Corporation was set up within the NIRA in 1933, and it made appropriations to cities for slum clearance projects. Detroit received the first of such grants, and in December, 1933, the corporation appropriated $12 million for use in Cleveland. It continued to make grants until the NIRA was declared unconstitutional by the Supreme Court in 1935. Following its enactment in 1933, the Civil Works Administration (CWA) spent money on work relief projects, and in January, 1934, it hired people to make an inventory of buildings and housing in sixty cities. Although the CWA was abolished three months later, its preliminary report proved to be useful for other New Deal programs concerned with housing. In this category, no agency was more important than the Federal Housing Administration (FHA). Established in 1934 under the National Housing Act of that year, it insured mortgages on homes that it approved for loans of up to 80 (later 90) percent of their appraised value. The

Works Progress Administration (WPA, or the Works Projects Administration, as it also was called), which originated in June, 1935, provided work relief jobs and was engaged in public works projects. By the end of 1935, it had spent more for public works in ten cities than the cities themselves had spent during 1930.

Cities also benefited from government appropriations for airports, which totaled $100 million spent on some 1,000 airports across the nation during the depression. The work was done by the WPA, Federal Emergency Relief Administration (FERA), and the CWA. At the end of World War II, the airports were declared surplus and were turned over to cities, counties, or states for civilian airport use. The government later enacted the Federal Airport Act of 1946 providing for grants to states, counties, or public agencies for airport construction and maintenance—one of the many grant programs which aided municipalities.

These measures were passed despite the New Deal's ambivalence about urban America; they represented the administration's reaction to a particular situation and its responsiveness to the pressures put upon it by certain interest groups. Throughout the 1930s, local officials made frequent pilgrimages to Washington in an attempt to secure the enactment of favorable legislation. The degree of their individual success depended on a combination of factors, but one group that Washington had to take seriously by virtue of its numerical strength was the United States Conference of Mayors. Together with groups like the American Municipal Association, it saw to it that the interests of cities were given a hearing on Capitol Hill.

The conference was the result of the efforts of Mayor Frank Murphy of Detroit, who invited the mayors of sixty-seven large cities to a meeting in Detroit in May, 1932. Twenty-six mayors attended, and they drafted an appeal to Washington for a $5 billion construction program to aid the cities. Following the adjournment of the meeting, Mayors Murphy, James Michael Curley of Boston, James J. Walker of New York, and Daniel W. Hoan of Milwaukee went to meet with Hoover to discuss the question of federal assistance. Their plea was made in vain, but in February, 1933, a month before Roosevelt's first inauguration, a group of fifty mayors met in Washington and set up a permanent organization. It became the first group of public officials to urge a major public works program, and, this time, both the President and Congress paid close attention to its demands for financial help.

Its membership was open only to mayors of cities over 50,000, but the fact that most big-city mayors in the 1930s were Democrats facilitated its relationship with top administration officials. During his presidency, Roosevelt was in the habit of sending annual greetings to the conference, and in 1935 he invited its members to the White House. The bargaining power that it held was a factor in obtaining money for cities, including a $3.3 billion appropriation from the NIRA for public works and $400 million in CWA projects organized in cities and counties.

The achievements of groups like the United States Conference of Mayors did not allay the misgivings of those persons who believed that the New Deal was remiss in its failure to formulate a national urban policy. Expressions of this kind of sentiment can be found in the National Resources Committee, a relatively unknown New Deal agency. It originated in 1933 as the National Planning Board of the PWA, and the following year it was renamed the National Resources Board. In 1935, it was known as the National Resources Committee, and from 1939 until its expiration in 1943, it was called the National Resources Planning Board.

It was concerned with assessing and directing the expanded role of the federal government in the economic life of the country, and in 1937 its Urbanism Committee published *Our Cities: Their Role in the National Economy*. The book reflected the thinking of urbanists like Louis Wirth and Louis Brownlow, who were associated with the committee, and it called for a reappraisal of the federal-city relationship. As its report pointed out,

> . . . the relations between cities and the Federal Government still remain in an amorphous and anachronistic state. Although a substantial majority of our population is urban, we continue to live politically in a rural society. The city has been taken for granted as a necessary and inevitable byproduct of a developing industrialism. The Federal Government's perspective has traditionally divided the national scene into the agricultural and industrial spheres; and while rural life was, on the whole, synonymous with agriculture, the city and urban existence were never completely covered by industry. Accordingly, governmental measures designed to aid agriculture generally promoted the welfare of the rural population, whereas those designed to

assist industry benefited only a narrow segment of city life or even aggravated the conditions of urban existence.[17]

For a while, the National Resources Planning Board enjoyed moderate success in trying to direct federal attention to the urban scene. It sponsored studies relating to urban problems, and in 1943 it put out *Action for Cities: A Guide for Community Planning*, which, it was hoped, would encourage local officials and citizens to formulate planned programs for their communities. One of its most ambitious undertakings occurred in 1942, when it funded three experimental urban planning projects in Corpus Christi, Salt Lake City, and Tacoma. Nevertheless, there was opposition to its work from interest groups like the National Association of Real Estate Boards, rural Congressmen, and various congressional critics of planning. In 1943, with the country in the midst of World War II, Congress refused to grant it any more funds, and the National Resources Planning Board went out of existence. In its brief career, it had failed to demonstrate that federal planning could prove to be a solution for city problems. However, in urging the federal government to focus sharply and coherently on the needs of its urban populace, it gave voice to a point of view that has found increasing support over the last several decades.

Postwar Housing and Urban Renewal

After the crescendo reached by the New Deal, many of the federal programs in the postwar period appeared to be anticlimactic. Renewed prosperity after World War II assuaged the fear that hard times would return, and few citizens seriously considered the question of restructuring American society—a question that was discussed by some New Dealers and would be taken up again beginning in the 1960s. The "urban crisis" was not yet identified, and if significant portions of it already were simmering, it was not recognized as a crisis. The major area of concern in the cities was the acute housing shortage, which was aggravated by the baby boom after World War II. Consequently, the federal government stepped up its financing of public housing and added a new feature to its municipal agenda—urban renewal.

The Taft-Ellender-Wagner Housing Act, or the Housing

Act of 1949, was passed by Congress as an omnibus bill. It contained provisions benefiting a variety of blocs and interests. It authorized the federal government to provide for the construction of 810,000 housing units over a six-year period, while Title I of the Housing Act, "Slum Clearance and Community Development and Redevelopment," provided up to $500 million to assist cities in launching urban renewal projects. The public housing provisions of the act were bitterly opposed by real estate and construction groups, and it took four years before President Harry S Truman was able to help push it through Congress. In spite of the opposition to the bill, Title I contained several favorable provisions for private builders, and it was this group that received some of the substantial benefits from urban renewal.

In terms of the accomplishments of the Housing Act of 1949, it is important to consider its stated goals. Although the act said that ". . . Congress hereby declares that the general welfare and security of the Nation and the health and living standards of its people require . . . a decent home and suitable living environment for every American family," it also specified that Congress should assist private enterprise to build as much of the needed housing as possible.[18] As it turned out, the two goals were mutually incompatible. Private enterprise built housing primarily for those people able to afford a "decent home," making it exceedingly difficult for the other goal of "suitable" housing for every American family to be realized.

Under urban renewal, the government authorized local housing authorities to acquire property in slum areas, which by the terms of the act had to be at least 50 percent residential. The procedure involved was a lengthy one, for the plans had to be approved by the local renewal agency, the local governing body, and federal authorities in Washington. A public hearing also was held, and once the project was approved, the city acquired the property by purchasing it from its owner, or invoking the right of eminent domain if the owner refused to sell. The city authorities next cleared and improved the land and offered it for sale to a private developer either by direct negotiation or by competitive bidding. Private developers put up new buildings in the area, which had to conform to local specifications and design, and then offered them for sale.

The land was usually sold to private builders for about 30 percent of what it had cost the city to acquire, clear, and improve it, and the federal government assumed two thirds of the difference between the costs to the city and the price realized from the sale, with the city government assuming the remaining one third. The federal government later contributed three fourths of the costs to cities under 50,000, but made no such adjustments for larger cities.

By 1954, urban renewal was foundering. Of the $500 million available for grants, only $74 million had been committed. The cumbersome method of filing for a grant sometimes resulted in a four-year delay before the proposal was put into contract form. Moreover, many people were disturbed that renewal projects were displacing the poor at a time when there was a scarcity of housing. The Housing Act of 1954 was passed in response to some of the criticisms. To qualify for federal aid, the community was called upon to present "a workable program," which was to include detailed plans for the resettlement of those persons displaced by urban renewal. In addition to providing funds for the development or redevelopment of a community, the federal government sponsored the rehabilitation of an area, for which private builders would receive FHA-insured financing. The idea behind this provision was that rehabilitation would speed up the process of removing blight much faster than would the development or redevelopment of a neighborhood. Another section of the act specified that 10 percent of federal funds (later increased to 30 percent in 1961) could be used for renewal projects in nonresidential areas—an attempt to remove blight from business districts.

The act further sought to provide inducements for local communities to solve their own housing problems. According to terms of Section 701, grants-in-aid of up to 50 percent of the total costs were given to small cities and to all official state, metropolitan, or regional agencies to engage in metropolitan or regional planning. As a result, local, state, and regional planning associations started to hire consultants to produce master plans and other proposals, although the first agencies to take advantage of Section 701 were agencies already in existence. Detroit, for example, previously had established a metropolitan area planning commission, and it was able to receive a grant of $35,000 within a short time after the Housing Act of 1954 was passed. By 1969, the federal government had given over 5,000 grants, for which it spent a total of $236.4 million.

Urban renewal produced some notable achievements, as

well as some striking failures. The physical appearance of many cities was considerably improved, downtown business areas were revitalized, and municipalities received additional income in property taxes from the new structures that were built. New Haven had a particularly vigorous program, largely thanks to the endeavors of Mayor Richard C. Lee. By the mid-1960s, it had received $120 million in urban renewal funds, an amount exceeded only by New York, Philadelphia, Boston, and Chicago, and on a per capita basis, New Haven was first in the country at $790.

In New York, urban renewal turned out to be a mixed blessing. The first director of the city's program was Robert Moses, who served as chairman of the Mayor's Committee for Slum Clearance from 1948 to 1960. Due to Moses' skill in obtaining funds, New York soon had the biggest Title I program in the country. As of 1957, the federal government had spent $267 million on urban renewal in New York, as compared with a combined total for all other cities in the United States of $178 million. Robert A. Caro, whose critical book in 1974 about Moses has received much attention, has stated that New York was so far ahead that when scores of huge buildings constructed under the urban renewal program were already occupied, administrators from other cities were still borrowing New York's contract forms to learn how to draw up the initial legal agreements with interested developers.[19] The first ten Title I projects in New York boosted tax revenues by $5 million, an achievement that did not alter the fact that most of the program became highly controversial. Moses was accused of showing little concern for the people who were evicted to make way for urban renewal. In one Title I project—Manhattan South, west of Central Park in the Nineties—the developers (a former slum furniture dealer and a Tammany clubhouse politician) made millions in rents on property for which they paid $1 million, but which was valued at $16 million.

To critics of urban renewal, New York presents an excellent illustration of the disadvantages of the program, although they were quick to point out other shortcomings as well. A frequent charge was that it became "black removal," since blacks constituted a large percentage of the people who were evicted from their homes. Others alleged that in the process of evicting tenants, urban renewal often had the effect of moving them from one slum to another one. This situation arose because there was no provision in the original act providing housing for the people forced to move, and until the late 1960s only an estimated 6 percent of the construction in urban renewal projects was for public housing. As of that time, most of the new units were either buildings for commercial use or high-rise luxury apartments for upper middle income and affluent families. Urban renewel also was a lengthy process, and in view of the urgency of the housing crisis, it was disconcerting to find out that most projects eventually took from six to nine years to complete.

Nevertheless, even some of its most vocal critics are in favor of urban renewal, although they want it to be used in conjunction with other programs. Sociologist Herbert J. Gans has argued that urban renewal should be transformed from a program of slum clearance and rehabilitation into a program of urban housing. He suggested that the government build low and moderate cost housing on vacant land in cities, suburbs, and new towns beyond the suburbs, and that it undertake to help slum dwellers move into existing housing outside the slums. When a portion of the low income population has left the slums, Gans would like to see the government clear and rehabilitate the area.[20]

Gans' proposals serve as a reminder that urban renewal is just one approach to housing, and, as the facts attest, a relatively minimal one as compared with what has been undertaken by the private sector. While the government has spent upward of $10 billion on urban renewal since 1949, it accounted for only 1.3 percent of all construction activity in cities during the first decade of its existence. At the same time, the government has managed to tear down more housing than it has put up. During the first eighteen years that it was in operation, urban renewal, together with other government programs such as highway construction, destroyed one-half million more homes than the government subsequently built.

The federal government has not been indifferent to some of the criticisms that have been directed against urban renewal, and, accordingly, has made several changes in the program. Congress passed an act in 1958 providing payments to people and businesses displaced by urban renewal. Families received up to $100 for moving expenses (later increased to $200), and businesses received $1,800 (later raised to $3,000, with a maximum of $25,000). Under the terms of the Housing Act of 1968, at least one half of all housing units built in urban renewal projects must be for low and moderate income families, and at least 20 percent for low income groups.

Federal–City Relations: The 1950s

By the early 1950s, there was a degree of caution in Washington about its urban commitment. Dwight D. Eisenhower, like Republican Presidents before and after him, had misgivings about federal involvement in municipal affairs. Eisenhower felt that the time had come for the states to assume more of their share of municipal responsibilities. He made frequent reference to his fear that the federal government had improperly invaded the rights of the states when it came to overseeing urban matters, a theme which he stressed in a major talk on this subject delivered before a meeting of the Governors' Conference in Williamsburg, Virginia, in 1957. Although he recognized that "the needs of our cities are glaringly evident," and that "urban problems will soon almost defy solution," he looked to the states to solve the problems. After referring briefly to the fact that municipalities needed services that "ranged far beyond city boundaries," he said that he was "earnestly hopeful" that the task of providing these services to the metropolitan community would be assumed by the states and not by the federal government.[21]

In March, 1953, two months after Eisenhower had assumed the presidency, he asked Congress to appoint a commission to study the means of achieving a sounder relationship between federal, state, and local governments. Congress complied with the request, and later set up the Commission on Intergovernmental Relations, also known as the Kestnbaum Commission. In a report to the President issued in 1955, it advocated a reduction of federal grants-in-aid so as to encourage greater self-reliance at both the state and local levels. It made a reference to the need to reorganize local government but also noted that the federal government had an obligation to facilitate state action with respect to metropolitan problems. The following year, Eisenhower acted upon the recommendation of the Kestnbaum Commission that a special assistant be named for intergovernmental affairs, and he appointed Howard Pyle, former Republican governor of Arizona, to the position. Pyle functioned in an advisory capacity only, and had little influence on national policy.

At his Williamsburg address in 1957, Eisenhower had suggested to the governors that they join with members of his administration in creating a committee to look into the question of shifting functions from the federal government to the states. Subsequently, a Joint Federal State Action Committee was set up, and its first meeting was held in August, 1957. The committee consisted of seven members representing the federal government and ten state governors, with Secretary of the Treasury Robert Anderson and New Hampshire Governor Lane Dwinell serving as co-chairmen. After two years of study, it recommended that the states assume the major responsibility in slum clearance, urban renewal, and municipal waste treatment plants. The latter proposal had the approval of the President, for in a letter to Democratic House Speaker Sam Rayburn in May, 1958, Eisenhower urged that Congress discontinue federal grants to cities for the construction of water treatment facilities, as authorized by the Water Pollution Control Act of 1948. In spite of the recommendations from both the committee and the President, there were no cutbacks in either slum clearance, urban renewal, or municipal waste treatment plants.

Another commission established during the Eisenhower presidency was the Advisory Commission on Intergovernmental Relations, set up by an act of Congress in 1959. The commission's authorizations included giving critical attention to grant programs and making technical assistance available to the federal government in reviewing proposed legislation. Its membership was composed of twenty-six individuals representing all levels of government, and since its establishment it has published several reports, including *Urban and Rural America: Policies for Future Growth* (1968), and *Urban America and the Federal System* (1969).

While the federal government was appraising the question of its relationship with other branches of government, cities were attempting to solve their own problems. They were aided in their efforts in a substantial way by their state governments, which continued to channel funds to local communities. In 1950 and 1960, state payments to local governments totaled $4.2 billion and $9.4 billion, respectively, as compared with federal payments to local governments in 1950 of $211 million and $592 million in 1960. The figures indicate that while federal aid to cities was increasing during the 1950s, local governments were still getting nearly ten times as much money from the states as from the federal government. However, since states traditionally discriminated against urban areas in the per capita disbursements of these funds, cities were becoming more inclined to regard Washington as a more reliable source for funds. Municipalities sometimes sought financial assistance from both the state and federal governments as a means of insuring the survival of locally sponsored projects, for cities were far from averse to taking action in matters like housing, planning, government reform, and cleanup and beautification projects. Yet the sheer magnitude of metropolitan problems made traditional approaches seem outdated and had the effect of undercutting local activity. As Blake McKelvey has wrtten, "local clubs and bureaus of municipal research that had provided leadership in the 20's and a sense of need in the 30's lost much of their effectiveness as cities exploded into vast metropolises."[22] Therefore, the leading municipal associations of the 1950s and 1960s, as their counterparts had done during the 1930s, tried to secure more help from the federal government, even if they also shared Eisenhower's apprehensions at the trend toward national control of municipal functions. The best of both worlds—local initiative and federal financing—was proving to be a difficult task.

In spite of Eisenhower's objections, federal participation in municipal life was reaching significant proportions by the end of the 1950s. In an attempt to determine the actual extent of Washington's involvement in one particularly important region, Robert H. Connery and Richard H. Leach asked the United States Bureau of the Budget to furnish them with some figures on federal expenditures in the New York metropolitan area during the late 1950s.* The Budget Bureau cited, among other statistics, the following items: The Urban Renewal Administration gave grants of $120 million for slum clearance and urban renewal projects; the Public Housing Administration supported the construction of 90,000 units of low-rent public housing by pledging contributions of $30 million a year for forty years; the federal government contributed $10 million from 1947 to 1957 for the construction of ten airports; the Army Corps of Engineers had some thirty projects, involving expenditures of over $100 million for port improvements; and the Bureau of Public Roads had allocated

---

*The Budget Bureau took the New York Regional Plan Association's definition of "metropolitan area," which included more territory than the definition used by the Bureau of the Census.

grants of $129 million since 1953 for the federal government's share of $270 million for highway and bridge programs.[23]

Federal Policy and Suburban Growth

At the same time that it was expending substantial funds in urban areas, the federal government embarked on other programs that had the ultimate effect of contributing to the growth of the suburbs. The suburbs drew residents, businesses, and vital sources of income away from the cities, creating a situation which was difficult to remedy without additional funds from Washington. To various observers, this action represented just one aspect of the government's inconsistency, and it later prompted people like Daniel P. Moynihan to urge that federal authorities formulate a national urban policy and consider, among other things, the long-range implications of all legislation and programs.[24]

One act that proved to have a significant effect on suburban growth was the Federal-Aid Highway Act of 1956. Although it was not the first federal program for highways—the earliest one dated back to 1917—it was the most expensive program enacted up to that date. The Highway Act of 1956 authorized an expenditure of over $33 billion to construct 41,000 miles of interstate roads and highways during the next thirteen years. The major portions of the funds were to be spent in urban areas, and in keeping with Eisenhower's philosophy, the responsibility for the program was to be divided between the federal government and the states—with the federal government assuming 90 percent of the costs, and the states the remaining 10 percent.

The act had the support of pressure groups like the oil, rubber, automobile, and construction industries, trucking and bus concerns, and labor unions. It financed the building of excellent highways and facilitated access to the suburbs, but, as some would argue, it opened up a Pandora's box of social and environmental problems. In addition to displacing families forced to move as a result of the highway construction, it encouraged the adoption of the kind of policy in which, as one writer noted, "over 60 percent of the land surface in many major cities has been turned over, without plans and without restrictions, to auto-related functions such as roads, super highways, bridges, parking garages and open lots, billboards, motels, service stations, and car washes. Ecologically, economically, and socially, this practice can spell disaster."[25]

The exodus to suburbia also was made possible by the lending policies of two federal agencies, the FHA and the Veterans Administration (VA). The VA, during its first thirty years in operation, financed over eight million homes, mainly in the suburbs. This agency was created as part of the Serviceman's Readjustment Act of 1944, and it guaranteed mortgages for veterans. In similar fashion, most of the FHA-backed loans have been for suburban homes. New home loans, with accompanying long-term mortgages, were relatively easy to obtain from the FHA, and as of October, 1974, the FHA insured loans for nearly 11.5 million homes.

The FHA was careful about the areas in which its loans were made, and thereby established four categories for ratings, the highest of which were given to homogeneous and new neighborhoods far removed from the tensions of the inner cities. Since it shied away from lending in neighborhoods occupied by what its Operation Manual termed "inharmonious racial or national groups,"[26] only 1 percent of FHA loans went to black persons between 1945 and 1965. Its lending policies for builders of apartment houses also were stringent, thus tending to discourage this type of construction.

The tax policies of the federal government offer still another example of how the suburban home market has benefited from policies adopted in Washington. By permitting income tax deductions for mortgage interest charges and real estate taxes, the federal government made it economically feasible for many families to buy their own homes. Ironically, the government has lost more money by allowing these deductions than it has spent on housing programs for low income families. Alvin L. Schorr, who was a staff member in the Office of Economic Opportunity, said that the federal government spent $820 million in 1962 to subsidize housing for the poor. In the same year, the government lost $2.9 billion because of the tax deductions it allowed to homeowners, which mostly helped families from the middle and upper classes.[27] A decade later, the situation was unchanged. In *The President's Fourth Annual Report on National Housing Goals* (1972), the federal government estimated that in 1971 it had lost $4.7 billion by allowing homeowners these same kinds of deductions.[28]

Urban Problems in the 1960s

Cities received more attention during the 1960s than at any other time since the depression, as the public suddenly became aware of an urban crisis. The concern started during the administration of John F. Kennedy, whose interest in urban problems intensified when he became aware of the importance of big-city votes in his successful campaign for the presidency in 1960. The following year, he appointed the President's Committee on Juvenile Delinquency and Youth Crime, which sponsored research and demonstration projects in several cities. It was the first of many federal attempts during the decade to help youngsters in ghetto areas. In January, 1962, Kennedy called for the creation of a Department of Housing and Urban Affairs, telling Congress: "We neglect our cities at our peril, for in neglecting them we neglect our nation."[29] He leaked out news that he intended to nominate Robert C. Weaver, whom he named the preceding year to be director of the Housing and Home Development Agency, to head the department. The bill creating the department was defeated in the House Rules Committee, partly because Kennedy had linked civil rights to urban affairs by indicating that Weaver, a black man, was his choice for the new position. The bill was later passed in September, 1965, at the urging of President Lyndon B. Johnson, who also named Weaver to head the department, now called the Department of Housing and Urban Development (HUD). In January, 1966, Weaver became head of HUD and was the first black person to hold a cabinet position in the United States government.

Shortly before Kennedy's assassination in November, 1963, he had decided to launch an anti-poverty campaign and make it one of the themes in his reelection bid in 1964. In his decision to act, he had been influenced by Michael Harrington's book, *The Other America* (1962), an account of rural and urban poverty in the country. It had been given to him by Walter Heller, chairman of the Council of Economic Advisers. Two days before his death, Kennedy told Heller to proceed with plans for the program. Johnson learned about it within days after becoming President and told Heller to go ahead. "That's my kind of program," he said.[30]

Johnson, who had been a protégé of FDR's, seemed determined to outdo his former mentor and demonstrate to the public that he was qualified to serve as President in his own right. The product of a boyhood that had been spent on a small farm in the southwestern part of Texas, he may have shared rural America's traditional distrust of cities. Nevertheless, he personally understood some of the hardships of poverty and, skilled politician that he was, realized the political value of an urban base. The result was the greatest burst of legislative activity since the early days of the Roosevelt presidency. Unlike what happened during the New Deal, Johnson's War on Poverty, or his Great Society program, emphasized social issues and focused mostly on poor youth, a large portion of whom were black.

The first important act dealing with the War on Poverty was the Economic Opportunity Act, passed in 1964. It set up the Office of Economic Opportunity (OEO), headed by Peace Corps Dirctor R. Sargent Shriver. Congress had appropriated $800 million for the first year, and $1.5 billion in 1965. When plans for the OEO first were being discussed with various interested parties, Richard Boone, a former Cook County, Illinois, police captain, who had joined the Ford Foundation's delinquency program, suggested the phrase, "maximum feasible participation of the poor." It became an important concept of the War on Poverty, which sought to enlist the aid of poor people in planning poverty programs in their own neighborhoods. Before long, the OEO had set up several programs, some of which it ran itself and several of which it coordinated with the assistance of other agencies. Whenever possible, it tried to bypass the state and local governments in order to establish a direct line of communication between the people and the federal government.

One of the ways in which "maximum feasible participation" was to be achieved was through the organization of Community Action Programs (CAPs), whose membership was comprised of neighborhood people in a given target area. They might be chosen in elections or could be appointed by the mayor. In 1965, there already were 700 CAPs in existence. At first, it was hoped that the CAPs would have flexibility as to what programs would be established. They were asked to set up their own "demonstration" projects, for which the federal government paid 90 percent of the cost. But in time there was a shift in emphasis. The federal government decreased its share to 50 percent, requiring a matching sum which many communities could not afford, and some of the projects were dropped. The OEO also decided to prepackage some relatively popular projects, which the CAPs were expected to adopt in preference to devising alternative ones. By the end of the first year, most government funds were expended for ongoing programs.

Organizing the poor in local communities often led to confrontations with municipal authorities and groups. In time, many officials began to equate the CAPs with rent strikes, marches on City Hall, and demands for more city jobs for minorities. Some communities had experiences similar to what took place in Syracuse in 1965. The city already had a youth-oriented poverty program called the Crusade for Opportunity, when the OEO gave Syracuse University a grant to establish a community action training center to help the poor participate more widely in local programs. Within a short time, there was fear that the university had trained the poor too well, especially after the Crusade for Opportunity, operating under the guidance of black militants, began putting out remedial reading manuals advocating the use of violence. Amid protests by the local branch of the National Association for the Advancement of Colored People, further trouble broke out over finances when it was disclosed that of the $8 million spent by the center by mid-1967, about $7 million had gone for salaries. In July, 1967, the OEO stepped in and appointed three trustees to take over the program.

Some of the other programs funded by the OEO were the Jobs Corps and VISTA (Volunteers in Service to America). The Jobs Corps provided residential training centers for school dropouts between the ages of fourteen to twenty-two to help them complete their studies and learn a trade. When figures became available indicating that the federal government was spending $8,000 anually to train an enrollee, Congress put a lid of $6,900 on the costs. VISTA was intended as the domestic counterpart of the Peace Corps, which Shriver had headed since its adoption in 1961. Participants were expected to work in places like urban slums, migrant camps, rural outposts, and Indian reservations. Among other services set up by the OEO were legal aid to the poor, neighborhood centers, and one very popular program, Head Start, designed to provide preschool training for children.

Although the OEO attempted to work directly with poor people, it had to face the fact that government agencies like HUD, Department of Health, Education, and Welfare, Office of Education, the Children's Bureau, Department of Labor, and the Public Health Service had initiated some of the same kinds of programs. In 1967, the Department of Labor began plans to launch a crash employment program in urban slums after it received news that inner city unemployment was three times the total in the rest of the country. It was given an appropriation of millions by Congress to set up Concentrated Employment Program (CEP) centers. The CEPs offered services similar to HUD's Neighborhood Service Centers (NSCs), established by Johnson in 1966, and in Washington, the Labor Department was constructing a $54 million CEP center two blocks away from where a $5 million NSC was being planned. Both the NSCs and the CEPs resembled many OEO agencies, and several larger cities soon had a variety of centers, which sometimes were competing with each other in providing services relating to manpower training, human resources, health care, youth opportunity, rehabilitation, employment, mental health, and supplementary education. There was an additional complication because most communities already had made available some form of assistance and guidance in the areas of education, vocational training, counseling, public health, and welfare.

The War on Poverty never reached its full potential, as huge sums were diverted from it, beginning in 1967, for the Vietnam War. The OEO was revamped by Richard M. Nixon, who was elected President in 1968, although most of its programs remained in operation. Finally, in March, 1974, Nixon asked Congress to dismantle it; in the previous year its appropriations had totaled $1.9 billion, which was approximately the same amount funded during Johnson's last year in office.

In assessing the War on Poverty, some of its defenders, including Shriver, maintained that poverty would have been eliminated completely by the late 1970s had the government increased its appropriations to a figure of $6 billion per year. It also can be claimed that the programs did have an impact on poverty. In 1975, there were 25.9 million poor people—or a total of 12.3 percent of the population—in the United States, "poor" being defined by the government's inflation-related price index as all those nonfarm families earning less than $5,500 annually. Although the number of poor people increased by 2.5 million between 1974 and 1975, there has been a steady decline over the years in the percentage of people living in poverty. In 1959, 22.4 percent of the national population was classified as poor, but in 1969, following the

War on Poverty, the figure decreased to 12.1 percent.* Black Americans, in particular, also appear to have been helped by the War on Poverty. Thanks to massive federal funds spent on public education in ghetto schools,† financial aid to black students, and assistance provided by groups like the Ford Foundation, in 1972, for the first time, the percentage of black and other minority high school graduates enrolled in colleges was the same as for whites.

Those persons who remained unconvinced about the merits of the poverty programs justified their position by pointing to the record. They asserted that the people who really profited from the War on Poverty were the ones who ran its programs, a list that included bureaucrats as well as neighborhood people. Other forms of criticism were along the lines offered by Allen E. Pritchard, executive director of the National League of Cities, who complained that the programs "had a peculiar frantic quality" about them,[31] and by sociologist Nathan Glazer, who argued that "a democratic polity cannot take the position that the major way to improve its institutions of government and welfare is to finance guerilla warfare against them."[32]

Many of the difficulties that beset the War on Poverty were evident in the Demonstration Cities and Metropolitan Development Act (model cities), another of the pillars of Johnson's Great Society. The original proposal, which Johnson had sent to Congress in January, 1966, called for the concentration of large sums of money in a few cities over a six-year period to be spent on areas that included housing, education, health, and job training programs. There were many justifications for this approach, since it sought to demonstrate how one massive program, as opposed to a series of uncoordinated efforts, could revive the staggering metropolitan city. However, the proposal, as formulated, defied political realities. When the act was signed in November, it appeared that a large portion of model city funds had been distributed

---

*Poverty figures have fluctuated between 1970 and 1975 on account of the recession. However, the difference between 1959, when the federal government began keeping poverty statistics, and 1975 is still striking.

†Title I of the Elementary and Secondary Education Act of 1965 authorized federal funds for children from low income families as a supplement to local and state funds. By the early to mid-1970s, its annual appropriations amounted to approximately $1.8 billion.

to cities on the basis of their political clout. A total of $400 million was to be spread over seventy-five cities in the first round, with others to be named later. Listed in the first-round selection were Butte (population 27,000) and Helena (population 22,000) for Montana's Senate Majority Leader Mike Mansfield; McAlester (population 17,000) for House Speaker Carl Albert of Oklahoma; and Texarkana (population 32,000) for Texas' Wright Patman, chairman of the House Banking and Currency Committee, which held hearings on the bill.

The widespread disbursement of money over so many areas made the concept of model cities virtually impossible to achieve. In several first-round "problem" cities, there were complaints that model cities was a skeletal program that did not provide enough funds to do an adequate job. To cite one case, the target area selected for the model cities program in Detroit was a relatively small one, and, according to Robert Conot, even with four other target areas in the city already receiving appropriations from the anti-poverty programs, "the other poor—a significant number of Negroes and a large number of whites—who lived in low-income enclaves scattered throughout the city remained as separated and alienated from the social programs as they had been before the War on Poverty got under way."[33]

Consistent with some of the goals of the War on Poverty, model cities required "widespread citizen participation." This led to the election of neighborhood planning councils in each community, which were supposed to work in conjunction with the newly created demonstration agency in the targeted city. It was not unusual for both groups to fight over the distribution of funds, and since the OEO often regarded model cities as a rival, the CAPs and the city demonstration agencies also were frequently at odds. Other complications arose because, under the HUD guidelines, the planning councils were expected to produce a comprehensive neighborhood plan within one year, making it difficult, particularly at the beginning, to arrive at a workable formula. It has been argued that during its first years model cities "produced only a collection of warmed-over anti-poverty and urban renewal proposals,"[34] and early in 1973 the Nixon administration announced that the program would expire as of August 30, 1974.

The fact that the riots of the mid-1960s followed some of the most intensive efforts to alleviate poverty ever undertaken by the national government led to both a feeling of disillusionment and a renewed interest in solving urban problems. In August, 1967, after rioting had erupted in Detroit, a group of over 1,000 municipal officials, urban specialists, and business leaders met and founded the National Urban Coalition. At the beginning of 1968, John Gardner, Secretary of Health, Education, and Welfare, agreed to serve as president, and later that year the coalition set up a Commission on the Cities to undertake a study of urban problems. In 1972, the Commission on the Cities put out a report entitled, *The State of Our Cities*.

The National Commission on Urban Problems, appointed by Johnson in January, 1967, has published several studies, including *Building the American City* (1968). As early as March, 1965, Johnson had called for the creation of a commission to study building and housing codes, zoning, and local and federal tax policies. When he established the commission nearly two years later, he also asked it to consider how the efforts of the federal government, private industry, and local communities could be marshaled to increase the opportunities for low-cost housing. This latter area once again became a prime concern of the administration in the aftermath of the racial outbursts.

One of the immediate responses of the federal government to the riots of 1967 was the passage of the National Housing Act of 1968, which set as a goal the availability of home ownership to low income persons, mostly city dwellers. Earlier, the Housing Act of 1965 had supplemented the rent of poor tenants, but nothing was said about home ownership. The 1968 act specified that the government would repay lenders who underwrote mortgages for low income people if the mortgagee defaulted. In practice, handsome profits were made by the people who undertook to finance these mortgages, while very few low income families became homeowners. Poor people often were encouraged to buy homes, sometimes on a fraudulent basis, only to learn that the homes required the kind of upkeep that they could not afford. Many subsequently defaulted on the mortgages, but the lender was fully reimbursed by the federal government.

The program was administered by the FHA, which functioned under the jurisdiction of HUD, so that when the mortgagee defaulted, HUD acquired the property. Consequently, HUD has become one of the largest owners of property in the country, and, as several of its critics allege, one of the country's largest slumlords.

A Nation of Suburbs: The 1970s

By the time that Nixon became President, it was beginning to look as if the federal government had a talent for spending money on many programs of dubious value, and the public was left wondering whether there was any way out of the urban crisis. Moreover, persons who were interested in city affairs were having a hard time keeping abreast of developments and the already voluminous writings on the subject. There was also confusion in Washington. Robert Conot reported that during the 1960s it was not unusual for the staffs of congressional committees to be approached by supposedly knowledgeable people who asked their support for legislation that had already been enacted.[35]

Nixon astutely understood these frustrations and was aware of the fact that his presidency coincided with a period in which the United States was rapidly becoming a nation of suburbs. In 1960 the population of the country had been divided almost equally among central cities, suburbs, and nonmetropolitan areas, each of which had approximately 60 million people. But in 1970, the suburbs pulled ahead with 76 million people, in comparison to 64 million in cities, and 63 million in rural areas. With the growth of suburban areas, the problems of the biggest cities were beginning to appear remote to the "silent majority" of Americans, for by the mid-1970s, only 15 percent of the nation's population lived in central cities with over 500,000 people. Many of Nixon's policies, while hardly ignoring urban America, were largely designed to appeal to the views of suburbanites. By talking about the need to tone down the powers of the federal goverment, as he did in his first inaugural address, he was uttering a sentiment that found an especially warm reception among those not directly involved in the daily turmoil of big-city living. Yet Nixon was also caught up in an era that witnessed increasing agitation over urban problems, and his knowledge of this fact foreshadowed aspects of his policy.

Although his pace was not as frenetic at Johnson's, Nixon manifested a concern for the social ills plaguing the American urban community, at least until the end of 1972. The first official act of his administration in January, 1969, was to establish an Urban Affairs Council. The function of the council was to "advise and assist" the administration on urban matters, and to develop a national urban policy. With regard to the War on Poverty, Nixon redirected its focus and sought the advice of Daniel P. Moynihan, his adviser on urban affairs. Federal outlays continued to go to the poor, but no longer was there an emphasis on training programs for youths. Instead, the administration increased expenditures for food stamps and made more funds available for services which sometimes benefited the non-poor as well, such as Social Security and Medicare. His chief proposal to alleviate poverty took the form of a Family Assistance Plan, an alternative to welfare. It called for a guaranteed income for every American family, including the working poor who were ineligible for welfare. It was never passed due to dissatisfaction over provisions such as the guaranteed amount ($1,600 for a family of four, or $2,460 when food stamps were added) and the requirement that recipients, except mothers with preschool children, had to register for work or job training.

Other aspects of Nixon's urban program revealed a desire to get around some of the administrative red tape that had bogged down so many of the projects of earlier years. The President's references to a "New Federalism," or the call for the states and cities to assume more control over matters pertaining directly to their own needs, made him sound like Eisenhower, but he proved himself capable of spending money like Roosevelt and Johnson. The cornerstone of his New Federalism was the State and Local Fiscal Assistance Act (revenue sharing), passed three weeks before his landslide victory in 1972. This act provided for the distribution of $30.2 billion over a five-year period to state and local governments on the basis of their population, retroactive to January 1, 1972. Two thirds of the money was given to local governments (counties, cities, and towns) to be used in any or all of nine priority areas: public safety, environmental protection, transportation, recreation, health, libraries, social services, financial assistance to the poor and elderly, and capital expenditures. The remaining one third of the money was for state use, without any restrictions, provided that it was used for legal purposes only. Another provision in the act specified that there could be no racial, sex, ethnic, and religious discrimination in the application of these funds.

There were some doubts on both sides about the relative merits of revenue sharing. Washington had apprehensions

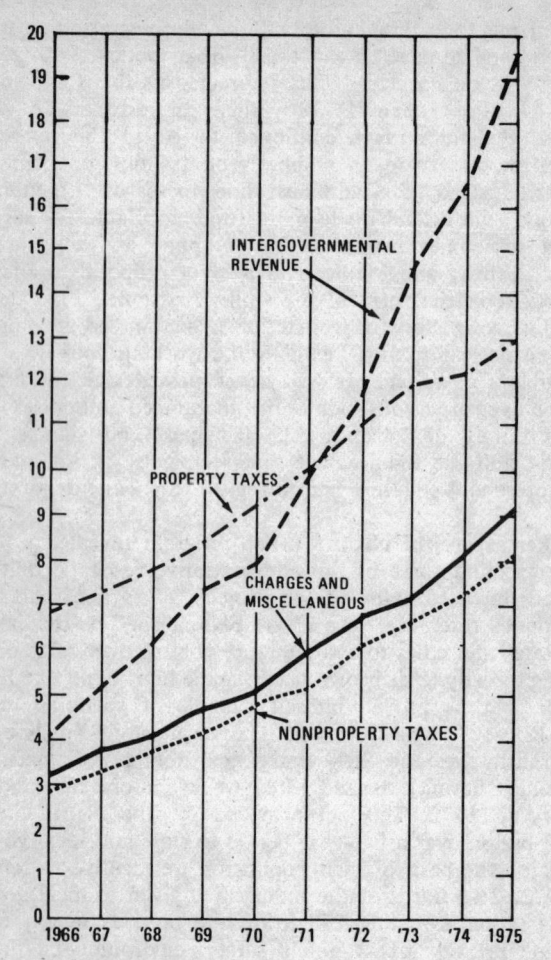

Figure 10.3 Trends in City General Revenue from Selected Major Sources: 1966–1975*

*Figures given in billions of dollars.

SOURCE: U.S. Department of Commerce

that the money might be spent in such a way as to circumvent the intention of the act. Municipalities and towns feared that the more affluent suburbs would benefit most from it, while larger cities felt that they would find it difficult to obtain

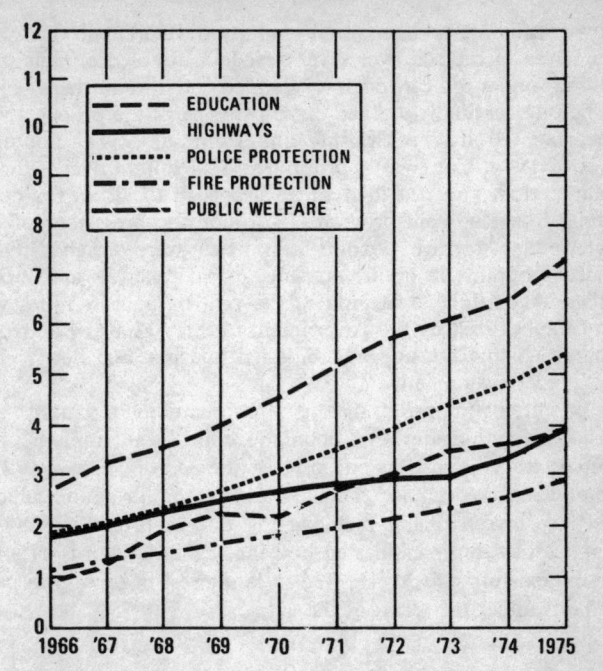

Figure 10.4 Trends in City General Expenditure for Selected Major Functions: 1966–1975*
*Figures given in billions of dollars.
SOURCE: U.S. Department of Commerce

other funds from the federal government. Objections were also voiced that the undercount of black persons in the census (an estimated 7.7 percent of the total black population in 1970) was depriving many cities of their fair share of revenue sharing funds. This argument was taken up in a 1973 report issued by the Urban League, which alleged that millions of dollars were lost in this way to cities like New York, Chicago, Los Angeles, Philadelphia, Detroit, Washington, and Baltimore.[36] Nevertheless, revenue sharing, together with the lump sum payments under the Housing and Community Development Act of 1974, has proved useful to cities in helping them to find a way out of some of their difficulties.

After the enactment of revenue sharing, Nixon requested Congress to appropriate special revenue sharing funds to state and local governments for education, law enforcement, manpower training, and urban community development. The purpose was to replace over seventy federal grant programs providing similar aid for narrowly defined activities in these fields. When it was finally worked out by Congress, the proposal was incorporated in the Housing and Community Development Act of 1974. Congress appropriated $8.4 billion over a three-year period, and provided single grants to localities for community development programs. The housing provisions of the act were set forth in Section 8, and they were designed to replace programs in public housing, urban renewal, and model cities. According to Section 8, the rent of poor families was to be subsidized by the government in three kinds of housing: sound existing housing, rehabilitated housing, and newly constructed developments.

In spite of the government's good intentions in making provisions for housing the poor, Section 8, as implemented, failed to accomplish its purpose. By the end of 1975, only 200 families had occupied housing under the program, chiefly because investors and financial institutions found it risky to finance new or rehabilitated housing, while landlords offering sound existing housing showed little interest in renting to poor tenants under the terms of the act.

Whither Urban America?

It is impossible to view the urban crisis without a measure of caution. Wishful thinking will not make it go away, even had the administration of President Gerald R. Ford indulged in thoughts along that line. A headline on page one of the *New York Times on* March 23, 1975, stated: "Urban Crisis of the 1960s Is Over, Ford Aides Say"—a statement that flew in the face of reality. Several months later, Mayor Abraham D. Beame of New York disclosed that the "Empire City" was on the verge of bankruptcy, and it took an appropriation of $2.3 billion in loans to New York, passed by Congress in December of that year, to prevent the city's default. New York State likewise came across with financial aid, leaving the state in the city's former position of monthly encounters with impending economic disaster.

If New York's close encounter with default caught the country off guard, its situation played up the plight of several of the nation's largest metropolitan centers. As of the mid-1970s, the suburbs remained the mainstay of metropolitan growth, as they had been in the 1960s. They have accounted for all the growth in the North and in the South, while only in the West has there been any discernible increase in the population of the central cities. Economically, the cities continue to lose out to other sections of the metropolitan community. The *Population Bulletin* reported that during the decade of the 1960s, approximately 70 percent of the total increase in employment, and 95 percent of the increase in manufacturing, occurred in large metropolitan areas outside the central city.[37] These economic problems have been further aggravated by the increasing numbers of urban families on relief. New York's near financial disaster was not helped by the fact that one out of every seven people in the city was on welfare, a sizable jump over the one out of every sixteen reported in 1965. Even if the states and the federal government eventually assume more of the costs of welfare, which, of course, is only hypothetical, cities must still contend with their swelling municipal payrolls and pension costs. At the annual meeting of the National League of Cities in February, 1975, at Houston, one of the most widely discussed topics was the question of how city officials should deal with public unions. Many cities were approaching the situation faced by Detroit, where 50 percent of its public safety budget was eaten up by pension costs. Rising budgets also have resulted in an increase in taxes, causing city residents to pay more in taxes than their suburban neighbors. Unfortunately, these increased taxes never seem to keep up with soaring municipal costs, which have increased by nearly 550 percent since 1945.

Politically, the cities find themselves in a minority status with respect to their state and national governments. The suburbs, rather than the cities, have gained the greatest representation by virtue of the Supreme Court's legislative reapportionment decisions in the early 1960s, and it is the suburbs, and not the cities, that are sending more representatives to Congress. In 1973, the biggest geographic grouping of House of Representatives districts consisted of 161 predominantly suburban areas, 130 rural areas, 119 central cities, and 25 towns.[38] In order to give the cities more political power and to increase the efficiency of municipal services, suggestions have been made that there be a reorganization of the over 78,000 units of local governments (counties, municipalities, and townships) into a composite metropolitan government. It may be a logical solution, but it is a solution that has met with repeated and fierce opposition from the very groups involved.

Many of the long-range prospects for the cities are tied to the general state of their economy. To some extent, the problem has geographic boundaries, with cities in the northeast and north-central regions being particularly hard-pressed because of the changes that have taken place within their metropolitan areas. A study completed by the Brookings Institution in 1975 actually rated twelve out of fifty-eight central cities surveyed as being better off than their suburbs with regard to employment, welfare, crowded housing, poverty, and income and educational level of the populace. However, of the twelve cities (including Houston, Phoenix, and Dallas), eleven were located in the southern and western portions of the country.[39]

If urban America is to find a way out of several of its major problems, it is conceivable that it will be through some form of growth planning. Many of the industrial countries of western Europe—notably England, France, Italy, Holland, and Sweden—have growth policies as a way of redistributing population, decentralizing industry, and preventing metropolitan congestion. These growth policies usually take the form of incentives to industry, covering a portion of the cost of investment in areas in which growth is to be encouraged, followed up by appropriations for roads, ports, utilities, and public facilities within the targeted region. This type of planning previously has been anathema to many Americans, but there may be no other choice. With growth projections for the United States indicating that there will be a shift in income away from the northeastern and north-central portions of the country, the cost of providing essential municipal services in these older areas will become increasingly prohibitive for the average wage-earning urban residents. Other projections foresee a total United States population of 300 million in the year 2020, the continuation of urban sprawl, and the concentration of about 85 percent of the country's population into 16 percent of the nation's land areas—a situation that many urbanologists regard as disastrous from the point of view of the energy crisis. In terms of the gloomy nature of these predictions, the statement made by Daniel P. Moynihan in 1969 appears to be especially pertinent at the present time. "The conviction that in the cities will be found a paramount threat to the life of the Republic," he wrote, "has changed hardly at all. What has perhaps changed is that at long last what they have been saying may be beginning to be true."[40]

On the more positive side, several proposals for rescuing urban America, in addition to growth planning, are worthy of note. Edward K. Hamilton, former budget director of New York City, believes that the federal government can—and must—assume more fiscal management over cities, rather than come forth with a narrow response that is tailored to a particular city, as was the case with New York in 1975. Hamilton's argument is that cities are in financial trouble because their operating revenues have come to outstrip their incomes by a ratio of approximately three to one, and not because they are guilty of gross mismanagement and incompetence. Nevertheless, he sees the need for greater efficiency in municipal affairs and looks to the federal government to act as a watchdog as well as to embark on a bold plan of action. His suggestions include the creation of a new class of "national cities" or metropolitan areas with a federal charter and special procedures for federal monitoring, regulation, and assistance; the establishment of national incentives and guidelines for effective and equitable collective bargaining procedures, efficient local administration, and comprehensive efforts to improve local government productivity; assessments by the federal government of the feasibility of assuming the costs for services like welfare, medical care for the indigent, and mass transit; and consideration of a federal banking and guarantee agency which could regulate and stand behind state and local securities if the issuers agreed to meet federal standards and criteria.[41] Other viewers, like Richard P. Nathan of the Brookings Institution, favor the enactment by the federal government of a "Marshall Plan" for inner cities. Nathan has further advocated giving direct income assistance to the poor in urban areas, revising formulas under existing aid programs in order to concentrate grants in distressed central cities, and calling upon state governments, county governments, business, labor, and civic organizations to devise an urban strategy.[42]

The urgency behind these proposals is apparent, although many Americans—particularly those who live in areas far removed from the turmoil of inner city life—may be tired of being told about the urban crisis. To ignore the cities, however, is also to ignore various aspects about American life that are dynamic, including its problems. In the past, it was the resolution of these problems that sparked the economic development of the country, and made possible the spirit of community that enabled the cities to accommodate the diverse groups of people who congregated in them. When cities are viewed from this perspective, it can be maintained that the failure to deal with urban problems—rather than the existence of them—forebodes ill for the future.

Notes

Chapter 1

1. Bernard Bailyn, *The New England Merchants in the Seventeenth Century* (Cambridge, Mass.: Harvard University Press, 1955), 86.
2. Kenneth T. Jackson and Stanley K. Schultz (eds.), *Cities in American History* (New York: Alfred A. Knopf, 1972), 41.
3. Jean Gottman, *Megalopolis: The Urbanized Northeastern Seaboard of the United States* (Cambridge, Mass.: M.I.T. Press, 1961), 102ff.
4. Julius Rubin, "Urban Growth and Regional Development," in David T. Gilchrist (ed.), *The Growth of the Seaport Cities, 1790–1825* (Charlottesville, Va.: University of Virginia Press, 1967), 3–21, quote on pp. 4–5.
5. Jackson and Schultz, *Cities in American History*, 42.
6. Page Smith, *As a City Upon a Hill: The Town in American History* (New York: Alfred A. Knopf, 1966).
7. John W. Reps, *The Making of Urban America: A History of City Planning in the United States* (Princeton, N.J.: Princeton University Press, 1965), 119–146.
8. Charles N. Glaab, *The American City: A Documentary History* (Homewood, Ill.: Dorsey Press, 1963), 36.
9. James T. Lemon, "Urbanization and the Development of Eighteenth Century Southeastern Pennsylvania and Adjacent Delaware," *William and Mary Quarterly*, XXIV (October, 1967), 501–542.
10. See Curtis Nettels, "The Economic Relations of Boston, Philadelphia, and New York, 1680–1715," *Journal of Economic and Business History*, 3 (1930–1931), 185–215; Bernard Bailyn, "Communications and Trade: The Atlantic in the Seventeenth Century," *Journal of Economic History*, 13 (1953), 378–387; Carl Bridenbaugh, *Cities in the Wilderness: The First Century of Urban Life in America, 1625–1742* (New York: The Ronald Press, 1938), *passim.*; and Jacob M. Price, "Economic Function and the Growth of American Port Towns in the Eighteenth Century," *Perspectives in American History*, VIII (1974), 123–186.
11. Aubrey C. Land, "Economic Base and Social Structure: The

Northern Chesapeake in the Eighteenth Century," *Journal of Economic History*, 25 (1965), 639–654.
12. George Rogers Taylor, "American Economic Growth Before 1840: An Exploratory Essay," *Journal of Economic History*, 24 (1964), 427–444; see also Price, "Economic Function and the Growth of American Port Towns in the Eighteenth Century."
13. Sam Bass Warner, Jr., *The Private City: Philadelphia in Three Periods of its Growth* (Philadelphia: University of Pennsylvania Press, 1968), 14–19.
14. Carl Abbott, "The Neighborhoods of New York, 1760–1775," *New York History*, LV (January, 1974), 35–54. See also Bruce M. Wilkenfeld, "New York City Neighborhoods, 1730," *New York History*, LVII (April, 1976), 165–182. Using the tax assessment list prepared in February, 1730, among other evidence, Wilkenfeld suggests that clearly defined neighborhoods, based on socio-economic distinctions, emerged at an early date in America's cities.
15. Bridenbaugh, *Cities in the Wilderness*, 49, 95, 163, 200, 249–50, 409–10, 417; Gary B. Nash, "Slaves and Slaveowners in Colonial Philadelphia," *William and Mary Quarterly*, XXX (April, 1973), 223–256.
16. James A. Henretta, "Economic Developments and Social Structure in Colonial Boston," *William and Mary Quarterly*, 22 (January, 1965), 75–92; also see Allan Kulikoff, "The Progress of Inequality in Revolutionary Boston," *William and Mary Quarterly*, XXVIII (July, 1971), 375–412.
17. Warner, *The Private City*, 8–9.
18. *Ibid.*, 3.
19. Gerard B. Warden, *Boston, 1689–1776* (Boston: Little, Brown and Co., 1970), 25.
20. Taylor, "American Economic Growth Before 1840," *passim*.
21. Richard G. Miller, "Gentry and Entrepreneurs: A Socio-Economic Analysis of Philadelphia in the 1790s," *Rocky Mountain Social Science Journal*, 12 (January, 1975), 71–84.
22. Reps, *The Making of Urban America*, Chap. 9

Chapter 2

1. George Rogers Taylor, "American Urban Growth Preceding the Railway Age," *Journal of Economic History*, XXVII (1967), 309–335; quote on p. 328.
2. Charles N. Glaab, *The American City: A Documentary History* (Homewood, Ill.: Dorsey Press, 1963), 135.
3. Constance M. Green, *American Cities in the Growth of the Nation* (New York: Harper and Row, 1965), 87.

4. Richard Wade, "The City in History—Some American Perspectives," in Werner Z. Hirsch (ed.), *Urban Life and Form* (New York: Holt, Rinehart, and Winston, 1963), 59–79; quote on p. 64.
5. Richard Wade, *The Urban Frontier: Pioneer Life in Early Pittsburgh, Cincinnati, Lexington, Louisville, and St. Louis, 1790–1830* (Chicago: University of Chicago Press, 1964), 45–48.
6. *Ibid.*, 322, 323–336.
7. *Ibid.*, 70.
8. Louis L. Tucker, "Cincinnati, Athens of the West, 1830–1861," *Ohio History*, 75 (Winter, 1966), 16–25, 67–68; quotes on p. 16. See also Richard T. Farrell, "Cincinnati, 1800–1830: Economic Development through Trade and Industry," *Ohio History*, 77 (Autumn, 1968), 111–129, 171–174.
9 *The Cleveland Herald*, October 13, 1831, as quoted in Edmund H. Chapman, *Cleveland: Village to Metropolis* (Cleveland: Western Reserve University Press, 1965), 46.
10. Margaret Walsh, "Industrial Opportunity on the Urban Frontier: 'Rags to Riches' and Milwaukee Clothing Manufacturers, 1840–1880," *Wisconsin Magazine of History*, 57 (Spring, 1974), 174–194; tables on p. 179.
11. Richard Wade, *Slavery in the Cities: The South, 1820–1860* (New York: Oxford University Press, 1964).
12. Eugene Genovese, "The Significance of the Slave Plantation for Southern Economic Development," *Journal of Southern History*, XXVIII (November, 1962), 422–437; quote on pp. 436–437.
13. Lewis Mumford, *The City in History: Its Origins, Its Transformations, and Its Prospects* (New York: Harcourt Brace Jovanovich, 1961), 422, 424.
14. Quoted in Warner, *The Private City*, 53, Note 5.
15. *Ibid.*, Chap. 3.
16. Sam Bass Warner, Jr., "The Feeding of Large Cities in the United States, 1860–1960," *Third International Conference of Economic History*, Munich, 1965, 83–96.
17. Sam Bass Warner, Jr., *The Urban Wilderness* (New York: Harper and Row, 1972), 71.

Chapter 3

1. Stephan Thernstrom, *The Other Bostonians* (Cambridge: Harvard University Press, 1973), 225.
2. Daniel Boorstin, *The National Experience* (New York: Random House, 1965), 116–121.
3. Clarence H. Danhof, "Agriculture," in Harold F. William-

son (ed.), *The Growth of the American Economy* (New York: Prentice Hall, 1951), 151.
4. Richard Wade, *Slavery in the Cities; the South, 1820–1860* (New York: Oxford University Press, 1964), *passim.*
5. Leon Litwack, *North of Slavery* (Chicago: University of Chicago Press, 1961), 90.
6. *Ibid.*, 70.
7. *Ibid.*, 187–190.
8. Robert Albion, *The Rise of New York Port* (New York: Charles Scribner's Sons, 1939), 349–353.
9. John R. Commons, *History of Labor in the United States* (New York: The Macmillan Co., 1918–1935), Vol. I, 495.
10. *Ibid.*, Vol. I, 9–11.
11. Sam Bass Warner, Jr., *The Private City* (Philadelphia: University of Pennsylvania Press, 1968), 61.
12. Christopher Tunnard and Henry Hope Reed, *American Skyline* (Boston: Houghton Mifflin Co., 1955), 99.
13. J. Thomas Scharf, *Chronicles of Baltimore* (Baltimore: Turnbull Brothers, 1874), 523.
14. Herbert Asbury, *The Gangs of New York* (New York: Alfred A. Knopf, 1928), 49.
15. As cited in Daniel Bell, *The End of Ideology* (New York: Collier Books, 1962), 172.
16. As cited in Henry Still, *The Dirty Animal* (New York: Hawthorn Books, 1967), 141.
17. Mrs. Frances Trollope, *Domestic Manners of the Americans* (New York: Vintage Books, 1949), 39.
18. As cited in Howard D. Kramer, "Early Municipal and State Boards of Health," *Bulletin of the History of Medicine,* XXIV (November–December, 1950), 512.
19. Henry Still, *op. cit.*, 34.
20. "Sanitary Reform," *North American Review,* LXXIII (July, 1851), 124.
21. Earl Niehaus, *The Irish in New Orleans* (Baton Rouge: Louisiana State University Press, 1965), 147.
22. Robert Ernst, *Immigrant Life in New York City, 1825–1863* (New York: King's Crown Press, 1949), 141.
23. *New American State Papers, Labor and Slavery* (Wilmington, Del.: Scholarly Resources, 1973), Vol. II, 195.
24. Carl Wittke, *The Irish in America* (Baton Rouge: Louisiana State University Press, 1956), 183.
25. *New American State Papers, Labor and Slavery,* Vol. II, 196–197.

Chapter 4

1. The term was used by William B. Munro, *The Government of American Cities* (4th ed., New York: The Macmillan Co., 1926), 431. See also Frank Mann Stewart, *A Half-Century of Municipal Reform: The History of the National Municipal League* (Berkeley and Los Angeles: University of California Press, 1950), 195.
2. James Bryce, *The American Commonwealth* (2 vols., New York: The Macmillan Co., 1888), Vol. I, 608.
3. Sam Bass Warner, Jr., *The Private City: Philadelphia in Three Periods of its Growth* (Philadelphia: University of Pennsylvania Press, 1968), 9.
4. Edward Pessen, "Who Governed the Nation's Cities in the 'Era of the Common Man'?" *Political Science Quarterly*, LXXXVII (December, 1972), 591–614; D. Clayton James, *Antebellum Natchez* (Baton Rouge: Louisiana State University Press, 1968); and Michael H. Frisch, "The Community Elite and the Emergence of Urban Politics: Springfield, Massachusetts, 1840–1880," in Stephan Thernstrom and Richard Sennett (eds.), *Nineteenth-Century Cities: Essays in the New Urban History* (New Haven: Yale University Press, 1969).
5. Horace E. Deming, *The Government of American Cities: A Program of National Democracy* (New York: G. P. Putnam's Sons, 1909), 35.
6. *Ibid.*, 32.
7. E. L. Godkin, "Dumb Legislation," *The Nation*, XLIV (June 2, 1887), 465.
8. James Parton, "The Government of the City of New York," *North American Review*, CIII (October, 1866), 456.
9. Cited in Clifford W. Patton, *The Battle for Municipal Reform: Mobilization and Attack, 1875 to 1900* (Washington, D.C.: American Council of Public Affairs, 1940), 9.
10. Quoted in Zane L. Miller, *Boss Cox's Cincinnati: Urban Politics in the Progressive Era* (New York: Oxford University Press, 1968), 92.
11. Quoted in William L. Riordon, *Plunkitt of Tammany Hall*, introduction by Arthur Mann (New York: McClure, Phillips and Co., 1905: Dutton paperback edition, 1963), ix.
12. *Ibid.*, 37.
13. Harold Zink, *City Bosses in the United States: A Study of Twenty Municipal Bosses* (Durham, N.C.: Duke University Press, 1930), 3–61.
14. Lincoln Steffens, *The Shame of the Cities* (New York: Mc-

Clure, Phillips and Co., 1904: Hill and Wang paperback edition, 1969), 138.
15. Quoted in Gore Vidal, Review of Robert A. Caro, *The Power Broker: Robert Moses and the Fall of New York*, in *The New York Review of Books*, XXI (October 17, 1974), 3.
16. Riordon, *Plunkitt of Tammany Hall*, 3.
17. *Ibid.*, 30.
18. Bryce, *The American Commonwealth*, Vol. II, 103.
19. Quoted in Lincoln Steffens, *The Autobiography of Lincoln Steffens* (New York: Harcourt, Brace and Company, Inc., 1931), 618.
20. Quoted in Francis Russell, "Honey Fitz," *American Heritage*, XIX (August, 1968), 31.
21. Quoted in Zink, *City Bosses in the United States*, 17
22. Quoted in Lyle W. Dorsett, *The Pendergast Machine* (New York: Oxford University Press, 1968; paperback edition, 1970), 41.
23. John W. Pratt, "Boss Tweed's Public Welfare Program," *The New-York Historical Society Quarterly*, XLV (October, 1961), 411.
24. Steffens, *The Shame of the Cities*, 164–165.
25. Miller, *Boss Cox's Cincinnati*, 63.
26. Frederick C. Howe, *The City: The Hope of Democracy* (New York: Charles Scribner's Sons, 1905), 3.
27. Steffens, *The Shame of the Cities*, 126.
28. Quoted in Arthur M. Schlesinger, *The Rise of the City, 1878–1898*, Vol. X: *A History of American Life* (New York: The Macmillan Co., 1933), 388.
29. Quoted in Walton Bean, *Boss Ruef's San Francisco: The Story of the Union League Party, Big Business, and the Graft Prosecution* (Berkeley and Los Angeles: University of California Press, 1967), 6.
30. See Diana Klebanow, "E. L. Godkin, the City, and Civic Responsibility," *The New-York Historical Society Quarterly*, LV (January, 1971), 67–68.
31. Quoted in Alexander B. Callow, *The Tweed Ring* (New York: Oxford University Press, 1966), 254.
32. Stephan Thernstrom, *The Other Bostonians: Poverty and Progress in the American Metropolis, 1880–1970* (Cambridge, Mass.: Harvard University Press, 1973), 143.

Chapter 5

1. U.S. Bureau of the Census, *Fourteenth Census of the U.S.: 1920*, I, *Population.* (Washington D.C., 1921), 63–64, 72, 80.
2. Anselm L. Strauss, *Images of the American City* (New York:

NOTES

The Free Press of Glencoe, 1961), 240.
3. U.S. Bureau of the Census, *Statistical Abstract of the U.S.: 1962* (Washington, D.C., 1962), 21.
4. Lawrence Larsen and Robert Branyan, "The Development of an Urban Civilization on the Frontier of the American West," *Societas,* I (Winter, 1971), 33–50.
5. Quoted in Charles Glaab, *The American City: A Documentary History* (Homewood, Ill.: Dorsey Press, 1963), 162.
6. Quoted in Richard Wade, "The City in History—Some American Perspectives," in W. Z. Hirsch (ed.), *Urban Life and Form* (New York: Holt, Rinehart and Winston, 1963), 62.
7. Robert V. Hine, *The American West: An Interpretative History* (Boston: Little, Brown and Co., 1973), 253.
8. David G. Taylor, "Boom Town Leavenworth: The Failure of the Dream," *Kansas Historical Quarterly,* XXXVIII (Winter, 1972), 389–415.
9. Robert R. Dykstra, *The Cattle Towns* (New York: Alfred A. Knopf, 1968).
10. *Ibid.,* 142–148, esp. 144.
11. Howard Chudacoff, "Where Rolls the Dark Missouri Down," *Nebraska History* (Spring, 1971), 1–30.
12. Duane Smith, *Rocky Mountains Mining Camps: The Urban Frontier* (Bloomington: University of Indiana Press, 1967).
13. Gilbert Stelter, "The Birth of a Frontier Boom Town: Cheyenne in 1867," *Annals of Wyoming,* 39 (April, 1967), 5–33; see also Carl Abbott, "Boom State and Boom City: Denver's Growth," *Colorado Magazine,* L (Summer, 1973), 12–30.
14. Thomas J. Noel, "The Multifunctional Saloon, Denver, 1858–1876," *Colorado Magazine,* LII (Spring, 1975), 114–136; see also Elliott West, "The Saloon in Territorial Arizona," *Journal of the West,* XIII (July, 1974), 61–73.
15. Dykstra, *The Cattle Towns,* 121–131.
16. Quoted in Kenneth Hammer, "Territorial Towns and the Railroads," *North Dakota History,* 36 (Fall, 1969), 359.
17. Quoted in Gilbert Stelter, "The City and Westward Expansion: A Western Case Study," *The Western Historical Quarterly,* IV (April, 1973), 191.
18. James B. Allen, *The Company Town in the American West* (Norman: University of Oklahoma Press, 1966).
19. Kenneth Wheeler, *To Wear a City's Crown: The Beginnings of Urban Growth in Texas 1836–1865* (Cambridge: Harvard University Press, 1968).
20. Roger Lotchin, "San Francisco, 1846–1856: The Pattern and Chaos of Growth," in Kenneth Jackson and Stanley Schultz (eds.), *Cities in American History* (New York: Alfred A. Knopf, 1972), 143–163.
21. Robert M. Fogelson, *The Fragmented Metropolis: Los Angeles, 1850–1930* (Cambridge: Harvard University Press, 1967).

22. Stuart Bruchey, *Growth of the Modern American Economy* (New York: Dodd, Mead and Co., 1975), 85.
23. *Report of the Board of Park and Boulevard Commissioners of Kansas City, Missouri, 1893*, quoted in Charles Glaab, *The American City*, 258.
24. Kenneth Jackson, "The Crabgrass Frontier: 150 Years of Suburban Growth in America," in Raymond Mohl and James Richardson (eds.), *The Urban Experience* (Belmont, Calif.: Wadsworth Books, 1973), 200, 206.
25. Edmund H. Chapman, *Cleveland: Village to Metropolis* (Cleveland: Western Reserve University Press, 1965), 21.
26. Quoted in Bernard J. Sauers, "A Political Process of Urban Growth: Consolidation of the South Side with the City of Pittsburgh, 1872," *Pennsylvania History*, XLI (July, 1974), 285.
27. Eleanor S. Bruchey, "The Development of Baltimore Business, 1880–1914," *Maryland Historical Magazine*, LXIV (Spring, 1969), 18–42; (Summer, 1969), 144–160.
28. Sam Bass Warner, Jr., *The Urban Wilderness* (New York: Harper and Row, 1972), 71.
29. Zane Miller, *The Urbanization of Modern America* (New York: Harcourt, Brace, Jovanovich, 1973), 66.
30. Alfred D. Chandler, Jr., "The Beginning of 'Big Business' in America," in Carl Degler (ed.), *Pivotal Interpretations of American History* (New York: Harper and Row, 1966), II, 107–138; see also Stuart Bruchey, *Growth of the Modern American Economy*, 98–100, 106.
31. Daniel J. Boorstin, *The Americans: The Democratic Experience* (New York: Random House, 1973), 110.
32. *Ibid.*, 121–129.
33. Chandler, "The Beginnings of 'Big Business' in America," 132; Bruchey, *Growth of the Modern American Economy*, 98–100, 106.
34. Edward C. Kirkland, *Industry Comes of Age, 1860–1897* (Chicago: Quadrangle Books, 1967), 239.
35. *Ibid.*, 238, 258.
36. Blake McKelvey, *The Urbanization of America, 1860–1915* (New Brunswick, N.J.: Rutgers University Press, 1963), 81, 107.
37. *Ibid.*, 236.
38. Quoted in Charles Glaab and A. Theodore Brown, *A History of Urban America* (New York: The Macmillan Co., 1967), 148–149.
39. George Hilton and John Due, *The Electric Interurban Railways in America* (Stanford, Calif.: Stanford University Press, 1960).
40. Glaab and Brown, *A History of Urban America*, 183.
41. Quoted in David Nord, "The Experts Versus the Experts: Conflicting Philosophies of Municipal Utility Regulation in

the Progressive Era," *Wisconsin Magazine of History,* 58 (Spring, 1975), 223.
42. Forrest McDonald, *Insull* (Chicago: University of Chicago Press, 1962), 118–119.
43. Quoted in Nord, "The Experts Versus the Experts . . . ," 231.
44. See Ernest S. Griffith, *A History of American City Government, 1900–1920* (New York: Praeger, 1974), Chap. 7, "Taming the Public Utility."
45. McDonald, *Insull,* 118–119.
46. J. E. Vance quoted in Maurice Yeates and Barry Garner, *The North American City* (New York: Harper and Row, 1971), 218.
47. Quoted in Glaab, *The American City,* 233–234.
48. Sam Bass Warner, Jr., *Streetcar Suburbs: The Process of Growth in Boston, 1870–1900* (Cambridge: Harvard University Press, 1962), 8–9, 129.
49. Graham R. Taylor, *Satellite Cities: A Study of Industrial Suburbs* (New York: D. Appleton and Co., 1915), 91.
50. Warner, *Streetcar Suburbs,* quote on p. 151. See especially pp. 126–141.
51. *Ibid.,* 163–164.
52. Clay McShane, *Technology and Reform: Street Railways and the Growth of Milwaukee, 1887–1900* (Madison: State Historical Society of Wisconsin, 1974).
53. Fogelson, *The Fragmented Metropolis,* 144.
54. John B. Rae, *The Road and the Car in American Life* (Cambridge, Mass.: M.I.T. Press, 1971), 50–51, 202–207, 250–252; see also Blaine Brownell, "A Symbol of Modernity: Attitudes Toward the Automobile in Southern Cities in the 1920s," *American Quarterly,* XXIV (Summer, 1972), 20–44.

Chapter 6

1. Stephan Thernstrom and Peter Knights, "Men in Motion," in Tamara Haraven (ed.), *Anonymous Americans* (Englewood Cliffs, N.J.: Prentice-Hall, 1971), 29.
2. Howard P. Chudacoff, *Mobile Americans: Residential and Social Mobility in Omaha, 1880–1920* (New York: Oxford University Press, 1972), 57.
3. As cited in John R. Commons *et al., History of Labor in the United States* (New York: The Macmillan Co., 1918–1935), Vol. III, 331.
4. As cited in John A. Garraty, *The New Commonwealth* (New York: Harper and Row, 1968), 184.
5. Maldwyn Allen Jones, *American Immigration* (Chicago: University of Chicago Press, 1960), 220.

6. William F. Whyte, *Street Corner Society: The Social Structure of an Italian Slum* (Chicago: University of Chicago Press, 1943), XVIII.
7. Chudacoff, *Mobile Americans*, 67.
8. As cited in Thomas C. Cochran and William Miller, *The Age of Enterprise* (New York: Harper and Row, 1961), 231.
9. *Chicago Herald*, July 17, 1887, as cited in Humbert Nelli, *The Italians of Chicago, 1860–1920* (New York: Oxford University Press, 1970), 11.
10. John Higham, *Strangers in the Land* (New York: Atheneum, 1969), 143.
11. Nathan Glazer and Daniel Patrick Moynihan, *Beyond the Melting Pot* (Cambridge, Mass.: M.I.T. Press, 1963), 258–259.
12. Edward Steiner, *On the Trail of the Immigrant* (New York: F. H. Revell, 1906), 290.
13. Stephan Thernstrom, *The Other Bostonians: Poverty and Progress in the American Metropolis* (Cambridge: Harvard University Press, 1973), 254–255.
14. For a Summary and analysis of these findings, see Thernstrom, *The Other Bostonians*, 249–250.
15. Clarence Dickinson Long, *Wages and Earnings in the United States* (Princeton, N. J.: Princeton University Press, 1960), 109; Albert Rees, *Real Wages in Manufacturing, 1880–1914* (Princeton, N. J.: Princeton University Press, 1961), 3.
16. Harold Melvin Mayer and Richard Wade, *Chicago: Growth of a Metropolis* (Chicago: University of Chicago Press, 1969), 154.
17. Thernstrom and Knights, "Men in Motion," 30.
18. As cited in Bayrd Still, *Mirror for Gotham* (New York: New York University Press, 1956), 297.
19. Mayer and Wade, *Chicago*, 142.
20. "Housing Conditions in Cleveland," *Charities Magazine*, XII (April 2, 1904), 346.
21. Charles F. Zueblin, *American Municipal Progress* (rev. ed., New York: The Macmillan Co., 1916), 55.
22. Charles M. Glaab and A. Theodore Brown, *A History of Urban America* (New York: The Macmillan Co., 1967), 176.
23. Charles A. Beard, *American City Government; A Survey of Newer Tendencies* (New York: Century Company, 1912), 262–263.
24. As paraphrased in Blanche Coll, *Perspectives in Public Welfare; A History* (Washington: U. S. Government Printing Office, 1969), 64.
25. William B. Munro, *Municipal Government and Administration* (New York: The Macmillan Co., 1923), Vol. II, 319.
26. As cited in Arthur Meier Schlesinger, *The Rise of the City* (New York: The Macmillan Co., 1933), 349.

27. As cited in Moses King (ed.), *King's Handbook of New York City* (Boston: Moses King, 1893), 419.
28. Robert H. Bremner, *From the Depths: The Discovery of Poverty in the United States* (New York: New York University Press, 1956), 56–57.
29. Blake McKelvey, *The Urbanization of America* (New Brunswick, N.J.: Rutgers University Press, 1963), 151.
30. As cited in Bremner, *From the Depths*, 65.
31. Zueblin, *American Municipal Progress*, 163.
32. Robert H. Wiebe, *The Search for Order, 1877–1920* (New York: Hill and Wang, 1968), 166.
33. As cited in Lawrence A. Cremin, *The Transformation of the School: Progressivism in American Education, 1876–1957* (New York: Alfred A. Knopf, 1961), 118.
34. Robert E. Park and Herbert Miller, *Old World Traits Transplanted* (New York: Harper and Bros., 1921), 146.
35. Bayrd Still, *Milwaukee: The History of a City* (Madison: State Historical Society of Wisconsin, 1965), 259.
36. Will Herberg, *Protestant, Catholic, Jew: An Essay in Religious Sociology* (rev. ed., New York: Peter Smith, 1955).
37. Oscar Handlin, *Race and Nationality in American Life* (Garden City: Doubleday-Anchor, 1957), Chap. 5; Jones, *American Immigration*, 177–182.

Chapter 7

1. Brand Whitlock, *Forty Years of It* (New York and London: D. Appleton and Co., 1914), 162.
2. Richard Hofstadter, *The Age of Reform: From Bryan to F.D.R.* (New York: Alfred A. Knopf, 1955: Vintage paperback edition, 1960), 8–9; Arthur Mann, *Yankee Reformers in the Urban Age: Social Reform in Boston, 1880–1900* (New York: Belknap Press of Harvard University Press, 1954: Harper Torchbook edition, 1966); Robert H. Wiebe, *The Search for Order, 1870–1920* (New York: Hill and Wang, 1968), 170–171; Samuel P. Hays, "The Politics of Reform in Municipal Government in the Progressive Era," *Pacific Northwest Quarterly*, LV (October, 1964), 157–169; J. Joseph Huthmacher, "Urban Liberalism and the Age of Reform," *Journal of American History*, XLIX (September, 1962), 231–241. See also James Weinstein, "Organized Business and the City Commission and Management Movements," *Journal of Southern History*, XXVIII (May, 1962), 166–182, and John D. Buenker, *Urban Liberalism and Progressive Reform* (New York: Charles Scribner's Sons, 1973).

3. Quoted in Allen F. Davis, *Spearheads for Reform: The Social Settlements and the Progressive Movement, 1890–1914* (New York: Oxford University Press, 1968), 173.
4. See, for example, Clifford W. Patton, *The Battle for Municipal Reform: Mobilization and Attack, 1875 to 1900* (Washington, D.C.: American Council on Public Affairs, 1940); William B. Munro, *The Government of American Cities* (3rd ed., New York: The Macmillan Co., 1920), 22; and Albert Shaw, "Our 'Civic Renaissance,'" *Review of Reviews*, XI (April, 1895), 415–427.
5. Quoted in Frank Mann Stewart, *A Half-Century of Municipal Reform: The History of the National Municipal League* (Berkeley and Los Angeles: University of California Press, 1950), 17.
6. Quoted in Thomas C. Devlin, *Municipal Reform in the United States* (New York: G. P. Putnam's Sons, 1896), 11–12.
7. Quoted in Stewart, *A Half-Century of Municipal Reform*, 18.
8. Quoted in Whitlock, *Forty Years of It*, 158.
9. Quoted in Justin Kaplan, *Lincoln Steffens: A Biography* (New York: Simon and Schuster, 1974), 130.
10. Quoted in *ibid.*, 143.
11. Bessie L. Pierce, *A History of Chicago*, Vol. III: *The Rise of a Modern City, 1871–1893* (New York: Alfred A. Knopf, 1957), 380.
12. Lincoln Steffens, *The Shame of the Cities* (New York: McClure, Phillips and Co., 1904; Hill and Wang paperback edition, 1969), 185.
13. Quoted in Allen F. Davis, "Jane Addams vs. the Ward Boss," *Journal of the Illinois State Historical Society*, LIII (Autumn, 1960), 263.
14. Jane Addams, *Democracy and Social Ethics*, in Blaine A. Brownell and Warren E. Stickle (eds.), *Bosses and Reformers* (Boston: Houghton Mifflin Co., 1973), 120.
15. *Ibid.*, 122.
16. Quoted in Melvin G. Holli, *Reform in Detroit: Hazen S. Pingree and Urban Politics* (New York: Oxford University Press, 1969), 159.
17. *Ibid.*, 158.
18. Quoted in Whitlock, *Forty Years of It*, 164.
19. Quoted in Ernest Crosby, *Golden Rule Jones: Mayor of Toledo* (Chicago: The Public Publishing Company, 1906), 11.
20. Quoted in Whitlock, *Forty Years of It*, 114.
21. Tom L. Johnson, *My Story*, edited by Elizabeth J. Hauser (New York: B. W. Huebsch, 1911), 124.
22. Lincoln Steffens, "Ohio: A Tale of Two Cities," *McClure's Magazine*, XXV (July, 1905), 302.

23. Bayrd Still, *Milwaukee: The History of a City* (Madison: The State Historical Society of Wisconsin, 1965), 320.
24. Quoted in Patton, *The Battle for Municipal Reform*, 74.
25. Steffens, *The Shame of the Cities*, 164.
26. Theodore J. Lowi, *At the Pleasure of the Mayor: Patronage and Politics in New York City, 1898–1958* (New York: The Free Press of Glencoe, 1964), 224.
27. Jacob A. Riis, *A Ten Years' War: An Account of the Battle with the Slum in New York*, in Brownell and Stickle, *Bosses and Reformers*, 101.
28. Steffens, *The Shame of the Cities*, 199.
29. *Ibid.*, 199–201.
30. Quoted in James Bryce, *The American Commonwealth* (2 vols., New York: The Macmillan Co., 1888), Vol. II, 94.
31. James Bryce, *Modern Democracy* (2 vols., London: Macmillan and Co., Ltd., 1921), Vol. II, 138–140.
32. Lyle W. Dorsett, *The Pendergast Machine* (New York: Oxford University Press, 1968; paperback edition, 1970), 103.
33. Quoted in Diana Klebanow, "Frank Hague," *Encyclopedia of World Biography* (New York: McGraw-Hill Book Co., 1973).
34. Rexford G. Tugwell, *The Art of Politics* (Garden City, N.Y.: Doubleday and Co., Inc., 1958), 15.
35. Julius Horowitz, "In One Month, 50,000 Persons Were Added to the City's Welfare Rolls," *New York Times Magazine* (January 26, 1969), 22, 24, 46, 48–49, 51, 54.
36. Quoted in *New York Times*, December 21, 1976, 27.

Chapter 8

1. Leo Schnore, *The Urban Scene* (New York: The Free Press, 1965), 88.
2. Jean Gottmann, "Megalopolis, or the Urbanization of the Northeastern Seaboard," *Economic Geography*, XXXXIII (July, 1957), 189–200; see also Jean Gottmann, *Megalopolis* (New York: Twentieth Century Fund, 1961).
3. "Grow Slow," *Newsweek*, LXXIX, part 2 (March 27, 1972), 75.
4. Robert Fogelson, *The Fragmented Metropolis* (Cambridge: Harvard University Press, 1967), 161.
5. John Dyckman, "Transportation in Cities," *Cities; A Scientific American Book* (New York: Alfred A. Knopf, 1966), 136.
6. Frederick Lewis Allen, "The Suburban Nightmare," *Independent*, CXIV (June 13, 1925), 671.
7. Harold M. Mayer and Richard Wade, with the assistance of

Glen E. Holt, *Chicago: Growth of a Metropolis* (Chicago: University of Chicago Press, 1969), 326.

8. Gregory Singleton, "The Genesis of Suburbia: A Complex of Historical Trends," in Louis Masotti and Jeffrey K. Hadden (eds.), *The Urbanization of the Suburbs*, Vol. 7, *Urban Affairs Annual Reviews* (Beverly Hills, Calif.: 1973), 40–41.

9. Christopher Tunnard and Henry Hope Reed, *American Skyline* (Boston: Houghton Mifflin Co., 1955), 167.

10. As cited in John Hamer, "Restrictions on Urban Growth," *Editorial Research Reports*, Vol. I (1973), 97–98.

11. Janet Roebuck, *The Shaping of Urban Society* (New York: Charles Scribner's Sons, 1974), 193.

12. Daniel Elazar, "Are We a Nation of Cities?" in H. R. Mahood and Edward L. Angus (eds.), *Urban Politics and Problems: A Reader* (New York: Charles Scribner's Sons, 1969), 26.

13. John Kramer, *North American Suburbs* (Berkeley, California: Glendessary Press, 1972), XIV.

14. Graham Taylor, "Satellite Cities," in Charles M. Glaab (ed.), *The American City: A Documentary History* (Homewood, Ill.: Dorsey Press, 1963), 439.

15. Louis H. Masotti, "Prologue: Suburbia Reconsidered—Myth and Counter-Myth," in Masotti and Hadden (eds.), *The Urbanization of the Suburbs*, 19.

16. *New York Times*, February 10, 1976.

17. *New York Times*, February 9, 1976.

18. Beverly Duncan and Stanley Lieberson, *Metropolis and Region in Transition* (Beverly Hills, Calif.: Sage Publications, 1970), 216.

19. Kenneth T. Jackson, "Metropolitan Government versus Suburban Autonomy: Politics on the Crabgrass Frontier," in Kenneth T. Jackson and Stanley K. Schultz (eds.), *Cities in American History* (New York: Alfred A. Knopf, 1972), 456.

20. *New York Times*, February 13, 1976.

21. News story by Jack Rosenthal in the *New York Times* of May 30, 1971, reprinted in Louis H. Masotti and Jeffrey K. Hadden (eds.), *Suburbia in Transition* (New York: New Viewpoints, 1974), 27.

22. Unpublished 1975 paper in the possession of the authors.

23. "Why Houston Voters Vetoed Mass Transit," *Business Week*, October 13, 1973, 28.

24. B. Bruce-Briggs, "Mass Transportation and Minority Transportation," *The Public Interest* 39 (Summer, 1975), 48.

25. "Why Houston Voters Vetoed Mass Transit," 28.

26. Tunnard and Reed, *American Skyline*, 188.

27. As cited in Mel Scott, *American City Planning Since 1890* (Berkeley, Calif.: University of California Press, 1967), 79.

28. As cited in John Reps, *The Making of Urban America: A*

NOTES 389

History of City Planning in the United States (Princeton, N. J.: Princeton University Press, 1965), 501.
29. David Shipler in the *New York Times*, December 14, 1969, reprinted in Masotti and Hadden, *Suburbia in Transition*, 117.
30. Obituary of Paul Windels, *New York Times*, December 16, 1967.
31. The comment is by Robert Herman, as cited in William H. Whyte, *The Last Landscape* (Garden City, N. Y.: Anchor-Doubleday, 1970), 275.
32. Quoted in Thomas H. Reed (ed.), *Government in a Depression: Constructive Economy in State and Local Government* (Chicago: University of Chicago Press, 1933), 7.
33. Daniel R. Grant, "Urban Needs and State Response: Local Government Reorganization," in Alan K. Campbell (ed.), *The States and the Urban Crisis* (Englewood Cliffs, N. J.: Prentice-Hall, Inc., 1970), 65.
34. See Morton and Lucia White, *The Intellectual Versus the City: From Thomas Jefferson to Frank Lloyd Wright* (Cambridge, Mass.: Harvard University Press and M.I.T. Press, 1962).
35. Lewis Mumford, *The City in History: Its Origins, Its Transformations, and Its Prospects* (New York: Harcourt, Brace and World, Inc., 1961), 572–573.
36. Lewis Mumford, "The Wilderness of Suburbia," *The New Republic*, XXVIII (August–November, 1921), 44–45.
37. "Cities, Worldwide, Can Vie with New York for Urban Problems," *New York Times* (International Economic Survey Section), January 25, 1976, 23.

Chapter 9

1. Irving Kristol, "The Negro Today Is Like the Immigrant Yesterday," *New York Times Magazine* (September 11, 1966), 50–51, 124–142.
2. Philip M. Hauser, "Demographic Factors in the Integration of the Negro," *Daedalus*, 94 (Fall, 1965), 863.
3. James Weldon Johnson, *Along This Way: The Autobiography of James Weldon Johnson* (New York: The Viking Press, 1933; Viking Compass edition, 1968), 206–207.
4. Gunnar Myrdal, *An American Dilemma: The Negro Problem and Modern Democracy* (2 vols., New York: Harper and Row, 1944; Harper Torchbook edition, 1969), Vol. I, 282. The research for this book was begun in 1937, under a grant from the Carnegie Corporation.
5. *Ibid.*, I, 283.
6. St. Clair Drake and Horace R. Cayton, *Black Metropolis: A*

Study of Negro Life in a Northern City (2 vols., New York: Harcourt, Brace and Co., 1945; New York: Harper Torchbook edition, 1962), Vol. I, 223.

7. Myrdal, *An American Dilemma*, I, 294–295.

8. Unlike other northern cities in the 1920s, New York's black population did not come primarily from the South. About 25 percent of Harlem's population was foreign-born, mostly of West Indian origin. This large foreign-born population led historian Gilbert Osofsky to call Harlem "America's largest Negro melting pot." At this time, Harlem was also set apart from other black areas, in that large groups of white visitors went there to partake of the great outpouring of black music, poetry, and literature in the period known as the Harlem Renaissance. See Osofsky, *Harlem: The Making of a Ghetto, Negro New York, 1890–1930* (New York: Harper and Row, 1967; Harper Torchbook edition, 1971), 131, 179–187.

9. The committee conducted the first major federal investigation of black housing ever undertaken. It recommended urban renewal and rehabilitation, but its report was ignored. See Gilbert Osofsky (ed.), *The Burden of Race: A Documentary History of Negro–White Relations in America* (New York: Harper and Row, 1967; Harper Torchbook edition, 1968), 269–274.

10. See Abram Kardiner and Lionel Ovesey, *The Mark of Oppression: Explorations in the Personality of the American Negro* (New York: W. W. Norton and Co., 1951; World Publishing Co. paperback edition, 1962).

11. Kenneth T. Jackson, *The Ku Klux Klan in the City, 1915–1930* (New York: Oxford University Press, 1967), 236–241.

12. Cited in Myrdal, *An American Dilemma*, Vol. I, 499.

13. Quoted in Osofsky, *Burden of Race*, 277.

14. Quoted in Osofsky, *Harlem*, 149.

15. Quoted in Robert Conot, *American Odyssey: A Unique History of America Told Through the Life of a Great City* (New York: William Morrow and Co., 1974), 379.

16. Quoted in June Sochen (ed.), *The Black Man and the American Dream: Negro Aspirations in America, 1900–1930* (Chicago: Quadrangle Books, 1971), 129.

17. Quoted in Kenneth T. and Barbara B. Jackson, "The Black Experience in Newark: The Growth of the Ghetto, 1870–1970," in William C. Wright (ed.), *New Jersey Since 1860: New Findings and Interpretations* (Trenton, N.J.: New Jersey Historical Commission, 1972), 53.

18. The episode is related in Conot, 435–438.

19. Charles Tilly, "Migration to American Cities," in Daniel P. Moynihan (ed.), *Toward a National Urban Policy* (New York and London: Basic Books, Inc., 1970), 161.

20. Stanley Lieberson, *Ethnic Patterns in American Cities* (New York: The Free Press of Glencoe, 1963), 16, 64.

21. Karl E. Taeuber and Alma F. Taeuber, *Negroes in Cities: Residential Segregation and Neighborhood Change* (Chicago: Aldine Press, 1965; Atheneum paperback edition, 1969), 2.
22. Kenneth B. Clark, *Dark Ghetto: Dilemmas of Social Power* (New York: Harper and Row, 1965; Harper Torchbook edition, 1967), 87.
23. *Report of the National Advisory Commission on Civil Disorders* (New York: Praeger, 1968; Bantam paperback edition, 1968), 128–129.
24. *Ibid.*, 1, 203, 2.
25. Quoted in *Time* (August 11, 1975), 6.
26. The Harris results were reported in Robert B. Hill, "Who Are More Prejudiced: WASPS or White Ethnics?" *The Urban League Review*, I (Spring, 1975), 26–29. Campbell's study is set forth in his book, *White Attitudes Toward Black People* (Ann Arbor: University of Michigan Institute for Social Research, 1971). However, white Protestants in New York had a far more favorable attitude toward black people than did white ethnic groups, according to Louis Harris and Bert E. Swanson in their work, *Black-Jewish Relations in New York City* (New York: Praeger, 1970). These studies can be compared with the findings of Neil Betten and Raymond A. Mohl with regard to racism in Gary, Indiana, between 1906 and 1940. Betten and Mohl contend that beginning in 1906, immigrants and black workers lived in mixed neighborhoods without resultant strife. Yet by World War I Gary had become a fully segregated city with staunch racist attitudes. They allege that white racism was introduced by the city's elite, i.e., realtors, professionals, businessmen, and officials of the United States Steel Company, and that prejudice was taught to the immigrants in the course of their assimilation into American society. See Neil Betten and Raymond A. Mohl, "The Evolution of Racism in an Industrial City, 1906–1940: A Case Study of Gary, Indiana," *The Journal of Negro History*, LIX (January, 1974), 51–64.
27. Nathan Glazer and Daniel P. Moynihan, *Beyond the Melting Pot: The Negroes, Puerto Ricans, Jews, Italians, and Irish of New York City* (Cambridge, Mass.: M.I.T. Press, 1963; M.I.T. Press paperback edition, 1970), 84.
28. See Daniel P. Moynihan, *The Negro Family: The Case for National Action* (Washington, D.C.: Government Printing Office, 1965).
29. Edward C. Banfield, *The Unheavenly City Revisited: A Revision of The Unheavenly City* (Boston: Little, Brown and Co., 1973), 78, 87, 97. See also Banfield, *The Unheavenly City: The Nature and Future of Our Urban Crisis* (Boston: Little, Brown and Co., 1970).
30. Stephan Thernstrom, *The Other Bostonians: Poverty and*

Progress in the American Metropolis, 1880–1970 (Cambridge, Mass.: Harvard University Press, 1973), 258.

Chapter 10

1. Quoted in Andrew Sinclair, *The Available Man*: *The Life Behind the Masks of Warren Gamaliel Harding* (New York: The Macmillan Co., 1965; Quadrangle paperback edition, 1969), 8.
2. Cited in Blake McKelvey, *The Emergence of Metropolitan America, 1915–1966* (New Brunswick, N.J.: Rutgers University Press, 1968), 62.
3. [Herbert Hoover], "A Statement from Secretary Hoover to Readers of the American City," *The American City*, XXXVII (November, 1927), 575–576.
4. Robert H. Connery and Richard H. Leach, *The Federal Government and Metropolitan Areas* (Cambridge, Mass.: Harvard University Press, 1960), 129.
5. Quoted in McKelvey, *The Emergence of Metropolitan America*, 80.
6. See Walter S. Gifford, "Cities, Counties, States Can Handle the Situation," *Survey Graphic*, LXVII (February 1, 1932), 466.
7. Quoted in Clarke A. Chambers, *Seedtime of Reform*: *American Social Service and Social Action, 1918–1933* (Minneapolis: University of Minnesota Press, 1963), 200.
8. Quoted in Kenneth S. Davis, *FDR: The Beckoning of Destiny, 1882–1928, A History* (New York: G. P. Putnam's Sons, 1971; Capricorn paperback edition, 1975), 636.
9. Quoted in Dixon Wecter, *The Age of the Great Depression, 1929–1941*, Vol. XIII: *A History of American Life* (New York: The Macmillan Co., 1948), 127.
10. Gunnar Myrdal, *An American Dilemma*: *The Negro Problem and Modern Democracy* (2 vols., New York: Harper and Row, 1944; Harper Torchbook edition, 1969), Vol. I, 350.
11. William E. Leuchtenburg, *Franklin D. Roosevelt and the New Deal, 1932–1940* (New York: Harper and Row, 1963; Harper Colophon edition, 1963), 136.
12. Lewis Mumford, *The Urban Prospect* (New York: Harcourt, Brace and World, Inc., 1968), 182.
13. See, for example, Catherine Bauer Worster, "Framework for an Urban Society," in United States President's Commission on National Goals, *Goals for Americans* (New York: Prentice-Hall, Inc., 1960), 225–247.
14. Quoted in Joseph P. Lash, *Eleanor and Franklin*: *The Story*

of Their Relationship Based on Eleanor Roosevelt's Private Papers (New York: W. W. Norton and Co., 1971; Signet paperback edition, 1973), 524.

15. Quoted in *ibid.*, 394.
16. Wesley Stout, "The New Homesteaders," *Saturday Evening Post*, CCVII (August 4, 1934), 5–7, 61–65.
17. Report of the Urbanism Committee to the National Resources Committee, *Our Cities, Their Role in the National Economy* (Washington, D.C.: Government Printing Office, 1937), 52.
18. The Housing Act of 1949, As Amended Through June, 1961 (Public Law 171, 81st Congress), Sec. 2.
19. Robert A. Caro, "Annals of Politics: The Power Broker, I—The Best Bill-Drafter in Albany," *The New Yorker*, L (July 22, 1974), 35. This article was based on Caro's book, *The Power Broker: Robert Moses and the Fall of New York* (New York: Alfred A. Knopf, 1974).
20. Herbert J. Gans, "The Failure of Urban Renewal: A Critique and Some Proposals," *Commentary*, XXXIX (April, 1965), 29–37.
21. Quoted in Connery and Leach, *The Federal Government and Metropolitan Areas*, 131.
22. McKelvey, *The Emergence of Metropolitan America*, 137.
23. Connery and Leach, *The Federal Government and Metropolitan Areas*, 7.
24. Daniel P. Moynihan, "Toward a National Urban Policy," in Moynihan (ed.), *Toward a National Urban Policy* (New York and London: Basic Books, Inc., 1970), 3–25.
25. Betty D. Hawkins, "Cities and the Environmental Crisis," in Melvin I. Urofsky (ed.), *Perspectives on Urban America* (Garden City, N.Y.: Anchor Books, 1973), 166.
26. Quoted in Edward C. Banfield, *The Unheavenly City Revisited: A Revision of the Unheavenly City* (Boston: Little, Brown and Co., 1973), 15.
27. Alvin L. Schorr, "National Community and Housing Policy," *The Social Service Review*, XXXIX (December, 1965), 434.
28. *The President's Fourth Annual Report on National Housing Goals*, 92d Congress, 2d Session, House Document No. 92-319, June 29, 1972.
29. Quoted in McKelvey, *The Emergence of Metropolitan America*, 206.
30. Quoted in Mark R. Arnold, "The Good War That Might Have Been," *New York Times Magazine* (September 29, 1974), 56.
31. Quoted in the *New York Times*, March 23, 1975, 46. Pritchard's remark had been made before a National League of Cities convention in Puerto Rico in 1973.
32. Nathan Glazer, "The Grand Design of the Poverty Program,"

in Glazer (ed.), *Cities in Trouble* (New York: Quadrangle Books, 1970), 187.
33. Robert Conot, *American Odyssey: A Unique History of America Told Through the Life of a Great City* (New York: William Morrow and Co., 1974), 500.
34. John N. Kolesar, "The States and Urban Planning and Development," in Alan K. Campbell (ed.), *The States and the Urban Crisis* (Englewood Cliffs, N.J.: Prentice-Hall, Inc., 1970), 122.
35. Conot, *American Odyssey*, 646.
36. Urban League Data Service, "Estimating the 1970 Census Undercount for State and Local Areas." Presented at the Annual Conference of the National Urban League on July 23, 1973 in Washington, D.C. (Washington, D.C.: National Urban League, 1973).
37. Editorial Research Reports on the Future of the City, *The Future of the City* (Washington, D.C.: Congressional Quarterly, 1974), 7.
38. *Ibid.*
39. For a summary of the report, see Richard P. Nathan, "For Cities, No Single Problem or Solution," *New York Times*, August 23, 1975, 21. According to the report, the ten worst cities, in ranking order, as compared to their suburbs, are: Newark, Cleveland, Hartford, Baltimore, Chicago, St. Louis, Atlanta, Rochester, Gary, and New York.
40. Daniel P. Moynihan, "The City in Chassis," in Moynihan (ed.), *Toward a National Urban Policy*, 325.
41. Edward K. Hamilton, "Big City Finance: The Next President's Hidden Agenda," *The Stanford Magazine*, IV (Spring/Summer, 1976), 14–19.
42. Richard P. Nathan, "An Agenda for the Cities," *New York Times*, November 10, 1976, p. A29.

Selected Bibliography

[*There is a paperback edition of this work.]

*Abrams, Charles, *The City Is the Frontier*. New York: Harper & Row, 1967.

Adrian, Charles R., and Griffith, Ernest S., *A History of American City Government: The Formation of Traditions, 1775–1870*. New York: Praeger, 1975.

Albion, Robert G., *The Rise of New York Port, 1815–1860*. New York: Charles Scribner's Sons, 1939.

*Anderson, Martin, *The Federal Bulldozer: A Critical Analysis of Urban Renewal, 1949–1962*. Cambridge, Mass.: M.I.T. Press, 1964.

Arnold, Joseph L., *The New Deal in the Suburbs: A History of the Greenbelt Town Program, 1935–1954*. Columbus: Ohio State University Press, 1971.

*Asbury, Herbert, *The Gangs of New York: An Informal History of the Underworld*. New York: Alfred A. Knopf, 1927.

*Banfield, Edward D., *The Unheavenly City: The Nature and Future of Our Urban Crisis*. Boston: Little, Brown and Co., 1970.

*———, *The Unheavenly City Revisited: A Revision of the Unheavenly City*. Boston: Little, Brown and Co., 1973.

Barton, Josef, *Peasants and Strangers: Italians, Rumanians, and Slovaks in an American City, 1890–1950*. Cambridge, Mass.: Harvard University Press, 1975.

*Bean, Walton, *Boss Ruef's San Francisco: The Story of the Union League Party, Big Business, and the Graft Prosecution*. Berkeley: University of California Press, 1967.

Belcher, Wyatt W., *The Economic Rivalry Between St. Louis and Chicago, 1850–1880*. New York: Columbia University Press, 1947.

Bender, Thomas, *Toward an Urban Vision: Ideas and Institutions in Nineteenth-Century America*. Lexington: University of Kentucky Press, 1975.

*Berger, Bennett M., *Working-Class Suburb: A Study of Auto*

    Workers in Suburbia. Berkeley: University of California Press, 1968.
Blake, Nelson M., *Water for the Cities: A History of the Urban Water Supply Problem in the United States.* Syracuse: Syracuse University Press, 1956.
Blumin, Stuart M., *The Urban Threshold: Growth and Change in a Nineteenth-Century American Community.* Chicago: University of Chicago Press, 1976.
*Boskin, Joseph (ed.), *Urban Racial Violence in the Twentieth Century.* Beverly Hills, Calif.: Glencoe Press, 1969.
*Bracey, John H., Jr., Meier, August, and Rudwick, Elliott (eds.), *The Rise of the Ghetto.* Belmont, Calif.: Wadsworth, 1971.
*Bremner, Robert H., *From the Depths: The Discovery of Poverty in the United States.* New York: New York University Press, 1956.
*Bridenbaugh, Carl, *Cities in the Wilderness: The First Century of Urban Life in America, 1625–1742.* New York: The Ronald Press, 1938.
*———, *Cities in Revolt: Urban Life in America, 1743–1776.* New York: Alfred A. Knopf, 1955.
*———, *The Colonial Craftsman.* Chicago: University of Chicago Press, 1950.
Brown, A. Theodore, *Frontier Community: A History of Kansas City to 1870.* Columbia: University of Missouri Press, 1964.
Brownell, Blaine A., *The Urban Ethos in the South, 1920–1930.* Baton Rouge: Louisiana State University Press, 1976.
*Brownell, Blaine A., and Goldfield, David R. (eds.), *The City in Southern History: The Growth of Urban Civilization in the South.* Port Washington, N.Y.: Kennikat Press, 1976.
*Brownell, Blaine A., and Stickle, Warren E. (eds.), *Bosses and Reformers: Urban Politics in America, 1880–1920.* Boston: Houghton Mifflin Co., 1973.
*Buder, Stanley K., *Pullman: An Experiment in Industrial Order and Community Planning, 1880–1930.* New York: Oxford University Press, 1967.
Buenker, John D., *Urban Liberalism and Progressive Reform.* New York: Charles Scribner's Sons, 1973.
*Callow, Alexander B., *The Tweed Ring.* New York: Oxford University Press, 1966.
*——— (ed.), *American Urban History: An Interpretative Reader with Commentaries,* 2nd edition. New York: Oxford University Press, 1974.
Cassedy, James H., *Charles V. Chapin and the Public Health Movement.* Cambridge, Mass.: Harvard University Press, 1962.
*Chudacoff, Howard P., *The Evolution of American Urban Society.* Englewood Cliffs, N.J.: Prentice-Hall, Inc., 1975.
———, *Mobile Americans: Residential and Social Mobility in*

SELECTED BIBLIOGRAPHY

    Omaha, 1880–1920. New York: Oxford University Press, 1972.

Clark, Dennis, *The Irish of Philadelphia: Ten Generations of Urban Experience*. Philadelphia: Temple University Press, 1974.

*Cole, Donald B., *Immigrant City: Lawrence, Massachusetts, 1845–1921*. Chapel Hill: University of North Carolina Press, 1963.

*Condit, Carl W., *The Chicago School of Architecture: A History of Commercial and Public Buildings in the Chicago Area, 1875–1925*. Chicago: University of Chicago Press, 1964.

*Conot, Robert, *American Odyssey: A Unique History of America Told Through the Life of a Great City*. New York: William Morrow and Co., 1974.

*———, *Rivers of Blood, Years of Darkness: The Unforgettable Classic Account of the Watts Riot*. New York: William Morrow and Co., 1968.

Cowan, Michael H., *City of the West: Emerson, America, and the Urban Metaphor*. New Haven: Yale University Press, 1967.

Crooks, James B., *Politics and Progress: The Rise of Urban Progressivism in Baltimore, 1895 to 1911*. Baton Rouge: Louisiana State University Press, 1968.

*Cross, Robert (ed.), *The Church and the City, 1865–1910*. New York: Bobbs-Merrill Co., 1967.

*Dahl, Robert E., *Who Governs: Democracy and Power in an American City*. New Haven: Yale University Press, 1961.

*Davies, Richard O. (ed.), *The Age of Asphalt: The Automobile, the Freeway, and the Condition of Metropolitan America*. Philadelphia: J. B. Lippincott Co., 1975.

*Davis, Allen F., *Spearheads for Reform: The Social Settlements and the Progressive Movement, 1890–1914*. New York: Oxford University Press, 1968.

DeForrest, Robert W., and Veiller, Lawrence, *The Tenement House Problem*, 2 vols. New York: The Macmillan Co., 1903.

*Dobriner, William M., *Class in Suburbia*. Englewood Cliffs, N.J.: Prentice-Hall, Inc., 1963.

*Donaldson, Scott, *The Suburban Myth*. New York: Columbia University Press, 1969.

*Dorsett, Lyle W., *The Pendergast Machine*. New York: Oxford University Press, 1968.

Douglass, Harlan Paul, *The Suburban Trend*. New York: Century, 1925.

*Drake, St. Clair, and Cayton, Horace R., *Black Metropolis: A Study of Negro Life in a Northern City*, 2 vols. New York: Harper Torchbook, 1962.

Dubofsky, Melvyn, *When Workers Organize: New York City in the Progressive Era*. Amherst: University of Massachusetts Press, 1968.

Duffy, John, *A History of Public Health in New York City, 1625–1866*. New York: Russell Sage Foundation, 1968.

*Duhl, Leonard J. (ed.), *The Urban Condition: People and Policy in the Metropolis*. New York: Basic Books, Inc., 1963.

Duncan, Beverly, and Lieberson, Stanley, *Metropolis and Region in Transition*. Beverly Hills, Calif.: Sage Publications, 1970.

Duncan, Otis D., and Duncan, Beverly, *The Negro Population of Chicago*. Chicago: University of Chicago Press, 1957.

*Dykstra, Robert R., *The Cattle Towns*. New York: Alfred A. Knopf, 1968.

*Eldredge, H. Wentworth (ed.), *Taming Megalopolis*, 2 vols. Garden City, N.Y.: Doubleday, 1967.

Ernst, Robert, *Immigrant Life in New York City, 1825–1863*. New York: King's Crown Press, 1949.

Esslinger, Dean R., *Immigrants and the City: Ethnicity and Mobility in a Nineteenth Century Midwestern City*. Port Washington, N. Y.: Kennikat Press, 1975.

Fairlie, John A., *Municipal Administration*. New York: The Macmillan Co., 1910.

Farley, Reynolds, *Growth of the Black Population: A Study of Demographic Trends*. New York: The Macmillan Co., 1970.

Fogelson, Robert M., *The Fragmented Metropolis: Los Angeles, 1850–1930*. Cambridge, Mass.: Harvard University Press, 1967.

*————, *Violence as Protest: A Study of Riots and Ghettos*. Garden City, N.Y.: Doubleday, 1971.

*Fortune (eds.), *The Exploding Metropolis*. Garden City, N.Y.: Doubleday, 1958.

Frieden, Bernard J., and Kaplan, Marshall, *The Politics of Neglect: Urban Aid from Model Cities to Revenue Sharing*. Cambridge, Mass.: M.I.T. Press, 1975.

Friedman, Lawrence M., *Government and Slum Housing: A Century of Frustration*. Chicago: Rand McNally, 1968.

Frisch, Michael H., *Town into City: Springfield, Massachusetts, and the Meaning of Community, 1840–1880*. Cambridge, Mass.: Harvard University Press, 1972.

*Gans, Herbert J., *The Levittowners: Ways of Life and Politics in a New Suburban Community*. New York: Pantheon, 1967.

*————, *The Urban Villagers: Group and Class in the Life of Italian-Americans*. New York: Free Press, 1962.

Garrett, Charles, *The La Guardia Years: Machine and Reform Politics in New York City*. New Brunswick, N.J.: Rutgers University Press, 1961.

Gelfand, Mark I., *A Nation of Cities: The Federal Government's Response to the Challenges of Urban America, 1933–1965*. New York: Oxford University Press, 1975.

Gilchrist, David T. (ed.), *The Growth of Seaport Cities, 1790–1825*. Charlottesville, Va.: University Press of Virginia, 1967.

SELECTED BIBLIOGRAPHY

*Gitlin, Todd, and Hollander, Nanci, *Uptown: Poor Whites in Chicago.* New York: Harper and Row, 1971.

*Glaab, Charles N., and Brown, A. Theodore, *A History of Urban America,* 2nd edition. New York: The Macmillan Co., 1967.

*Glazer, Nathan, and Moynihan, Daniel P., *Beyond the Melting Pot: The Negroes, Puerto Ricans, Jews, Italians, and Irish of New York City,* 2nd edition. Cambridge, Mass.: M.I.T. Press, 1970.

Goldstein, Sidney, *Patterns of Mobility, 1910–1950: The Norristown Study.* Philadelphia: University of Pennsylvania Press, 1958.

*Gordon, Mitchell, *Sick Cities: Psychology and Pathology of American Urban Life.* Baltimore: Penguin Books, 1972.

*Gottmann, Jean. *Megalopolis: The Urbanized Northeastern Seaboard of the United States.* Cambridge, Mass.: M.I.T. Press, 1961.

*Green, Constance M., *American Cities in the Growth of the Nation.* New York: Harper and Row, 1965.

———, *Holyoke, Massachusetts: A Case History of the Industrial Revolution in America.* New Haven: Yale University Press, 1939.

*———, *The Rise of Urban America.* New York: Harper and Row, 1965.

———, *Washington, Village and Capital, 1800–1878; Washington, Capital City, 1879–1950.* Princeton: Princeton University Press, 1962–1963.

*———, *The Secret City: A History of Race Relations in the Nation's Capital.* Princeton: Princeton University Press, 1969.

*Greer, Scott, *Urban Renewal and American Cities: The Dilemma of Democratic Institutions.* Indianapolis: Bobbs-Merrill Co., 1965.

Griffith, Ernest S., *A History of American City Government:* Vol. 1, *The Conspicuous Failure, 1870–1900;* Vol. 2, *The Progressive Years and Their Aftermath, 1900–1920.* New York: Praeger, 1974.

Groh, George W., *The Black Migration: The Journey to Urban America.* New York: Weybright and Talley, 1972.

Gutman, Herbert G., *The Black Family in Slavery and Freedom, 1750–1925.* New York: Pantheon, 1976.

*Haar, Charles M. (ed.), *The End of Innocence: A Suburban Reader.* Glenview, Ill.: Scott, Foresman, 1972.

*Handlin, Oscar, *Boston's Immigrants: A Study in Acculturation.* Cambridge, Mass.: Harvard University Press, 1943.

*———, *The Newcomers: Negroes and Puerto Ricans in a Changing Metropolis.* Cambridge, Mass.: Harvard University Press, 1959.

*———, *The Uprooted.* Boston: Little, Brown and Co., 1951.

*———, and Burchard, John (eds.), *The Historian and the City.*

Cambridge, Mass.: Harvard University Press and M.I.T. Press, 1963.

*Hareven, Tamara K. (ed.), *Anonymous Americans: Explorations in Nineteenth-Century Social History*. Englewood Cliffs, N.J.: Prentice-Hall, Inc., 1971.

*Harrington, Michael, *The Other Americans: Poverty in the United States*. New York: The Macmillan Co., 1962.

Hauser, Philip M., and Schnore, Leo F., *The Study of Urbanization*. New York: John Wiley and Sons, 1965.

Hawes, Joseph M., *Children in Urban Society: Juvenile Delinquency in Nineteenth Century America*. New York: Oxford University Press, 1971.

*Headley, Joel Tyler, *The Great Riots of New York, 1712–1873*. New York: E. B. Treat, 1873.

*Higham, John, *Send These to Me: Jews and Other Immigrants in Urban America*. New York: Atheneum, 1975.

Hirsch, Werner Z. (ed.), *Urban Life and Form*. New York: Holt, Rinehart and Winston, 1963.

*Hofstadter, Richard, *The Age of Reform: From Bryan to F.D.R.* New York: Alfred A. Knopf, 1955.

*Holli, Melvin G., *Reform in Detroit: Hazen S. Pingree and Urban Politics*. New York: Oxford University Press, 1969.

Holt, Michael F., *Forging a Majority: The Formation of the Republican Party in Pittsburgh, 1848–1860*. New Haven: Yale University Press, 1969.

*Hoover, Dwight W., *A Teachers' Guide to American Urban History*. Chicago: Quadrangle Books, 1971.

Huggins, Nathan Irwin, *Protestants Against Poverty: Boston's Charities, 1870–1900*. Westport, Conn.: Greenwood, 1970.

*Hunter, Robert, *Poverty: Social Conscience in the Progressive Era*. New York: The Macmillan Co., 1907.

*Huthmacher, J. Joseph, *Senator Robert F. Wagner and the Rise of Urban Liberalism*. New York: Atheneum, 1968.

*Jackson, Kenneth T., *The Ku Klux Klan in the City, 1915–1930*. New York: Oxford University Press, 1967.

*——— and Schultz, Stanley K. (eds.), *Cities in American History*. New York: Alfred A. Knopf, 1972.

*Jacobs, Jane, *The Death and Life of Great American Cities*. New York: Random House, 1961.

*———, *The Economy of Cities*. New York: Random House, 1969.

*Jacobs, Paul, *Prelude to Riot: A View of Urban America. From the Bottom*. New York: Random House, 1968.

James, D. Clayton, *Ante Bellum Natchez*. Baton Rouge: Louisiana State University Press, 1968.

Jensen, Arthur, *The Maritime Commerce of Colonial Philadelphia*. Madison: The State Historical Society of Wisconsin, 1963.

Kaestle, Carl F., *The Evolution of an Urban School System*:

SELECTED BIBLIOGRAPHY

New York City, 1750–1850. Cambridge, Mass.: Harvard University Press, 1973.

*Kardiner, Abram, and Ovesey, Lionel, *The Mark of Oppression: Explorations in the Personality of the American Negro*. New York: W. W. Norton and Co., 1951.

*Katzman, David M., *Before the Ghetto: Black Detroit in the Nineteenth Century*. Urbana, Ill.: University of Illinois Press, 1973.

Katznelson, Ira, *Black Men, White Cities: Race, Politics and Migration in the United States, 1900–1930 and in Britain, 1948–1968*. New York: Oxford University Press, 1973.

*Kessner, Thomas, *The Golden Door: Italian and Jewish Immigrant Mobility in New York City, 1880–1915*. New York: Oxford University Press, 1977.

Kirschner, Don S., *City and Country: Rural Responses to Urbanization in the 1920's*. Westport, Conn.: Greenwood, 1970.

*Knights, Peter R., *The Plain People of Boston, 1830–1860: A Study in City Growth*. New York: Oxford University Press, 1973.

Korman, Gerd, *Industrialization, Immigrants and Americanizers: The View from Milwaukee, 1866–1921*. Madison: The State Historical Society of Wisconsin, 1967.

*Kouwenhoven, John, *The Columbia Historical Portrait of New York: An Essay in Graphic History*. New York: Harper and Row, 1972.

*Lane, Roger, *Policing the City: Boston, 1822–1885*. Cambridge, Mass.: Harvard University Press, 1967.

Lazerson, Marvin, *Origins of the Urban School: Public Education in Massachusetts, 1870–1915*. Cambridge, Mass.: Harvard University Press, 1971.

Lebergott, Stanley, *Manpower in Economic Growth: The American Record Since 1800*. New York: McGraw-Hill Book Co., 1964.

Lieberson, Stanley, *Ethnic Patterns in American Cities*. New York: Free Press, 1963.

*Liston, Robert A., *Downtown: Our Challenging Urban Problems*. New York: Delacorte Press, 1970.

*Litwack, Leon F., *North of Slavery: The Negro in the Free States, 1790–1860*. Chicago: University of Chicago Press, 1961.

Livingood, James W., *The Philadelphia–Baltimore Trade Rivalry, 1780–1860*. Harrisburg, Pa.: Pennsylvania Historical and Museum Commission, 1947.

*Lowe, Jeanne R., *Cities in a Race with Time: Progress and Poverty in America's Renewing Cities*. New York: Random House, 1967.

*Lowenstein, Louis K. (ed.), *Urban Studies: An Introductory Reader*. New York: Free Press, 1971.

Lowi, Theodore J., *At The Pleasure of the Mayor: Patronage* and Politics in New York City, 1898–1958. New York: The Free Press, 1964.

*Lubove, Roy, Community Planning in the 1920's: The Contribution of the Regional Planning Association of America. Pittsburgh: University of Pittsburgh Press, 1964.

———, The Progressives and the Slums: Tenement House Reform in New York City, 1890–1917. Pittsburgh: University of Pittsburgh Press, 1962.

*———, Twentieth-Century Pittsburgh: Government, Business, and Environmental Change. New York: John Wiley and Sons, 1969.

*——— (ed.), The Urban Community: Housing and Planning in the Progressive Era. Englewood Cliffs, N.J.: Prentice-Hall, Inc., 1967.

Lynch, Hollis R. (ed.), The Black Urban Condition: A Documentary History, 1866–1971. New York: T. Y. Crowell, 1973.

*Lynch, Kevin, The Image of the City. Cambridge, Mass.: M.I.T. Press, 1960.

*Mandelbaum, Seymour J., Boss Tweed's New York. New York: John Wiley and Sons, 1964.

*Mann, Arthur, Yankee Reformers in the Urban Age: Social Reform in Boston, 1880–1900. New York: Harper Torchbook, 1966.

Martin, Robert L., The City Moves West: Economic and Industrial Growth in Central West Texas. Austin: University of Texas, 1969.

*Marx, Leo, The Machine in the Garden: Technology and the Pastoral Idea in America. New York: Oxford University Press, 1964.

*Masotti, Louis H., and Hadden, Jeffrey K. (eds.), Suburbia in Transition. New York: New Viewpoints, 1974.

*Mayer, Harold M., and Wade, Richard C., with the assistance of Glen E. Holt, Chicago: Growth of a Metropolis. Chicago: University of Chicago Press, 1969.

*McKelvey, Blake, American Urbanization: A Comparative History. Glenview, Ill.: Scott, Foresman, 1973.

———, The Urbanization of America, 1860–1915. New Brunswick, N.J.: Rutgers University Press, 1963.

———, The Emergence of Metropolitan America, 1915–1966. New Brunswick, N.J.: Rutgers University Press, 1968.

McKenzie, Roderick D., The Metropolitan Community. New York: McGraw-Hill Book Co., 1933.

Merwick, Donna, Boston's Priests, 1848–1910: A Study of Social and Intellectual Change. Cambridge, Mass.: Harvard University Press, 1973.

Miller, William D., Memphis During the Progressive Era, 1900–1917. Memphis: Memphis State University Press, 1957.

SELECTED BIBLIOGRAPHY

———, *Mr. Crump of Memphis*. Baton Rouge: Louisiana State University Press, 1964.

*Miller, Zane L., *Boss Cox's Cincinnati: Urban Politics in the Progressive Era*. New York: Oxford University Press, 1968.

*Miller, Zane L., *The Urbanization of Modern America: A Brief History*. New York: Harcourt, Brace, Jovanovich, 1973.

Mohl, Raymond A., *Poverty in New York, 1783–1825*. New York: Oxford University Press, 1971.

Mohl, Raymond A., and Betten, Neil (eds.), *Urban America in Historical Perspective*. New York: Weybright and Talley, 1970.

*Mohl, Raymond A., and Richardson, James F. (eds.), *The Urban Experience: Themes in American History*. Belmont, Calif.: Wadsworth, 1973.

Monkkonen, Eric H., *The Dangerous Class: Crime and Poverty in Columbus, Ohio, 1860–1885*. Cambridge, Mass.: Harvard University Press, 1975.

*Moynihan, Daniel P., *Maximum Feasible Misunderstanding: Community Action In the War on Poverty*. New York: The Free Press, 1969.

——— (ed.), *Toward a National Urban Policy*. New York: Basic Books, Inc., 1970.

*Mumford, Lewis, *The City in History: Its Origins, Its Transformations, and Its Prospects*. New York: Harcourt, Brace, and World, 1961.

*———, *The Urban Prospect*. New York: Harcourt, Brace, and World, 1968.

Munro, William B., *The Government of American Cities*, 4th edition. New York: The Macmillan Co., 1926.

*Murphy, Thomas, and Rettfuss, John, *Urban Politics in the Suburban Era*. Homewood, Ill.: Dorsey Press, 1976.

Mushkat, Jerome, *Tammany: The Evolution of a Political Machine, 1789–1865*. Syracuse: Syracuse University Press, 1971.

*Myrdal, Gunnar, *An American Dilemma: The Negro Problem and Modern Democracy*, 2 vols. New York: Harper and Row, 1944.

Olton, Charles S., *Artisans for Independence: Philadelphia Mechanics and the American Revolution*. Syracuse: Syracuse University Press, 1975.

*Osofsky, Gilbert (ed.), *The Burden of Race: A Documentary History of Negro–White Relations in America*. New York: Harper and Row, 1967.

*———, *Harlem: The Making of a Ghetto, Negro New York, 1890–1930*. New York: Harper and Row, 1966.

*Nelli, Humbert S., *The Italians in Chicago, 1880–1930: A Study in Ethnic Mobility*. New York: Oxford University Press, 1973.

*Park, Robert E., Burgess, Ernest W., and McKenzie, Roderick D. (eds.), *The City*. Chicago: University of Chicago Press, 1925.

Patton, Clifford W., *The Battle for Municipal Reform: Mobilization and Attack, 1875 to 1900*. Washington, D.C.: American Council on Public Affairs, 1940.

Pierce, Bessie L., *A History of Chicago*, Vol. I: *The Beginnings of a City, 1673–1848*; Vol. 11: *From Town to City, 1848–1871*; Vol. III: *The Rise of a Modern City, 1871–1893*. New York: Alfred A. Knopf, 1937–1957.

Pierson, G. W. *The Moving American*. New York: Alfred A. Knopf, 1972.

*Piven, Frances Fox, and Cloward, Richard A., *Regulating the Poor: The Functions of Public Welfare* (original title, *Relief and Civil Disorder*). New York: Pantheon, 1971.

*Powell, Sumner C., *Puritan Village: The Formation of a New England Town*. Middletown, Conn.: Wesleyan University Press, 1963.

Pred, Allan R., *The Spatial Dynamics of United States Urban-Industrial Growth, 1800–1914: Interpretative and Theoretical Essays*. Cambridge, Mass.: M.I.T. Press, 1966.

———, *Urban Growth and the Circulation of Information: The United States System of Cities, 1790–1840*. Cambridge, Mass.: Harvard University Press, 1973.

Quiett, Glenn C., *They Built the West: An Epic of Rails and Cities*. New York: D. Appleton-Century, 1934.

*Rae, John B., *The American Automobile: A Brief History*. Chicago: University of Chicago Press, 1965.

*Ravitch, Diane, *The Great School Wars, New York City, 1805–1973: A History of the Public Schools as Battlefield of Social Change*. New York: Basic Books, Inc., 1974.

Reed, Merl E, *New Orleans and the Railroads: The Struggle for Commercial Empire, 1830–1860*. Baton Rouge: Louisiana State University Press, 1966.

Reiser, Catherine E., *Pittsburgh's Commercial Development, 1800–1850*. Harrisburg, Pa.: Pennsylvania Historical and Museum Commission, 1951.

Report of the National Advisory Commission on Civil Disorders. New York: Praeger, 1968.

Reps, John W., *The Making of Urban America: A History of City Planning in the United States*. Princeton: Princeton University Press, 1965.

Richardson, James F., *The New York Police: Colonial Times to 1901*. New York: Oxford University Press, 1970.

*———, *Urban Police in the United States: A Brief History*. Port Washington, N.Y.: Kennikat Press, 1974.

*——— (ed.), *The American City: Historical Studies*. Waltham, Mass.: Xerox College Publishing, 1972.

*Riis, Jacob, *How the Other Half Lives: Studies Among the Tenements of New York*. New York: Charles Scribner's Sons, 1902.

Ringenbach, Paul T., *Tramps and Reformers, 1873–1916: The*

Discovery of Unemployment in New York. Westport, Conn.: Greenwood, 1973.

*Riordon, William L., *Plunkitt of Tammany Hall*. New York: McClure, Phillips and Co., 1905.

*Rischin, Moses, *The Promised City: New York City's Jews, 1870–1914*. Cambridge, Mass.: Harvard University Press, 1962.

*Roebuck, Janet, *The Shaping of Urban Society: A History of City Forms and Functions*. New York: Charles Scribner's Sons, 1974.

*Rosenberg, Charles, *The Cholera Years: The United States in 1832, 1849, and 1866*. Chicago: University of Chicago Press, 1962.

*Rothman, David J., *The Discovery of the Asylum: Social Order and Disorder in the New Republic*. Boston: Little, Brown and Co., 1971.

*Royko, Mike, *Boss: Richard J. Daley of Chicago*. New York: E. P. Dutton, 1971.

Rubin, Julius, *Canal or Railroad? Imitation and Innovation in the Response to the Erie Canal in Philadelphia, Baltimore, and Boston*. Philadelphia: American Philosophical Society, 1961.

*Rubinstein, Jonathan, *City Police*. New York: Farrar, Straus and Giroux, 1973.

*Schlesinger, Arthur M., *The Rise of the City, 1878–1898*, Vol. X: *A History of American Life*. New York: The Macmillan Co., 1933.

Schmitt, Peter J., *Back to Nature: The Arcadian Myth in Urban America*. New York: Oxford University Press, 1969.

*Schnore, Leo F. (ed.), *The New Urban History: Quantitative Explorations by American Historians*. Princeton: Princeton University Press, 1974.

Schultz, Stanley K., *The Culture Factory: Boston Public Schools, 1789–1860*. New York: Oxford University Press, 1973.

*Scott, Mel, *American City Planning Since 1890*. Berkeley: University of California Press, 1969.

Sellers, Leila, *Charleston Business on the Eve of the American Revolution*. Chapel Hill: University of North Carolina Press, 1934.

*Sennett, Richard, *Families Against the City: Middle Class Homes of Industrial Chicago, 1872–1890*. Cambridge, Mass.: Harvard University Press, 1970.

Shaw, Ronald, *Erie Water West: A History of the Erie Canal, 1792–1854*. Lexington: University of Kentucky Press, 1966.

*Spear, Allan H., *Black Chicago: The Making of a Negro Ghetto, 1890–1920*. Chicago: University of Chicago Press, 1967.

Stave, Bruce M., *The New Deal and the Last Hurrah: Pittsburgh Machine Politics*. Pittsburgh: University of Pittsburgh Press, 1970.

*Steffens, Lincoln, *The Shame of the Cities*. New York: McClure, Phillips and Co., 1904.

Still, Bayrd, *Milwaukee: The History of a City*, revised edition. Madison, Wisc.: The State Historical Society of Wisconsin, 1965.

———, *Mirror for Gotham: New York as Seen by Contemporaries from Dutch Days to the Present*. New York: New York University Press, 1956.

*———, *Urban America: A History with Documents*. Boston: Little, Brown and Co., 1974.

Strauss, Anselm, *Images of the American City*. New York: The Free Press, 1961.

*Taeuber, Karl E., and Taeuber, Alma F., *Negroes in Cities: Residential Segregation and Neighborhood Change*. Chicago: Aldine Press, 1965.

*Tager, Jack, and Goist, Park Dixon (eds.), *The Urban Vision: Selected Interpretations of the Modern American City*. Homewood, Ill.: Dorsey Press, 1970.

Tarr, Joel A., *A Study in Boss Politics: William Lorimer of Chicago*. Urbana, Ill.: University of Illinois Press, 1971.

*Taylor, George R., *The Transportation Revolution, 1815–1860*. New York: Holt, Rinehart and Winston, 1951.

Teaford, Jon C., *The Municipal Revolution in America: Origins of Modern Urban Government, 1650–1825*. Chicago: University of Chicago Press, 1975.

Thernstrom, Stephan, *The Other Bostonians: Poverty and Progress in the American Metropolis, 1880–1970*. Cambridge, Mass.: Harvard University Press, 1973.

*———, *Poverty and Progress: Social Mobility in a Nineteenth Century City*. Cambridge, Mass.: Harvard University Press, 1964.

*———, and Sennett, Richard (eds.), *Nineteenth Century Cities: Essays in the New Urban History*. New Haven: Yale University Press, 1969.

*Tunnard, Christopher, and Reed, Henry Hope, *American Skyline: The Growth and Form of Our Cities and Towns*. Boston: Houghton Mifflin Co., 1955.

*Urofsky, Melvin I. (ed.), *Perspectives on Urban America*. Garden City, N.Y.: Doubleday, 1973.

*Wade, Richard C., *Slavery in the Cities: The South, 1820–1860*. New York: Oxford University Press, 1964.

*———, *The Urban Frontier: Pioneer Life in Early Pittsburgh, Cincinnati, Lexington, Louisville, and St. Louis*. Chicago: University of Chicago Press, 1964.

*Wakstein, Allen M. (ed.), *The Urbanization of America: An Historical Anthology*. Boston: Houghton Mifflin Co., 1970.

*Ward, David, *Cities and Immigrants: A Geography of Change*

SELECTED BIBLIOGRAPHY

in Nineteenth Century America. New York: Oxford University Press, 1971.

*Warner, Sam Bass, Jr., *The Private City: Philadelphia in Three Periods of Its Growth*. Philadelphia: University of Pennsylvania Press, 1968.

*———, *Streetcar Suburbs: The Process of Growth in Boston, 1870–1900*. Cambridge, Mass.: Harvard University Press and M.I.T. Press, 1962.

*———, *The Urban Wilderness: A History of the American City*. New York: Harper and Row, 1972.

*———, (ed.), *Planning for a Nation of Cities*. Cambridge, Mass.: M.I.T. Press, 1966.

*Waskow, Arthur I., *From Race-Riot to Sit-In: 1919 and the 1960s, A Study in the Connections Between Conflict and Violence*. New York: Doubleday, 1966.

*Weaver, Robert C., *Dilemmas of Urban America*. Cambridge, Mass.: Harvard University Press, 1965.

*Weber, Adna F., *The Growth of Cities in the Nineteenth Century: A Study in Statistics*. New York: The Macmillan Co., 1899.

*Weimer, David R. (ed.), *City and Country in America*. New York: Appleton-Century-Crofts, 1962.

*Wertenbaker, Thomas J., *The Golden Age of Colonial Culture*. New York: New York University Press, 1942.

———, *Father Knickerbocker Rebels: New York During the Revolution*. New York: Charles Scribner's Sons, 1948.

Wheeler, Kenneth, *To Wear a City's Crown: The Beginnings of Urban Growth in Texas, 1836–1865*. Cambridge, Mass.: Harvard University Press, 1968.

*White, Morton, and White, Lucia, *The Intellectual Versus the City: From Thomas Jefferson to Frank Lloyd Wright*. Cambridge, Mass.: Harvard University Press, 1962.

*Wiebe, Robert H., *The Search for Order, 1870–1920*. New York: Hill and Wang, 1968.

*Wilson, James Q. (ed.), *The Metropolitan Enigma: Inquiries into the Nature and Dimensions of America's "Urban Crisis."* Cambridge, Mass.: Harvard University Press, 1968.

*Wilson, William H., *Coming of Age: Urban America, 1915–1945*. New York: John Wiley and Sons, 1974.

*Wirth, Louis, *The Ghetto*. Chicago: University of Chicago Press, 1928.

Woods, Robert A., and Kennedy, Albert J., *The Zone of Emergence: Observations of Lower Middle and Upper Working Class Communities of Boston, 1905–1914*, abridged and edited by Sam Bass Warner, Jr. Cambridge, Mass.: M.I.T. Press, 1962.

*Young, James Sterling, *The Washington Community, 1800–1828*. New York: Columbia University Press, 1966.

Zink, Harold, *City Bosses in the United States*: *A Study of Twenty Municipal Bosses*. Durham, N.C.: Duke University Press, 1930.

*Zuckerman, Michael, *Peaceable Kingdoms*: *New England Towns in the Eighteenth Century*. New York: Alfred A. Knopf, 1970.

Index

A

Abolitionists, 102
Accidents, industrial, 205
Addams, Jane, 227-228
AFL-CIO, 214, 312
Air pollution, 88-89, 273-275
Akron, Ohio, 269
American Indians, 313-314
Appalachia, 314
  commerce and industry, 54-55
Atlanta, 140, 177
  blacks, 181, 192
Atlantic trading region, 3, 30, 44-52
Austin, Texas, 148-149
Automobiles
  air pollution and, 275-279
  effects on suburbs, 173-175, 255, 258

B

Baltimore, 5, 48-52
  colonial period, 5, 22, 34-35, 63
  economy, 48-52, 155-157
  housing, 197
  population, 40-41, 63, 132
Baltimore and Ohio Railroad, 51
Birmingham, Alabama, 140

Black Legion, 312-313
Black Muslims, 308-309, 325
Blacks, 298-330
  anti-black feelings, 102-104
  churches, 75
  demonstrations in 1960s, 323-326
  depression of 1930s, 309-313
  desegregation, 319
  discriminatory practices, 304-307
  employment of, 74, 314-315
  female family head, 323
  housing, 182, 328, 341-343
  migration patterns, 73, 181, 300-304
    depression of 1930s, 309-310
    1960-1970, 320-323
  migration to suburbs, 262, 318, 328
  organizations, 307-309
  political power, 326-327
  population patterns
    1860, 76
    1880-1970, 298-299
    1950-1960, 217-219
  prejudice, 330
  professionals and entrepreneurs, 73
  race riots, 305-306, 311-312, 315, 323-326
  segregation, 182, 321-323
  sit-ins, 323-326

Blacks (*Cont.*)
  socioeconomic position, 327-330
  upward mobility, 192, 327-328, 330
  urban settlements, 72-75, 181, 313-317, 327-330
  welfare programs, 323, 360-364
Blue collar workers, 192
Bossism *see* Machine politics
Boston, 6, 291
  colonial period, 6-7, 19, 33-34
  commerce and industry, 44-46
  death rates, 90
  grid plan, 66
  machine politics, 122*n*, 136
  mass transit, 167
  metropolitan area, 195
  population, 22-24, 25, 31, 40-41, 132
  reform movement, 224
  suburban communities, 171-173
Bryce, James, 105, 217, 220
Buffalo, N.Y., 48
Business, decentralization, 262-266

C

Canadian immigrants, 186
Canals and waterways, 43, 48-49
Cattle towns, 144
Central cities
  economic activities, 264-266
  exodus of corporations, 265
  influx of blacks and Hispanics, 270
  office-building boom, 265
Chain stores, 158-159, 161
Charitable activities, 206-207
Charles Town, S.C., 4-5, 18-19, 63
  blacks, 72
  population, 22-24, 31
Charlotte, N.C., 269
Cheyenne, Wyoming, 146, 148
Chicago, 113
  blacks, 181
  commerce, 60-63
  expansion, 152-154
  housing, 197
  machine politics, 120, 128, 133-134, 247
  mass transit, 83, 167
  population, 40-41, 60-61, 132, 177
  race riots, 182
  railroad center, 61-62
  reform movement, 220, 225-228
  World's Columbian Exposition, 225
Chicanos, 329
Child labor laws, 209
Chinese immigrants, 182, 313, 321
Cincinnati, 52, 55-56, 58, 113
  blacks, 74
  machine politics, 121, 128-129
Cities
  black settlements, 72-75
  colonial, 1-38
    effects of Revolution, 33-36
  decline of older, 269-272
  depression of 1930s, 336-339
  dilemmas of urban policy, 331-374
  growth planning, 372
  immigrants, 75-79
  long-range prospects, 370-375
  in 1920s, 332-336
  preindustrial, 24-29
  See also Urban growth
Civic organizations, 218-221
Civil service reform, 242
Civil War, 102
Clean Air Act, 275-276
Cleveland, 59, 138
  pattern of growth, 153-154
  reform movement, 232
Colonial period, 1-38
  community spirit, 32-33

Colonial period (*Cont.*)
  economic activities, 29-32
  effects of Revolution, 33-36
  leaders, 30-31
  municipal government, 106-108
  preindustrial city, 24-29
  social structure, 29-32
  urban growth, 1-6
  urban merchants, 19-21
  urban network, 14-19
Commerce and industry, 39-69
  Atlantic seaports, 44-52
  Boston, 44-46
  Chicago, 60-63
  Cincinnati, 57
  colonial period, 29-32
  emerging industrial city, 65-69
  factors contributing to, 41-44
  Great Lakes cities, 58-63
  lagging Southern urbanization, 63-65
  New York, 46-48
  Philadelphia and Baltimore, 48-52
  rising centers of, 36-39
  St. Louis, 57-58
Communications, rapid spread, 43
Communism, 215, 311
Communities
  divisions and conflicts, 95-102
  ethnic groups, 96-98
  political machines and, 125-128
Community Action Programs, 360-361
Company-owned towns, 147-149
Constitution of U.S., 36
Cooper, Peter, 219
Crime and violence, 205
  in older cities, 271-272
Cultural activities, 97, 265-266

D

Dallas, Texas, 149, 268
Daly, Richard J., 247
Death penalty, 95
Death rates, 89-90, 178, 204
Denver, 140, 143, 145
Depression of 1930s
  blacks and, 309-313
  effect on cities, 336-339
  New Deal, 310, 346-349
Detroit, 177, 269
  black population, 315-319
  reform movements, 229-231
Dodge City, 144

E

Economic development, 39-69
  circular and cumulative growth process, 27, 50
  colonial period, 29-32
  urban blight and, 81-83
Education, public, 93-94, 210-211
  urban school systems, 210-211
Eisenhower, Dwight D., 354-356
Elderly, in older cities, 272
Electric power systems, 164-166
Elites, 108
  business, 162
  colonial period, 30-32
  municipal government and, 130-133
  and rural migrants, 71-72
Employment agencies, 179
Energy crisis, 372
Environmental problems, 88-93, 272-277
  blight and pollution, 81-83
  slums, 81-83
Environmental Protection Agency (EPA), 274-275
Epidemics and disease, 90
Erie Canal, 48
Ethnic communities, 214

Ethnic groups, 96-98, 211-216
Expressways, 256-257, 272

F

Factories and plants, 68-69
Fair Employment Practices Commission, 315
Family Assistance Plan, 367
Farms and farming
 exodus from rural areas, 179-182, 250-251
 transformation of, 71-72
Federal policy
 environmental controversies, 274-277
 highway trust fund, 357-358
 housing programs, 339-340
 municipal problems and, 331-336, 348-349, 373
 in the 1950s, 354-357
 in the 1960s, 359-365
 pollution control, 274-277
 suburban growth and, 357-358
Federal Housing Administration, 346-347, 358
Fire protection, 86-87, 200
 fire-resistant buildings, 200
Food industries, 68-69
Ford, Gerald R., 370
Foreign-born
 dominant nationalities in cities, 187
 patterns of adjustment, 183-189
 population (1920), 185
 See also Emigrants
Franchises, 168-170
Freeways, 272-273
Future of cities, 294-297

G

Galveston, Texas, 148-149
Gardner, John, 365
George, Henry, 228-229
German immigrants, 184

Ghettos, 75, 305, 322-323
Gilded Age, political turmoil, 105
Great Britain, "dumping" campaign, 46
Great Lakes cities, 58-63
 commerce and industry, 58-59
Great Plains
 agricultural settlements, 143
 cities and towns, 141-149
Great Society programs, 360-363
Greek immigrants, 184
Greenbelt towns, 259, 286, 343-345

H

Hague, Frank, 245-246
Hartford, Conn., 8-9, 17
Health programs, 203-210
Hispanic Americans, 320, 321, 323-329
Hoan, Daniel W., 233
Home Owners Loan Corporation, 346
Home rule, 112, 237, 290
Hoover, Herbert, 335-339
Hospitals, 203-204
Housing
 abandoned, 271
 apartment houses, 196-197
 blacks, 182
 comprehensive laws, 199-200
 construction techniques, 25
 "Chicago" or balloon frames, 25, 61
 skyscrapers, 163-164
 deterioration of central cities, 271-272
 in 1860s, 163
 FHA and VA loans, 358
 federal programs, 336, 339-346, 358
 greenbelt towns, 259, 286, 343-345
 National Housing Act, 365
 New Deal programs, 339-346

INDEX

Housing (*Cont.*)
  new towns, 286, 288
  postwar and urban renewal, 349-354
  public, 342-343
  shanty-dwellings, 83
  slum or tenement districts, 197-198
  subsistence homesteads, 345-346
  suburbs, 195
  tenements, 83, 196-197
    dumbbell style, 198
    reforms, 198-199
  urban blight, 81-83
Housing and Community Development of 1974, 369-370
Houston, Texas, 148-149, 255, 268, 277-278
HUD (Department of Housing and Urban Development), 359, 365
Hull House, Chicago, 227-228

I

Immigrants, 75-79
  Americanization programs, 215
  anti-foreign attitudes, 189
  conflicts between native-born and, 98-102, 189-193
  discriminatory practices, 304-307
  employment opportunities, 188-189
  ethnic communities, 96-98
  German immigrants, 79, 96-97
  "greenhorn" workers, 192
  immigrant aid societies, 77
  influx of, 75-76
  Irish immigrants, 78, 96-97, 184
  Italian immigrants, 184, 188
  labor contractors or *padrones*, 188
  mobility, 191-192
  National Origins Act, 215
  nativism and restrictionism, 98-102, 189-193
  organizations, 77, 213-216
  population of foreign-born, 76
    1870-1920, 183
    1960-1970, 320
  right to vote, 126
  from Southern and Eastern Europe, 183-184, 215
  unskilled workers, 77-78
Income
  of blacks, 328
  of metropolitan families, 329
Industrial growth, 65-69
  colonial period, 24-29
  major business innovations, 159-162
  manufactured products, 68
  metropolitan districts, 157-159
  nationwide corporations, 158-162
  "threshold industries," 27-28
Initiatives and referendums, 241
Inventions or innovations, 28
Irish immigrants, 78, 96-97, 184
Italian immigrants, 184, 188

J

Jacksonville, Florida, 291
Jamestown colony, 4
Jersey City, N.J., 245-246
Jewish communities, 96-97
Jewish immigrants, 191, 209, 214
Job Corps, 361
Johnson, Lyndon B., 359-360, 363
Johnson, Tom L., 232-233
Jones, Samuel M., 231-233
Juvenile delinquency, 205

K

Kansas City (Missouri), 140, 143-144
    cattle town, 144
    machine politics, 245
Kennedy, John F., 359
Kerner Commission, 325-326
Kindergartens, 211
King, Martin Luther, Jr., 319, 325
Know-Nothing movement, 101
Ku Klux Klan, 305-306, 312-313

L

Labor force
    blacks, 181
    boys from farms, 180
    cheap immigrant labor, 185
    distribution of workers by industry (1870-1920), 160-161
    hours and wages, 192-193
    mobility, 179, 192
    purchasing power, 192-193
    unskilled workers, 79-81
Labor unions, 80-81, 214
    anti-black feelings, 102-104, 312
    political activity, 136
LaGuardia, Fiorello H., 246
Lake Erie, pollution, 273
Land companies, railroad, 147-148
Land use
    checkerboard pattern, 66
    gridiron plan, 52, 66
Law enforcement, 87-88
L'Enfant, Pierre, 36-37
Lincoln, Abraham, 102
Lindsay, John V., 246-247
Living standards, 95
Lodges and fraternal orders, 212
Los Angeles, 58, 149-150, 255
    environmental problems, 273-274
    growth of, 268-269
    suburban communities, 173
    Watts riot, 325
Louisville, Kentucky, 53, 55, 58, 140

M

Machine politics, 118-123, 244-248
    bossism and, 120-123
    effect of reform movement, 233-237
    graft and corruption, 123-125
    services provided by, 125-130
Mail-order businesses, 159
Manufacturing industry, 68-69, 160-161
    cities and towns, 68-69
    cottage-and-mill system, 29
    standardized parts, 44
"Marshall Plan" for inner cities, 373
Mass transit, 166-168, 278-279
    decline, 278
    federal subsidies, 279
    subways, 167
Mayors
    methods of selecting, 109-110
    powers of, 238-239
Mechanics, skilled, 50-51
Medical facilities and programs, 203
Medicare, 367
Megalopolises, 254-255
    decline of older cities, 269-272
Merchants, role in urban growth, 19-21
Metropolises, 137-175
    central cities, 151
        declining population, 250
        economic activities, 264-265
    decentralization of businesses, 262-266
    definition, 138-140

Metropolises (*Cont.*)
  geographical expansion, 152-156, 162-171
  growth and economy, 150-156, 251-257, 372
  industrial transformations, 157-159
  migrations to, 137-138
  population growth, 137-138, 249-251
  post-Civil War urbanization, 137-141
  problems in governing, 288-294
  Standard Metropolitan Area, 251-252
  Standard Metropolitan Statistical Areas, 252-254
  suburban communities, 171-175, 250, 257-262
  Sun Belt, 266-269
  "urban sprawl," 252
Metropolitan districts, 138
  central core city plus suburbs, 151
  governing, 288-294
Mexican Americans, 314, 321, 329
Miami, Florida, 290
Middle Atlantic region, 10
Migrations, 70
  rural to urban, 71, 178-192
Mill towns, 45
Milwaukee, 59-60
  reform movement, 233
Mining camps, 145-146
Minneapolis, 140, 292
Minority groups, 290
Mobility, 70, 104, 179
  among blacks, 192, 327-328, 330
  social, 191-192
Model cities programs, 363-364
Montgomery, Alabama, boycott, 219
Moses, Robert, 281-282, 352
Moynihan, Daniel P., 367, 372
Multiplier effect, 28

Municipal associations, 335, 356
Municipal government, 105-136
  bossism and machine politics, 118-120
    reformers and, 133-136
    services provided by, 125-130
  city councils, 239
  city government (1776-1850), 108-111
  city-state relations, 111-115
  colonial period, 106-108
  commission and council manager plans, 242-244
  consolidation movement, 289-290
  debts and administrative agencies, 115-117
  expansion of services, 117-118
  growth policies, 372
  graft and corruption, 105, 123-125, 132
  home rule, 112, 237, 290
  lack of interest in, 109
  mayors' role, 109-110, 238-239
  metropolitan area problems, 288-294
  obstacles to effective, 113-115
  office holders, 108-112, 130-132
  post-Civil War, 105
  progressivism, 224-228
  reform movements, 217-248
  reorganizations of, 290-291
  services provided by, 112-115
  structural changes, 237-239
  urban elite and, 130-133
  voting reforms, 239-241
  workingmen's parties, 111
Municipal Voters' League, 227

N

Nashville, Tenn., 140
Nast, Thomas, 124, 132

National Association for the Advancement of Colored People, 307, 308, 361
"National cities," 373
National Industrial Recovery Act, 345
National League of Cities, 355
National Municipal League, 221-222
National Resources Planning Board, 348-349
National Road, 49
Nativism (anti-foreign) movements, 99
  restrictionism and, 189-193
Neighborhoods, divisions and conflicts, 95-102
New Deal, 310, 346-349
  housing programs, 339-340
New England, 8
  labor force, 80
  mill towns, 45
  town meetings, 107-108
  urban growth, 5-10
New England Societies, 96
"New Federalism," 367
New Haven, 5, 8-9, 24, 30
  population, 40-41
New Orleans, 55, 57-58, 63-64, 72, 140
Newport, Rhode Island, 9, 17, 106
  population, 22-24, 34, 138
Newspapers, 216
New York City
  air pollutions, 273-274
  annexation of suburbs, 196
  black population, 73, 181
  Central Park, 93
  civic organizations for reform, 218-221
  colonial period, 10-12, 25, 29, 35
  commerce and industry, 46-48
  crime and vice, 88
  death rate, 89-90
  decline of, 270-271
  Draft riots of 1863, 102-103
  environmental problems, 273-274
  expansion of, 152-153, 196
  financial services, 47-48
  fiscal crisis, 370-371
  grid plan, 66-67
  Harlem race riots, 311-312, 324
  housing, 197-200
  immigrants, 183-184
  industrial transformations, 157
  machine politics, 120-125
  mass transit, 167, 195
  municipal government, 113-118
  neighborhoods, 26-27
  New Amsterdam, 10-12
  population growth, 22-24, 40-41, 177
  reform mayors, 246-247
  reform movement, 224, 234-235
  street cleaning, 200-202
  street railways, 83
  subways, 195
  water supply, 85
  urban renewal programs, 352
Nixon, Richard M., 362, 366-367, 369
Norfolk, Virginia, 5, 40-41
Northeast, 4-5, 42
  decline of older cities, 269-272

O

Office buildings and skyscrapers, 163-164, 265
Office of Economic Opportunity (OEO), 360
Ohio River towns, 52-53
Omaha, Nebraska, 140, 143, 145
Organizations, private, 212
Oriental immigrants, 313, 321

P

Parks and playgrounds, 92-93, 202
Peace Corps, 360-361
Pendergast, Thomas J., 245
Penn, William, 12-13
Philadelphia
  black community, 73, 181
  ctiy plan, 66-67
  colonial period, 12-14, 24, 25, 29, 32, 106-107
  commerce and industry, 48-52
  Constitutional Convention, 36
  expansion of, 152
  Fairmount Park, 93
  housing, 197
  machine politics, 119-123
  Penn's plan, 13
  population growth, 22-24, 31, 34-35, 40-41, 132, 177
  reform groups, 220-222
  water supply, 84
Phoenix, Ariz., 255, 268
Pingree, Hazen, 229-231
Pittsburg, Pa., 52, 55-56
  pattern of growth, 153-154
Planning movements, 279-283
  City Beautiful movement, 279-281
  federal aid and, 286-288, 349
  growth policies, 372
  new towns, 285-288
  1920s, 335
  regional planning, 283-288
  satellite cities, 287-288
Plantation-slave system, 18, 47, 64-65
Playgrounds, 202
Police protection, 87-88, 205
Political power, of cities, 371
Politics
  fraud and violence, 99-101
  machine politics *see* Machine politics
  municipal reform, 217-248
Pollution and blight, 81-83
  See also Environmental problems
Population growth, 22-24
  blacks in cities, 298-299
  cities (1790-1870), 40-41
  colonial America, 22-24
  comparison of shift in U. S. and Europe (1880-1930), 176
  1890-1920, 177-178
  foreign-born, 183-189
  metropolises, 137, 249-251
  metropolitan cities (1920), 137-140
  natural increase, 178
  urban and rural (1890-1920), 177-178
  urban and total (1790-1970), 333
Portland, Oregon, 149-150
Portsmouth, Rhode Island, 9
Poverty
  drive to combat, 204-208
  public assistance, 94-95
  vice and crime, 205
  War on Poverty programs, 360-364
Primaries, 230
  nonpartisan, 241
Prisons, 95
Privatism, 32
Progressive era, 217-218, 224-233
  changes in municipal government, 224-228, 237-239
  civil service reform, 242
  commission and council manager plans, 242-244
  radical reformers, 228-233
Prostitution and vice, 205
Protestants
  anti-Catholic views, 98-99
  anti-foreign conflicts, 99
  communities, 95-96
  social action, 208-209
Providence, Rhode Island, 9, 24, 40-41
Public education, 93-94, 210-211
Public health, 88-93, 203-210
Public utilities, 168-170

Public welfare departments, 209
Public Works Administration, 340
Puerto Rican immigrants, 314, 321

R

Race riots, 102, 182, 205, 305-306
  demonstrations and, 323-326
  Harlem, 311-312, 324
Radburn, New Jersey, 259, 268
Railroads, 43, 62
  construction, 43, 51-52
  effect on cities, 67-68, 147
  land grants, 147-148
  terminal towns, 147
  transcontinental, 141-142, 144, 146-147, 150
Railways, interurban, 168
Reconstruction Finance Corporation, 336, 338
Referendums and initiatives, 241
Reform movement, 133-136
  in Chicago, 225-228
  municipal government, 222-224
  problems, 233-235
  radical progressives, 228-233
Regional planning, 283-288
  land use, 284
  metropolitan areas, 284
  new towns, 285-287
  transportation, 284
Regional Planning Associations, 283-285
Relief programs
  depression of 1930s, 336-339
  housing programs, 339-346
  welfare payments, 337-338
Religious conflicts, 98-102
  colonial period, 12
  Protestant and Catholic, 98-99, 189
  sectarian divisions, 95-96
Retirement communities, 262

Revenue sharing programs, 367-370
Revolutionary War, effect on cities, 33-36
Richmond, Va., 181
Riis, Jacob, 234
River towns and cities, 52-58, 70
Roads and highways, 255-257, 277-278
  expressways, 256-257
  federal program, 357-358
Roman Catholics, 209, 214
  anti-Catholism, 98-99, 189
  charitable institutions, 97
  immigrants, 78-79
  parochial schools, 98
Roosevelt, Eleanor, 345
Roosevelt, Franklin D., 339-346
Roosevelt, Theodore, 131, 224
Ruef, Abraham, 130-131, 229
Rural exodus to urban areas, 179-182, 250-251
Russian immigrants, 186

S

St. Louis, 53, 58, 61, 138
  home rule, 237-238
  housing, 197
  machine politics, 120
  reform movement, 224
St. Paul, 292
Saloons, 146-147
San Antonio, Texas, 148-149
San Francisco, 58, 140, 149-150
  machine politics, 130
  reform movement, 229-230
Sanitation and health, 202-203
Satellite cities, 287-288
Savannah, 5, 19, 40-41
Schools, 93-94, 210-211
  curriculum, 211
  Dewey's influence, 211
  free, tax supported, 93
  private, 98
Seaport towns, 14-19, 44-52

INDEX

Seaport towns (*Cont.*)
  role of merchants, 19-21
  Western, 149-150
Seattle, Washington, 149, 292
Services, municipal, 84-95, 117-118, 161-162
  environmental problems, 88-93
  expansion of, 117-118
  fire protection, 86-87
  police protection, 87-88
  public assistance, 94-95
  public education, 93-94
  public health, 88-93
  water supply, 84-86
Settlement house movement, 207-208, 227
Sewage disposal, 89, 202-203, 289, 292
Shopping centers, 264, 279
Shriver, R. Sargent, 360-362
Skyscrapers, 264-265
Slaves and slavery, 31, 63
  plantation system and, 18, 47, 64-65
Slums, 81-83
  clearance and rehabilitation, 353
  disease and congestion, 92
Social Gospel movement, 208-210
Social mobility, 191-192
Social problems, 84, 207-210
  reforms, 208-210
Social Security, 367
Socialists, 228-229
South
  colonial period, 4-5, 15
  commerce and industry, 42
  lack of urban growth, 19, 63-65, 140
  municipal governments, 120
  segregation of races, 182
  slave-plantation system, 64-65
  slaves and slavery, 63
  Sun Belt, 266-269
  town and cities, 63-65
  white supremacy, 120
Southwest, 63

Spoils system, 109-110
Standard Metropolitan Area, 251-252
Standard Metropolitan Statistical Areas, 252-254
State-city relations, 111-115
Steamboat construction, 57
Steam-powered factories, 49-50
Steffens, Lincoln, 123, 127, 128, 223-224, 232, 234, 235
Streets, paving and cleaning, 200-202
Suburbia
  advent of ethnic groups, 195
  annexation to central cities, 196
  class and income, 195-196, 258
  community associations, 259
  counter-trend to, 272
  crime and violence, 272
  decentralization of business, 262-266
  development of, 82, 171-175
  effect of automobile, 258
  exodus of blacks to, 328
  exodus of corporations to, 265
  federal policy and, 357-358
  garden city concept, 258
  growth of, 193-196
    1920-45, 257-260
    since 1945, 260-262
    in the 1970s, 366-370
  home ownership, 261
  housing, 196-197, 261
  metropolitan districts, 151-152
  planned developments, 261-262
  population growth, 258
  racial segregation, 262
  Radburn and green belt towns, 259, 286, 343-345
  residential communities, 171-175
  retirement communities, 262
  transit systems, 195
  upward mobility, 193

Suburbia (*Cont.*)
  white migration to, 317
  zone of emergence, 199-200
Subways, 167, 168
Sun Belt, 266-269
  population growth, 266-267
Sweatshops, 189
Swedish immigrants, 186

T

Tacoma, Washington, 149
Tammany Hall, 119, 121, 124, 126, 132, 220, 235-236, 244
Tax policies, 358
Tennessee Valley Authority, 340
Texas towns and cities, 149
Textile industry, 43-44
Tilden Commission, 219
Tobacco trade, 18
Toledo, reform movement, 231
Town meetings, 107-108
Towns
  colonial, 14-19
  inland river, 52-58
  patterns of settlement, 8-9
Trade and commerce
  colonial period, 14-19
  effect of Revolution, 33-36
  New York City, 46-48
  rising centers (1800-1860), 36-39
  role of seaport merchants, 19-21
Trade-transportation-communication network, 14-19
  role of merchants, 19-21
Traffic and transit, 272-279
  control, 275-276
  pollution and, 272-279, 286
Trans-Appalachian West, 54
  commerce and industry, 54-55
  growth of cities, 140-141
Transportation, 166-168, 272-279
  See also Mass transit

Trolley cars, 170
Tweed, Boss (William Marcy), 120, 123-124, 128, 132, 218-220
Twin Cities Metro Council, 292

U

Underground Railroad, 73-74
Unemployment, 205
  depression of 1930s, 309-313, 336-338
United States Conference of Mayors, 348
Urban Affairs Council, 366
Urban crisis, 331, 349, 359, 370, 373
  role of federal government, 331-332
Urban Development Corporation, 293-294
Urban growth
  colonial period, 1-38
    effects of Revolution on, 33-36
    in the North, 5-6
    in the South, 4-5
  1800-1860, 39-69
    factors contributing to, 39-44
  post-Civil War, 137-141
  1870-1920, 177-216
    rise of metropolises, 137-175
  in the 1920s, 332-336
  population growth, 22-24
  preindustrial, 24-29
  role of merchants, 19-21
  role of towns, 14-19
Urban League, 307
Urban renewal, 349-354
  achievements, 352
  difficulties, 351
Urban sprawl, 252
Utility companies, 168-170
  franchises, 168-169
  public ownership, 169-170
  regulatory commissions, 170

INDEX

V

Violence, 205-206
VISTA, 361
Veterans Administration (VA)
    mortgages, 358
Votes and voting, 239, 241
    machine politics and, 122-123
    reforms, 239, 241
    secret ballot, 230

W

"Walking city," 81-82
War of 1812, 39, 44
War on Poverty program, 360-363
    criticism of, 362-364
Washington, D.C.
    black population, 316
    planning and construction, 36-38
    planning for future, 284-285
Water pollution, 273-274
Water supply, 84-86, 202, 272-274
Watts riot, 325
Welfare measures, 208-210
Welfare programs, 94-95, 208-210, 367
    public welfare departments, 209
Westward expansion, 70, 143
    commerce and industry, 42
    hucksters and confidence men, 52
    inland towns and cities, 52-58
    railroads and, 50-51
Wheeling, West Virginia, 56
Whitney, Eli, 44
Williams, Roger, 9
Women's clubs, 212
Work Progress Administration (WPA), 347
Workmen's Compensation, 210
World's Columbian Exposition, 225

Y

Yerkes, Charles T., 129, 227

Z

Zoning ordinances, 282-283

ABOUT THE AUTHORS

Diana Klebanow, a native New Yorker, received her PhD in history from New York University in 1965. She has published in leading academic journals and has taught at several universities, including the University of Connecticut and the University of Bridgeport.

Franklin L. Jonas received his doctorate degree in history from New York University in 1972. He has published several articles in academic journals and is currently teaching history at New York Institute of Technology.

Ira M. Leonard, born in New York City, received his PhD in history in 1965. Dr. Leonard has taught at several universities, and frequently makes lecturing appearances. He is currently Professor of United States Urban History at Southern Connecticut State College.

SIGNET and MENTOR Titles of Special Interest

☐ **HOW TO SAVE URBAN AMERICA: CHOICES FOR '76 edited by William A. Caldwell.** A Regional Plan Association book. This book confronts the major urban problems of housing, transportation, poverty, environment, cities, and government and provides a chance to choose among alternative policies for the future.
(#W5559—$1.50)

☐ **FROM KNOW-HOW TO NOWHERE: The Development of American Technology by Elting E. Morison.** An exploration of the ways in which machines have been shaped by and in turn shaped American society over the past two hundred years. (#MJ1539—$1.95)

☐ **POPULATION: A Clash of Prophets edited by Edward Pohlman.** Is increasing population the source of a nation's health, or a disease that must be checked? Are the world's resources about to run out, or are there virtually limitless possibilities of expansion? Overpopulation—menace or myth? Here's what the leading authorities think. (#MJ1183—$1.95)

☐ **TO LIVE ON EARTH: Man and His Environment by Sterling Brubaker.** A Resources for the Future Study. A vitally needed book that shows us where we are on the road to possible extinction. It offers a superbly balanced view of the mixed blessings of our industrial society, the cost of its achievements, and what we must be prepared to give up if we want to survive on Earth.
(#MW1137—$1.50)

☐ **OIL POWER: The Rise and Imminent Fall of an American Empire by Carl Solberg.** The great American oil companies and their influence on our country's social, political, economic, and military structures . . . "A gripping narrative . . . fact-filled . . . persuasive."—**Publishers Weekly** (#MJ1531—$1.95)

SIGNET Books You Will Want to Read

☐ **THE LIMITS TO GROWTH: A Report for the Club of Rome's Project on the Predicament of Mankind** by Donella H. Meadows, Dennis L. Meadows, Jørgen Randers, and William W. Behrens III. The headline-making report on the imminent global disaster facing humanity—and what we can do about it before time runs out. "One of the most important documents of our age!"—Anthony Lewis, **The New York Times** (#E6617—$1.75)

☐ **MANKIND AT THE TURNING POINT: The Second Report to the Club of Rome** by Mihajlo Mesarovic and Eduard Pestel. This successor to **The Limits to Growth** spells out clearly what we can and must do to avoid worldwide catastrophe in the near future. (#J7817—$1.95)

☐ **RIO: Reshaping the International Order—A Report to the Club of Rome,** Jan Tinbergen, coordinator. This successor to **The Limits to Growth** and **Mankind at the Turning Point** presents an all-inclusive working plan that can let us win our global race for survival—the first totally researched, completely practical alternative to our present way of doing things. (#E7708—$2.50)

☐ **GOALS FOR MANKIND: A Report to the Club of Rome on the New Horizons of Global Community** by Ervin Laszlo et al. Updated and revised. The successor to **The Limits to Growth, Mankind at the Turning Point,** and **RIO.** A vital guide to making the right decisions today for a better life tomorrow. (#E8023—$2.50)

☐ **BLUEPRINT FOR SURVIVAL** by the editors of *The Ecologist.* Introduction by Paul Ehrlich. Inspired by the warnings of **The Limits to Growth,** the first positive plan for solving the dire problems of our world energy crisis. "A storehouse of information about what needs to be done if we are to avoid turning the planet into a clinker." —**Washington Post** (#W7830—$1.50)

More SIGNET and MENTOR Books of Interest

☐ **THE DOWNTOWN JEWS: Portraits of an Immigrant Generation by Ronald Sanders.** An extraordinary evocation of life on the Lower East Side in its heyday. A vivid recreation of the years, the culture, and the people who in a brief and glorious period left us a legacy to be forever remembered. (#E7284—$2.50)

☐ **NOBODY'S HERO: A Puerto Rican Story by Lefty Barretto. Introduction by Piri Thomas.** A human document of raw and searing truth about coming of age in a world of slums and street gangs. (#E7357—$1.75)

☐ **STORIES OF THE AMERICAN EXPERIENCE edited by Leonard Kriegel and Abraham H. Lass.** These stories, by some of the greatest writers America has produced, give vivid insight into both our complex national character and our rich literary heritage. Authors included range from such nineteenth century masters as Nathaniel Hawthorne and Herman Melville to such moderns as Richard Wright and Nelson Algren. (#ME1605—$2.25)

☐ **GETTING JUSTICE: The Rights of People by Stephen Gillers. Foreword by Ramsey Clark.** Expanded and updated. A clear guide to your rights under the law—including recent Supreme Court decisions. "For your own sake and the future of freedom you should read this book!"—Ramsey Clark, former U.S. Attorney General (#MW1227—$1.50)

☐ **THE ASSAULT ON PRIVACY: Computers, Data Banks and Dossiers by Arthur R. Miller.** The author lays out the often indecent attitudes towards personal privacy that we can expect from information gatherers such as wiretaps, bugs, computers, and data banks. (#MW1284—$1.50)

☐ **THE PULSE OF FREEDOM—American Liberties: 1920-1970s edited by Alan Reitman. Foreword by Ramsey Clark.** From the beginnings of the organized civil liberties movement in World War I to the confrontations of citizen versus government in the civil rights revolution and Vietnam war protests, an analysis of five decades of the fight to preserve our basic human rights. (#MJ1484—$1.95)

Ⓟ

Quality Paperbacks from PLUME and MERIDIAN

☐ **STILL HUNGRY IN AMERICA** text by Robert Coles, photographs by Al Clayton. Introduction by Edward M. Kennedy. A moving documentary of the shocking, poverty-stricken conditions in which many Americans still live.
(#Z5142—$3.95)

☐ **IN SEARCH OF THE AMERICAN DREAM** edited by Jane L. Scheiber and Robert C. Elliott. This volume traces through our history the persistence—for good or for bad—of the utopian spirit which animated America's beginnings and helped shape her development. Included are selections from Thomas Jefferson, Abraham Lincoln, F. Scott Fitzgerald, and John Steinbeck. (#F421—$4.50)

☐ **THE FUTURE OF ARCHITECTURE** by Frank Lloyd Wright. In this volume the master architect looks back over his career and explains his aims, his ideas, his art. Also included is a definition of the Language of Organic Architecture as the architect has employed it throughout a lifetime of work.
(#F446—$3.95)

☐ **THE LIVING CITY** by Frank Lloyd Wright. Here, Mr. Wright unfolds his revolutionary idea for a city of the future, a brilliant solution to the ills of urbanization whereby man can attain dignity in his home, his work, his community. Includes Wright's amazing plans for his model community, Broadacre City. (#F444—$3.95)

☐ **THE NATURAL HOUSE** by Frank Lloyd Wright. Here, shown in photographs, plans, and drawings, are houses for people of limited means, each individually designed to fit its surroundings and to satisfy the needs and desires of its owners.
(#F445—$3.95)

THE NEW AMERICAN LIBRARY, INC.,
P.O. Box 999, Bergenfield, New Jersey 07621

Please send me the books I have checked above. I am enclosing $_____ (check or money order—no currency or C.O.D.'s). Please include the list price plus the following amounts per copy for postage and handling: 35¢ for SIGNETS and MENTORS; 50¢ for PLUMES and MERIDIANS. Prices and numbers are subject to change without notice.

Name_____

Address_____

City_____State_____Zip Code_____

Allow at least 4 weeks for delivery